WAR IN THE AIR

Francis K. Mason

**Temple Press
Aerospace**

Published by Temple Press
an imprint of Newnes Books
84-88 The Centre, Feltham, Middlesex TW13 4BH,
England
and distributed for them by
Hamlyn Distribution Services
Rushden, Northants, England

Produced by David Donald
Aerospace Publishing Ltd
179 Dalling Road
Hammersmith
London W6 0ES

First published 1985

ISBN: 0 600 35115 7

All correspondence concerning the content of this
volume should be addressed to Aerospace Publishing
Ltd. Trade enquiries should be addressed to Temple
Press.

Printed in Italy

Picture acknowledgements

The Publishers would like to thank the following individuals and organisa-
tions for their help in supplying photographs for this book.

Bell Helicopter Textron: 186
Boeing Aircraft Company: 171
Cessna Aircraft Company: 149
ECPA: 124, 125, 134, 135
Fleet Air Arm Museum: 85, 141
Gamma: 174, 175
Imperial War Museum: 12, 15, 20, 22, 24, 40, 41, 43, 45, 50, 51, 55, 57, 59,
61, 64, 65, 70, 71, 73, 77, 83, 84, 85, 87, 91, 95, 113
Israel Defence Force: 184, 185
Robert L. Lawson: 101, 106, 108, 143, 158, 159, 177
MARS, Lincs: 30, 34, 35, 36, 37, 38, 46, 49
John MacClancy Collection: 39, 44, 48, 65, 66, 67
McDonnell Douglas: 187
MoD: 121, 123, 126, 127, 128, 131, 132, 133, 138, 139, 160, 161, 171, 173
D. Nicolle: 129, 164, 165
Herman Potgieter: 182, 183
Press Association: 167, 179, 180, 181 185
RAF Museum, Hendon: 42, 56, 57, 58, 76, 82, 120
Bruce Robertson: 8, 10, 11, 13, 16, 17. 18, 19, 23, 29, 31, 33, 54, 79, 110, 125
Warren Thompson: 75, 140, 141, 144, 145
United States Air Force: 68, 69, 72, 74, 75, 80, 81, 86, 87, 90, 93, 98, 99, 105,
109, 116, 118, 119, 121, 122, 136, 137, 142, 145, 146, 147, 148, 149, 150, 151,
152, 153, 154, 155, 156, 157, 170, 171, 172, 173, 177
United States Navy: 51, 71, 92, 93, 96, 97, 100, 101, 103, 105, 107, 109, 110,
111, 114, 115, 117, 141, 159, 176, 177
Lt K.P. White: 178

Contents

World War I and The Interval Years

World War II in Europe

World War II in the Pacific

The Post-War Period

Index

THE ITALO-TURKISH WAR 1911-12

Long before World War I the aeroplane was being seen as likely military equipment, the US Army calling for demonstration by Orville Wright of his aircraft as far back as 1908; indeed it was during such a flight at Fort Myer that he crashed on 17 September that year, killing Lieutenant Thomas E. Selfridge, US Signal Corps, and was himself injured. Thus died the first military man in an aeroplane.

It was just three years later, on 25 September 1911, that Italy moblized a special expeditionary Army Corps with an Air Flotilla for despatch to Libya to counter Arab-Turkish occupation of the town of Tripoli. Under the command of Captain Carlos Piazza, the Air Flotilla comprised five operational pilots, six reserve pilots and 30 groundcrew; their aircraft were three Nieuports, two Blériots, two Farmans and two Etrich Taubes.

Tripoli was stormed on 5 October, and 10 days later work started to unload the crated aircraft from ships anchored offshore, the first being air tested a week later. In the meantime the Turks had counterattacked and the Italian beachhead was becoming precarious when, on 23 October, Piazza took off on a dawn flight in his Blériot with orders to discover the exact whereabouts of the enemy's main forces, a mission successfully accomplished when he discovered a number of Turkish encampments and reported his findings on landing after a 59-minute flight. Six reconnaissance flights were carried out during 23-25 October, a flight by Captain Ricardo Moizo in a Nieuport on the third day being met by rifle fire, three shots passing through his wings. The location of some 8,000 enemy troops opposing the Italian forces was vital in re-arranging the Italian line, and before the end of the month Lieutenant Guilio Gavotti and naval Lieutenant Ugo de Rossi had also made ready their aircraft.

The next role undertaken by the Air Flotilla was artillery observation when Piazza and Moizo performed spotting duties for the Italian warship *Sardegna* bombarding the Zanzur Oasis, but this was handicapped by the pilots' inability to signal the effects of the gunnery until Piazza hit on the idea of dropping small tins containing messages to the gunnery officer. By the end of November successful artillery spotting was being carried out as a matter of routine.

On 1 November the first bombs ever dropped by an aeroplane on operations were released by Lieutenant Gavotti in his Etrich Taube. On that occasion he dropped three 4.4-lb (2-kg) Cipelli grenades over the Taguira Oasis and another at Ain Zara. Refinements in weapons followed when an engineer, Lieutenant Bontempelli, produced a cylindrical bomb containing explosive and shrapnel, of which 10 could be carried aloft in a box container which, after operation of a lever in the cockpit, would drop them singly or in a 'stick'.

Atrocious weather at the turn of the year did not prevent the Italian pilots from supporting the Italian advance towards Ain Zara, working out a system of flying manoeuvres to indicate the presence of threatening enemy forces. Occasional instances in which the ground forces would not believe the pilots' reports prompted Piazza to have a camera fitted to his Blériot, the only difficulty being that the aircraft had to land after taking each photograph as it was impossible to change plates in the air. The Italian aircraft were also used to drop propaganda leaflets among tribal groups in successful efforts to win their support for the Italian cause.

During the winter two replacement Farmans were received at Tripoli to allow maintenance on other aircraft which were beginning to show signs of considerable wear and tear. With them came Lieutenant Oreste Salomone, newly trained in Italy and who was to gain fame in World War I with the award of Italy's highest gallantry decoration, the Gold Medal for Valour.

At the end of 1911, as the campaign moved east and north into Cyrenaica, a new flotilla came into being at Homs, near Benghazi under the command of Captain Montu. It was in this theatre that the Turks began using anti-aircraft artillery, and it was in one of the first Bristol two-seaters to reach Africa that naval Lieutenant Roberti was flying a reconnaissance sortie when his aircraft was hit and his propeller struck by shrapnel; in a congratulatory gesture typical of the time, Roberti dived low over the enemy battery scattering his personal visiting cards (some of which he found on display in a Turkish museum 14 years later).

The first operational night flights were made by the Cyrenaica Flotilla, Captain Marengo making five night reconnaissance sorties between May and July 1912, and on 11 June he dropped several bombs on a Turkish camp in moonlight shortly before dawn, the first night bombing attack in history. Tragedy struck on 12 August, when the first Italian pilot was killed during an operational flight, although the accident was caused by loss of control (probably due to a severe thermal near the ground).

As the Libyan campaign drew to an end the achievements of the Italian air flotillas were hailed by the international press as a new chapter in warfare, and certainly gained military attention throughout Europe. Though no evidence can be found to confirm the presence of any British observer with the Italians, one cannot be blind to the coincidence that it was in April 1912 that the formation of the Royal Flying Corps was announced, followed almost immediately by the opening of the Central Flying School; at this, reconnaissance, artillery spotting and night flying were the main constituents of the military flying training course, all of which were being practically demonstrated by the Italians in Libya with their tiny air flotillas.

The first casualty of war in the air occurred during the Italo-Turkish war when this Italian crewman in a Caproni bomber was hit by ground fire. The aircraft was based at Tripoli in Libya.

Blériot monoplanes were used by the Italians during the war with Turkey, principally on scouting duties. The power was provided by an 80-hp (60-kW) Gnome rotary engine. Blériots were fitted with cameras to become the first photo-reconnaissance aircraft.

Captain Moizo is seen standing by his Nieuport scout at Tripoli in 1911. Moizo and his fellow pilots were engaged in carrying out reconnaissance flights over Turkish lines when his aircraft took three hits through the wings.

THE OPENING ROUNDS 1914-5

To many of the pioneer air enthusiasts the very concept of using aeroplanes as weapons of war was not only distasteful but a prostitution of a sporting machine. Such was to ignore the fact that the Italo-Turkish War had ever been fought, and that soldiers and sailors of a score of nations had already become proficient in the skills of flying. In America five Curtiss A-1s had been employed for reconnaissance during the Vera Cruz incident in April 1914, and the French had employed aeroplanes during a colonial campaign in Morocco early that year.

In Europe alone France, Germany, Russia, the UK, Turkey, Belgium, Italy and Bavaria already had military air arms in being, the purpose of these being almost exclusively reconnaissance, the two first-named nations being measurably the most advanced both in equipment and tactical concept. Even so, no aeroplane existed at the outbreak of war equipped with a gun of any sort, it being generally thought unlikely that a rifle or pistol shot from one moving aircraft would prove fatal against another.

In the French Aviation Militaire more than 30 *escadrilles* were equipped with a variety of aircraft, of which Blériot XIs, Maurice Farman MF.7s and MF.11s, and Caudron G.3s existed in the largest numbers. The British Royal Flying Corps, whose Nos 2, 3 and 4 Squadrons moved to France in August 1914, employed these aircraft together with Deperdussins, Sopwith Tabloids, Bristol Boxkites, RAF B.E.2 and many others, being assigned the task of visual reconnaissance over the swiftly moving German advance. The first British aeroplane to be lost to enemy action was an Avro 504, shot down by enemy small arms fire from the ground on 19 August.

The Germans, whose Military Aviation Service had formally existed since October 1912, went to war with 246 first-line aeroplanes of numerous types, of which the Taube monoplane, and Albatros and Aviatik biplanes predominated; the service possessed an established operational strength of 254 pilots and 271 observers, distributed among units deployed to support the defences of the great German fortress towns.

There being no specific organization or plan in being to commit any of these air services to armed combat duties, no attempt was made by either side in the early weeks of the war to interfere with the enemy's use of the skies over the Western Front, other than the instinctive use of the infantryman's rifle. The employment of the aeroplane as a bomber had not been overlooked, however, and it was not long before individual pilots started out on what can only be regarded as courageous, if foolhardy ecapades, one Leutnant Franz von Hiddeson dropping (by hand) two light bombs from his Taube over Paris on 13 August. The first bomb to fall from an aeroplane on English soil was another such light bomb which dropped into a Dover garden on Christmas Eve, 1914. By then a number of planned

bombing attacks had been executed, notably the attack on 8 October by two pilots of the British RNAS based at Antwerp who, in Sopwith Tabloids, bombed Cologne railway station and the airship shed at Düsseldorf; in the latter attack Flight Lieutenant R.L.G. Marix destroyed the brand-new German airship Z IX.

Inevitably airmen of the opposing air services encountered each other in the air, and it soon became customary for the observers, if not the pilots themselves, to carry rifles and pistols with which to persuade their opponents to vacate that particular part of the sky. The first aeroplane to be shot down (as distinct from being forced down by 'aggressive manoeuvres') was a German Aviatik, shot down by the French pilot Sergeant Joseph Franz in a Voisin over Reims using a free-mounted Hotchkiss gun on 5 October. (A British pilot, Lieutenant L.A. Strange, had fitted his Farman biplane with a Lewis gun in the very first days of the war, but had been ordered to remove it as it severely restricted the aircraft's performance.)

Elsewhere drastic means were being adopted to destroy enemy aircraft. Staff Captain Nesterov of the Imperial Russian Air Service, flying an unarmed Morane-Saulnier, rammed an Austrian two-seater over Galicia flown by Leutnant Baron von Rosenthal; both pilots were killed. An even more unorthodox method was employed by another Russian, Staff Captain Kazakov, who trailed a grapnel below his Morane-Saulnier MS 5; with this he engaged the wing of an Albatross two-seater near Gusov and then struck the enemy aircraft with his landing gear.

Notwithstanding these primitive forms of combat, efforts were being made to fit guns in aeroplanes early in the war, rifles and machine-guns at first being mounted on makeshift pylons for use by the observer. In France Roland Garros became the world's first pilot to destroy an opponent using a fixed, forward-firing machine-gun in his Morane Type L parasol monoplane; with steel deflector wedges bolted to the propeller blades to deflect bullets that would otherwise damage them, Garros shot down an Aviatik over the Western Front on 1 April 1915. The era of true air combat had opened.

The Caudron G.3 was widely used on spotting duties by both the French Aviation Militaire and the Royal Flying Corps. The aircraft was unarmed but the observers often carried rifles for taking pot shots at enemy aircraft.

One of the most widely used aircraft of the early years was the B.E.2c. It had many shortcomings and was frequently referred to as 'Fokker fodder', as so many fell to the guns of the *Eindeckers*.

2633

Blériot XIs were employed by the Royal Flying Corps on light spotting duties in the early months. This type was made famous by its designer's flight across the English Channel, but was soon to be no match for the new German scouts.

293

BATTLE OF THE FRONT GUN 1915

Although the idea of mounting a machine-gun in the nose of an aeroplane to fire forward through the propeller had been conceived before World War I, only the French had ordered such an aircraft (the Morane Type I) for service. This had proved unreliable and it was not until the Frenchman Roland Garros, flying a Morane Type L with Escadrille MS 23, shot down three German aircraft in April 1915, that the era of dedicated air combat opened. His aircraft was equipped with a machine-gun on the nose and steel deflector plates on the propeller blades to prevent the bullets shooting off the blades, a device evolved by Saulnier. Garros was forced down behind the German lines on 19 April and taken prisoner, his Morane being closely examined by the enemy.

In the meantime the German engineer Schneider had already developed an interrupter gear which mechanically prevented the gun from firing at the instant a propeller blade passed the gun muzzle, and this was being incorporated in a small monoplane fighting scout then being produced by Anthony Fokker for the Germans.

When originally conceived, the Fokker E-type monoplane was not intended for offensive air combat but simply as an escort for reconnaissance aircraft which were becoming ever more widely used over the Western Front, and was initially issued in small numbers to the *Fliegerabteilungen*. It was when such men as Boelcke, Immelmann and Kastner came to fly the new scout that they appreciated the supreme advantage of the synchronized gun as an offensive weapon and quickly mastered the basic skills necessary to stalk and shoot down unsuspecting enemy pilots.

As more German pilots learned these rudimentary tactics with the Fokker E I, losses among British and French observation aircraft increased rapidly, with little in the way of immediate remedy in sight. The first French aircraft fell to the new German 'fighting scout' in June, and the following month two British B.E.2c aircraft were forced down. By November the depredations of the Fokker monoplanes had given rise to the 'Fokker Scourge', though in fact at that time there were probably fewer than 80 Fokkers in service over both Eastern and Western Fronts. Already the first Allied pilots were becoming known to the public for their prowess in air combat, the legendary Georges Guynemer having shot down his first victim while flying a Morane-Saulnier Type N on 19 July; he had survived being shot down once when, on his 19th birthday on Christmas Eve 1915, he was awarded the Cross of the Légion d'Honneur for having destroyed two enemy aircraft. During the next three months he shot down six more.

None of the Allied pilots attracted the adulation commanded by the German Max Immelmann, dubbed by his colleagues 'the Eagle of Lille'. Taught to fly the Fokker monoplane by Oswalde Boelcke, Immelmann was regarded with almost spectral awe by his enemies, and shot down 15 Allied aircraft before finally being killed near Lens on 18 June 1916. His mentor, Boelcke, was however the true originator of air combat tactics and, with his extraordinary gifts of patience and meticulous instruction, brought a new level of flying

discipline to the pilots whom he personally coached. He, like Immelmann, was awarded the coveted Pour le Mérite, before he met his death on 28 October 1916 with a score of no fewer than 40 victories. He has remained to this day the father figure of German fighter aviation.

The British were slow to introduce the sychronized front gun and, unlike the French and German, perpetuated a myth (originating in a number of pre-war accidents) that the monoplane was unavoidably and fundamentally unsound. Several constructors persisted in producing biplanes of the pusher type, a layout whose origins lay in the Wright Flyer of 1903, and could point to the ease with which a front gun could be mounted without the need for any interrupter gear. Thus it was that the Airco D.H.2 pusher biplane equipped the Royal Flying Corps' first true fighter squadron, No. 24, commanded by Major Lanoe G. Hawker VC; it did not reach the Western Front from England until February 1916.

Losses among B.E.2c aircraft of the RFC over the Western Front had reached alarming proportions during the latter half of 1915, for this type of aircraft (a veritable forest of struts and wires) retained no more than a modest performance provided it was not encumbered by a defensive gun; when such a gun was fitted, perforce unable to fire through the propeller, the aircraft was so slow and cumbersome as to invite swift destruction should a German scout appear. Both this and the F.E.2b were in truth two years out of date when they reached the front, and it speaks volumes that Lanoe Hawker's pilots in their ungainly D.H.2s were able partly to redress the balance of superiority, first during the early stages of the Battle of Verdun and, more important, during the great Battle of the Somme in 1916.

In the fact that such aircraft as the B.E.2c and F.E.2b had taken so long to appear lay the reasons for the prolonged success of the Fokker E-types. Petty squabbling was rife in the British aircraft industry, and where the Royal Aircraft Factory at Farnborough should have provided guidance and leadership there was little but acrimony and jealousy, compounded by inter-Service rivalry for aircraft contracts. It fell to the commercial firm of Sopwith Aviation to provide a remedy, but it was not until February 1916 that the first Pup appeared with its single front gun and Sopwith-Kauper interrupter gear, and even this had been ordered by the Admiralty. Moreover, not until September of that year did the Pups of RNAS squadrons finally put paid to the Fokkers' superiority.

The final 'Eindecker' variant was the E IV, which featured a more powerful engine. This example is being held back by ground crew while the pilot climbs aboard. The machine-gun can be seen mounted under the king-post.

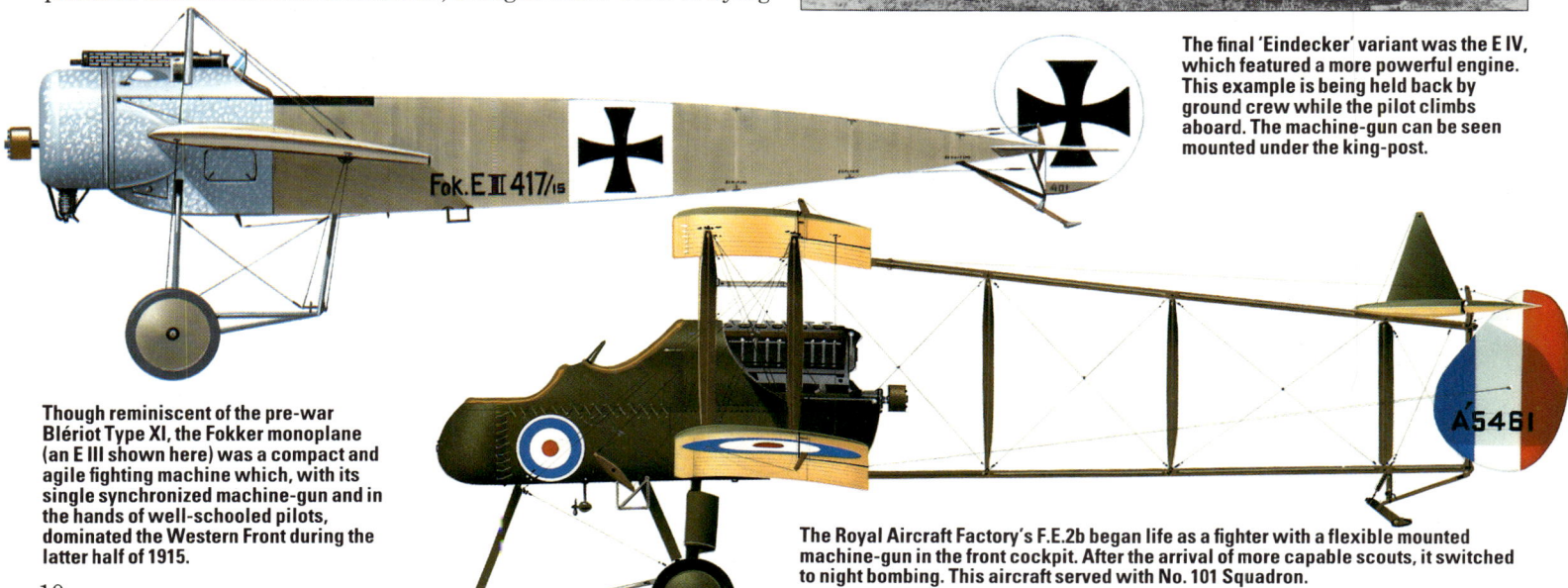

Though reminiscent of the pre-war Blériot Type XI, the Fokker monoplane (an E III shown here) was a compact and agile fighting machine which, with its single synchronized machine-gun and in the hands of well-schooled pilots, dominated the Western Front during the latter half of 1915.

The Royal Aircraft Factory's F.E.2b began life as a fighter with a flexible mounted machine-gun in the front cockpit. After the arrival of more capable scouts, it switched to night bombing. This aircraft served with No. 101 Squadron.

THE YEAR OF THE SOMME 1916

The first true British fighter Squadron was No. 24 whose commanding officer, Major Lanoe Hawker, had won the Victoria Cross on 25 July 1915 when, flying a Bristol Scout armed with a single-shot cavalry carbine, he forced down three machine gun-armed enemy two-seaters. The Bristol Scout was not a fighter in the true sense but had been supplied in small numbers for the protection of observation aircraft. In February 1916 Hawker took No. 24 Squadron to France equipped with the D.H.2, a single-seat pusher biplane armed with a free-firing front gun. The aircraft was manoeuvrable and sensitive on the controls, and although fitted with a movable gun in the nose its pilots soon adopted the practice of fixing the gun to fire along the line of flight and aiming the aircraft directly at the target. Lieutenant Tidmarsh was the first to open the Squadron's score with a victory near Bapaume on 2 April; thereafter No. 24 achieved a fast-growing reputation for determination and skill in countering the 'Fokker Scourge', being joined shortly after by two more D.H.2 squadrons, Nos 29 and 32.

The Germans meanwhile, recognizing that the superiority of the Fokker E-type monoplanes must soon be disputed by the Allies, were already early in 1916 introducing the Fokker D I and Halberstadt D II biplanes with single synchronized 'Spandau' (LMG 08/15), machine-guns, aircraft of neat but conventional appearance, and with better handling characteristics than the monoplanes. The whole concept of air fighting was undergoing reappraisal in the German air force, however, largely as a result of representations by Oswald Boelcke who, having demonstrated (with Immelmann) the superiority of the E-types in 1915, on return from a tour of the front early in 1916 was given command of a new fighting unit, Jasta 2 equipped with Fokker D Is and D IVs. This represented the beginning of the creation of a large number of dedicated air combat units (after the formation of the first RFC fighter squadrons, it should be noted).

Notwithstanding the success of the relatively small number of D.H.2s, the French were the first among the Allies to introduce a truly successful fighting scout, the Nieuport 17 which arrived at the front late in March. It was faster by 10 mph (16 km/h) than any British aircraft and was armed with a single synchronized front gun. It also served in large numbers with the RFC, and among the British pilots who gained their first victories in this excellent little aeroplane was Captain Albert Ball (later VC, DSO and MC), who destroyed an Albatros D I in May and a Roland C II on 2 July.

The prolonged Battle of Verdun had started late in February 1916, and was to drag on for many months. Inevitably the increasing dependence on aircraft for artillery observation by both sides led to frequent air combats between opposing Fokkers, Halberstadts, Nieuports and D.H.2s, not to mention the widespread destruction of poorly-armed reconnaissance aircraft. By the start of the bloody

Battle of the Somme in July there were dozens of dedicated fighter squadrons in action over the Western Front.

Operations by both sides took much the same form, with single observation aircraft sent to cover closely defined sections of the front line, their pilots seldom being instructed to penetrate more than a mile or so into enemy airspace. They would occasionally be escorted by a flight of fighting scouts, but more often a flight or even a squadron would patrol within sight of the reconnaissance aircraft, the pilots keeping watch for enemy scouts. Some use was made of decoy aircraft which it was hoped would lure the defending scouts away from their charges, after which the lumbering B.E., F.E., Voisin or Aviatik would be easy meat for prowling scouts.

This was the era of the lone 'stalker', of whom Ball in his Nieuport was one of the most deadly, while McCudden of No. 29 Squadron in a D.H.2 scored the first of his 57 victories on 6 September. The Frenchman Charles Nungesser had been flying Nieuports of various types since late 1915, and by the end of 1916 had destroyed 20 enemy aircraft, this despite constant pain from unhealed wounds. In the German air service, Immelmann had been killed on 18 June, followed by Boelcke on 28 October; but a new star was in the ascendant. Rittmeister Manfred, Freiherr von Richthofen, the greatest German flying name to emerge from the War, had joined Jasta 2 under Boelcke in September, and scored the first of 80 air victories on 17 September while flying an Albatros D II. It has been estimated that by the end of that year more than a dozen German scout pilots had gained at least a dozen victories.

It was in September that the German superiority in the skies over the Western Front was ended, at least for about six months, with the eventual arrival in France of such excellent Allied fighting scouts as the Sopwith Pup which, though in no way radical, proved such a delightfully manoeuvrable aircraft that in even only moderately skilled pilots' hands it could outfly and outfight almost any German aircraft extant. Pups of the RNAS were in action over the Belgian and French coast in September, and the following month No. 8 (Naval) Squadron was formed in the Somme area; within 50 days 'Naval Eight' had destroyed 20 German aircraft.

Following on from the successful 'E' series, Fokker produced the biplane D I, with a synchronized LMG 08/15 'Spandau' machine-gun above the neatly cowled engine. These aircraft began equipping the *Jastas* in 1916 and, along with other types, were to revolutionize air combat tactics under the guidance of Oswald Boelcke.

The delightful Sopwith Pup first appeared in RFC markings early in 1917 with No. 66 Squadron, one of whose aircraft is shown here.

First of the British dedicated fighting scouts was the Airco D.H.2, the example shown here being one of the first aircraft to be delivered to No. 24 Squadron at Hounslow at the end of 1915. Commanded by Major Lanoe Hawker VC, this squadron did a great deal to wear down the effects of the 'Fokker Scourge'.

HUNTERS AND ACES 1917

The year 1917 brought home to the Western nations all the horrors of modern warfare, with the start of unrestricted submarine operations, the first major aeroplane raids against civilian targets and the first use of tanks on the Western Front. On that dismal front trench warfare ensured a continuation of bloody stalemate, while overhead the Allied air forces began the year with a tenuous possession of air superiority.

Yet both the British and the French were slow to exploit the limited tactical successes they had achieved in the air during the autumn of 1916, and persisted in using slow and vulnerable bombing and reconnaissance machines in the mistaken assumption that small numbers of fighting scouts, patrolling nearby, would be adequate to defend them. Air fighting tactics were not developed, other than by individual example, with the result that the Germans were able to gain the measure of such aircraft as the Sopwith Pup and Nieuport 17, and in so doing quickly evolved improved combat tactics which were embraced in the flying training programmes.

The Royal Aircraft Factory R.E.8 was introduced before the end of 1916 and, despite shortcomings that immediately became apparent, was delivered in fast-growing numbers in the new year to the RFC. Other patently outdated aircraft, such as the B.E.2e, F.E.2b and F.E.8, continued in service, while promising aircraft like the S.E.5a, Sopwith Camel and Sopwith Triplane suffered persistent delays before delivery got under way to the RFC, a situation that resulted in searching questions in the British parliament.

In the meantime the German air force had set its sights on creating an impressive force of *Jagdstaffeln* (*Jastas*, or 'hunting squadrons'), aiming to establish 37 such units by April 1917, each with 14 aircraft of which the new Albatros D III was to provide the principal equipment. When this formidable force started concerted operations over the Western Front it achieved absolute mastery and took the Allies totally unawares. The R.E.8 was to suffer terrible casualties for, having apparently learned from previous experience, its designers had so increased the aircraft's stability that its manoeuvrability suffered disastrously. Good fighters were too few in number to afford protection with the result that April 1917 became known in RFC annals as 'Bloody April'. Squadron after squadron were decimated, and within the space of one month no fewer than 316 pilots and observers were lost. By the same token an increasing number of German pilots achieved fame on account of their mounting victory tallies; there is no doubt that this period marked the summit of German achievement in the air that was not to be matched again until the advent of the Fokker D VII in 1918.

Forced by the events of April to take drastic action, the RFC now introduced the new scouts and, with commendable speed, the Sopwith F1 Camel, with 130-hp (97-kW) Clerget rotary, appeared over the Western Front and was in time to join combat in July over the great 3rd Battle of Ypres which lasted until November, a battle which cost the Allies almost half a million casualties, and gained

little more than the capture of a ridge between Armentières and Dixmude. It did nevertheless serve to reduce the German pressure on the French after the collapse of their spring offensive.

This was the period of swiftly improving combat training in the RFC and, with such aircraft as the improved S.E.5a, the Camel and the Bristol F.2B Fighter, the balance began to swing back in the Allies' favour. Men like Mannock, Bishop, McCudden, Fullard and Collishaw became household names in the UK no less than those of von Schleich, Manfred von Richthofen and Berthold in Germany. Against the new British scouts, and the French SPADs and Nieuports, were flown the new Albatros D Vs and Fokker Dr I triplanes (the latter flown by von Richthofen himself, and its most dashing exponent, Werner Voss). In the French air force the legendary Georges Guynemer failed to return from combat in his SPAD on 11 September when his score stood at 54 victories, but the superb marksman René Fonck and the indomitable Charles Nungesser were already far along the road to stardom among fighter pilots. Yet for all these supreme individual achievements, usually the product of the pilots' preference for lone patrol and single-handed combat, the pattern of air fighting was undergoing change, and the era of combat between formations of fighters had already dawned. The Germans had in July created a menacing new tactic with the formation of their first 'flying circus', in effect a wing of *Jastas*, commanded by Manfred von Richthofen, the purpose of this large fighting formation being in its ability to switch quickly from sector to sector of the front to achieve local air superiority. As much as anything else, this tactic convinced the RFC (and RNAS) of the importance of training for squadron combat, and it was significant that many of the British high-scoring pilots were posted home to training units at which to put their experience to good effect in the combat training of new squadrons.

An interesting design to gain better agility, the Sopwith Triplane proved deadly in the hands of the RNAS squadrons. This line-up is of the aircraft of No. 201 Squadron, RNAS, seen at Bailleul in France.

Below: The Albatros D V fighter flown by Vizefeldwebel Clausnitzer of Jagdstaffel 4. Projecting above the upper wing centre-section is part of the radiator; this was offset to starboard to ensure that in the event of combat damage the pilot would not be drenched by a stream of scalding water.

Above: A good scout, the SPAD VII served in several air forces. This example of Escadrille SPA 81 is in the grey finish of the Aviation Militaire in 1917. The developed SPAD XIII gained much success with the American Expeditionary Force.

One of the most famous aircraft of all time, this is the Fokker Dr I flown by Rittmeister Freiherr von Richthofen at the time of his death. The Dr I was designed to emulate the success of the Sopwith Triplane but apart from those flown by Richthofen and Voss, was never to achieve this, its performance being overshadowed by other German scouts.

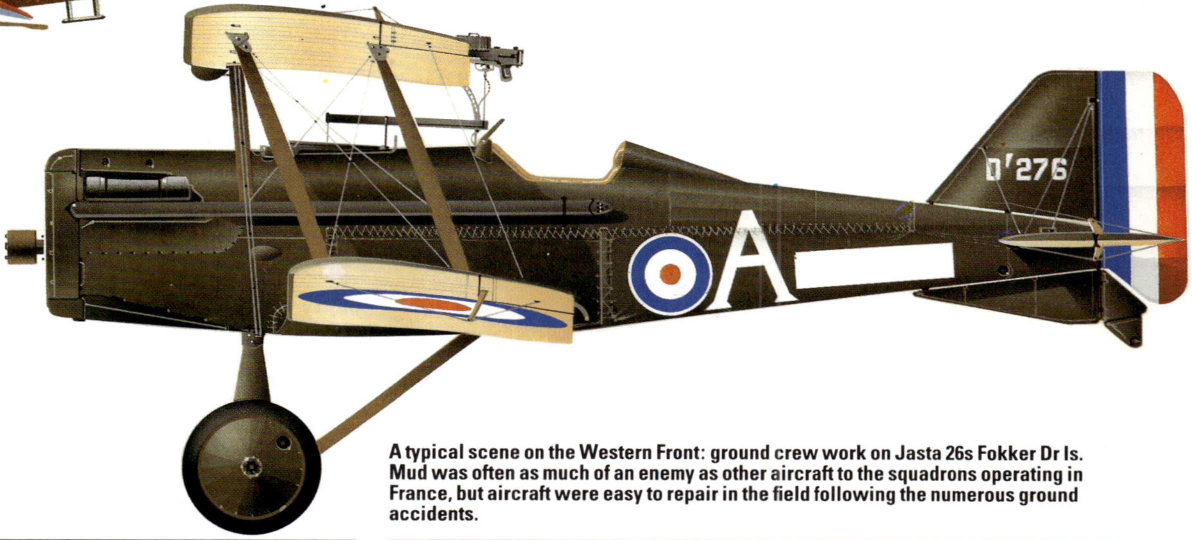

Powered by the Wolseley Viper engine, the Royal Aircraft Factory S.E.5a was one of the finest fighters to appear over the Western Front. This aircraft was flown by No. 74 Squadron.

Although not as glamorous as the single-seat scouts, the two-seat observation types played an important part in the war, providing up-to-date information for ground commanders. This is an LVG C II.

A typical scene on the Western Front: ground crew work on Jasta 26s Fokker Dr Is. Mud was often as much of an enemy as other aircraft to the squadrons operating in France, but aircraft were easy to repair in the field following the numerous ground accidents.

Typical of the 'heavy' bombers used by the Allies was the Breguet 4, which featured a defensive machine-gun mounted in a large open cockpit in the nose. This particular aircraft was forced down by the well-known pilot, Ernst Udet.

The forerunner of the famous 19 series of post-war days, the Breguet XIV was an excellent two-seat observation post and light bomber. This served with the Belgians.

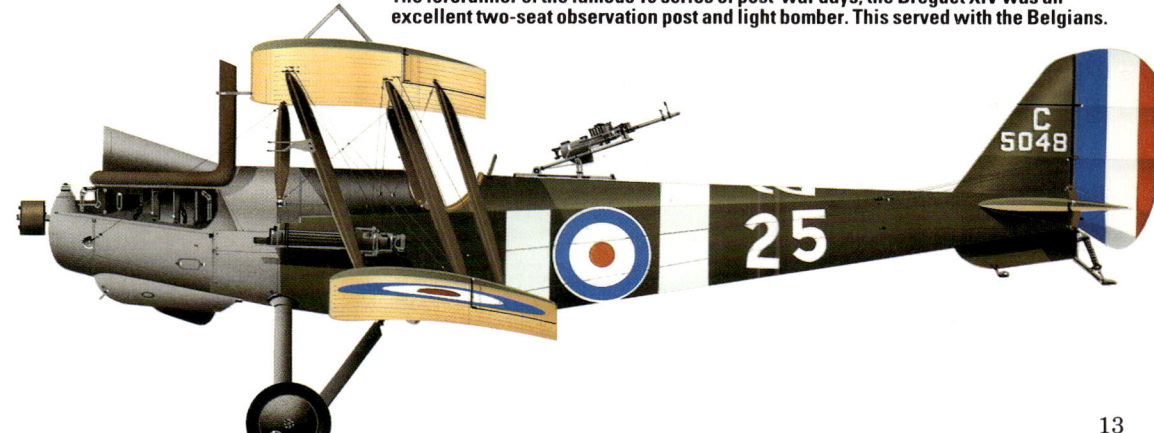

The R.E.8 served in large numbers on Corps duty over the Western Front, universally known as the 'Harry Tate'. This aircraft carries the two white bars of No. 16 Squadron.

THE GERMAN SPRING OFFENSIVE 1918

After the end of the 3rd Battle of Ypres in November 1917 there followed a relative lull in the air fighting over the Western Front. The British, French and Germans set about strengthening their air forces, the Germans for their part preparing for a final great offensive to defeat the Allies before the arrival in France of the Americans who were expected to be ready to enter the fighting early the following summer.

As already mentioned, the German air force had created the first of its *Jagdgeschwader* (popularly known as the 'flying circuses', literally hunting wings) in July 1917 under Manfred von Richthofen, and such had been the success gained by this formidable fighting formation that two more (JG 2, initially comprising Jastas 12, 13, 15 and 19, and JG 3 with Jastas 2, 26, 27 and 36) were formed on 1 February 1918 under Rudolf Berthold and Bruno Loerzer respectively. Simultaneously another type of formation came into being: this was the *Jagdgruppe*, usually of no more than two or three *Jastas*; this unit was of a more transient nature and was created simply for convenience during a specific operation or offensive; a total of 12 such *Jagdgruppen* (nos 1 to 12) was formed from time to time during 1918.

Elsewhere in Germany trials were held in January 1918 to decide on new fighter equipment for the *Jastas*, and the choice fell on the Fokker D VII, one of the best German fighting scouts to achieve major production during the last year of the war. Unfortunately it did not achieve significant deliveries in time for the beginning of the great German offensive in March. Instead, the majority of the 80 *Jastas* were equipped with Albatros D Vs and D Vas, Pfalz D IIIs and D IIIas, and Fokker Dr I triplanes.

At the time of the German offensive there were 2,047 aircraft facing the Allies, of which 1,680 were deployed on the British Front; of the latter, 475 were single-seat fighting scouts flying with 51 *Jastas*.

The RFC and RNAS, on the other hand, contented themselves with building up their strength of Camel, S.E.5a and Bristol Fighter squadrons, and by March there were in France nine squadrons with the Camel (151 aircraft), 10 with the S.E.5a (163 aircraft), six with the Bristol Fighter (79 aircraft) and nine with other miscellaneous fighting scouts (130 aircraft, including the excellent SPAD S.13, Nieuport 17 and Nieuport 27). These squadrons bore the brunt of the air combat over the British front, but were also assisted by a number of French *escadrilles* on a short-term basis.

The German offensive opened on 21 March, by which time the establishment of RFC scout squadrons had been increased by 50 per cent to 24 aircraft each. Already heavy air fighting had broken out as the Germans sought to prevent Allied reconnaissance aircraft of V Corps from exposing the massive assembly of troops and artillery. As the enemy barrage opened on 21 March, Camels of No. 46 Squadron attacked the German gun batteries north of Bourlon Wood as No. 3 Squadron strafed enemy infantry. No. 54 Squadron was tasked with escort of the corps reconnaissance machines. The following day Camels of Nos 73 and 80 Squadrons shot down six German scouts, and on 24 March Captain J.L. Trollope of No. 43 Squadron set a new record by alone shooting down six aircraft in one day, a feat equalled by Captain H.W. Woollett of the same squadron on 12 April. Nine days later fell the greatest of the war's legendary scout pilots when a Canadian Camel pilot, Captain A.R. Brown of No. 209 Squadron, shot down a Fokker Dr I triplane near Corbie; in it died Manfred von Richthofen, victor of 80 air combats.

Now fully aware of the serious nature of the German offensive, the RAF (which had formally come into being on 1 April) now rushed eight more scout squadrons to France, the American squadrons, which had already started arriving in France, not yet being considered battle-ready.

On the French front the Aéronautique Militaire, facing 367 German aircraft (of which 168 were scouts in 18 *Jastas*), successfully denied the enemy unrestricted reconnaissance over the battlefield, and it was now that the French pilot René Fonck began his extraordinary spell of multiple victories, and on 9 May alone destroyed six of the enemy (despatching three in 45 seconds); by the end of the German offensive Fonck's score was approaching 50, and he was to continue up to 75 to become the leading Allied ace by the end of the war.

By now air combats frequently involved more than 100 aircraft, and these huge fights certainly accounted for the large individual victory scores being achieved by British, French and German pilots, for the days were ending when pilots would be ordered off on lone patrols; the large formations could be sighted at long range and accordingly engaged by equally large formations of defending scouts.

As the German offensive ground to a halt on 14 June it quickly became clear that the enemy ground forces had run out of steam, possibly for good, and that, with the Americans now streaming into France in large numbers, it might require no more than one great 'push' eastwards to end the war.

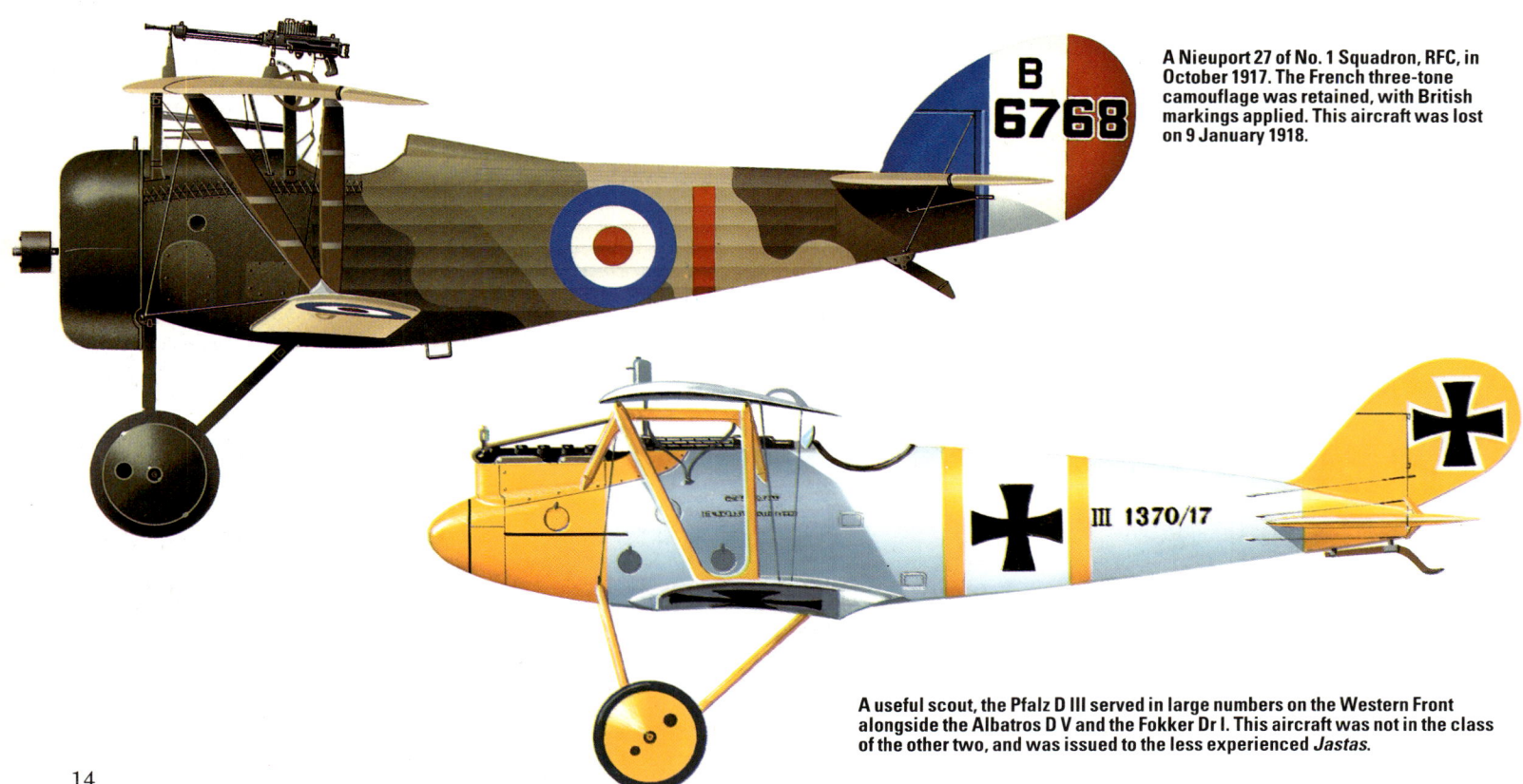

A Nieuport 27 of No. 1 Squadron, RFC, in October 1917. The French three-tone camouflage was retained, with British markings applied. This aircraft was lost on 9 January 1918.

A useful scout, the Pfalz D III served in large numbers on the Western Front alongside the Albatros D V and the Fokker Dr I. This aircraft was not in the class of the other two, and was issued to the less experienced *Jastas*.

WESTERN FRONT

A Sopwith-built 2F.1 Camel flown by the high-scoring Canadian pilot William Alexander with 'A' Flight, No. 10 (Naval) Squadron, RNAS at Treizennes, a squadron that was to become No. 210 Squadron RAF on the amalgamation of the RFC and RNAS on 1 April 1918.

Wearing a typical lozenge camouflage, this Fokker D VII was flown by Josef Raesch, Jastaführer of Jasta 43. The introduction of this aircraft to the front was a major coup for the Germans, being the best scout on either side.

This Albatros D V was flown by Vzfw Clausnitzer of Jasta 4. The centre section of the fuselage was varnished natural plywood with black stripes.

Ground and air crew sort out their gear at a hastily improvised airfield in France. The aircraft are R.E.8s of No. 15 Squadron, RFC, one of the most widely used observation types in the last years of the war.

THE FINAL CURTAIN 1918

If the defeat of the German offensive of March-June 1918 suggested that the energy of the enemy army had been catastrophically sapped, such was by no means evident in the air, although a number of *Jastas* were certainly withdrawn from the front to re-man and re-equip for, by June, deliveries of the superb new Fokker D VII were well under way; by the end of that month no fewer than 270 had been received by the fighting units. Indeed, at the moment that Manfred von Richthofen was killed on 21 April, JG 1 was already scheduled to receive the new aircraft, and did so during the remainder of that month.

It was now that the first American scout squadrons took their place in the line. In fact the 94th and 95th Squadrons (of the 1st Pursuit Group) had arrived at Villeneuve in February and March, and had carried out their first combat sortie on 15 March when Major Raoul Lufbery led an unarmed patrol over the lines in Nieuport 28s. The Americans disliked this aircraft (as they did the Camel), however, and opted to change to the SPAD S.13, and during the summer and autumn of 1918 began to accumulate an impressive score of victories, their leading aces, Captain Eddie Rickenbacker and Lieutenant Frank Luke gaining scores of 26 and 21 respectively; third in the list was Lufbery himself, with 17, but this pilot was killed on 19 May.

On 18 August the great British offensive ('the Big Push') opened in Flanders. In support, either directly or at longer ranger, were 13 squadrons with the S.E.5a, 17 with the Camel, six with the Bristol Fighter four with the new Sopwith Dolphin, 14 with the R.E.8, four with the F.K.8, five with the D.H.4, 14 with the D.H.9/9A, seven with the F.E.2b/d and seven with O/400 heavy bomber for a total of 91 squadrons fielding almost 1,700 aircraft.

On the French front, where an initial counteroffensive had opened on 18 July, the Aéronautique Militaire had undergone continuous strengthening with almost complete standardization among the scout *escadrilles* with the SPAD S.13, there being 49 subordinate *escadrilles* and 10 independent *escadrilles* thus equipped. In addition there were 23 bomber *escadrilles* flying Breguet 14s, Caproni 10s and Voisin 10s, the Breguets being used in the 'ground attack' role; there were also almost 140 artillery and army co-operation *escadrilles*, the majority of which flew Breguet 14s and Salmson 2s. By the beginning of August the Aéronautique Militaire possessed a front-line strength of over 2,800 aircraft, a total that would grow to 3,222 within four months.

From the beginning of this final phase of the air war the Allies possessed air superiority, as much on account of excellent fighting aircraft as of the much improved standard of combat training, following the rotation of experienced pilots to training units in the rear. For their part the Germans formed a fourth *Jagdgeschwader*, this time under the command of Ritter Eduard von Schleich, the veteran Bavarian who had won the *Pour le Mérite* a year earlier and gained a score of 35 victories. Indeed during those last months of the war the 'flying circuses' inflicted very heavy casualties among the Allied air forces, not least among the relatively inexperienced Americans. When the American land forces launched an attack west of Metz on 20 September JG 2 alone destroyed 89 American aircraft in two days.

It was in September that the RAF began to receive the first examples of the new Sopwith Snipe fighting scout, a derivative of the successful Camel and one which was to survive in service for some years after the war. In the event very few reached operational squadrons in France, and its place in the history of the war is almost entirely filled by the epic fight by a lone pilot, Major W.G. Barker who, attached to No. 201 Squadron to gain experience in the new aircraft, was on patrol high above the Forêt de Mormal on 27 October when he became involved in a prolonged fight with more than 15 enemy aircraft. Despite being severely wounded, he shot down at least four of the enemy (including three Fokker D VIIs), before crash landing behind the British lines; he survived to be awarded the Victoria Cross.

Like the Snipe, the German Fokker D VIII parasol monoplane scout also failed to reach operational squadrons in significant numbers but, with a speed some 10 mph (16 km/h) higher than that of the Snipe and much lighter on the controls, there is little doubt but that this aircraft would have otherwise given the Allied pilots a great deal of trouble. Be that as it may it was the D VII that came to be most respected by the Allies, so much so that the terms of the Armistice specifically named this aircraft (*in erster Linie alle apparate D VII*, or particularly first-line aircraft known as D VII) to be handed over.

The fighting on the Western Front was the key to the war's outcome. With internal strife inside Germany, shortages of food and the loss of the Hindenburg Line in October, the strength and power of the German air force had become superfluous. On 11 November the war ended when armistice terms were negotiated in France.

The French used the Salmson 2.A2 widely over the front on all forms of observation and artillery spotting. It was well armed, sporting a forward-firing gun as well as one mounted in the rear cockpit.

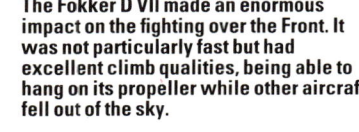

The Fokker D VII made an enormous impact on the fighting over the Front. It was not particularly fast but had excellent climb qualities, being able to hang on its propeller while other aircraft fell out of the sky.

Refinements to the SPAD VII design led to the SPAD XIII, an excellent fighter which was used by the French, British and Americans.

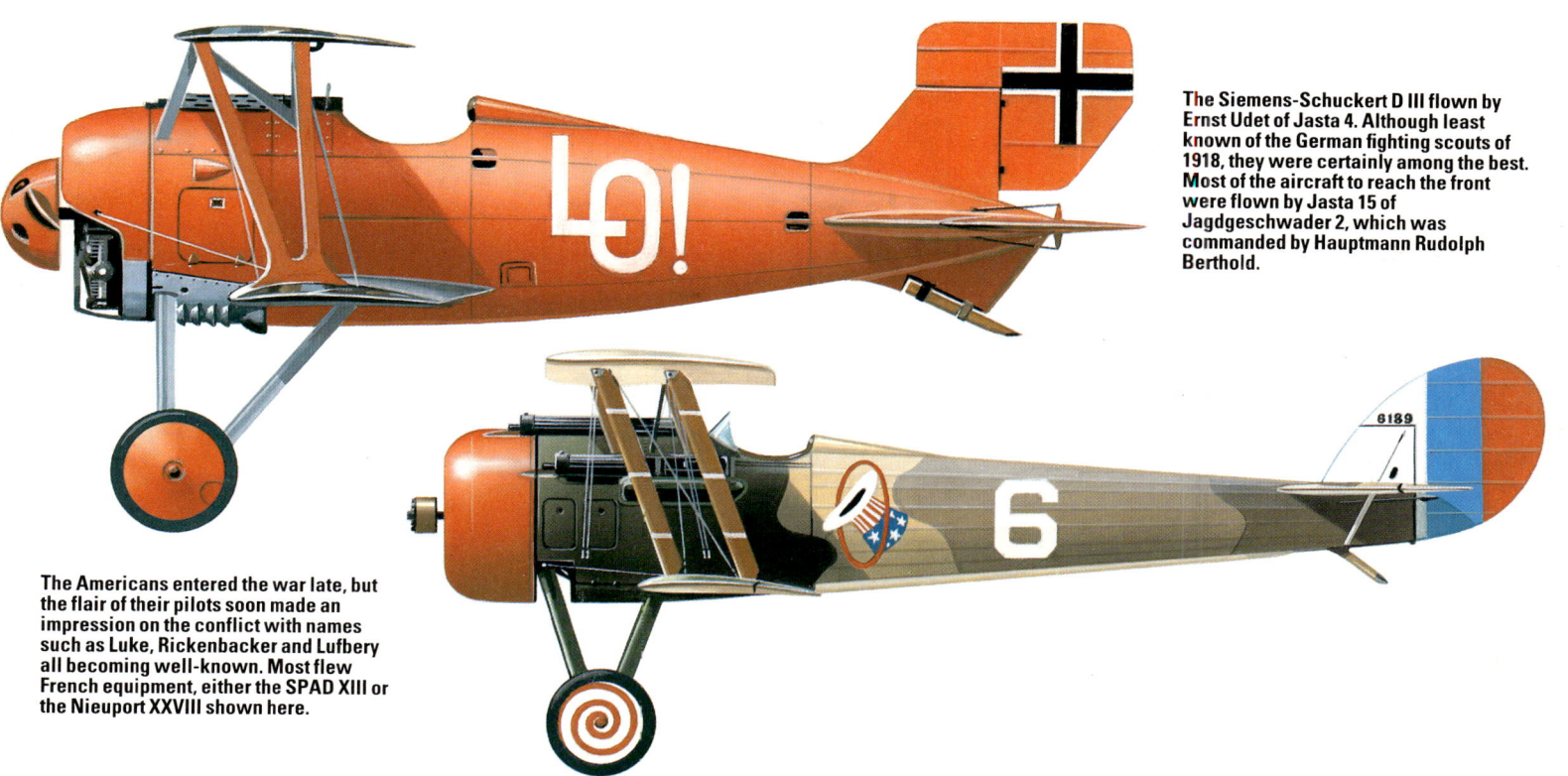

The Siemens-Schuckert D III flown by Ernst Udet of Jasta 4. Although least known of the German fighting scouts of 1918, they were certainly among the best. Most of the aircraft to reach the front were flown by Jasta 15 of Jagdgeschwader 2, which was commanded by Hauptmann Rudolph Berthold.

The Americans entered the war late, but the flair of their pilots soon made an impression on the conflict with names such as Luke, Rickenbacker and Lufbery all becoming well-known. Most flew French equipment, either the SPAD XIII or the Nieuport XXVIII shown here.

Five Royal Aircraft Factory S.E.5as overfly their airfield in a scene typical of the Western Front. This type proved to be a good fighter, as it was fast, manoeuvrable and could absorb damage well.

Originally known as the Fokker E V, the D VIII did not arrive at the front in any great numbers. It was the fastest scout to see service and possessed good agility but suffered from structural problems.

This Fokker D VII was flown by Uffz Piel of Jasta 13; this particular unit was identified by the green nose. The wings were covered with the pre-printed lozenge fabric, in common with most D VIIs.

The most successful two-seat fighter of World War I was the Bristol Fighter, which doubled as a reconnaissance aircraft. This machine belonged to No. 139 Squadron, based at Villa Verla on the Italian front.

THE RUSSIAN FRONT 1914-18

The war between Germany and Austria-Hungary on the one hand and Tsarist Russia on the other lasted for three years before dying out with the onset of the Russian Revolution in October 1917. At the outbreak of war the frontier dividing the two empires stretched from midway between Riga and Danzig on the Baltic coast, running west of Warsaw south through Galicia (now southern Poland) and finally south east to the mouth of the Danube on the Black Sea coast. Early air fighting predominated in Galicia and the north, the Germans at first deploying little air strength in the east, and the Russians possessing even less of an air force in any case. When the war opened the Imperial Russian Air Service had a total of 244 aeroplanes, 12 airships and 46 kite balloons, of which 145 aeroplanes were in the field; most were of French design, produced under licence by such companies as Duks, Russo-Baltic and Lebedev. Notable exceptions were the four-engine Sikorsky bombers which started bombing operations over the Eastern Front on 15 February 1915; no fewer than 73 of these huge aeroplanes were produced by the Russo-Baltic Wagon Works during the war.

Early combat was no less primitive in its tactics than in the West, the first Russian pilot to achieve fame being Piotr Nesterov (a pre-war pilot of renown) who was killed while gaining his only air victory near his airfield at Sholkiv by ramming a German aircraft in his Nieuport; Sholkiv was later renamed in his honour. Relentless pressure by the Central Powers forced the Russian armies back in the Ukraine where constant operations were flown in the Lutsk and Kovel regions, with frequent attacks being made to destroy the railway centre at Kovel. One of the great Russian pilots, Aleksandr Kazakov, spent most of his combat career in this area and became the top-scoring pilot on the front, some of his early victims being Fokker monoplanes when they arrived in the East late in 1915. In 1917 he commanded the newly-formed No. 1 Fighter Group, but this broke up at the time of the revolution and Kazakov made his way north to Archangelsk to join the British who landed there in 1918; he died needlessly while practising aerobatics in a Camel the following year. His decorations included the British DSO, MC and DFC.

The bomber designer Igor Sikorsky was later to make his home in the USA, and another to do so was Alexander de Seversky who had an outstanding combat record on the Eastern Front, much of it spent in the Riga region with the Imperial Naval Air Service. During his first night bombing flight he was shot down into the sea and his bomb exploded, blowing off his right leg; yet despite this he returned to command fighter aviation in the Baltic area and went on to destroy 13 German aircraft. He was in the USA at the time of the revolution and so decided to apply for American citizenship, later creating the Seversky Aero Corporation in 1922.

There is no doubt that the Russian air forces possessed many fine pilots, no less courageous and skilled than their opponents in the German and Austro-Hungarian air services. And their aircraft, though generally lagging about six months behind those in the West (as was the German equipment), were adequate and well serviced. The weakness lay in the command structure, a failing that permeated all the forces of Tsarist Russia. The officer corps was treated with elitism far beyond that of other nations, so that when setbacks, and ultimate disaster faced the Russian forces, disintegration followed in numerous units, although the air force was probably less disaffected than the army.

Collapse of discipline, particularly in the Ukraine, immediately before the October Revolution literally cut the ground from under the air force. Despite orders forbidding the continuation of hostilities against the Germans, many Russians fought on. One such incident involved Lieutenant Commander Viktor Utgov of the Black Sea Fleet who, flying a Grigorovich M-9 seaplane from the carrier *Imperator Nicolai Pervyi*, attacked a German U-boat with bombs, only to be summoned before the sailors' revolutionary executive to explain his conduct. (He also emigrated to the USA and joined Sikorsky, only to be killed in a flying accident with the US Marine Corps.)

Many Russian airmen served on the Western Front, and others learned to fly with the RFC in the UK. Likewise, a number of individual French pilots (as well as some French squadrons) served in Russia. The Imperial Russian air forces also numbered a few women among their pilots, the most famous (or infamous) being Princess Eugine Shakhovskaya; one of the first women to learn to fly in Russia before the war, she became a reconnaissance pilot on the Riga front; after the revolution it is said that she was chief executioner in the Tcheka at Kiev.

By the summer of 1918 German forces occupied a gigantic area of Russia, including the entire Ukraine and almost all the territory to the west of the River Don. However, if Germany had 'killed herself by victories' (*Wir siegen uns zum Tod*), the skills and courage of the Imperial Russian air forces may have unwittingly contributed to the widespread popular appeal of revolutionary opportunism in the armed forces simply on account of the adulation the officer corps attracted.

Nieuport XVIIs were the best fighters available to the Russians in 1917. After the revolution, some aircraft still fought on in Bolshevik colours, the first aircraft to bear the famous red star.

The Imperial Russian Flying Corps received from France large numbers of Nieuport fighters. This Nieuport 17c, an improved increased-span version of the Nieuport XI, was flown by No. XIX Gruppa, No. 1 Ostryad, but was subsequently captured by the Austrians.

Albatros C.III flown by Leutnant Bruno Maass of Flieger Abteilung 14 on the Eastern Front against Russia in January 1917. Most extensively-built of the Albatros C-type two-seaters, the C.III entered service in late 1916. Like many similar aircraft it had an angular, drag-inducing engine installation.

THE ITALIAN FRONT 1914-18

The outbreak of war in the south in May 1915 found the Italian army poorly prepared for action, despite fielding a total of 35 divisions against 25 Austrian. The frontier was largely Alpine, the four Italian armies being deployed in the Trentino, Cadore, Carnia and Isonzo sectors, of which the last-named absorbed 14 divisions, with seven in reserve. The Austrians, however, possessed a considerable superiority in artillery.

In the air the Italian Aeronautica del Regio Esercito (Royal Army Air Service) was better prepared, with 14 *squadriglie* of Nieuports, Maurice Farmans and Blériots in the field, and with ineffective opposition by the Austro-Hungarian air force these *squadriglie* gave a good account of themselves, particularly in reconnaissance duties, during the first general offensive which involved a combined advance by all four armies. Gradually the fighting concentrated on the eastern flank where the Isonzo plain provided the best opportunities for greatest gain, and indeed it was in this sector where the Italians made their biggest gains in the early months. By the autumn, however, following Russian defeats in Galicia, Austrian forces had been freed for service on the Isonzo, including increasing numbers of German aircraft including Rumpler and Aviatik C Is, which now provided the Austrian artillery with fairly effective spotting services. In this, the 2nd Battle of the Isonzo, the Italians had greatly reorganized their air force, greater emphasis being placed on bombing and reconnaissance, employing Capronis and Farmans in the former tasks, and Macchis, Farmans and Caudrons in the latter.

The Italians reduced their fighting scout strength progressively early in 1916, retaining two squadrons of Nieuport 11s for the defence of Santa Caterina and Aquileia. Successive battles were fought on the Isonzo front, as gradually the Austro-Hungrians built up their ground and air forces. As the Italian Capronis flew daylight bombing raids over the Alps a small number of Fokker E I monoplanes became available to mount token opposition; increasing numbers of Lohner and Lloyd reconnaissance aircraft were introduced into service, together with Fokker B IIs and D IIs, but the first aircraft to make its mark on the front was the Brandenburg D I, the famous 'Star-Strutter'. This was flown by the top-scoring Austrian, Godwin Brumowski, who led Fliegerkompanie (Flik) 12 and whose aim it was to create an élite fighting unit on the same lines as those beginning to appear on the Western Front. Opposite him the great Italian ace, Francesco Baracca (whose personal emblem, the *Cavallino Rampante* or prancing horse, is to this day adopted in the Italian air force) had by November 1916 destroyed five enemy aircraft; before the end of the war, while flying Nieuports and SPADs, he was to top the Italian scout fighters with a score of 34 victories.

After the desperate battles of the winter of 1916-7, in which appalling weather conditions and the freezing hardships sapped

morale of Italian fighting personnel from the warmer south, the fortunes of Italy continued to deteriorate. However, the failure of the Austrian Bainsizza offensive also took its toll and Austria was forced to seek assistance from Germany, a massive build-up that was to result in the crushing defeat of the Italians at Caporetto in October 1917, they being utterly unprepared for the use against them of gas shells. As the entire front threatened to collapse under the weight of attack by five armies, the Allies rushed reinforcements to Italy, particularly from France; these included 11 British and French divisions and four RFC squadrons (of Camels and Bristol Fighters) and three French *escadrilles*.

By a supreme effort of bravery and sacrifice the Italians eventually mended the front and held the Austro-Hungarian assault on the Piave. Fighting in the air continued to rage furiously, the Italians having resurrected their fighting scout *squadriglie* such that by the time of Caporetto they possessed eight Hanriot HD 1 *squadriglie*, four of SPAD S.7s and three of Nieuports. Caproni bombers equipped 14 *squadriglie*, and the excellent Ansaldo light reconnaissance bomber entered service in January 1918, later performing a number of epic missions. Air combat in the theatre brought to the fore numerous great pilots, Baracca continuing to score heavily until his death on the Piave front on 19 June. Teniente Silvio Scaroni, who only opened his air fighting score in November 1917 and flew Nieuports and Hanriots, survived the war with 26 victories, and reached the rank of general before World War II.

In the Austro-Hungarian air force Brumowski had progressed from the Brandenburg D I to the two-gun Albatros D III, leading a 'flying circus' of these aircraft during the Caporetto campaign. Julius Arigi, whose victory score reached 32, also flew Albatros D IIIs, and survived beyond World War II having numbered among his flying students the Luftwaffe's Walter Nowotny and Hans-Joachim Marseille. Third highest-scoring pilot was the Polish-born Frank Linke-Crawford, commander of Flik 60, whose combat score increased rapidly over Caporetto but who was killed on 31 July 1918.

Following the great Italian victory at Vittorio Veneto on 30 October an armistice was signed between Austria and Italy on 4 November.

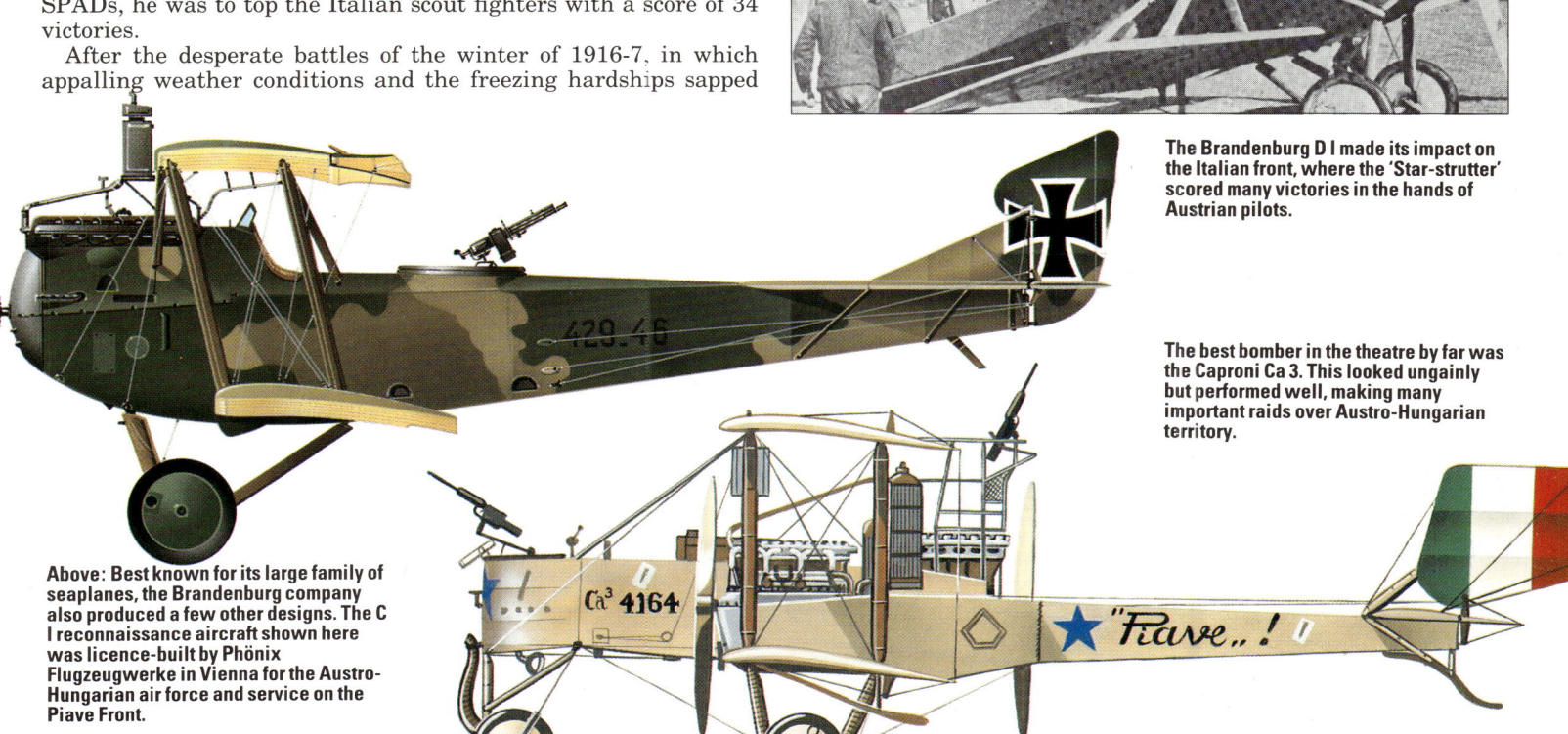

The Brandenburg D I made its impact on the Italian front, where the 'Star-strutter' scored many victories in the hands of Austrian pilots.

The best bomber in the theatre by far was the Caproni Ca 3. This looked ungainly but performed well, making many important raids over Austro-Hungarian territory.

Above: Best known for its large family of seaplanes, the Brandenburg company also produced a few other designs. The C I reconnaissance aircraft shown here was licence-built by Phönix Flugzeugwerke in Vienna for the Austro-Hungarian air force and service on the Piave Front.

ZEPPELINS AT WAR 1915-18

Paradoxically it was not the Germans but the French (or rather a Brazilian who lived in France) who first produced a practical airship, Alberto Santos-Dumont building some 15 non-rigid dirigibles by 1904 before being diverted to heavier-than-air craft. In Germany Count Ferdinand von Zeppelin, pursuing earlier theories of the Austrian engineer David Schwartz, began trials with a compartmented, rigid airship in 1900, the LZ 1, but it was not for several years that success attended his trials.

By the beginning of World War I, however, more than a score of very large airships had been produced in Germany, seven of them by Luftschiffbau Zeppelin for its associated airship-operating company Deutsche Luftschiffahrts AG (Delag), an airline that made 1,588 flights totalling 107,205 miles (172,525 km) in the five years before the war and carried 32,722 passengers. As early as 1909 the German war ministry took over two airships, the LZ 3 and LZ 5, for crew training, and it was Kapitän Kahlenberg of the 1st Prussian Airship Battalion who was in fact in command of LZ 7 *Deutschland* when it crashed in June 1910, though without loss of life.

The outbreak of war put an end to anything resembling commercial airship operation in Germany, although as late as 1917 a naval craft, the L 59, was called on to carry supplies to German forces in East Africa; it was recalled, when near Khartoum, having flown 4,200 miles (6760 km). Among the seven airships on army charge in August 1914 were the LZ 11 *Viktoria Luise*, taken over by the XVIII Corps, LZ 13 *Hansa* by the VII Corps (and used for training) and the LZ 17 *Sachsen* by the XIX Corps; in addition the LZ 25 (IX) was being completed to an army order. The Imperial navy had suffered catastrophe in 1913 when LZ 14 was lost at sea and LZ 18 exploded near Berlin, killing most of the service's trained crews. During the war Luftschiffbau Zeppelin built a total of 95 rigid airships, production of their giant craft (most of which were about 492 ft/150 m long) continuing at the rate of about one every fortnight. German army and navy airship stations had been established before the war (some of which were taken over from Delag) at Baden-Baden, Berlin, Bremen, Brunswick, Dresden, Düsseldorf, Emden, Hamburg, Cologne, Leipzig, Mannheim, Nordholz, Potsdam and Stuttgart.

Most of the early wartime operations by the German airships were navigation exercises, but on the night of 2/3 September 1914 LZ 17, flying from Cologne, dropped three bombs of about 200 lb (91 kg) on Antwerp before returning safely to base. Three months later this airship was transferred to the Eastern Front where it is said to have made half a dozen bombing raids before being handed over to the navy for training duties.

Of the two airships LZ 25 (IX) and LZ 26 (XII), the former was destroyed in its shed at Düsseldorf on 8 October by the epic attack by Flight Lieutenant R.L.G. Marix, RNAS, in a Sopwith Tabloid; of the latter, delivered to the army in December, it is said that this craft, a 500-ft (153-m) airship, was one of the first to fly a sortie over the British Isles.

The first authenticated raids over the UK were by the naval Schutte-Lanz L 3 and L 4, flying from Hamburg and Nordholz on 19 January 1915; their bombs fell in the area of Great Yarmouth, Norfolk, causing numerous casualties. A third airship turned back following engine trouble. L 3 and L 4 were later wrecked on the coast of Jutland during a second raid attempt.

As explained elsewhere, all German air raiding policies at the beginning of the war were under tight political control, the Kaiser himself withholding sanction for indiscriminate bombing. Nevertheless, despite an almost total lack of black-out precautions in the UK, the German naval airships (soon followed by those of the army), began flights over East Anglia, southern England and northern France. The first bombs to fall on London were dropped by a German army airship on 31 May 1915.

A week later the first German airship, LZ 37 (captained by Oberleutnant Otto van de Haegen, and flying in company with LZ 38 and LZ 39), was destroyed in 'air combat' over Ghent, Belgium, on the night of 6/7 May when Flight Sub-Lieutenant R.A.J. Warneford, RNAS, flying a Morane-Saulnier parasol monoplane from Dunkirk, struck the craft's hull with a small bomb, an action fraught with hazard and one for which the British pilot was recommended for the Victoria Cross. Warneford, who had had to force land after his successful exploit, lost his life in a flying accident a fortnight later, before his award was gazetted.

Further German airships were lost in action at an increasing rate as the frequency of attacks was stepped up, but it was not until the night of 2/3 September 1916 that one was shot down over British soil when Lieutenant William Leefe Robinson of No. 39 (Home Defence) Squadron, RFC, shot down SL XI at Cuffley, Hertfordshire; Leefe Robinson was also awarded the Victoria Cross.

By the end of 1916 the German airships, of which about 50 were in service, were carrying bombs of up to 600-lb (272-kg) weight, roughly twice the size of those capable of being carried by the early twin-engine bombing aeroplanes. On 27/28 November that year two German naval airships were destroyed in a single night over the English East Coast, the same night that six tiny bombs fell for the first time on London from an aeroplane. The airship raids continued throughout 1917, being launched wholly independently of the Gotha raids which started on 25 May. On 21 August the German naval airship L 23 was shot down off the Danish coast by a Sopwith Pup launched from a platform on the light cruiser HMS *Yarmouth* and flown by Flight Sub-Lieutenant B.A. Smart, RNAS.

It was perhaps ironic that it was the build-up of the UK's home defences against the aeroplane raids that eventually led to the discontinuation of the airship raids on the UK, the last to cause casualties being on 12 April 1918.

L 10 was a Zeppelin-built airship which made several raids on Britain.

The Zeppelin airships were the most accomplished of the war, and led to a successful civil line until the fateful crash of the *Hindenburg*.

L59 was a Zeppelin-built craft operated by the navy. It was used on an abortive resupply mission to East Africa.

GERMAN LONG-RANGE BOMBING 1915-18

Although the origins of strategic bombing probably lie in the Russian use of the Sikorsky four-engine bombers early in 1915, the Germans sought to extend the operations by their growing fleet of airships with development of the large aeroplane, of whose manufacturers the Siemens-Schuckert, Gothaer-Waggonfabrik and Zeppelin-Staaken companies were actively engaged in producing experimental examples at that time. Origins of the German use of bombers lay in the so-called battleplanes which equipped the first *Kampfstaffeln* (battle squadrons) of mid-1915, and although such large aircraft were generically referred to as K-types, such as the AEG K I, the first operational bombing units were codenamed Carrier Pigeon Units (*Brieftauben Abteilungen*), one of which was based at Ostend, ostensibly for attacks against south east England and the busy Channel ports; because of delays in bringing the larger aircraft up to reliable service standard, these units continued to fly relatively small aircraft of the B- and C-type and were therefore capable of no more than nuisance raids with very small bombs.

On the Eastern Front the large multi-engine battleplanes, such as the Siemens Forssman (obviously inspired by the Sikorsky bombers), Siemens-Schuckert Steffen R I and Zeppelin-Staaken VGO (Versuchs Gotha Ost) had undergone operational trials over the front with both the army and navy, and although most were either found to be altogether unsatisfactory or in need of further development, establishment of frontline *Kampfgeschwader* (battle wings) went ahead in 1916 for the purpose of launching worthwhile bombing raids on strategic targets well behind the Russian and French fronts. Such a policy of carrying the war to the rear areas, and the consequent endangering of civilian lives by premeditated acts of war, was the outcome of persistent pressure by the German military and naval staffs upon the Kaiser to permit military targets within cities remote from the battle theatres to be attacked from the air. Such a policy ignored the absence of any workable bomb-aiming equipment, so that any damage of a military value would be quite fortuitous.

The Brieftauben Abteilung Ostende was withdrawn to Bulgaria in mid-1916 and redesigned Kampfgeschwader Nr 1 (KG 1), three of its *Staffeln* (squadrons) being detached to form the basis of KG 3 (known as Kagohl 3), which in turn moved to Ghent with the stated purpose of starting raids on the UK with Gotha and Friedrichshafen bombers under the command of Hauptmann Ernst Brandenburg, the first of which was launched on 25 May 1917. On that day 23 Gotha G IVs set out for London but, on finding the British capital obscured by cloud and haze, turned for home and dropped their bombs on Folkestone, killing 95 and injuring 260 – higher casualties than in any previous raid by airship or aeroplane.

As an outcry erupted in the British Parliament at the defences' inability to counter this daylight raid, Brandenburg launched an attack on the naval town of Sheerness on 5 June by 22 Gothas; little damage was done, but 45 people were killed. One of the raiders was shot down by the ground defences. The next raid, flown on 13 June, marked the climax of Kagohl 3's fortunes: 20 Gothas set out for London, where the majority of bombs fell on the dock area and East End, one bomb falling on an infants' school at Poplar, killing 16 young children. Other bombs fell in the City, causing damage and casualties near St Paul's cathedral and Liverpool Street station. As Brandenburg brought his bombers home without loss, London counted 162 dead and 432 injured.

The clamour in the UK caused the defences to be strengthened by withdrawal of fighters from France and the establishment of gun and balloon belts around London and other Home County targets. The result in turn was to encourage the Germans to attack by night, and on the evening of 3 September 1917 four Gothas attacked Chatham, one bomb falling on a naval barracks, killing 131 ratings and injuring 90 others in the worst single bomb incident of the war. During the following 30 nights the Gothas flew 64 sorties over England, reaching London on six occasions.

Meanwhile the Germans had been making ready a new weapon, the R-type bomber (*Riesenflugzeug*, or giant aeroplane). These truly colossal aircraft, most of which were built by Zeppelin-Staaken, originated in the VGO 1 that had flown in 1915, and in various forms were powered by four (and sometimes five) Maybach or Mercedes engines. They formed the equipment of two units, Riesenflugzeug-abteilungen 500 and 501, and operated from the Ghent area both over France and south east England. With a wing span of over 138 ft (42 m) and a crew of at least seven, Rfa 501's R VIs carried out a total of 11 raids on the UK between 18 December 1917 and 20 May 1918. On 28 January an R VI, with the unit commander Hauptmann Richard von Bentivegni aboard (he was not himself a pilot), dropped a 661-lb (300-kg) bomb on a printing works in London, killing 38 and injuring 85. On the night of 16/17 February an R VI dropped a 2,205-lb (1000-kg) bomb on the Royal Hospital, Chelsea, the heaviest bomb to fall on the UK during the war.

Although these raids achieved little in terms of military value (other than diverting small numbers of aircraft from France) they focused attention on the potential value of strategic bombing, and incidentally encouraged the British authorities to amalgamate their air forces into a single service, the Royal Air Force, which came into being on 1 April 1918.

The Gotha G IV and G V were the main production variants of this famous family of German bombers (Gotha G V shown here). Powered by a pair of 260-hp (194-kW) Mercedes D IVa inline, water-cooled engines, their bombload varied from 600 to 1,000 lb (272 to 454 kg) according to mission range.

The Zeppelin-Staaken R VI was the largest aircraft ever to have attacked the British Isles. Luckily, for Britain, these were used only in very small numbers as they carried a large bomb load.

This Gotha G IV is typical of those which attacked Britain in 1917 and 1918. The effect of these raids was minimal in a military sense, but the effect on British morale was huge.

ALLIED BOMBING 1915-18

It was not until 1915, when in August that year Colonel Hugh Trenchard assumed command of the RFC in France, that a single British squadron was specifically assigned the task of supporting the army by bombing operations. And with nothing better than the Royal Aircraft Factory B.E.2 available, such long-distance raids that could be undertaken fell to the French to launch. The only aircraft that existed in any numbers were Voisin IIIs which could carry a bomb load of 132 lb (60 kg); this archaic single-pusher biplane, of which no fewer than 2,162 were ultimately built in France alone, served on the Western Front as well as in Russia and Italy.

In December 1915 the first purpose-built heavy bomber made its maiden flight in the UK. This design had been ordered by the Admiralty, yet it was not until November of the following year that the first example reached an operational unit. In the meantime little more than sporadic short-range bombing operations by B.E.2c and R.E.7 aircraft could be carried out by the RFC. The majority of bombs dropped were the 20-lb (9-kg) Hales weapon, but from early in 1916 an increasing number of 112-lb (50.8-kg) bombs became available and, on 30 June, six R.E.7s of No. 21 Squadron each dropped one of the new 336-lb (152.4-kg) RAF heavy-cased bombs over Lille railway station.

Meanwhile the RNAS' 3rd Wing had assembled under Captain W.L. Elder, RN, with the intention that from bases in the Vosges its 35 Sopwith 1½-Strutters and Short bombers would be able to reach the Saar industrial area. However, demands for aircraft to support ground operations on the Western Front resulted in most RNAS 1½-Strutters being transferred to the RFC, and it was not until October 1916 that the 3rd Wing was strong enough to launch a powerful bombing raid, nine 1½-Strutters and six French Breguet bombers attacking the Mauser factory at Obendorf on 12 October.

It was the RNAS 5th Wing at Dunkirk that received the first Handley Page O/100 heavy bomber in November 1916, followed shortly afterwards by the 3rd Wing, then based at Luxeuil; and it was the latter that carried out the first British night raid by a heavy bomber when a single O/100 bombed Moulin-les-Metz railway station on 16/17 March 1917. Four days later the RFC's first squadron (No. 100) formed and trained specifically for night bombing arrived in France, albeit without aircraft.

In October 1917 there was formed the RFC's 41st Wing under Lieutenant Colonel (later Marshal of the RAF Lord) C.L.N. Newall with the expressed purpose of mounting a strategic bombing campaign against German industrial targets, it being intended ultimately that this wing would operate independently of the tactical elements of the RFC so as to avoid its strength being squandered by local military commanders. The initial components of this wing were No. 55 Squadron (Airco/de Havilland D.H.4 day bombers), No. 100 (Royal Aircraft Factory F.E.2b night bombers) and No. 16 (Naval), (O/100 night bombers); in February 1918 the wing was reorganized as VIII Brigade and three months later Nos 99 and 104 Squadrons (both with D.H.9s) were added.

During the period between October 1917 and May 1918 this force carried out 142 raids, of which 57 were over German territory, and included such cities as Koblenz, Cologne, Mainz, Mannheim and Stuttgart.

With the creation on 1 April 1918 of the Royal Air Force by the amalgamation of RFC and RNAS, the way was clear to extend further the independence of VIII Brigade and, on 6 June, under the command of Major General Sir Hugh (later Marshal of the RAF Lord) Trenchard, was formed the Independent Force; this comprised Nos 55, 99, 100, 104 and 216 Squadrons (the last-named was previously No. 16 (Naval) Squadron), to which were added in August and September Nos 97, 115 and 215 Squadrons with Handley Page O/400 bombers and No. 110 Squadron with D.H.9a aircraft. No. 100 Squadron also converted to O/400s.

This force continued with the bombing task, begun by the 41st Wing, right up to the Armistice. In the last five months of the war it dropped a total of 550 tons of bombs, of which 390 tons were delivered at night. Among the targets were Bonn, Darmstadt, Frankfurt, Kaiserslautern, Karlsruhe, Rombas, Saarburg, Wiesbaden and Zweibrücken, as well as further visits to the cities attacked by the 41st Wing.

That these bombing raids began to have a serious effect on the German morale, already severely strained by civil unrest, was evidenced by a rapid increase in the enemy fighter defences, to counter which it was proposed to add a squadron of Sopwith Camels as escort to the force. Casualties were high, with a total of 109 aircraft (of which 69 were the big Handley Pages) lost.

During the last five months of the war the weight of RAF bombs increased dramatically, the most notable being the 1,600-lb (726-kg) (later increased to 1,800-lb/816-kg) bomb capable of being carried by the O/400. Shortly before the Armistice deliveries began of a new, much larger bomber, the Handley Page V/1500, capable of lifting the 3,360-lb (1524-kg) bomb, and it was intended that No. 166 Squadron with V/1500s would bomb Berlin. On the day the war ended three of these huge aircraft were bombed-up and ready for take-off from Bircham Newton.

Seen here in the company of a comparatively diminutive S.E.5 is this experimental version of the Handley Page O/400 bomber (3117), in this instance powered by four 200-hp (149-kW) Hispano-Suiza engines in place of the more usual pair of Rolls-Royce Eagles or Sunbeam Maori engines.

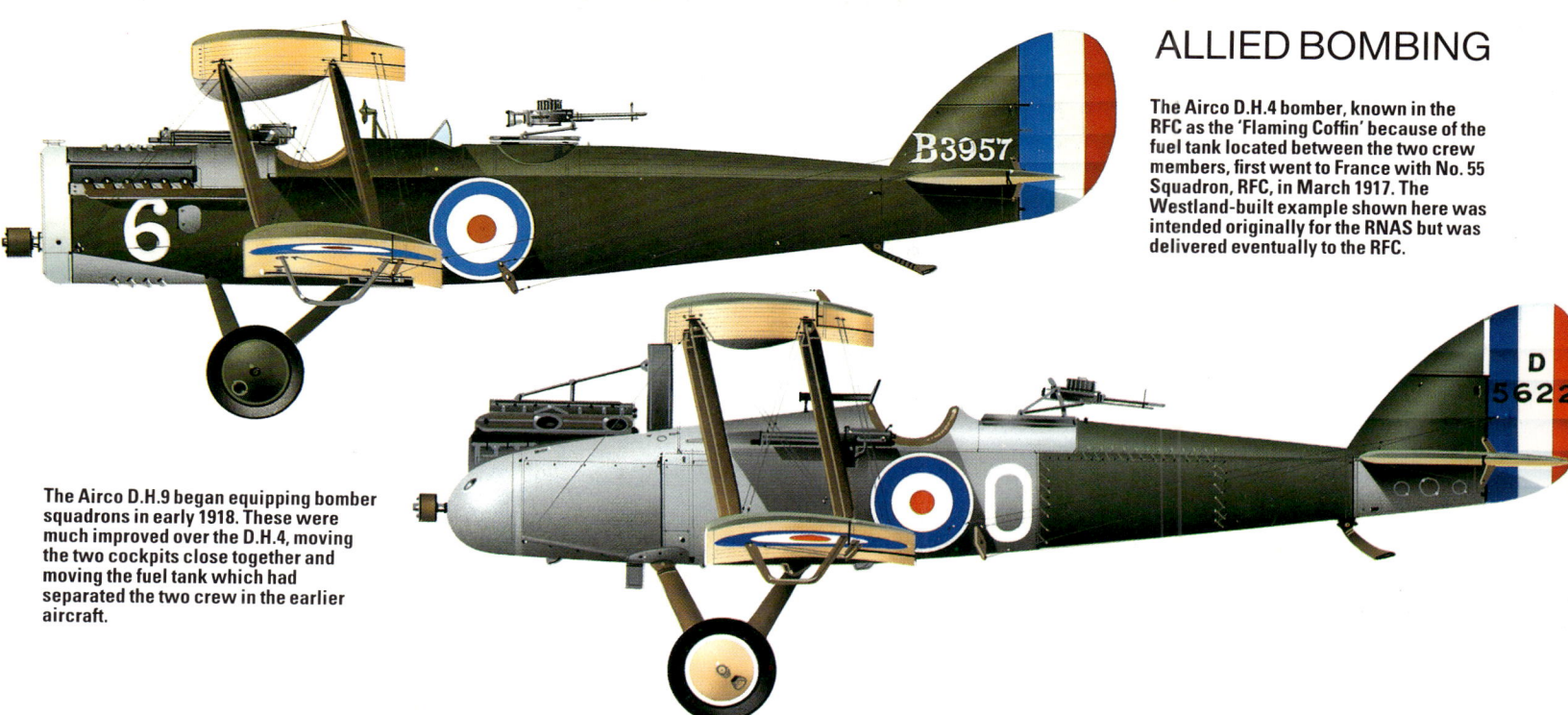

The Airco D.H.4 bomber, known in the RFC as the 'Flaming Coffin' because of the fuel tank located between the two crew members, first went to France with No. 55 Squadron, RFC, in March 1917. The Westland-built example shown here was intended originally for the RNAS but was delivered eventually to the RFC.

The Airco D.H.9 began equipping bomber squadrons in early 1918. These were much improved over the D.H.4, moving the two cockpits close together and moving the fuel tank which had separated the two crew in the earlier aircraft.

The Handley Page O/100 was a marvellous creation and was soon in action against German installations flying from airfields in France. The first units equipped were the 5th and 3rd Wings of the Royal Naval Air Service.

Members of the 11th Squadron, American Expeditionary Force, pose by their Airco D.H.4 aircraft at an airfield in France during 1918.

At the time that the RAF was formed, on 1 April 1918, the RFC's standard day bomber was the O/400, an aircraft from No. 207 Squadron at Ligescourt, France, being shown here. This was the first British squadron used solely for long-range night bombing, and the first to operate Handley Page bombers.

Handley Page O/400s carried the brunt of the bombing offensive during 1918 and many were lost to the increased defences. These were introduced as the newly-formed RAF stepped up its bombing campaign.

The giant V/1500 was issued to No. 166 Squadron just before war's end. This equal-span biplane, which could hit Berlin from its British base at Bircham Newton, carried the 3,360-lb (1524-kg) bomb.

COLONIAL OPERATIONS 1918-39

The UK's Royal Air Force emerged from World War I the most powerful air force in the world, having taken a major part in the air campaigns in the West, yet within a couple of years of the Armistice the RAF was faced with a far more sinister fight for survival as the generals and admirals squabbled to acquire for their own services the slender defence funds allowed by the British Treasury. Sir Eric Geddes, wartime First Lord of the Admiralty and for long an opponent of an autonomous RAF, achieved almost total emasculation of the RAF, reducing its squadrons from 188 to 25, and its personnel from 291,000 to 28,300, inclusive of overseas deployment.

It was indeed overseas that Sir Hugh Trenchard saw his opportunity to foster the survival of his service, first during the Chanak Crisis of 1920 in Turkey, when a small force of RAF personnel lent stability in a flashpoint situation, and then in the age-old trouble spots in the Middle East. Ever since the end of hostilities with the Turks the British Army had waged a costly and exhausting campaign against warring factions in Iraq in efforts to stabilize the area. Trenchard's policy was to concentrate a major part of the surviving RAF in the Middle East (there was only a single fighter squadron left in the UK in 1920) and use his resources sparingly but firmly in a wide-ranging campaign of air policing. For this he deployed the Snipes of No. 1 Squadron, Bristol F2Bs of No 6 Squadron and D.H.9As of Nos 8, 30 and 55 Squadrons in Iraq, all World War I aircraft but representative of the RAF's equipment until the mid-1920s. Faced initially with little more than inter-tribal strife, the RAF squadrons quickly evolved a pattern of 'benevolent policing', seldom firing a gun in anger and more often than not simply staging a demonstration; frequently, however, the wear of sand and dust caused engine failures far out over the desert, and a burst of Lewis gun from a downed F2B was sometimes needed to keep inquisitive tribesmen at a respectful distance until help arrived from the nearest British army post. Very soon relative peace reigned in the area, an achievement that had previously cost the army much time and money. The RAF proved itself a highly cost-effective force, gaining a fine reputation on which Trenchard played heavily to acquire new aircraft. The big Vernons of No. 70 Squadron gave excellent service, moving units about the Middle East, and in 1926 these were replaced by Victorias at Hinaidi; two years later they evacuated 500 British nationals caught up in the Afghan civil war. Also in 1928 the old D.H.9A began giving place to the Westland Wapiti, a process that continued until 1932.

In Egypt and India the pattern had been much the same. To provide defence for the Suez Canal a total of eight squadrons served in Egypt during the 1920s, while No. 14 Squadron was based in Palestine until the outbreak of World War II, latterly co-operating with the Palestine Police in maintaining some semblance of peace between Jew and Arab and re-equipping with Fairey Gordons in 1932.

Deployment of the RAF in India was more extensive throughout the inter-war period, most squadrons serving some time on the North West Frontier; stations such as Risalpur, Peshawar and Kohat became familiar postings for RAF flying personnel. The majority of squadrons in India were on permanent deployment, Nos 5, 20, 28 and 31 taking out Bristol F2Bs in 1919-20, and keeping them until 1929-30 when they received Wapitis; No. 5 continued to fly these until the beginning of World War II, but Nos 20 and 28 changed to Audaxes in the mid-1930s, and No. 31 became a transport squadron with Valentias in 1939. No. 60 Squadron was equipped in turn with D.H.10s, D.H.9As and Wapitis. As the strength of the RAF increased perceptibly during the late 1920s Nos 11 and 39 Squadrons, both with Wapitis, were sent out to India so that by the mid-1930s there were 13 RAF squadrons serving on the sub-continent.

A minor crisis in China threatened the safety of the international settlement at Shanghai and prompted the despatch of No. 2 Squadron with Bristol Fighters from Manston in April of that year, but it was returned later that year to re-equip with Atlases.

The continued presence of the RAF in Iraq (on aerodromes at Mosul, Baghdad, Hinaidi, and elsewhere) prompted the construction of a single large, centralized base at Habbaniyah in 1934, and this became in effect the focal point of the British military presence in the country, not only providing maintenance and training facilities but also becoming the base of No. 30 Squadron equipped with Hardy aircraft, developed specifically for the air policing role.

The last major Imperial deployment of the RAF overseas before World War II was undertaken when the Italian adventure in Abbyssinia threatened the security of the sea route through the Red Sea. Accordingly, so as to reinforce the British presence in the Canal Zone and at Aden, Nos 12 (Harts) and 41 (Demons) Squadrons were sent to Aden, No. 45 (Harts) to Kenya, No. 35 (Gordons) to the Sudan, and Nos 29 (Demons) and 33 (Harts) to Egypt; No. 22 Squadron with Vildebeests was based on Malta to cover any hostile movement by the Italian fleet. The following year, with the subjugation of Abyssinia, the immediate crisis passed and these RAF squadrons returned home where preparations for possible world war were now under way.

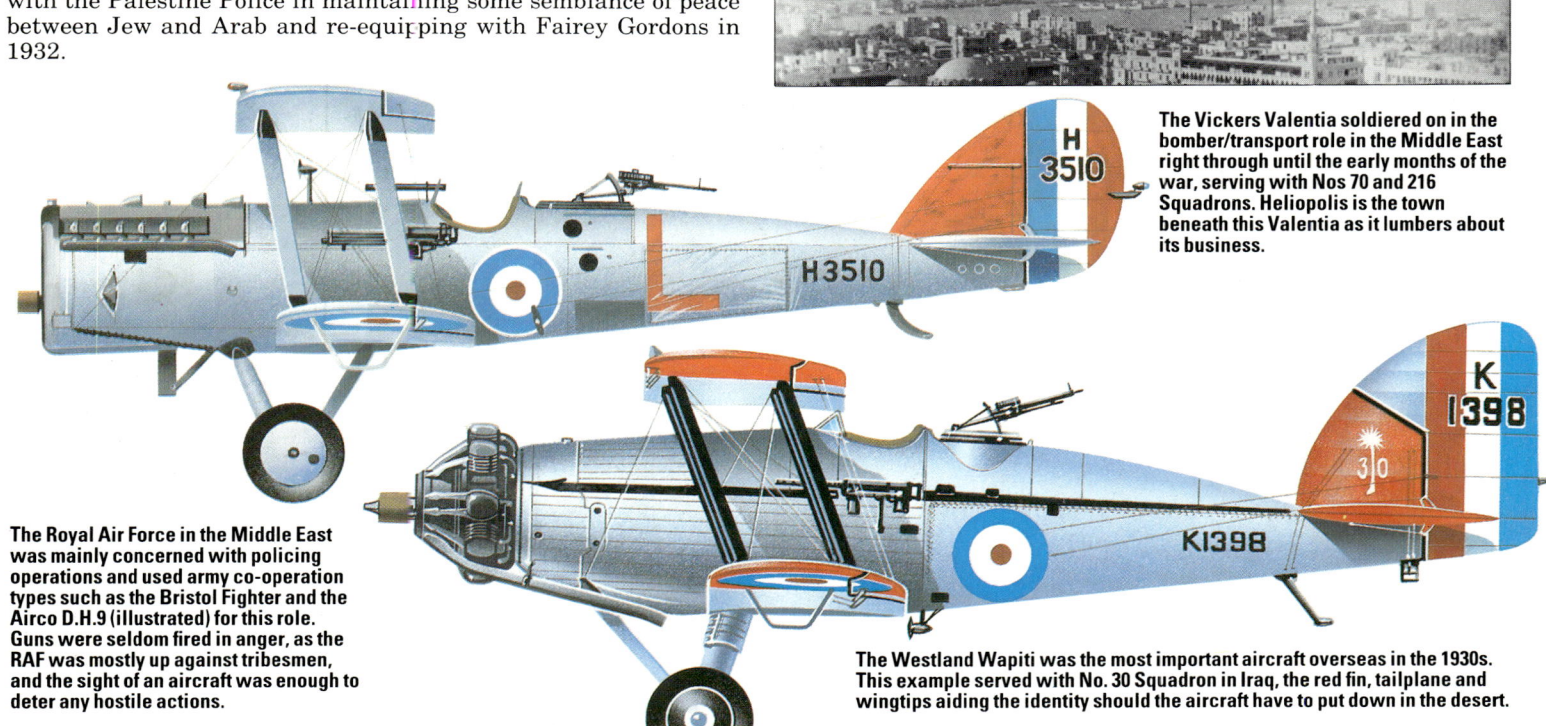

The Vickers Valentia soldiered on in the bomber/transport role in the Middle East right through until the early months of the war, serving with Nos 70 and 216 Squadrons. Heliopolis is the town beneath this Valentia as it lumbers about its business.

The Royal Air Force in the Middle East was mainly concerned with policing operations and used army co-operation types such as the Bristol Fighter and the Airco D.H.9 (illustrated) for this role. Guns were seldom fired in anger, as the RAF was mostly up against tribesmen, and the sight of an aircraft was enough to deter any hostile actions.

The Westland Wapiti was the most important aircraft overseas in the 1930s. This example served with No. 30 Squadron in Iraq, the red fin, tailplane and wingtips aiding the identity should the aircraft have to put down in the desert.

AMERICAN FLASHPOINTS 1922-35

Aviation had come early to South America, one of the early pioneers of flight being indeed the Brazilian Alberto Santos-Dumont who had contributed so much to European flying in the first decade of the 20th century. Military air forces had, before World War I, been created in Argentina, Brazil, Chile and Peru, to which Uruguay was added in 1916. It was not long thereafter that the age-old abrasive politics arising from contentious border demarcation, arbitrary ethnic divisions and external industrial exploitation involved the Central and South American states in self-imposed strife, though relatively few of the coups and revolutions were staged by more than a few troops. Military aircraft were scarcely in evidence during the continuous internal strife that existed in Mexico between 1922 and 1926, or during the bloodless coup in Guatemala of 1924, or the Cuban revolution of 1930.

In 1932, however, conflict between Peru and her neighbour, Colombia, broke out when the border territory of Leticia (previously awarded to Colombia in a 1922 treaty) became a source of disputed sovereignty. Peruvian forces entered Leticia in 1932 and ejected Colombian officials, installing their own provincial administration. Colombia at that time possessed a small air force comprising a handful of Curtiss Hawk biplane fighters, Curtiss O-1 Falcon reconnaissance biplanes and a small number of other American and European aircraft. Peru on the other hand had been strengthening her air force, the Cuerpo de Aeronautica del Perú (CAP), since 1929, and already possessed Curtiss Hawk and Nieuport 121 fighters, Vought O2U-1E Corsair observation aircraft, Douglas M-4 bombers and Boeing 40B-4 transports; orders had also been placed in the UK for Fairey Fox II bombers and some Fairey Gordon general-purpose aircraft.

Flying proficiency was generally lacking on both sides, though there were a number of incidents involving air combat but, while the Colombian air force was handicapped by the lack of established aerodromes within 200 miles (320 km) of the disputed border territory, the CAP contrived to use its fighters and observation aircraft in support of the ground forces to some effect; its bombers, being seaplanes and based on the coast some 600 miles (960 km) from the war zone, were not used. When, in April 1933 the Peruvian president Luis Sánchez Cerro was murdered, Peru became more conciliatory and hostilities died down; a year later Leticia was formally returned to Colombia.

While the Peruvian-Colombian conflict was at its height a major war was raging between Bolivia and Paraguay. Both nations had for many years been disputing sovereignty of the Chaco Boreal, a dispute fuelled by the belief by foreign interests that large oil deposits lay undeveloped in the territory. In 1928 Paraguayan forces had seized a Bolivian fort, and immediately a series of isolated but bloody clashes followed. A truce had been negotiated by the Pan American Conference and League of Nations, but this failed to hold and in 1932 all-out warfare between the two states erupted.

The small Paraguayan air force possessed a number of Italian Fiat CR.30 biplane fighters, Bergamaschi AP.1 monoplane fighters, Caproni Ca 101 three-engine bombers and Breda Ba 44 transports, while the larger Bolivian Cuerpo de Aviación flew about 60 Curtiss-Wright Osprey general-purpose aircraft, Curtiss Hawk IA fighters and Junkers W.34s converted as bombers. From 1933 onwards both sides made considerable use of their air forces, a high proportion of the aircrews being foreign mercenaries although, with the assistance of an Italian military aviation mission, the standard of training among Paraguayan flying personnel quickly improved. Numerous air combats took place, particularly when both sides began flying bombing raids, and it has been suggested that each air force lost about 30 aircraft. Best known pilot of the war was undoubtedly Major Rafael Pavon who, in Curtiss Hawks, was credited with three combat victories and came to be dubbed the Bolivian 'ace of aces'.

A further truce was arranged in 1935 and the Chaco Treaty was signed at Buenos Aires dividing the Chaco Boreal between the two belligerents, Paraguay gaining by far the greater area. Both sides had suffered heavy casualties (Paraguay 36,000 men and Bolivia 52,000), and both were rendered economically exhausted by the Chaco War which achieved precious little, as the oil interests that had led to such bitter jealousies were not to be realized for many years to come.

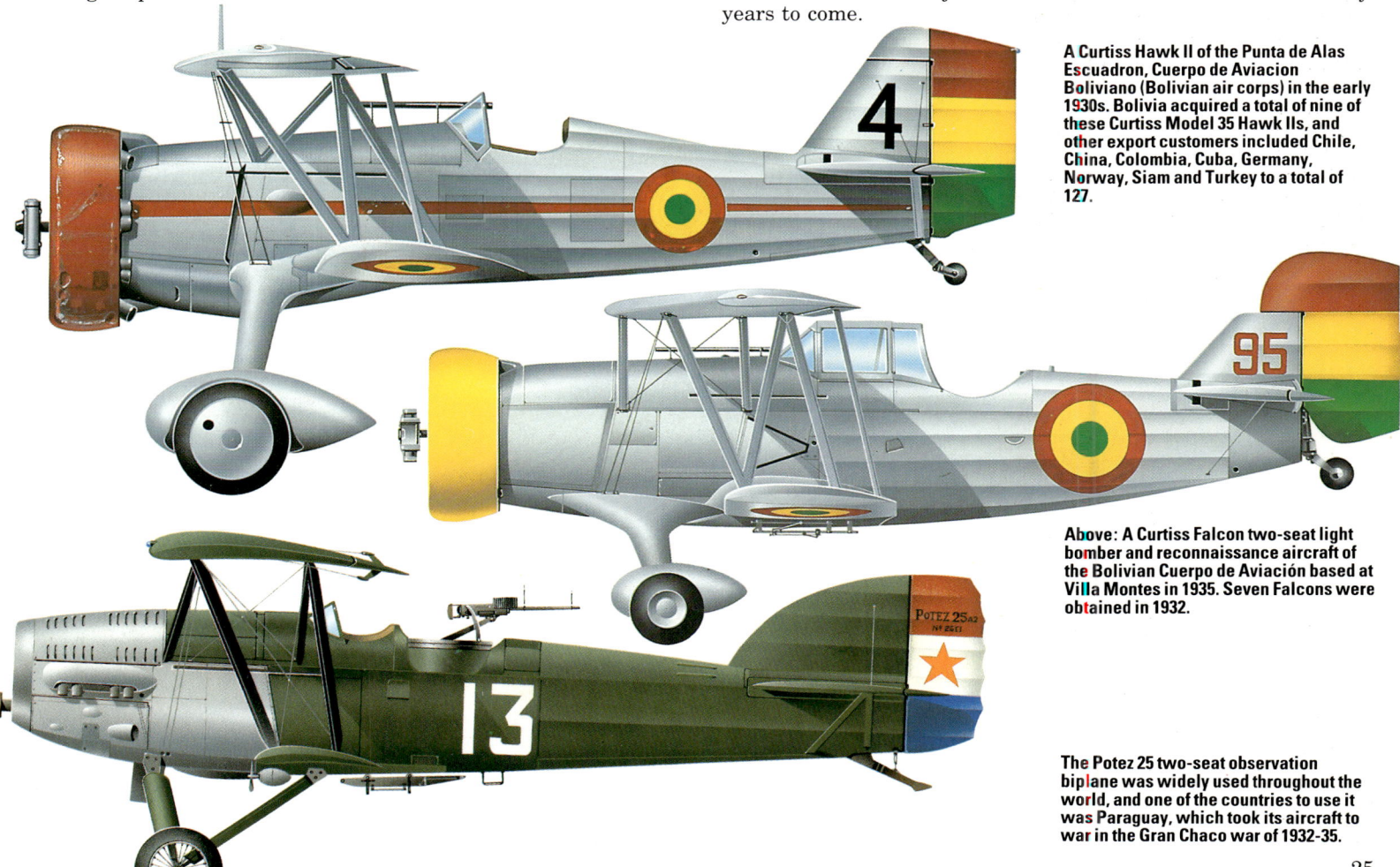

A Curtiss Hawk II of the Punta de Alas Escuadron, Cuerpo de Aviacion Boliviano (Bolivian air corps) in the early 1930s. Bolivia acquired a total of nine of these Curtiss Model 35 Hawk IIs, and other export customers included Chile, China, Colombia, Cuba, Germany, Norway, Siam and Turkey to a total of 127.

Above: A Curtiss Falcon two-seat light bomber and reconnaissance aircraft of the Bolivian Cuerpo de Aviación based at Villa Montes in 1935. Seven Falcons were obtained in 1932.

The Potez 25 two-seat observation biplane was widely used throughout the world, and one of the countries to use it was Paraguay, which took its aircraft to war in the Gran Chaco war of 1932-35.

THE NOMONHAN INCIDENT 1939

Fought out over the remote steppelands of Mongolia, the conflict now usually known as the Nomonhan Incident occupied 129 days just as World War II was breaking out in Europe in 1939. Yet despite its involvement of tens of thousands of troops and hundreds of aircraft, the incident is scarcely recorded in the history books of the West. Moreover, like the Spanish Civil War, it provided practical experience for combatant nations that were to be involved in World War II.

At a point where the Khalkha river formed the border between the Soviet-Mongolian province of Dorcnod and Japanese-administered Manchukuo, a band of nomadic tribesmen strayed into Soviet territory on 10 May 1939 and were pursued back by Mongolian border guards. *Ad hoc* Japanese air reconnaissance disclosed an unexpected build-up of military forces on the west bank of the Khalkha river and, smarting from previous humiliations by the Soviet Union, the Kanto-gun (the Japanese defence command in China) forthwith created a local detachment comprising about 50 aircraft in the area, with its headquarters at Hailar, some 100 miles (160 km) behind the border; the majority of these aircraft were Type 97 (Nakajima Ki-27) fighters.

The Soviet forces comprised a cavalry division, a rifle corps and an armoured brigade, supported by three air regiments, also of about 50 aircraft, of which about 40 were Polikarpov I-15 biplane and Polikarpov I-16 monoplane fighters. Following the shooting down of a V-VS reconnaissance aircraft by the Japanese, a number of isolated air combats took place during May, in which the Type 97 fighters confirmed their superiority by shooting down a score of Soviet aircraft without loss to themselves.

The Soviets replied by sending a further fighter regiment of I-16s to the war zone, and at the same time established a group of airfields (little more than strips cleared on the steppeland) around the township of Tamsag Bulag. On 22 June the V-VS staged a number of sweeps and raids on the Japanese ground positions lining the Khalkha river and fierce air battles developed. The Soviet attacks stung the Kanto-gun into retaliation, and on 27 June 30 Japanese bombers with an escort of 74 fighters twice raided the V-VS airfields around Tamsag Bulag.

On 2 July two Japanese divisions attacked across the Khalkha and came under heavy air attack by up to 60 Tupolev SB-2 bombers. Air combats between the opposing air forces were now frequently involving up to 100 fighters on each side, but still the Japanese proved superior, their fighters taking heavy toll of the I-15 biplane

fighters opposing them. At the end of July the V-VS introduced 20-mm cannon-armed I-16 Type 17 monoplane fighters, and these to a large extent redressed the balance.

As Japanese losses in the air began to mount during August (particularly among their more experienced pilots), the Soviets, now commanded by Komkor Georgi Zhukov, mounted a large-scale attack by 100,000 troops and 800 tanks across the Khalkha, aiming to trap the Japanese forces in a giant pincer movement. Supporting this offensive were more than 500 aircraft, including a half-regiment of Tupolev TB-3 four-engine heavy bombers which began night raids on Japanese supply lines in the rear. Through sheer tenacity and skill the Japanese managed to cling to a slender air superiority, although the SB-2s and TB-3s started making raids from 19,685 ft (6000 m), which gave them some immunity, but when the Soviet fighters began strafing attacks on the forward Japanese airfields losses among the Type 97 fighters increased rapidly.

Just as it seemed that the Soviet forces were poised to destroy the two Japanese divisions on the eastern side of the Khalkha the first heavy snow of the winter began falling on 11 September, effectively halting all activity on the ground. Air combat continued until 16 September, when peace negotiations between Tokyo and Moscow brought the conflict to an end.

The small war had been extraordinarily vicious, involving 120,000 Soviets and 80,000 Japanese on the ground, while each side lost upwards of 200 aircraft. The fighting had demonstrated unequivocally to the Soviets that the age of the biplane fighter was at an end (although the I-15 continued in service for almost two more years); it also confirmed the SB-2 as an efficient light bomber by the standards of the day. The Japanese could take comfort in the excellence of their pilots, while the Type 97 fighter had continued to dominate the skies in the absence of really modern fighters.

The real lesson was missed. Foreign correspondents and observers were forbidden access to the war front, with the result that Western staffs remained blissfully ignorant of the high standard of training and equipment in the Imperial Japanese army air force. This standard was to enjoy further progressive improvement, so that when the Pacific war broke out two years later the Japanese proved immeasurably superior to the Allied forces ranged against them.

A formation of Nakajima Ki-27s on patrol. This type held air superiority for the Japanese throughout the conflict, largely on account of the superior training of the Japanese pilots, many of whom had fought Polikarpov aircraft previously, over China.

In common with its Japanese opponents, the Polikarpov I-152 (also known as the I-15bis), featured both sturdiness and agility. This aircraft served with the 70 IAP of the V-VS (Soviet air force) during the Nomonhan Incident on the Manchukuoan-Mongolian border in the summer of 1939.

A lightly constructed and armed fighter which possessed phenomenal manoeuvrability, the Nakajima Ki-27 made its operational debut over China in 1938, proving an instant success. This Ki-27b was the mount of the Chutai leader, 10th Direct Command Chutai, based in Manchuria in 1938.

The Polikarpov I-16 was the principal fighter employed by the Soviets over Nomonhan, and the best. It was a good match performance-wise for the Nakajima Ki-27 (Type 97) but its pilots were not as well trained.

The Mitsubishi Ki-15 light bomber saw much action over Nomonhan and China and its performance was good for its day. But bombload was limited, and it could offer little defence against well-flown fighters.

Japan acquired Fiat BR.20 Cicognas from Italy and used these along the Manchurian border on bombing raids. The BR.20 also fought with Nationalist forces in Spain.

SPANISH CIVIL WAR 1936-1939

Years of international antagonism between extremist socialism and fascism throughout continental Europe sparked into bloody civil war in Spain on 18 July 1936, when right-wing army officers rose against an effete and corrupt socialist administration. The government (Republican) air force was poorly equipped with a hotch-potch of obsolete Nieuport-Delage NiD.52 fighters, Breguet 19 reconnaissance bombers, some Vickers Vildebeest torpedo-bombers and a handful of other old foreign aircraft.

Sensing that the Nationalist forces were even worse equipped, Nazi Germany quickly assembled a force of modern aircraft and volunteers for support of General Francisco Franco, and within a week the first Junkers Ju 52/3m bomber-transports were on their way to Morocco to airlift large numbers of troops from Africa to bolster the Nationalists. Some of the NiD.52 pilots had also joined the Nationalists and one of these, Teniente Miguel Guerro Garcia, shot down half a dozen Republican aircraft in the first fortnight of the war. In August the nationalist air force quickly gained strength with six Heinkel He 51 fighters and further Ju 52/3m bomber-transports from Germany, and a dozen Savoia-Marchetti S.81s and a similar number of Fiat CR.32s from Fascist Italy. The S.81s went into action on 5 August, bombing a Republican warship; soon after, their initial trooping completed, the Ju 52/3m aircraft started bombing raids in support of Franco's northward advance.

The Republicans had also appealed for foreign assistance, and during August about 60 French aircraft (Dewoitine D.371s, D.372s, D.501s and D.510s, Potez 54s, Loire-Nieuport LN.46s and Blériot-Spad S.510s) arrived.

By the end of the year the flow of foreign aircraft to both sides was well established, the German contingent having been organized into the Legion Cóndor, under General Hugo Sperrle, with Ju 52/3ms, He 51s, He 45s, He 46s, He 59s, He 70s and Henschel Hs 123s. The Italians, now formed into an autonomous Aviazione Legionaria, had added Meridionali Ro 37bis reconnaissance bombers to further CR.32s and S.M.81s. The Soviet Union, demanding full payment in gold, had supplied the first of a large number of Polikarpov I-15 biplane and I-16 monoplane fighters and some Tupolev SB-2 twin-engine bombers.

Most of these aircraft were deployed on the Madrid front in October where the Nationalists threatened the capital. Indeed it was the superiority of the I-15 and I-16 fighters that frustrated Nationalist air operations around Madrid, and it was the failure by such aircraft as the He 51 and CR.32 to secure air superiority that prompted despatch of 45 Messerschmitt Bf 109B monoplane fighters early in 1937, as well as 30 Heinkel He 111B and 15 Dornier Do 17F bombers, from Germany.

Stalemate around Madrid in 1937 was followed by a Nationalist offensive in the north; many of the He 51s and CR.32s were handed over to the Spaniards with the arrival of the Bf 109Bs, and delivery of the new SM.79 allowed the more vulnerable Ju 52/3m aircraft to confine their operations to night bombing, while a shipload of Czech Aero A.101 bombers, intended for the Republicans, was captured and put into service with Franco's forces. It was during the Nationalist drive in the north that an air attack on the small fortified town of Guernica was seized on by the socialist propagandists to point to the supposedly indiscriminate bombing by the fascists, yet neither side was innocent of such lapses.

Three main Republican counteroffensives in 1937 gained only limited success and did not succeed in diverting Nationalist air strength from the northern front, which crumbled in August. However, licence production of the excellent I-16 fighter had contributed to a numerical superiority in Republican aircraft during the summer and led to yet further acceleration of German aircraft deliveries to the Legion Cóndor, including Junkers Ju 87 dive-bombers and further Bf 109s, and Fiat BR.20 bombers to the Aviazione Legionaria.

During the spring of 1938, heartened by their victory in the north, the Nationalists succeeded in reaching the Mediterranean coast between Barcelona and Valencia, thereby cutting Republican-held territory in two. That April the first Bf 109Cs replaced the last of the German-flown He 51s and, led by the great German pilot, Werner Mölders, succeeded at last in mastering the I-16. As the Republican forces desperately fought to avoid defeat, the majority of Soviet volunteer pilots melted away and returned home; all the while the Nationalist air force grew in strength, taking over German equipment as newer aircraft arrived in the country. On the central front in particular the Legion Cóndor proved almost invincible, and in November Franco crossed the Ebro and soon after was driving on Barcelona. Early in 1939 the Germans introduced the first cannon-armed Bf 109Es and the Italians delivered a few Fiat G.50s, and these (together with the earlier Bf 109Bs and Bf 109Cs now being flown by Spanish pilots) effectively dominated the air, Mölders himself becoming the highest-scoring German with 14 victories.

On 27 March the Nationalists fought their way into the centre of Madrid and on the next day the war ended. Whatever the wider ramifications of the Spanish Civil War, it had proved the ideal testing ground for the infant German Luftwaffe, conceived as it was as an aerial support arm for the German army, and the success of close-support aircraft was classically demonstrated, German propagandists being loud and quick to point to the devastating power of the dreaded Ju 87 dive-bomber, soon to terrorize half of Europe.

A handful of Tupolev SB-2 light bombers was supplied to the Republicans. The Soviet Union demanded full payment for all the aircraft it supplied, whereas the forces of Italy and Germany gladly contributed aircraft and crew free in order to gain valuable combat experience.

Below: This Junkers Ju 52/3mg4e was flown by the Grupo de Bombardeo Nocturno 2-G-22 of the 1ª Escuadra, Nationalist Arma de Aviacion. The Ju 52 made an effective bomber when out of the way of fighters, and carried a gunner in a ventral dustbin which was swung into position after take-off.

Below: Messerschmitt Bf 109D flown by Hauptmann Gotthard Handrick, Gruppenkommandeur JG 88, Legion Condor, Calamocha, in February 1938. The zylinder Hut (top hat) identified 2. Staffel, JG 88, and the motif on the spinner recalls Handrick's Modern Pentathlon Gold Medal at the 1936 Olympic Games in Berlin.

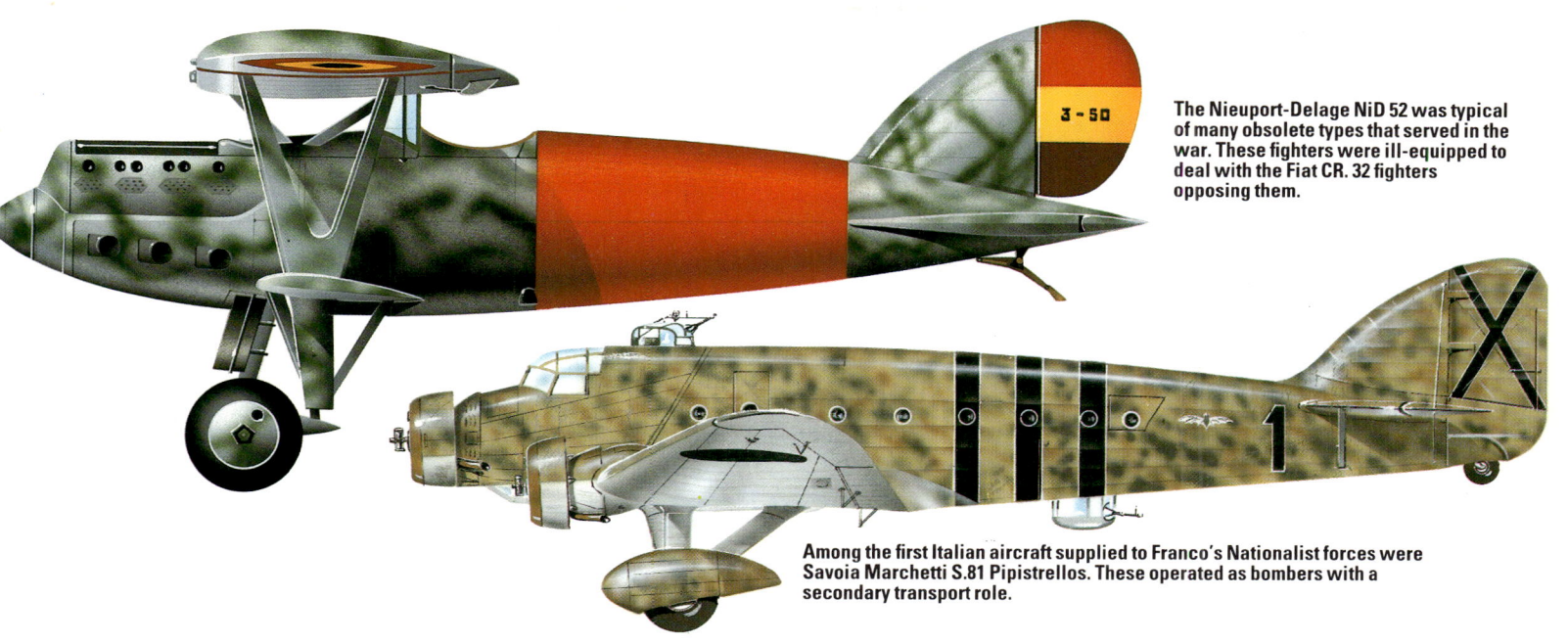

The Nieuport-Delage NiD 52 was typical of many obsolete types that served in the war. These fighters were ill-equipped to deal with the Fiat CR. 32 fighters opposing them.

Among the first Italian aircraft supplied to Franco's Nationalist forces were Savoia Marchetti S.81 Pipistrellos. These operated as bombers with a secondary transport role.

Although it suffered during World War II, the Savoia Marchetti S.M.81 proved useful as a bomber during the war in Spain. This example flies over a burning Republican target while escorted by Fiat CR.32s.

Some of the trench warfare employed in Spain resembled that of World War I, but the sleek Messerschmitt Bf 109B buzzing the trench is a harbinger of the doom and despair that would befall the rest of Europe as it plunged into a modern war in 1939.

The 'Double Six' emblem on the fin identifies this Spanish I-16 as a Super Mosca operated by the 3ª Escuadrilla de Mosca based at Albacete during 1937. The I-16 was to play a significant role in early air operations during the Spanish Civil War, with Republican aircraft like this helping to regain air superiority.

An enormous number of types flew during the Civil War, and many of these were used by both sides. This Polikarpov I-16 was captured by Nationalist forces and hastily impressed into service.

One of the great fighters of the 1930s, the Fiat CR.32 saw much action during the war, being the main Italian fighter. They had excellent performance for their day but could not wrest air superiority from the Polikarpov I-16. It was this failure, and that of the Heinkel He 51, that hastened the deployment of the Messerschmitt Bf 109 to the theatre.

BLITZKRIEG ON POLAND 1939

At 04.15 on 1 September 1939 World War II shattered an uneasy European peace as the German 3rd, 4th, 8th, 10th and 14th Armies burst across Poland's western frontiers as the components of two army groups embarking on a huge pincer movement designed to close successively at Kutna, Warsaw and Brest Litovsk, thereby encircling the ill-prepared Polish armies under General Smigly-Rydz. From the first moments of the crushing attack the young Luftwaffe hurled some 2,000 modern aircraft into the battle with scant worry from the opposing Lotrictwo Wojskowe (Polish air force) which was quickly seen to be not only poorly equipped but badly organized and deployed; the Poles could field fewer than 200 obsolete PZL P.7 and P.11 fighters and a similar number of light bombers.

Over the battlefields themselves roared nine *Gruppen* of Junkers Ju 87 dive-bombers (some 366 aircraft), spearheading and supporting the devastating *Blitzkrieg* tactic whose theory had been proved in the Spanish Civil War. As aircraft and armour blasted its way through the Polish defences, the German bomber force ranged far afield against vital lines of communication, against the Polish war factories and against airfields in the rear. Three *Kampfgeschwader* of Heinkel He 111 heavy bombers (about 300 aircraft) and four of Dornier Do 17s (400 aircraft) were active on the first day: 60 He 111s of I and III/KG 4 bombed Krakow airfield as 30 similar aircraft of II/KG 4 dropped 22 tons of bombs on Lemburg airfield, destroying six Polish fighters on the ground. The Putzig/Rahmel naval base was heavily hit from the air by I/KG 1, and the all-important PZL fighter factory was badly damaged in a raid by II/LG 1 on Warsaw/Okecie airport.

The main fault in the Polish air force deployment lay in the rigid affiliation of fighter and bomber squadrons, bound tightly into autonomous regiments, to specific armies themselves regionally deployed. There was thus no flexibility in air defence, more than half the air force being withheld from battle until imminently threatened by the German advance. The Poles' trouble was that the Luftwaffe recognized no such parochial niceties and was frequently free to attack its targets with scarcely any opposition. Quickly realizing the fatal flaw in their organization, some of the Polish fighter squadrons abandoned their assigned bases and sought to attack the German bomber formations wherever they were reported.

Unfortunately the aged P.7 and P 11 fighters on which Poland's air defence rested almost exclusively were no match for the German Messerschmitt Bf 109Es, whose pilots were given free rein to hunt the Polish skies. Nevertheless there were numerous instances of reckless courage by the defending pilots who, with scant heed of appalling odds, waded into the big German formations.

By the end of the third day the Luftwaffe had lost a total of 55 aircraft destroyed, 71 aircrew killed, 39 wounded and 94 missing. Polish casualties, on the other hand, had reached the loss of 46 fighters and about 60 light bombers, roughly a quarter of the entire air force in just three days. The light bomber force (the only arm of the Polish air force to be tightly reined within its regional deployment) had carried out several setpiece raids against German armour assembly areas with some success, but with crippling losses to *Flak* and fighters. In one memorable attack by 28 P.23 light bombers in the Radomski-Piotrków area more than half the aircraft failed to return.

After 10 days the invading armies had virtually isolated a dozen Polish divisions in the Kutno area, and the Poles attempted to mount a concerted counterattack against the German forces, now nearing Warsaw itself. This proved to be the last fully sustained resistance by the Polish army in the field, now desperately handicapped by the surging masses of civilian refugees seeking escape from the ravaged towns and villages. No more than about 100 Polish fighters and bombers remained airworthy, and these were flown into battle piecemeal, their pilots seldom briefed as to the strength or presence of the enemy's air force. By 13 September German aircraft losses had risen to 150 aircraft destroyed, but as the German army closed its ring of steel around the capital, resistance by the Polish air force dwindled to nothing. Those pilots who could made good their escape to neighbouring countries, and thence to the West, later joining the French and British air forces to continue their fight.

With tacit agreement on partitioning rights with Germany, the Soviet Union invaded Poland from the east on 17 September and, although Warsaw continued to resist until 27 September, the last concentration of Polish forces in the Modlin fortress was defeated on the following day and the campaign ended.

The short Polish campaign sparked World War II, with the UK and France siding with Poland against Germany on 3 September, though neither country was in any position, militarily or geographically, to offer any assistance during the four short weeks needed by Germany to crush all opposition. Those weeks witnessed a demonstration of total war. If the world had thus far been indifferent to the portents of Spain, the flames of Warsaw and the whine of Stukas were to be the harbingers of hell that would not be quenched or quelled for six long years to come.

Dornier Do 17s head for a Polish target at a relatively low altitude. Operating under the aerial umbrella of the Luftwaffe's fighter units, the Do 17 squadrons proved themselves to be quite effective in this campaign.

PZL P.23 light bombers were used in retaliation against the advancing German hordes. The aircraft was totally outclassed by the modern opposition and was cut down in droves. German flak was as deadly as its fighters and the P.23s stood no chance.

Although of monoplane configuration, the PZL P.11 was scarcely in the class of the excellent Messerschmitt Bf 109. Although flown with bravery by the few pilots who managed to get airborne during the onslaught, the Luftwaffe was never challenged for air superiority.

The Stuka in classic pose, with its cluster of one 551-lb (250-kg) SC 250 and four 110-lb (50-kg) SC 50 bombs dropping away just before the aircraft pulls out of its steep dive. The terrifying aspect of the aircraft was enhanced by the 'Jericho trumpet' sirens mounted at the top of the landing gear legs.

Above: The PZL P.23 Karaś (Crucian Carp) was numerically the most important bomber/reconnaissance aircraft in service with the Polish air force: on 1 September 1939 the Dispositional Air Force had 50 of the type, and the Armies' Air Force 68. Illustrated is a P.23B of No. 42 Squadron, attached to the Pomorze Army.

Above: Messerschmitt Bf 109E-3 of IV Gruppe, Jagdgeschwader 51, later named 'Molders' in honour of Germany's first great ace of World War II. This variant appeared soon after the Polish surrender, and differed only a little from the Bf 109E-1 and E-1/B fighters equipping the fighter units deployed in that campaign.

PZL P.11s were the most modern fighters that the Poles could muster, and suffered at the hands of the Luftwaffe. German pilots had been fighting in Spain, and many unbeatable tactics had been worked out. Had the Poles possessed better aircraft, the revolutionary tactics of the Germans would still have resulted in a massive victory.

THE WINTER WAR 1939-40

Opportunist intervention by the Soviet Union in the latter stages of Poland's rape by Germany was to be expected following the Ribbentrop-Molotov Pact of August 1939. The Winter War between Finland and the USSR, which broke out on 30 November that year, was the outcome of the Soviet Union's failure to steamroller Finland into giving her the use of land and bases to safeguard her approaches to Leningrad through the Gulf of Finland in the event of an attack by Germany.

The conflict, which lasted for 14 weeks, was fought largely on the shores of the huge Lake Ladoga and on the vital Karelian Isthmus in the south. The Finns, conscious of the hazards implicit in resistance to Soviet demands, had built a formidable line of defence, the Mannerheim Line, across the Karelian Isthmus, this neck of land constituting the direct line of approach to Viipuri and the capital itself, Helsinki. In the air the Finns possessed a small but well-trained air force of some 145 aircraft, of which 114 were operational when war broke out. These comprised three squadrons of Fokker C.X reconnaissance biplanes and two squadrons of Bristol Blenheim Mk Is which constituted the bombing force. Two fighter squadrons were equipped with Fokker D.XXIs, although one squadron still had a flight of aged Bristol Bulldogs. Obsolete Blackburn Ripons and Junkers K.43s were employed for coastal duties.

Against Finland was ranged a total of 696 Soviet aircraft in support of ground forces, plus some 20 aircraft operating from Estonian bases. Main equipment consisted of Tupolev SB-2 and Ilyushin DB-3 medium bombers, Tupolev TB-3 heavy bombers and about 230 Polikarpov I-15bis biplane fighters, deployed along virtually the length of frontier from north to south.

Air attacks against targets in southern Finland by Estonian-based bombers on the first day found the defences unprepared but, when repeated on the following day, met a spirited defence by the D.XXIs, whose pilots destroyed 10 of the raiders; a Bulldog was lost and a D.XXI was shot down by Finnish ground defences in error. Atrocious weather now set in, preventing any further air action for three weeks, a period spent by both sides in building up their strength. On the ground the Finnish army, better equipped to fight in the fierce snowstorms, held the Soviet attacks almost everywhere, small infiltrating forces inflicting enormous losses on Soviet convoys moving up to the Karelian Front. In the Soviet air force, Polikarpov I-16 monoplane fighters started arriving at the front, and early in the New Year the total number of Soviet aircraft in the Finnish theatre grew to around 1,500.

By the end of 1939 the Finnish air force had been credited with destroying more than 50 enemy aircraft, almost all falling to the D.XXIs, but also two or three to the ancient Bulldogs. On 6 January, as the Finns counterattacked fiercely in Karelia and to the north of Lake Ladoga, eight DB-3s raided the Utti area; all were shot down by D.XXIs, six of them by one pilot.

It was at this point in the war that help arrived from Finland's allies. Eleven Blenheim Mk IV bombers, 24 Gloster Gauntlets and 30 Gloster Gladiators were sent from the UK; 30 Morane-Saulnier MS.406 fighters arrived from France and, from Sweden, a volunteer force of four Hawker Harts and a dozen Gladiators arrived to fight in the north. Some Italian Fiat G.50s had also arrived in December.

As the Finnish counterattack stabilized the front line, the Soviets stepped up the air attacks to cover a big build-up on the ground. On 17 January D.XXIs destroyed nine SB-2s, on 19 January five and on 20 January 13. Despite these significant successes, there were signs that the Soviets were beginning to avoid combat with the Finnish fighters, preferring to attack the bombers; in three weeks during January about half the Blenheims were lost.

In the first week of February the Soviet army launched a massive and ultimately decisive offensive towards Viipuri. As the Finnish fighters, now including Gladiators and G.50s, which first entered combat service on 2 and 26 February respectively, fought desperately to prevent the large Soviet bomber formations from interfering in the ground battle, air combat became perceptibly less one-sided than hitherto. There were still outstanding successes for the Finnish pilots, but their losses were mounting rapidly as when, on 29 February, a large formation of I-16s attacked one of the Gladiator bases, destroying five Gladiators and a D.XXI while they were taking off.

Despite defending Viipuri successfully right up to the end, the Finns recognized the war situation as hopeless. By the end of the first week in March the strength of the opposing Soviet air force was estimated at 2,000 aircraft, whereas that of the Finns was dwindling rapidly. Some 44 Brewster Buffalo fighters were on their way from the United States, but arrived too late. On 13 March the Finns agreed to an armistice, being forced to cede a large part of Karelia and other tracts in the north to the Soviet Union. It was perhaps strange, however, that Finland was permitted to retain her air force, in which the tardy Buffaloes were to form an important element.

The Ilyushin DB-3 bomber was widely used on the Finnish front by the Soviets. This example made a forced landing and was captured by the Finns; Finnish markings have been applied.

The Fokker C.X was used by the Finns on general reconnaissance and liaison duties. In common with most Finnish aircraft, these were fitted with skis for operations on snow.

Polikarpov fighters equipped all the fighter regiments facing Finland. Most were I-15s but some I-16 monoplanes were involved. This aircraft in winter camouflage served with the 4 IAP in the Lake Ladoga region.

Midway through the battle, help arrived from Britain in the shape of Bristol Blenheim Mk IVs, Gloster Gauntlets and Gloster Gladiators. One of the latter is illustrated, equipped with skis.

Blenheim Mk IVs drastically increased the Finnish bombing capabilities, which had hitherto rested on two squadrons of outdated Blenheim Mk Is. These continued in service for several years.

Augmenting the British aid, 30 Morane-Saulnier M.S. 406 fighters arrived from France and these were a welcome addition to the fighter forces, being able to hold their own against the Polikarpov opposition.

Despite its biplane configuration, the Gloster Gladiator had a lot of fight in it and proved a handful for the Russian fighters. However, as the war progressed, the effects of the Finnish defence grew less and less.

The Tupolev SB-2 possessed a similar performance to the Bristol Blenheim flown by the Finns. The aircraft was sluggish and underpowered, but carried out several telling raids on Finland.

Polikarpov I-16s became an ever more common sight over the battleground as the war progressed, and were often used in the fighter-bomber role armed with small bombs. A force of these destroyed several Finnish aircraft on the ground.

During the early part of the war, the Fokker D XXI represented the Finnish fighter force (in addition to a handful of obsolete Bristol Bulldogs). They performed admirably, scoring many victories until the odds became too great.

Below: The Tupolev SB-2 was successful in attacks on Finnish forces, as it had been over the Nomonhan region, but it was to receive a shock as it came up against the Luftwaffe when the Germans invaded the Soviet Union in 1941.

THE SCANDINAVIAN CONQUEST 1939-40

Motivated as much by concern for the continuing supply of Swedish iron ore along the Norwegian coast to the furnaces of the Ruhr as for the security of his left flank in his planned attack on the Soviet Union, Hitler decided to eliminate Norway as a potential enemy foothold in the north. Because of the long distances involved, the Junkers Ju 87 dive-bomber was scarcely to be used, ground support being provided by some 70 Messerschmitt Bf 110C heavy fighters and only 40 Ju 87Rs. A bomber force of 290 Heinkel He 111Hs and Junkers Ju 88As possessed the range to reach central Norway, and to the extreme north once Norwegian bases had been captured. In the likely absence of serious fighter opposition, no more than a single *Grupppe* (30 aircraft) of Bf 109Es was deployed.

By far the largest element of the air arm was to comprise about 500 Junkers Ju 52/3m transports, and these aircraft were to be employed to deliver waves of assault forces during the first 10 days of the campaign.

The UK for her part had been planning an occupation of northern Norway with the very object of denying German use of the port of Narvik and when, on 9 April, the German blow fell on Denmark and southern Norway, the Royal Navy was already at sea and an RAF squadron of Gloster Gladiators (No. 263) in the process of preparation for service in Scandinavia.

RAF aircraft were also already active in the German Bight as German naval forces were approaching the Norwegian coast but, as no troop transports were sighted, the sailing of British convoys was delayed. Such was the extent to which the Germans were able to conceal their preparations that Denmark was effectively overrun in a single day, paratroops being dropped on the airfields of Aalborg-Ost and Aalborg-West, followed by the arrival of further airborne infantry brought in by the swarms of Ju 52/3m transports. Denmark's handful of Gloster Gauntlets, Hawker Nimrods and Fokker D.XXIs had no chance to oppose the lightning attack.

Meanwhile, as German warships steamed up Oslo Fjord and seaborne landings were carried out along the south Norwegian coast, the Bf 110s strafed the airfields of Oslo-Förnebu and Stavanger-Sola, easily disposing of the small number of Norwegian Gladiators which rose in defence. The following day the airfield at Trondheim-Vaernes fell, and with the constant arrival of men, guns, fuel and ammunition brought in by the transport aircraft, it seemed that the whole of Norway would be quickly overrun within the next few days.

After the initial delay, however, British forces were quickly on the scene. A German advance force which had sailed to Narvik in the far north was isolated by the destruction of its supporting naval force.

Fleet Air Arm Blackburn Skuas of No. 803 Squadron dive-bombed and sank the *Königsberg* at Bergen, and the similar *Karlsruhe* was torpedoed by a British submarine. British land forces were put ashore at Narvik on 15 April at Namsos on 16 April and at Andalsnes on 18 April. At once the Luftwaffe retaliated with its Ju 87s, bombing the ports so heavily as to render them virtually unusable.

Five days later 18 RAF Gladiators of No. 263 Squadron landed on the frozen Lake Lesjaskog near Andalsnes, having flown off the carrier HMS *Glorious*. The Luftwaffe was again ready for them and, as a result of the extreme cold, difficulty was experienced getting the Gladiators into the air, most of them being destroyed on the ice in raids which started the next day. Although about half a dozen raiders were claimed shot down in 36 hours, the frozen lake was unusable by 25 April. The surviving aircraft were destroyed where they stood, and the wrecked ports of Andalsnes and Namsos were evacuated on 30 April and 2 May respectively. The members of No. 263 Squadron returned to the UK to re-equip with a fresh complement of Gladiators.

The British now decided to concentrate an attack on the port of Narvik, despite the rapid and relatively simple build up of German forces in the south. No. 263 Squadron with its new Gladiators embarked in HMS *Furious*, this time accompanied by No. 46 Squadron with Hawker Hurricanes, arriving at Bödo and Bardufoss on 26 May. An assault by British, Norwegian, French and Polish forces on 28 May succeeded in eliminating the German forces at Narvik, but such were the distances involved that it became all too obvious that to sustain what could be little more than an isolated garrison was out of the question. German air attacks were increasing daily, despite the RAF pilots' success in downing some 20 of the enemy raiders. In an effort to bring their aircraft home, the pilots volunteered to land aboard HMS *Glorious* for passage home, but within 48 hours the ship, the aircraft and all but two of the pilots were at the bottom of the ocean, sent there by salvoes from the German warships *Scharnhorst* and *Gneisenau*.

On 7 June King Haakon of Norway left his shores aboard HMS *Devonshire*, and on the following day Allied forces were extricated from Narvik. The campaign was over. Once more the overwhelming superiority of the Luftwaffe had contributed a vital weapon, this time the use of massive delivery of airborne infantry proving decisive. It was moreover but a dress rehearsal for worse to come.

The view through the nose glazing of a Heinkel He 111 sweeping in towards a small Norwegian port. Operating against minimal fighter opposition, the German *Kampfgruppen* provided ground forces with essential tactical support.

Norway's fighter arm was woefully deficient in modern aircraft at the time of the German onslaught. Seen here is a Gloster Gladiator Mk II of the Haerens Flyvevaben, based at Oslo-Förnebu in April 1940, and fitted with the ski landing gear that was so essential for winter operations in Norway.

Below: The Messerschmitt Bf 109E-3 introduced the more powerful DB 601Aa engine. This one was flown by the Gruppenkommandeur of II/JG 77, Hauptmann Henschel, from the captured Danish airfield complex at Aarlborg in July 1940. The unit badge of II/JG 77 was a shield marked with an eagle's head dipping towards water.

Above: A Hawker Nimrod fighter of the Marine Flyvevaesenets' 2. Luftflotille. Of the 12 Nimrods, designated L.B.V. in Danish service, two were supplied by Hawker and the other 10 built under licence by the Orlogsvaerftet. At the time of the German invasion they had been due for replacement by Italian Macchi C.200s.

Right: Some of Norway's most modern aircraft were a batch of Caproni Ca 310 Libeccio twin-engine bomber/reconnaissance aircraft. This Haerens Flyvevaben Ca 310 was based at Stavanger-Sola in April 1940, and was almost certainly destroyed by a Luftwaffe attack while the aircraft was still on the ground.

German *Fallschirmjäger* (paratroopers) come down in Norway. This campaign marked the first German use of such troops, whose shock value proved to be high, albeit at the cost of relatively heavy casualties.

Luftwaffe paratroops wait on an extemporized airfield in Norway as a Junkers Ju 52/3m comes in with reinforcements, ammunition and other supplies, and to pick up casualties.

Such was the urgency of the Scandinavian operations that all aircrew, including the pilot, were pressed into service for such tasks as refuelling. Only thus could a rapid turnaround be assured.

BLITZKRIEG IN THE WEST 1940

Following a massive and not wholly unobserved build-up of land and air forces along her frontiers with France and the neutral Low Countries, Germany on May 10 launched an overwhelming offensive westwards. Recognizing the futility of a frontal assault on the established Maginot Line, Hitler chose to attack through the Netherlands and Belgium, and strike directly at the Channel ports, thereby isolating the British army in the north, before striking south at Paris, so outflanking the French army concentrated on the border facing Germany.

Supporting the attack by some 75 divisions were Luftflotten II and III, comprising 4,000 front-line aircraft, of which more than 400 were Junkers Ju 52/3m transports, recently redeployed from the Norwegian campaign, as well as the full panoply of *Blitzkrieg*, the Ju 87s, Ju 88s, Dornier Do 17s, Heinkel He 111s, Messerschmitt Bf 109s and Bf 110s. Opposing this array of might were some 130 Dutch, 150 Belgian, 1,600 French and 450 British aircraft based in northern France; however, not only were the Allied airmen outnumbered by odds of about two to one, but two-thirds of their aircraft were at best obsolescent.

Moreover, the element of surprise enabled the Luftwaffe to concentrate its strength where needed, so that within a matter of four days, during which Rotterdam suffered a catastrophic raid by He 111s, the Netherlands had capitulated. Belgium, now the scene of powerful German armoured thrusts, quickly lost the key defence positions vital to its survival, the great Fort Eben-Emael falling to a dawn attack by gliderborne troops on the first day. Key crossing points on the Albert Canal were captured intact by the Germans and, despite frantic efforts by RAF Fairey Battle and Bristol Blenheim bombers to destroy them, this enabled the German columns to continue their swift advance, reaching Abbeville long before the end of the month. Within 10 days the Belgian air force had virtually ceased to exist, while losses among the RAF Battle squadrons had reached about 70 per cent. In the RAF only the Hawker Hurricane succeeded in matching the modern German aircraft, and it was estimated that around 200 of the enemy fell to their guns in the first fortnight.

In the French Armée de l'Air the Dewoitine D.520 fighter was of roughly equal quality to the British Hurricane, but only some 150 of these aircraft were available during the Battle of France. However, until the RAF's Supermarine Spitfire was committed to battle in the later stages, the German Bf 109 was the supreme fighter in French skies and this, together with highly effective mobile *Flak* which accompanied the advancing German columns, took tremendous toll of British and French light bombers. The latter, when not being clawed out of the smoke-filled skies over the land battle, were pulverized on their bases.

By 26 May the Belgian front had collapsed and almost 400,000 British and French soldiers were falling back on the port of Dunkirk. At this point Hermann Goering prevailed on Hitler to allow his air force to annihilate the Allied armies trapped with their backs to the sea. As orders were issued in the UK to evacuate these forces by sailing an armada of small vessels to Dunkirk, Spitfires, Hurricanes, Boulton Paul Defiants and Blenheim fighters, hitherto reserved for defence of the British Isles, were ordered to protect the great evacuation. Numerous heavy attacks by German He 111s, Ju 87s, Ju 88s and Do 17s were launched against the port and beaches during the following week, some of which inevitably penetrated the fighter defence. Casualties were very high on both sides, but by 3 June some 336,000 men of the British and French armies, though with scarcely any of their equipment, had been evacuated to safety.

As the German army closed swiftly on the Channel ports, which fell in rapid succession despite all possible support by RAF aircraft based in England, the remaining elements of the British air forces that had been deployed across the Channel fell back westwards through France, giving what cover they could to the ragged remains of the BEF and French force until eventually evacuated from Cherbourg, Brest, St Nazaire and other ports. The German army now swung south towards Paris, the first massive air raids on the capital being launched on 3 June; French fighter pilots claimed the destruction of 26 aircraft in the first attack, but lost almost as heavily. Despite great gallantry by the men of the Armée de l'Air, however, German air superiority was never threatened, and the final land assault opened on 5 June. On 14 June Paris fell, and eight days later an armistice was signed.

The campaign that had lasted just six weeks had cost the Luftwaffe the loss of 1,254 aircraft, but most of those aircrew who survived being shot down were now released by the French to return to their units. Much of the surviving French air force escaped to the unoccupied zone in France under a puppet government in Vichy, or to French territory in North Africa; some pilots made their way to the UK, where they joined the RAF.

The RAF itself had lost a total of 944 aircraft, of which 386 were Hurricanes and 67 Spitfires, fighters whose loss was to be sorely felt in the summer months to come. More important were the many professional pilots lost, whose peacetime training could never be matched by that of the men now rapidly filling the depleted ranks of RAF Fighter Command.

Dornier Do 17s seen in flight over the Low Countries. Though they carried a relatively small bombload, the Do 17Zs of the *Kampfgruppen* performed with credit when the German *Blitzkrieg* was launched against Western Europe in early May 1940. Do 17s deployed in Poland had suffered little from fighters, but were at a disadvantage when intercepted by aircraft such as the Spitfire.

Hawker Hurricane Mk I of No. 73 Squadron, one of the two component squadrons of the Advanced Air Striking Force's No. 67 (Fighter) Wing at the time of the German offensive. The AASF, commanded by Air Vice-Marshal P.H.L. Playfair, controlled one fighter and four bomber wings comprising Hurricanes, Battles and Blenheims.

Dewoitine D.520 no. 31 was on the strength of the Escadrille de Chasse de Défense, SNCASE, in June 1940. This semi-autonomous unit was tasked with the local defence of this important part of the French nationalized aircraft industry in the southern industrial city of Toulouse.

Fairey Battle I on the strength of the Belgian 5e Escadrille, III Groupe, 3e Régiment d'Aéronautique, based at Evère with 14 aircraft on 10 May 1940. Avions Fairey built 18 Battles in Belgium, and these differed from British production in revised engine cowlings and superior camouflage finish.

Messerschmitt Bf 109E-3 of I Gruppe of Jagdgeschwader 3 'Udet', based at Colombert in the autumn of 1940.

A *Schwarm* of Messerschmitt Bf 109E fighters skim low over the Channel as they cruise past a French coastal resort. All too soon for the French, their favourite beaches and hotels were to provide a playground for the victorious German troops.

BATTLE OF BRITAIN: THE ASSAULT 1940

Following the invasion of Norway and the fall of France and the Low Countries in May and June 1940, and as the RAF set about dressing its wounds, the Luftwaffe moved up to bases lining the coasts facing the British Isles. For the all-out air attack, intended to eliminate RAF Fighter Command in preparation for an invasion of the islands, the Luftwaffe disposed its forces in three air fleets, Luftflotte III based in north west France, Luftflotte II in north east France and the Low Countries, and Luftflotte V in Norway and Denmark.

By early July the German air forces facing the UK fielded about 2,800 aircraft, comprising 1,300 Heinkel He 111, Junkers Ju 88 and Dornier Do 17 bombers, 280 Junkers Ju 87 divebombers, 790 Messerschmitt Bf 109 single-seat fighters, 260 Messerschmitt Bf 110 and Junkers Ju 88C heavy fighters and 170 reconnaissance aircraft of various types; of these totals roughly half were immediately combat-ready. Facing them RAF Fighter Command possessed 640 fighters, the great majority of them Hawker Hurricanes and Supermarine Spitfires.

The daylight Battle of Britain opened at the beginning of July with relatively scattered raids by small formations of German bombers against coastal targets in southern England and against shipping in the English Channel, the initial object being to test the defences and to discover the extent to which they relied upon the coastal radar chain, known to have existed since before the war. As the month wore on the anti-shipping attacks increased in ferocity, as did the German losses, and it became clear that the British radar was not only highly efficient but gave substantial warning of approaching raids.

German losses in July amounted to some 220 aircraft and, as the Germans finalized plans for the all-out assault, scheduled for mid-August, there followed a lull in the fighting. The first heavy raids, against shipping in the Channel, were launched on 8 August by large formations of Ju 87s escorted by Bf 110s but, as was to be confirmed during the next few days, both these aircraft were found to be extremely vulnerable in the face of attacks by the Hurricanes and Spitfires, and losses were exceptionally heavy. Further shipping attacks were carried out on 11 August, but now the raiders were more adequately protected by Bf 109 single-seaters. This phase continued until 18 August, particularly severe fighting taking place on 12, 13, 15, 16 and 18 August. As a result of heavy losses suffered, the Ju 87 was largely withdrawn from the battle after 18 August.

By now raids were penetrating farther inland, and on 15 August the aircraft of Luftflotte V attempted to attack targets in northern England, but suffered so badly that such raids were not repeated during the Battle.

A reappraisal of the tactics being employed led to a marked shift during the next phase of the attack which began at the end of August. Following complaints by the Bf 109 pilots that they were badly handicapped when employed in the bomber-escort role, the *Jagdgeschwader* were allowed to resume the 'free chase' tactics over southern England, frequently catching the RAF fighters either during take-off or landing, or as they returned short of fuel and ammunition after combat.

This was unquestionably the most successful phase from the Luftwaffe's viewpoint and would have quickly brought the defences to their knees had the Germans persisted. However, exasperated at continuing losses, Goering ordered the attack to switch from the RAF to the British civilian population with a sudden massive attack on East London in the late afternoon of 7 September.

This marked the turning point of the whole battle, and the easing of pressure on the fighters allowed them a much-needed respite. In the course of further heavy daylight attacks on London, particularly on 15 September and on south east England at the end of the month, the Germans took a heavy beating; the British fighter pilots no longer had to fight over their airfields and could concentrate on the great armadas making their way ponderously towards some unfortunate town or city.

The very heavy losses of September constituted the Luftwaffe's first major setback of the war; survival by the British fighter defences led to postponement of the invasion (and its eventual abandonment), and the final phase, which occupied most of October, consisted of no more than nuisance raids by high-flying aircraft (usually Bf 109s) carrying single bombs, which were dropped with little hope of causing significant damage.

The daylight Battle of Britain cost the Luftwaffe a total of 2,020 aircraft destroyed, and more than 5,200 aircrew killed or missing; as with the RAF's losses in France, a high proportion of these men were the most experienced in the German air force, and had been responsible for evolving and proving the battle tactics employed. Nevertheless, whereas the British could regard the final outcome of the Battle of Britain as a resounding victory, it was by no means the end of the air assault, which now continued (with very different results) under cover of darkness.

Ground crew rush a bomb to a waiting Heinkel He 111, whose engines are already started. Such large bombs were carried externally, and began to feature prominently during the latter part of the bombing siege.

Employed as a long-range escort fighter, the Messerschmitt Bf 110 was somewhat shackled in this role and was easy meat for British fighters. However, when the aircraft was operated at high altitude away from the bombers, it was highly effective and scored many victories.

The Junkers Ju 87 was used early in the campaign against Britain but was soon realized to be extremely vulnerable in the company of enemy fighters. This aircraft served with 7./StG 41 in France at the outbreak of the bombing raids.

Losses by day forced the RAF and the Luftwaffe to turn to nocturnal bombing. This Junkers Ju 88A-1 served with II/KG 52 *Edelweiss* from Melun-Villaroche in the winter of 1940 during the night Blitz against Britain. National markings were obscured and lamp-black distemper applied to the undersurfaces.

Messerschmitt Bf 109E-3 of 7. Staffel, part of III Gruppe of Jagdgeschwader 2 'Richthofen', based in France during May and June 1940. Armament was fairly heavy: two or three 20-mm MG FF (Oerlikon) cannon and two 7.92-mm (0.31-in) MG 17 machine-guns.

Messerschmitt Bf 110C of the *Stabsschwarm* (staff flight) of I/Zerstörergeschwader 2, based at Amiens during July 1940. When its commander, Major Ott, was killed in action on 11 August, Hauptmann Heinlein assumed command of this Jagdfliegerführer Nr 3 (Luftflotte III).

BATTLE OF BRITAIN: THE DEFENCE 1940

The unexpected month long respite after the Dunkirk evacuation allowed RAF Fighter Command time to rest and re-equip most of its weary squadrons, and to some extent broadcast among its pilots vital information regarding German fighting tactics.

At the head of Fighter Command, Air Chief Marshal Dowding divided his air defences into three Groups, No. 11 in the south under Keith Park, No. 12 in the Midlands under Trafford Leigh-Mallory and No. 13 in the north under Richard Saul; a fourth Group, No. 10 under Quintin Brand, would shortly be added to cover the south west.

Dowding disposed a total of 640 fighters at the beginning of July 1940, including 347 Hawker Hurricanes, 199 Supermarine Spitfires, 69 Bristol Blenheim night-fighters and 25 Boulton Paul Defiants; slightly over half his strength was deployed in the south, the key airfields of Biggin Hill, Kenley, Croydon, Hornchurch, Manston and Tangmere constituting a defensive ring round London and the Thames estuary. To provide early warning and a degree of fighter control, the south and east coasts were covered by a network of radar stations which could detect approaching raids at a distance of about 100 miles (160 km).

The German attacks of July, aimed principally at shipping and coastal targets in the south, proved something of a strain on the British pilots who were obliged to fly standing patrols over the convoys until the German tactics were recognized for what they were, and orders given not to engage enemy fighters unnecessarily. British losses in the July combats amounted to 77 fighters, of whose pilots roughly half survived. A particularly savage combat on 19 July had shown the two-seat Defiant to be unsuitable for day fighting, and it was temporarily withdrawn out of harm's way.

The onset of the main assault on 8 August was competently countered by Park's squadrons, whose pilots quickly spotted the weaknesses of the Junkers Ju 87 and Messerschmitt Bf 110, and set about effective tactics to deal with them. The appearance of large formations of Messerschmitt Bf 109s, which were superior in most respects to the Hurricane, caused the British controllers, where possible, to order their Spitfires against the enemy fighters, while the Hurricanes fought the slower, lower-flying bombers.

The resumption of 'free chase' sorties by the Bf 109s at the end of August certainly posed a serious threat to Dowding's defences, so much so that by 5 September Fighter Command's losses were running at the rate of an equivalent of two whole squadrons every day. Moreover, there was little the RAF pilots could do to combat them. Losses during the past four weeks had deprived many squadrons of their most experienced members, and very young men with no more than two or three months' squadron service were being promoted to command; the aircraft themselves were now showing severe wear and tear, despite frantic efforts by their manufacturers and repair organizations. Bowing to the inevitable, Dowding was forced to withdraw some of his finest squadrons to the relative quiet of the north to rest and re-equip, bringing to the south newly-formed and inexperienced squadrons, among them the first Canadian, Polish and Czech squadrons of the RAF.

It was at this time that the differing tactics favoured by Park and Leigh-Mallory came into sharp focus, the former advocating use of single squadrons (because of the short time available in the south to assemble larger forces) and the latter favouring the committing of whole fighter wings to battle. Both men were probably justified in their own combat environments, and it must be said that, given adequate warning, Park himself tried to employ two or three squadrons simultaneously. There were, however, occasions when Leigh-Mallory's wing tactic failed to operate efficiently as a result of the time taken to assemble.

Be that as it may, the victory gained by RAF Fighter Command was achieved as much by the courage, resilience and skill of the RAF pilots and their groundcrews as by the extraordinarily close-knit organization that existed within the command, and there is no doubt that the extent to which the radar chain had been integrated into the fighting processes came as an unpleasant surprise to the enemy.

The cost of victory in the daylight Battle of Britain was heavy. Considerable damage was suffered at many of the key airfields, of which some were temporarily abandoned for operational purposes. The cost in aircrew lives was heavy, more than 500 men being posted killed or missing, yet on the last day of the Battle (31 October) Fighter Command possessed eight more squadrons in the front line than on the first day, and replacement pilots were arriving from the training schools twice as fast as in July to continue a tradition that would for ever be remembered by a grateful nation: survival had been achieved through the prowess in combat of just 3,030 airmen, forever remembered as The Few.

Supermarine Spitfire Mk IAs of No. 610 (County of Chester) Squadron, Royal Auxiliary Air Force, on patrol over Kent in the summer of 1940. During August No. 610 played a vital role in the defence of Biggin Hill before being withdrawn to Acklington at the end of the month for the defence of Newcastle.

Scramble! Hurricane pilots rush to their aircraft in answer to a telephone call from Fighter Control. The radar network along the South Coast gave good warning of impending attacks, and enabled the fighters to intercept the bombers before they got to London.

No. 85 Squadron, RAF, was better known as a night-fighter unit but during the Battle of Britain its Hurricanes were mainly employed by day against the Luftwaffe bombers. The squadron defended London from Debden and later Croydon, before (in September 1940) it was sent north to recuperate.

Hawker Hurricane Mk I of No. 85 Squadron, RAF Fighter Command, based at Debden and Croydon in August 1940. In the first phase of the battle, known to the Germans as the *Kanalkampf*, No. 85 Squadron was at Martlesham Heath under the command of Squadron Leader P.W. Townsend, who shot down six German aircraft in the battle.

Bristol Blenheim Mk IF of No. 25 Squadron, Fighter Command, based at North Weald in the early part of 1940. During the first phase of the battle the squadron was based at Martlesham Heath (in the North Weald sector), where it stayed for most of the battle under the command of Squadron Leader K.A.K. McEwan.

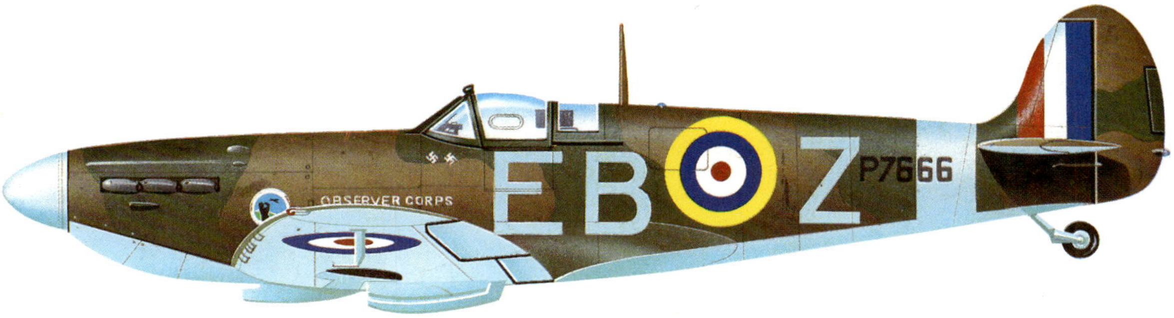

Supermarine Spitfire Mk IIA of Squadron Leader D.O. Finlay, commanding officer of No. 41 Squadron, RAF Fighter Command, based at Hornchurch in December 1940. The aircraft was presented by the Observer Corps, and notable is use of the colour 'sky' for the undersurfaces, code letters, spinner and rear fuselage band.

Hawkinge became too close to the action to base aircraft there permanently, and was used as a forward base. Here men from No. 610 Squadron relax near their Spitfires while waiting for the telephone to ring, calling them to action.

No. 56 Squadron was at North Weald for most of the Battle of Britain, flying its Hawker Hurricane Mk Is against the Luftwaffe's bomber streams. By September the squadron stood down for a well-earned rest.

EARLY BRITISH BOMBING 1940

The Royal Air Force went to war against Germany steeped in the Trenchard tradition that the heavy bomber was its principal weapon, yet the aircraft with which it was equipped (the Vickers Wellington, Armstrong Whitworth Whitley and Handley Page Hampden) proved to be wholly inadequate to impose any significant pressure upon the enemy, being not only poorly equipped to navigate and bomb accurately at night but disastrously vulnerable by day. Nor was the British Air Staff single-minded as how best to employ its so-called heavy bombers.

In September 1939 the RAF possessed 10 squadrons of Wellingtons, 10 of Hampdens and nine of Whitleys, of which the Wellington was undoubtedly the best. It was in the mistaken belief that it could defend itself in the presence of enemy fighters, however, that the Wellington was first committed to daylight attacks during the first four months of the war; in deference to government restrictions on endangering the enemy's civilian population, the targets were German naval forces in or near their home ports. From the outset German radar gave notice of the bombers' approach so that *Flak* and fighters were able to take a heavy toll. The last such raid, on 18 December, cost the loss of 12 out of 24 Wellingtons of Nos 9, 37 and 149 Squadrons. Scarcely any damage was inflicted on German ships, and thereafter the Wellingtons were confined to bombing at night.

If the efforts of the Wellington crews were disappointing, those of the RAF light bombers, the Bristol Blenheim Mk IVs, were more promising and from the first day of the war the type performed a number of outstanding raids, although the small number and size of their bombs (the largest of which was the 500-lb/227-kg weapon) severely limited the damage caused, yet the numerous attacks against targets off the north German coast, carried out with great gallantry and often in poor weather, probably achieved more than all the raids by the heavy bombers combined.

The Whitley was slowest of all the British bombers, though a rugged weight-lifter, and was assigned the nebulous task of dropping loads of propaganda leaflets over German towns at night, the bombing restrictions preventing the delivery of high explosive. Night after night these lumbering, angular aeroplanes set course from the UK to discharge their paper bundles with scarcely any interference from German defences, their worst enemy being bad weather. Early in 1940 Whitleys of No. 77 Squadron, flying from Villeneuve in France, dropped leaflets over Prague, Vienna and cities in Poland.

Third of the heavy trio was the Hampden, nicknamed the 'flying suitcase' on account of its deep, narrow fuselage, and this was the only British bomber not to be armed with a power-operated gun turret and was indeed appallingly vulnerable to enemy fighter attack. Fortunately the Germans possessed scarcely any night-fighter defence during the first eight months of the war.

Following the dropping of German bombs on British soil on 16 March 1940, which killed a civilian in the Orkneys, the RAF attacked an enemy land target four nights later when 26 Whitleys and 15 Hampdens attacked the seaplane base at Hörnum on Sylt. In the following month Wellingtons joined the attack with a raid on Stavanger airfield in Norway.

It was not until after the German offensive had opened in the West on 10 May that Bomber Command aircraft were permitted to attack the German mainland, although their targets were still strictly confined to military objectives. Moreover, because of inadequate navigation equipment and outdated bombsights, few bomber crews attacked their briefed targets. When eventually the War Cabinet lifted the restrictions on British bombing over Germany on 15 May, and 99 Wellingtons, Whitleys and Hampdens opened Bomber Command's strategic bombing offensive with attacks on oil and steel targets in the Ruhr, fewer than 30 crews claimed even to have identified their target. Bomber Command was further restricted in its attacks on Italian targets (when that nation entered the war on 10 June), and although Wellingtons deployed to the south of France the French government curtailed their attacks for fear of reprisal raids on their territory.

During the Battle of Britain a number of RAF bomber bases were attacked by the Luftwaffe and some bombers (mostly Whitleys) were destroyed. However, three achievements marked the climax (if such it can be called) of this stage of British bombing. On 11/12 June 36 Whitleys flew from the UK, refuelling in the Channel Islands, to attack targets in northern Italy and, although only 12 crews claimed to have bombed Turin or Milan, the long flight over the Alps in poor weather represented something of an epic of endurance. On 1 July a Hampden, flown by Flying Officer Guy Gibson (later Wing Commander, VC) dropped Bomber Command's first 2,000-lb (907-kg) bomb over Kiel, the heaviest bomb thus far carried by the RAF in World War 2. And on 25/26 August 81 Wellingtons, Whitleys and Hampdens set out for the first time for Berlin, and 29 of their crews claimed to have bombed the German capital.

Despite these very modest beginnings, Bomber Command was aware of its own shortcomings, and before the end of 1940 the first true heavy bombers, the Avro Manchester, Short Stirling and Handley Page Halifax, were arriving in the RAF. 1941 would see a significant strengthening of the bombing muscle, even though its aim would still be suspect.

Hampden Mk I of No. 455 (RAAF) Squadron airborne from Wigsley (Notts). Hampdens were coming to the end of their stalwart service in Bomber Command in 1942, and in April No. 455 Squadron was transferred, with No. 144 Squadron to Coastal Command.

An evening at an RAF base in the autumn of 1939. Ground crew and aircrew load packets of propaganda leaflets for a 'Nickelling' raid over Germany. Whitley units had this thankless task, starting on the night of 3/4 September 1939.

A Wellington Mk IA and two Mk ICs are seen early in World War II. The nearest two aircraft display the night black camouflage extended up the fuselage sides, the farthest with brown and green almost to the base of the fuselage.

R3612 was a Blenheim IV built by the Rootes shadow factory at Speke (today Liverpool Airport). It is shown after the fitting of the rear lower defence guns under the nose in December 1940 while serving with No. 40 Squadron at Wyton. Even the extra gun turret failed to make the Blenheim effective.

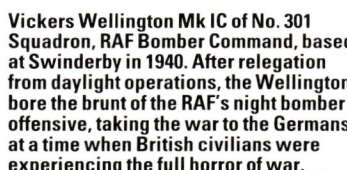

Vickers Wellington Mk IC of No. 301 Squadron, RAF Bomber Command, based at Swinderby in 1940. After relegation from daylight operations, the Wellington bore the brunt of the RAF's night bomber offensive, taking the war to the Germans at a time when British civilians were experiencing the full horror of war.

This Armstrong Whitworth Whitley Mk V flew with No. 78 Squadron in late 1939. It is painted in the all-black scheme adopted for night operations.

Taking off for Germany, the Whitley was one of the trio of types that handled the bombing in the early years. The Whitley had good range, which enabled it to reach Poland on clandestine missions, but suffered from poor bombload.

The best bomber available to the Royal Air Force was the Vickers Wellington. This No. 301 (Polish) Squadron aircraft awaits its bombs for a mission to Germany.

THE NIGHT BLITZ 1940-41

The German defeat in the daylight Battle of Britain frustrated plans to invade the British Isles in the early autumn of 1940. Instead Goering believed that his bomber force could impose a military solution to the war by repeated heavy attacks on London and other cities by night. The first such major attack was launched against the dock area of East London on the night of 7/8 September just as the Battle of Britain was reaching its decisive phase. Moreover, German bombers continued to visit London for more than 50 consecutive nights, creating infinitely greater damage and casualties than in the whole of the daylight assault.

Seldom more than 100 Heinkel He 111s, Dornier Do 17s and Junkers Ju 88s operated on any single night in this savage attack on the British capital yet, despite being without any form of fighter protection they were able to escape any significant loss, such was the poor state of the British night-fighter defences. Up to this stage the obsolescent Bristol Blenheim, flying with extremely rudimentary airborne radar, backed up by a few single-seat Hawker Hurricanes had constituted the fighter defence at night. In September the first purpose-designed night-fighter, the heavily armed Bristol Beaufighter, started arriving in service with more effective radar, together with some Boulton Paul Defiant turret-equipped two-seaters (discarded as day fighters), but it would be many months before these aircraft would achieve noticeable results against the night raiders.

Although the Nazi leadership espoused no pretence at achieving military damage in the night assault on London, the Luftwaffe itself recognized that worthwhile results from the night assaults could be gained only by striking at British industrial centres much farther afield, and had thus been developing navigation aids to enable its bombers to reach into the heart of the nation. Employing narrow radio beams transmitted from continental stations across the British Isles, the Germans started flying pathfinder He 111s of Kampfgruppe 100 specially equipped with radio receivers that enabled them to fly accurately towards distant targets, which they would mark with incendiary bombs to guide the crews of the main bombing force.

Despite the existence of this equipment being discovered by the British, the defences were caught unawares when, on 14/15 November, KGr 100 led 437 bombers against Coventry, causing enormous damage, killing 380 civilians and seriously injuring 800 others. In the final week of November further heavy raids were launched against London, Southampton, Bristol, Plymouth and Liverpool. In December Manchester and Sheffield were added to the list of stricken cities. Much in line with the growth of British bombs at this stage of the war, German weapons were in the main the

1,102-lb (500-kg) high explosive bomb, although huge numbers of 4.4-lb (2-kg) incendiary bombs were showered over British towns and cities during the Blitz. However, growing numbers of 2,205-lb (1000-kg) bombs were carried by the He 111s to short-range targets, as well as highly-destructive parachute 'mines', the latter being adaptations of the German sea mine fitted with a barostatic fuze to give maximum blast effect.

The year ended with a particularly vicious incendiary raid on the City of London which, carried out when the Thames was at low tide and during a weekend when few fire watchers were in their offices, caused grievous damage among centuries-old churches and other treasured buildings.

The second half of the Blitz brought about marked improvements in the British defences. Gradually the RAF night-fighters began to take a noticeable toll of the bombers: three in January, four in February, 22 in March, 48 in April and 96 in May. During the same five months the guns and balloons claimed a total of about 120 enemy aircraft. Meanwhile Nottingham, Avonmouth, Merseyside, Swansea, Belfast, Clydeside, Hull, Sunderland and Newcastle were all heavily raided, in addition to still further attacks on the previous victims. Not only were the night-fighter crews becoming proficient in operating their airborne radar in collaboration with the new ground-control radar stations; the gun defences were also being steadily strengthened throughout the country, and in February the first massed batteries of ground-to-air rockets went into action for the first time.

By May Hitler was completing his plans for the great assault on the Soviet Union, for which the Luftwaffe would be called on to support and, with no appearance of a crack in British morale, the bulk of German bomber forces was removed from Western Europe eastwards, and the night Blitz on the UK petered out.

The bombing itself had indeed done little lasting damage to the UK's ability to wage war. Most serious was that caused in the aircraft industry, whose output was reduced by about 20 per cent for almost six months (at the Supermarine, Short, Bristol, Avro and Vickers factories), while 70,000 tons of food stocks had been destroyed. However, no more than 0.5 per cent of the nation's oil stocks were destroyed and most of the damage caused to the railway network was quickly repaired. On the other hand no fewer than 52,000 civilians had been killed and almost 80,000 severely injured, not to mention well over 120,000 rendered temporarily homeless.

Keeping in company until reaching the coast, these Junkers Ju 88A-4s ride the clouds under a full moon. The navigation and bombing aids of the Luftwaffe in 1940-1 were technically far ahead of those of Bomber Command, and Goering's bombers were aided by the expert pathfinders of Kampfgruppe 100.

Seen from another bomber, this Heinkel He 111 shows the complicated disruptive camouflage applied for night operations over Britain.

The Boulton Paul Defiant put up a brave defence against the German raiders, but it lacked performance and the turret armament was not as effective as forward-firing armament.

This Heinkel He 111H-3 flew with 2./KGr 100 from Vannes in Brittany. It is equipped with *X-Gerät* pathfinder gear for steering other bombers on to the target. This electronic navigation aid was widely used during the night Blitz.

Boulton Paul Defiant Mk II of No. 151 Squadron, an RAF home night-fighter unit. Equipped, as in this example, with Airborne Interception radar, such Defiants enjoyed the highest number of victories per interception of any British night-fighter type deployed during the winter of 1940-1.

Right: The British Blenheim Mk IF made a valiant attempt to defend British skies at night until it could be replaced by the potent Beaufighter. Armament was carried in a ventral tray.

Below: Although devoid of interception aids, the Hawker Hurricane was widely used as a night fighter throughout the winter of 1940-41.

THE BALKANS AND CRETE 1941

Despite the eventual voluntary alignment by the other Balkan powers with the Axis, Hitler was aware that both Yugoslavia and Greece represented weak spots in his southern flank for his forthcoming attack on the Soviet Union. After weeks of little progress by the Italians in their own attack on Greece through Albania, Hitler accordingly decided to eliminate these potential Allied footholds in the Balkans.

Italy had struck at Greece on 28 October 1940, and in answer to appeals by the Greek government an RAF squadron of Blenheims was immediately sent from North Africa for the defence of Athens, and by the end of November two more Blenheim squadrons and two of Gladiators followed. Before the year was out the Gladiators were operating patrols over the Albanian frontier, though contact was seldom made with the Regia Aeronautica. Wellingtons, flying from Egypt, carried out occasional raids against Italian supply ports, but in general bad weather hampered air operations. Nevertheless the Gladiator pilots were credited with the destruction of around 30 Italian aircraft by the end of December, for the loss of 10 aircraft.

Fearing that the RAF might use Greek airfields from which to bomb the Romanian oil fields, Hitler began his move into the Balkans on 1 March 1941, with German troops entering Bulgaria. Within seven days three more RAF squadrons, including one of Hurricanes, were sent to Greece, followed by two more shortly after this. Before the end of the month a military coup in Yugoslavia threatened that country's ties with the Tripartite Pact and on 6 April the German army and air force attacked both Greece and Yugoslavia, launching a devastating and ruthless air attack on Belgrade. Supporting the Balkan campaign, Luftflotte IV fielded some 1,200 modern aircraft, which were opposed by fewer than 500 Yugoslav, British and Greek aircraft, all but a few of them (the Hurricanes and Blenheims) hopelessly outdated.

Despite all that these few aircraft could do, assisted by the long-range Wellingtons, the Germans had gained their first objectives (the occupation of Yugoslavia and the capture of Salonika) by 14 April. The previous day an entire formation of Blenheims had been shot down north of Monastir, and on 15 April enemy aircraft virtually wiped out a Blenheim squadron (No. 113) on the ground at Niamata.

Development of the German two-prong advance southwards decided the fate of Greece, and with overwhelming enemy air superiority quickly eroding the RAF's resources capable of supporting the British and Greek armies, the only question remaining was how much of the air forces could be evacuated. In the event the three fighter squadrons, Nos 33, 80 and 208, now equipped with Hurricanes, remained until the last moment. In one of the final air combats over the Piraeus the South African Squadron Leader M.T.St J. Pattle, the war's highest-scoring RAF pilot, was shot down and killed on 20 April. Four days later the last British fighters left Greek soil for the last time.

Some of the surviving aircraft from the Greek campaign landed on the island of Crete, and this soon became the next subject of German attention. On 20 May Luftwaffe Ju 52/3ms started dropping paratroops as gliders delivered infantry with the object of securing the island's landing grounds. To support the invasion the German air force mustered 650 first-line aircraft, 700 transports and 80 gliders. Opposing them were no more than a dozen Hurricanes, a handful of Fleet Air Arm Fulmars and some Gladiators dispersed on the two airfields and single rudimentary landing strip, although further limited support could be summoned from far-off Egypt. Since 14 May the Germans had made clear their intention to invade Crete, with constant air attacks on the airfields, which the Hurricane pilots did their utmost to counter. By the eve of the invasion only seven fighters remained airworthy, and these were reluctantly evacuated to Egypt.

Despite the elimination of the island's fighter defence, the invasion certainly did not go according to plan, and the paratroops dropped initially at the two airfields were either wiped out or beaten off, and the glider landings were effectively contained. It was only after repeated waves of paratroops had been dropped that the airfields were eventually captured, after which the hosts of Ju 52/3ms started landing. In spite of some fighter cover, provided at long range from Egypt, the Germans landed almost 30,000 troops and by the end of the month Crete was in enemy hands.

The campaign had cost the British forces dear. Apart from the loss of 38 RAF aircraft, the Royal Navy lost three cruisers and six destroyers sunk, and a battleship, carrier, six cruisers and eight destroyers damaged. About 15,000 Imperial troops were either killed or taken prisoner.

On the other hand the Luftwaffe suffered the loss of more than 200 aircraft, of which about half were Ju 52/3m transports. Of far greater significance, however, was the fact that the Balkan campaign had taken six weeks longer than planned and effectively delayed the opening of the great assault on the USSR. Apart from the severe losses among the vital transport aircraft, those six weeks may have been decisive in the conduct of Operation 'Barbarossa' before the onset of the dreaded Russian winter.

Operating from Greek and island airfields, the Ju 87B-2s of StG 2 were a key part of Germany's plan for the assault on Crete. They were not only heavily engaged in support of the ground forces, but made repeated attacks with heavy bombs against the ships of the Royal Navy's Mediterranean Fleet.

Vickers Wellington Mk IA of No. 37 Squadron, RAF, based in Egypt during December 1940. The squadron played a key part in the capture of Tobruk on 21 January 1941: for three hours its aircraft operated over the Italian perimeter to drown the noise of the assembling British armour and artillery.

Hawker Hurricane Mk I (licence-built by the Fabrika Aeroplana I Hydroplana at Zemun) of the Royal Yugoslav Air Force in April 1941. Yugoslavia initially procured 25 Hawker-built Hurricanes and also negotiated for and received licences to build 40 more at Rogozarski (Belgrade) and 60 at Zemun.

Transport around the rugged countryside in the Balkans was handled by the Junkers Ju 52. These slow and cumbersome aircraft were used for all the advances in this theatre, both dropping paratroops and towing gliders. These Ju 52s are loading for a fuel run.

The CANT Z.1007 was active over a wide area in the Aegean, used mainly for medium-level bombing attacks. The aircraft suffered from lack of performance and poor bombload but in this theatre proved successful due to the lack of real fighter opposition.

Macchi MC.200 of the 373ª Squadriglia, 153º Gruppo Autonomo. The star on the blue panel is the pennant of a General di Brigata and the *Assi di Bastoni* (ace of spades) badge distinguished the 153º Gruppo Autonomo; some aircraft also carried CLIII in large red characters forward of the fuselage band.

Bristol Blenheim Mk I of No. 113 Squadron, RAF, operational over the Macedonian Front (northern Greece) in the early part of 1941. Such bombers could have performed a useful role in North Africa, but were definitely outclassed by the German aircraft deployed against them in the forthcoming campaign.

Junkers Ju 52/3m g4e of the *Stabsschwarm* (staff flight) of IV/KGzbV 1, based around Corinth and Megara under the command of Oberst Buchholz in May 1941. KGzbV 1 suffered from the very real tactical disadvantage of operating from airfields of sand, whose effect on aircraft performance was disastrous.

47

INTO NORTH AFRICA 1940-41

Believing that he would be deprived of the spoils of war when German forces burst into northern France, Benito Mussolini entered the war alongside Hitler on 10 June 1940. At a stroke the balance of naval power in the Mediterranean swung in favour of the Axis, even more heavily after the French fleet refused to continue operations on the Allied side and was accordingly attacked by the Royal Navy in its North African ports.

Three immediate threats to British strategic interests were posed by Italy's entry into the war: the naval base at Malta would be threatened by Italian air forces in Sicily, Italian forces in Cyrenaica were uncomfortably close to the vital Suez Canal and the British naval base at Alexandria; and a large Italian colonial army (and air force) threatened British bases in East Africa and the Arabian peninsula at the southern end of the Red Sea.

Little could be done to strengthen Malta's defences immediately and the island was left much to its own devices, recourse being found in a handful of obsolete Gloster Sea Gladiators and some Hawker Hurricanes with which to provide a measure of air defence. Fortunately the Italians underestimated the strategic value of Malta and did little to attack the naval base from the air, at least for a month or so.

In the Western Desert, however, the position was more critical and in the face of considerable Italian numerical air superiority the RAF possessed an extraordinary hotch-potch of obsolescent aircraft with which to defend an enormous expanse of territory. Nevertheless, by dint of ingenious deployment and careful use of the resources available, the two Gladiator squadrons managed to exact a considerable toll of Italian aircraft during the early months of the desert war, while General Wavell was able to set about his brilliant campaign which took his army far into Cyrenaica. Gradually the RAF was able to send a trickle of reinforcements to the Middle East, at first by convoy through the Mediterranean and later to Takoradi in the Gold Coast for overland flight to the Canal Zone. Vickers Wellingtons and Lockheed Hudsons were flown out direct from the UK and Hurricanes and Bristol Blenheims arrived by the Takoradi route; other aircraft were crated and shipped out by the sea route round the Cape of Good Hope.

In East Africa the Italians gained early successes by invading and overrunning British Somaliland, and by doing so posed a threat to Aden. However, in support of another brilliant counteroffensive by Commonwealth forces, RAF Vickers Wellesleys and Gladiators, operating alongside aircraft of the South African Air Force, succeeded in defeating elements of the Italian air force in East Africa, and in due course the Italian presence in the horn of Africa was eliminated.

It was at the moment of triumph for Wavell's forces, which reached Benghazi in the first North African desert offensive, that RAF units were called on to go to the assistance of Greece (a campaign described elsewhere), a critical weakening that was to be compounded by events in Iraq in 1941.

Following a rebellion in support of the pro-Axis Rashid Ali, the large RAF base at Habbaniyah in Iraq came under attack supported by German and Italian aircraft, a threat only countered (and eventually overcome) by the deployment of ill-afforded Wellingtons, Blenheims, Gladiators and Hurricanes for defence of the base.

No sooner had the danger in Iraq been eliminated in the spring of 1941 than the Vichy French presence in Syria posed a threat to the Suez Canal (by possible defection to the Axis) as well as to important oil pipe lines, and it was decided to invade the country. This campaign, successfully completed in mid-July, involved the use of some 60 Hurricanes, Curtiss Tomahawks, Gladiators, Blenheims and Fairey Fulmars of the RAF, RAAF and the Fleet Air Arm.

Frustrated by the Italians' inability to gain a decisive victory in North Africa, the Germans moved the advance elements of a major force of aircraft to the Mediterranean (notably a *Geschwader*, JG 27, of Messerschmitt Bf 109Es) early in 1941, and these were quickly followed by Junkers Ju 87 and Junkers Ju 88 bombers, and it was the arrival of this *Fliegerkorps* in the theatre that first posed a major threat to Malta; for a period its use as a naval base was severely restricted, and it was only sustained by sailing aircraft-carriers into the Mediterranean and flying off fairly large numbers of Hurricanes to land on the island's airfields.

Meanwhile the RAF strength in the Middle East was growing steadily, and by November 1941, on the eve of the British 8th Army's second offensive into Cyrenaica against Erwin Rommel's Afrika Korps (Operation 'Crusader'), RAF, Middle East Command comprised 29 squadrons of Hurricanes, Tomahawks, Curtiss Mohawks, Morane-Saulniers, Blenheim fighters and Fulmars, and 11 squadrons of Wellingtons, Blenheim bombers, Wellesleys, Douglas Bostons and Martin Marylands, as well as a dozen second-line squadrons, a total of almost 1,000 aircraft. Ranged against them were some 600 German and 1,200 Italian first-line aircraft.

At sea both the RAF and Fleet Air Arm were at work constantly seeking out and attacking enemy supply vessels bringing troops and equipment from Europe to North Africa, a task carried out with increasing success, particularly in the waters between the Italian ports and Tripolitania. The Mediterranean had assumed the status of a major war theatre.

A Junkers Ju 88A-5 medium bomber, with a pair of 551-lb (250-kg) SC250 bombs under the wings, prepares to take off. The Ju 88 soon proved itself a superbly versatile aircraft, with a structure able to absorb massive combat damage.

Curtiss Tomahawk Mk IIB of No. 112 Squadron, RAF, based at Sidi Haneish, Egypt, in the autumn of 1941 as part of No. 258 Wing for the 'Crusader' offensive. The squadron had previously operated with its Gloster Gauntlet and Gladiator biplanes in Egypt, the Sudan, Greece and Crete.

Bristol Blenheim B.Mk IV of GRB 1, Free French air force, which was based at Abu Sueir (Egypt) in October 1941. By that time the Blenheim was obsolescent even in North Africa, but despite that it continued to form the major component of the Allies' light bomber elements operating in that theatre.

Fiat BR.20M of 1ª Squadriglia, 43º Gruppo, 13º Stormo Bombardamento Terrestre, Regia Aeronautica, based at Bir Dufan (Libya) in February 1942. In early 1942 the 13º Stormo suffered very heavy losses and was pulled back to Italy for re-equipment with the Caproni Ca 313 light reconnaissance-bomber.

The Fiat CR.42 Falco acquitted itself well over the deserts of North Africa, despite its biplane configuration. However, as fighter defences built up the CR.42 was diverted to ground attack duties. Several aircraft were used on the Eastern Front.

The Italians employed the Savoia-Marchetti S.M.82 Canguru as a troop transport in the desert from 1941 onwards. The type also had a bombing capability but was seldom employed in this role.

North Africa was brutal to aircraft. Dust and sand ruined engines, and torrential rain turned airfields into quagmires. When flying was possible the Luftwaffe was a formidable foe with good pilots, and with aircraft such as these Bf 109s.

TARANTO 1940

On the night of 11/12 November 1940 21 British Swordfish torpedo-bomber biplanes struck at the Italian fleet in Taranto harbour and, in the first major and successful strike by naval aircraft, effectively redressed in British favour the balance of sea power in the Mediterranean.

Italy's entry into the war in June 1940 and the subsequent elimination of the French fleet had given the Axis superiority at sea in the Mediterranean, a situation that seriously threatened British convoys sailing to the UK with vital food, forces and munitions from the dominions east of Suez. Moreover, following Italy's attack on Greece in October that year, undisputed use of the Aegean and Adriatic by the Axis powers posed considerable difficulties in the support of any British foothold in the Balkans that might be considered.

Key to any operations in the central Mediterranean by the Royal Navy lay in the continued use of Malta, both as a naval and air base, and it was with a fine sense of history that it had been intended to bring the Italian fleet to battle on 21 October (Trafalgar Day) with a British fleet of four battleships and battle-cruisers, two carriers (*Eagle* and *Illustrious*), 10 cruisers and four destroyer flotillas. Despite the sailing of two convoys through the Mediterranean, the Italian fleet (comprising five battleships, 14 cruisers and 27 destroyers) declined to leave its base at Taranto; moreover, following a number of near misses from Italian bombers, the carrier *Eagle* was suffering mechanical troubles, necessitating the transfer of her Swordfish aircraft to the *Illustrious*.

The action was accordingly postponed, and as a preliminary step a reconnaissance of Taranto was ordered on 10 November. A Maryland of No. 431 Flight, RAF, flown by Pilot Officer Adrian Warburton, was despatched from Malta that day and, following an epic wave-top tour of the enemy port carried out in the face of intense flak, full details of the Italian fleet's dispositions were brought back and reported to Rear Admiral Lumley Lyster, the flag officer aboard *Illustrious*. The same evening the crew of an RAF flying boat reported that a sixth Italian battleship had also entered Taranto.

Encouraged by the survival of the Maryland, Lyster decided to launch a strike against the Italian ships where they lay, and on the evening of 11 November two waves of Swordfish flew off *Illustrious* at a position 170 miles (274 km) south east of Taranto. The first formation, led by Lieutenant Commander Kenneth Williamson, comprised twelve aircraft (six with torpedoes, four with bombs and two with bombs and flares); the second wave of nine aircraft (five with torpedoes, two with bombs and two with bombs and flares) followed 40 minutes later, led by Lieutenant Commander John Hale.

Despite the obvious significance of the Maryland's appearance over the naval base on the previous day, the Italians were evidently caught completely unaware when Williamson's aircraft swept into Taranto harbour; added to this was the fact that the balloon barrage, which had been expected to cause some embarrassment during the attack, had been almost wholly destroyed by storms the day before. Moreover the Italians had decided against the use of anti-torpedo nets on the pretext that they restricted the movement of their ships.

Two flares quickly disclosed the position of the new battleship *Littorio* (35,000 tons), and this was promptly sunk at her moorings with three torpedoes. Two older battleships, *Conte di Cavour* and *Caio Duilio* (both of 23,600 tons) were also hit, the former never to sail again and the latter, beached to prevent her sinking, severely crippled. In the inner harbour a heavy cruiser and a destroyer were also hit.

In due course the gun defences came into action and two Swordfish were shot down, including that flown by Williamson himself, although he and his crewman survived to be taken prisoner. Another Swordfish failed to release its torpedo.

At a single blow half Italy's battlefleet had been put out of action, a blow from which the Italians never fully recovered. On numerous occasions during the following three years their fleet declined battle with the Royal Navy, having been deprived of capital ship superiority. In the naval Battle of Cape Matapan on 28 March 1941, when a powerful force of Italian battleships might otherwise have severely crippled Admiral Cunningham's Mediterranean Fleet, the two enemy capital ships (albeit one of them damaged) sought safety by flight, leaving three cruisers and two destroyers to be sunk by the Royal Navy. In the subsequent evacuation of Greece and Crete by British forces, losses among ships of the Royal Navy were grievous, being in the main inflicted from the air. Had the bulk of the Italian battlefleet been intact at that time, they would have been immeasurably worse.

HMS *Illustrious* was the carrier that launched the Swordfish aircraft that carried out the devastating attack on Taranto. She is seen here in the Mediterranean with full war paint and Swordfish on deck.

Martin Maryland Mk I of No. 431 Flight, based on Malta. This was the RAF's first operational Maryland unit when it formed on 19 September 1940 with three ex-French Martin 167Fs, and soon ranged the Mediterranean on reconnaissance sorties. AR707 illustrated here has an Armstrong Whitworth dorsal turret.

Fairey Swordfish Mk I of No. 813 Squadron, Fleet Air Arm. Normally based aboard HMS *Eagle*, the squadron operated from HMS *Illustrious* for the Taranto raid in November 1940. In this operation the slow speed and agility of the Swordfish proved an asset, allowing the aircraft to dodge through the balloon barrage.

MALTA 1940-43

Of all the British strategic bases overseas during World War II, the tiny rocky island of Malta, athwart the central Mediterranean, was probably the most important and, accordingly, the most savagely assaulted from the air. At the time of Italy's entry into the war on 10 June 1940 Malta served two purposes: a British naval replenishment base on the maritime route through the Mediterranean to and from the Suez Canal and the Far East, and as a limited staging point for long-range flights from the UK to the Middle East.

Despite the completion of four air bases (at Hal Far, Luqa, Takali and a flying-boat station at Kalafrana), there was no organized fighter defence and only a naval gunnery flight in June 1940. When the Italians began somewhat desultory air attacks in that month, however, four Sea Gladiators were hurriedly uncrated and used to fly patrols against the raids (three of them ultimately being dubbed *Faith*, *Hope* and *Charity*, though more with one eye on legend than with historical accuracy); before a fortnight was out four Hurricanes on their way out to North Africa were commandeered by the island for its defence.

These slender forces proved adequate to discourage the Italians from increasing their pressure on the island for several weeks, but it soon became obvious that, with major land operations imminent in North Africa, the need to reinforce both sides in Egypt and Cyrenaica would impose on Malta a vital role, lying as it did directly across the Italian supply route to Tripoli.

On 2 August 12 Hurricanes were flown off the carrier *Argus* to the island, where they formed No. 261 Squadron and, with adequate fighter defence now established, three reconnaissance Marylands of No. 431 Flight arrived from the UK. A second instalment of 12 Hurricanes, flown off the *Argus* on 17 November, was overtaken by tragedy, eight of them being lost at sea after running out of fuel. Meanwhile Wellingtons, which had been staging at Malta on their raids from North Africa against targets in Italy, were now allowed to remain on the island to form No. 148 Squadron. It was also a Maryland of No. 431 Flight that carried out the superb reconnaissance of Taranto harbour before the epic raid by Fleet Air Arm Swordfish on the night of 11/12 November.

Throughout General Wavell's brilliant offensive in Egypt and Cyrenaica during the winter of 1940-1 the Wellingtons from Malta constantly raided Tripoli and Castel Benito, operations that brought swift reaction by the Axis with the arrival in Sicily late in December of the advance units of the German Fliegerkorps X, a force that within a month had grown to some 250 modern aircraft. On 10 January 60 Ju 87s and He 111s attacked a British convoy in the Sicilian narrows, severely damaging the carrier *Illustrious* and the cruisers *Southampton* and *Gloucester*. The carrier limped into harbour at Malta where she became the target of heavy and repeated attacks by the Luftwaffe and Regia Aeronautica for more than a week. With losses increasing among the Hurricanes, the Wellingtons now had to be withdrawn to North Africa and, with Malta thus largely disarmed, the Germans were able to send about half of Fliegerkorps X to Cyrenaica to support Rommel's counter-offensive in the Western Desert.

The relief of pressure on Malta now allowed the British to sail a large convoy almost unscathed through the Mediterranean to Alexandria in May, by which time a second Hurricane squadron (No. 185 with Mk IIs) had been formed on the island. In June Fliegerkorps X was moved to Greece, Crete and the Dodecanese, a move that coincided with the arrival of Air Chief Marshal Sir Arthur Tedder to take over Middle East Command. At once the Wellingtons returned to Malta, together with Blenheims and further Marylands, and these aircraft renewed the attacks on the Italian ports and convoys, sinking over 70,000 tons of enemy shipping in the last two months of 1941. When two convoys reached Malta without loss Hitler resolved to eliminate the island once and for all, ordering Luftflotte II from the USSR to Italy before the end of the year under Albert Kesselring. There now started a four-month nightmare for Malta. Throughout January and February 1942 attacks by several dozen bombers were commonplace with never a day without raids, the targets in the main being the airfields. On 7 March 15 Spitfires reached the island from a carrier, but within a week the number of Hurricanes was down to 30, and at this point Kesselring started raids using 150 aircraft or more. The Wellingtons were withdrawn once more and April found the island seriously short of food, fuel and fighters, three out of four supply ships having been sunk. At the height of the assault, on 20 April, 47 more Spitfires arrived, followed by 62 on 9 May (having flown off the American carrier *Wasp*). Amidst rumours that the Germans were preparing to invade the island, Malta was awarded the George Cross for its sustained resistance.

It was now that Hitler stepped in with changed priorities (the first being the recapture of Cyrenaica) and Kesselring moved a large proportion of his aircraft to North Africa to support Rommel. The following month two convoys were sailed to Malta from east and west, of which one from Alexandria was forced to turn back. Two supply ships managed to reach the beleaguered island and the German offensive ran out of steam at El Alamein.

Following Montgomery's famous victory on November 1942, the aircraft on Malta, which had been preying on the supply convoys to North Africa, were further reinforced. For the next six months they took an increasing toll of Axis shipping in the central Mediterranean which was at first seeking to sustain the hard-pressed Axis forces and later desperately trying to extricate the beaten German and Italian forces from North Africa. The final irony of Malta's monumental achievement was reached when her fighter squadrons, numbering 12, provided air cover for the invasion of Sicily that was launched in July 1943.

The initial fighter defence of Malta rested on three Gloster Sea Gladiators hastily erected from four crated examples. The aircraft in the foreground is 'Faith', of the famed triumvirate of 'Faith', 'Hope' and 'Charity'.

A crowded flight deck aboard the USS *Wasp* as she enters the Mediterranean on 19 April 1942. Forward is its normal complement of Grumman F4F Wildcats plus, at the stern, some of 47 Supermarine Spitfires to be flown off to Malta.

OPERATION 'BARBAROSSA' 1941

Eclipsing all other German strategic planning during the first two years of the war was Hitler's determination to attack and defeat the Soviet Union. To do so it was necessary to eliminate any potential threat from the West to avoid the age-old German nightmare of war on two fronts. Following Italy's inability to impose a decisive solution in the Mediterranean and Balkans, Germany eventually launched her massive offensive in the East with the enemy still undefeated in the West and South and, as it transpired, with inadequate time to reach Moscow before the onset of the first Russian winter.

The assault on the Soviet Union was launched before dawn on 22 June 1941 along a front that stretched from the Baltic to the Black Sea, the three army groups (under Leeb, Bock and Rundstedt) advancing 50 miles (80 km) in the first 24 hours. Supporting the huge offensive were four *Luftflotten* (air fleets) which between them deployed 19 *Jagdgruppen* of Bf 109Es and Bf 109Fs (600 aircraft), seven *Stukagruppen* of Ju 87 dive-bombers (more than 200 aircraft) and 24 *Kampfgruppen* of He 111s, Do 17s and Ju 88s (about 850 aircraft), as well as more than 1,000 other transport and reconnaissance aircraft.

Despite warnings from the West and the impossibility of concealing the German preparations for the attack, the Soviet Union was taken by surprise and when, on the first day, the Luftwaffe set out to destroy the Soviet air force the German pilots found the enemy still on the ground. So widely dispersed were the Soviet airfields that the Luftwaffe was only able to send three or four aircraft against each yet, by use of large numbers of 2- and 10-kg (4.4 and 22-lb) fragmentation bombs, they were able to devastate the grounded aircraft. The relatively small numbers of outdated I-16 fighters which rose to defend their bases were swatted like flies by the experienced Luftwaffe pilots in their superb Bf 109s. During that first day the Soviets admitted the loss of more than 1,200 aircraft.

The airfield strikes were quickly followed by an attack by 127 He 111s and Ju 88s on Moscow, 104 tons of HE and 46,000 incendiary bombs being dropped; this was followed within 48 hours by two further raids by 115 and 100 aircraft. The massacre of Soviet aircraft continued to occupy the Luftwaffe throughout July and August, and not unnaturally huge personal victory tallies were amassed by individual pilots; by mid-August four of the *Jagdgeschwader* (JG 3, JG 51, JG 53 and JG 54) had each passed a score of 1,000 enemy aircraft destroyed. On the ground it seemed likely that the German army would be in Moscow before Christmas. The Soviet capital had not been Hitler's primary objective, however, and his orders to first secure the grain-rich Ukraine (which resulted in the capture of 650,000 Soviet troops) placed the entire campaign in jeopardy. In September the Finns advanced down the Karelian isthmus, thereby helping to complete the investment of Leningrad. Not until October did Hitler renew the advance towards the Soviet capital, but by then it was too late.

Despite the widespread use of the incisive *Blitzkrieg* tactics, which had hitherto overwhelmed so many armies in the previous two years, the German offensive slowed as autumn rains clogged the lengthening supply roads and organized partisan operations took their toll behind the German front. Increasing use was made of Ju 52/3m transports to bring up supplies, but serviceable landing grounds were few and far between.

On 23 September Ju 87s of Stukageschwader 2 based at Tyrkowo attacked the Soviet fleet at Kronstadt, and a single bomb dropped by Oberleutnant Hans Rudel sank the Soviet battleship *Marat*. By the end of that month the front stretched from the Crimea in an almost straight line north to Leningrad.

Despite the weather the German armies managed to struggle forward and by early December reached Rostov, Voronezh and the outskirts of Moscow itself just as the first snows fell. This effectively brought air operations to a halt, as well as catching the Germans hopelessly ill-prepared for the rigours of the cruel winter. Loathe to waste Luftwaffe resources where they would be useless, the Germans started moving some of their fighters and dive-bombers to the Mediterranean in December to support operations against Malta and the British forces in North Africa.

Then on 6 December the Soviet commander Georgi Zhukov (of Nomonhan fame) launched a counterattack with a fresh, well-equipped army in the Moscow area and, without the means to provide adequate air support for the ground forces, the Germans were forced to pull back. The bid to capture the Soviet capital was at an end.

At this time, however, both the Luftwaffe and V-VS were hurriedly introducing improved aircraft. The Bf 109E was now finally being replaced on all units by the Bf 109F; the Do 17 had almost disappeared from front-line service, being replaced by the Do 217, while new versions of the He 111, Ju 88 and Ju 52/3m were starting to arrive at the front. Among the Soviet aircraft the I-15 and I-16 were being withdrawn at last as deliveries of modern LaGG-3s, MiG-3s and Yak-1s were frantically stepped up. Production of the Il-4 bomber (which had first raided Berlin on 8 August 1941) and Il-2 close-support aircraft was accelerating, and the first British convoys bringing Hurricane fighters had been arriving at Murmansk since September. Hitler's dream of a speedy victory in the East was being shattered as his fighting men struggled to survive the frosts and snows of their first Russian winter.

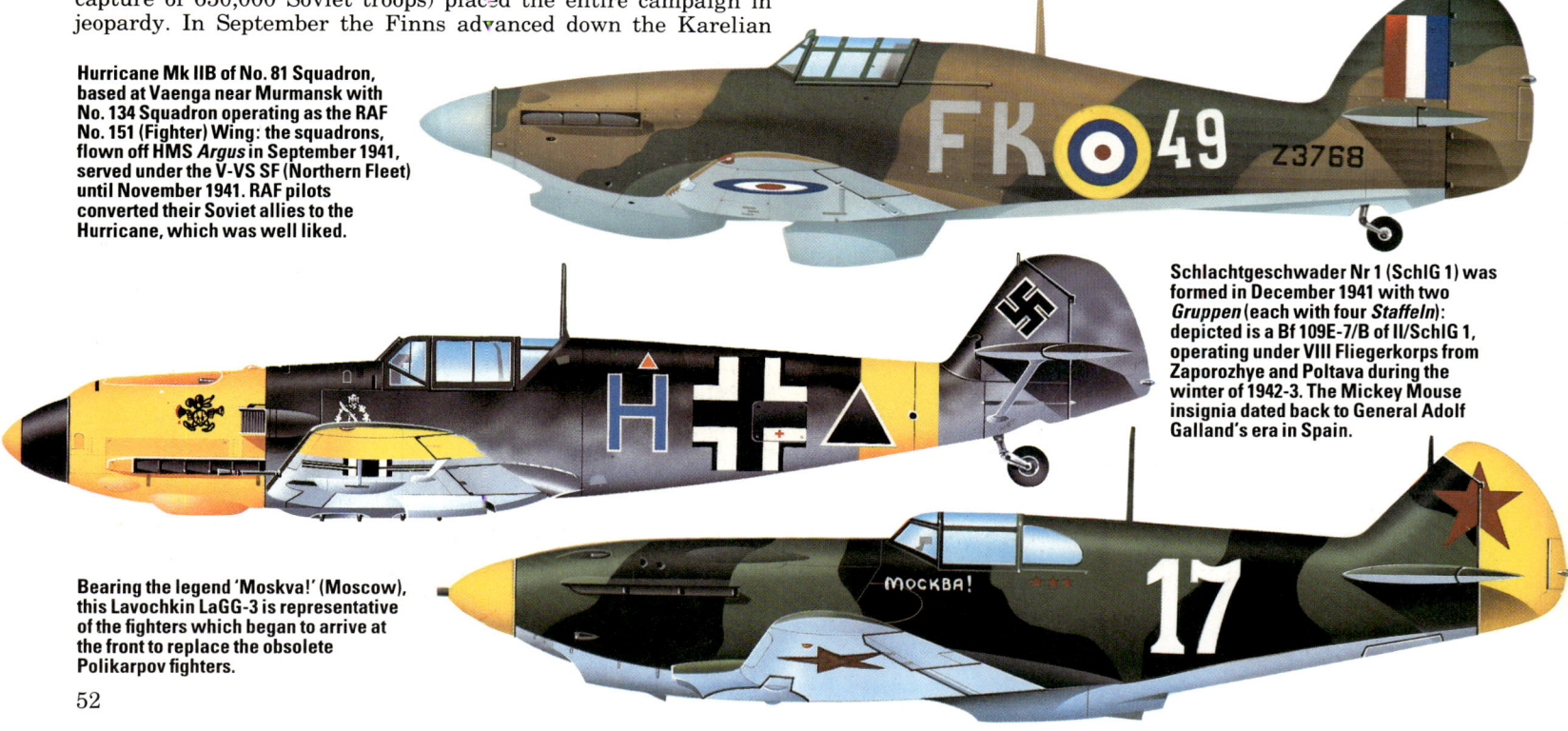

Hurricane Mk IIB of No. 81 Squadron, based at Vaenga near Murmansk with No. 134 Squadron operating as the RAF No. 151 (Fighter) Wing: the squadrons, flown off HMS *Argus* in September 1941, served under the V-VS SF (Northern Fleet) until November 1941. RAF pilots converted their Soviet allies to the Hurricane, which was well liked.

Schlachtgeschwader Nr 1 (SchIG 1) was formed in December 1941 with two *Gruppen* (each with four *Staffeln*): depicted is a Bf 109E-7/B of II/SchIG 1, operating under VIII Fliegerkorps from Zaporozhye and Poltava during the winter of 1942-3. The Mickey Mouse insignia dated back to General Adolf Galland's era in Spain.

Bearing the legend 'Moskva!' (Moscow), this Lavochkin LaGG-3 is representative of the fighters which began to arrive at the front to replace the obsolete Polikarpov fighters.

Dornier Do 17Z-2 of the Croatian-manned 10. Staffel of Kampfgeschwader 3 on the Central Sector of the Eastern Front in December 1941:

One of a number of glider-towing sub-variants was the He 111H-8/R2, this aircraft belonging to Schleppgruppe 4 based at Pskov-South on the Eastern Front in early 1942. Most of the glider operations were for transport purposes.

A tricky aircraft to fly, the Mikoyan-Gurevich MiG-3 was nevertheless welcomed into service as its high speed gave it some hope of catching the Messerschmitt Bf 109s that were holding air superiority over the Eastern Front.

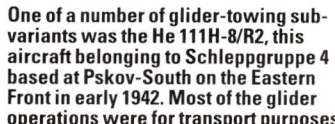

As the position in the East worsened for the Soviet Union, production of the LaGG-3 was stepped up. This was an unsatisfactory fighter but was available in quantity. It was underpowered and tricky but was to lead to the excellent La-5 and La-7.

MiG-3s lined-up on a Soviet airfield. Most aircraft are painted white for winter operations but two aircraft retain the dark green/dark brown summer camouflage.

This 72 AP I-16 Type 18 is inscribed 'Za Stalina' (for Stalin), while operating from Keg-Ostrov, Murmansk, on the Eastern Front in summer 1941. Initial losses in Operation 'Barbarossa' decimated the I-16 inventory, but it was still the most common V-VS fighter to oppose the Luftwaffe until October 1942.

Heinkel He 111H-6s were used widely on the Eastern Front, mainly as night bombers. This example is being loaded with two bombs which it will carry externally underneath the fuselage.

In the north, cold was the enemy of aircraft as much as the other side. The Russians were more used to these conditions, and these 4th Fighter Regiment, Baltic Fleet I-16s wear engine blankets to avoid freezing.

CHANNEL DASH 1942

In February 1942 there occurred what was for the Royal Navy and the Royal Air Force one of the most humiliating events of the entire war. Three German warships, *Scharnhorst*, *Gneisenau* and *Prinz Eugen*, escaped an elaborate blockade in Brest harbour, sailed through the Dover Straits in daylight and reached their German ports despite all the British could do to prevent them.

Since early 1941 the powerful battle-cruisers *Scharnhorst* and *Gneisenau* had lain in Brest, where they had put in after destructive forays in the Atlantic and where they were joined by the heavy cruiser *Prinz Eugen* on 1 June. Thereafter this trio posed a considerable threat to British convoys not only crossing the North Atlantic but sailing to and from Gibraltar and further afield. Accordingly, at the insistence of the British Admiralty, they had attracted the constant attention of RAF Bomber and Coastal Commands; however, in the first two months of attacks on Brest with over 1,100 sorties flown against the port, only four bombs damaged the ships, and it was decided to 'sew them in' using sea mines. On 6 April a single Beaufort, flown by Flying Officer Kenneth Campbell of No. 22 Squadron, managed to torpedo the *Gneisenau*, causing damage that took six months to repair. Throughout the remainder of 1941 an enormous tonnage of British bombs fell on Brest but caused little more than superficial damage to the warships, and in February 1942 the Germans decided on a bold bid to sail them back to Germany through the English Channel (Hitler being convinced that the UK was about to launch an invasion of Norway). The maritime operation was to be codenamed 'Cerberus', while 'Thunderbolt' covered the elaborate plans to provide air cover during the voyage. The breakout from Brest was scheduled for the late evening of 11 February.

To counter the threat of such an escape a British submarine lay off Ushant and the RAF covered the port with reconnaissance by day and operated radar watches ('Stopper') with Hudsons at night. Delayed by a Bomber Command raid on the port itself that night, the German ships slipped their moorings shortly before midnight and sailed out unseen by the submarine and set course north east up the Channel. Unfortunately at that critical moment the radar in the patrolling Hudson had become unserviceable and the German ships escaped undetected. By first light the following morning they had passed the Cherbourg peninsula. A further routine Coastal Command precaution, a patrol between Boulogne and Le Havre ('Habo'), had been recalled owing to the forecast of fog.

It was at this point that the first German day fighters arrived over the German ships to provide cover against the expected RAF attacks, and these were spotted on British coastal radar at 08.30 but were dismissed by Fighter Command (under Air Vice-Marshal Leigh-Mallory) as being some sort of German air-sea rescue exercise. Two hours later the pilots of two Spitfires on an *ad hoc* sweep over the Channel spotted the German fleet and, under orders not to break radio silence, sped back to their base at Kenley to report, landing at 11.10. Thus it was not until 11.25 that the British air and naval authorities were fully aware that the enemy ships were at large in the Channel. By then they were entering the Dover Straits under the protection of numerous destroyers and E-boats, as well as swarms of Fw 190As and Bf 109Fs of Adolf Galland's JG 2 and JG 26.

To counter such a break-out from Brest, the RAF (as part of Operation 'Fuller') had earmarked 100 Bomber Command aircraft and three squadrons of Beaufort torpedo-bombers, while the Fleet Air Arm had stationed a squadron (No. 815) of Swordfish at Manston. None of the Bomber Command aircraft were in the south of England and were only at four hours' standby; only seven of the Beauforts and the Swordfish were ready and loaded up with torpedoes.

As the German ships passed through the Dover Straits the heavy guns on the Kent coast opened up, but their shells all fell wide of the mark. Three fighter squadrons were ordered off to escort the Manston Swordfish which, at 12.20, took off and made for the enemy. Only one of the Spitfire squadrons, No. 72, arrived on time and was heavily engaged by the German fighters. Beset all around by Focke-Wulfs and Messerschmitts and faced by a veritable wall of flak, Lieutenant Commander Eugene Esmonde led his old torpedo biplanes into the attack. All were shot down and none of their torpedoes found their mark. Esmonde himself was awarded a posthumous Victoria Cross.

As the German ships passed out of British coastal radar cover a few Beauforts attacked with torpedoes, but again without success, as did a group of British destroyers. Between then and darkness on the evening of 12 February 242 RAF bombers set out to attack but fewer than 40 crews claimed even to have seen their targets. The enemy ships did not escape unscathed, however, the *Scharnhorst* exploding a mine off Walcheren in the early afternoon and another off Terschelling late that evening before limping into Wilhelmshaven; the *Gneisenau* also struck a mine but made Cuxhaven safely.

The bold Operations 'Cerberus' and 'Thunderbolt' had succeeded beyond all expectations, while 'Fuller', 'Stopper' and 'Habo' failed dismally. Ironically Bomber Command alone reaped an ill-earned reward: it no longer had the tiresome task of raiding Brest.

The Focke-Wulf Fw 190As of JG 26 were used to provide air cover for the break-out by the German ships. This example is seen just before the Channel Dash, during which this unit scored several victories over Spitfires and Swordfish.

The Bristol Beaufort was used for a number of torpedo attacks on the German ships. This No. 22 Squadron aircraft had managed to score a single hit on the *Gneisenau* in April 1941.

DIEPPE 1942

Since the moment of French capitulation in June 1940 and the loss of the UK's last foothold in continental Europe, the cornerstone of possible eventual victory against Germany was assumed to be a return in force by British forces across the English Channel. Such a major amphibious landing on a hostile coast was an unknown venture, particularly in the age of the military aeroplane.

It was therefore decided in 1942 to mount a major operation across the Channel as something of a rehearsal for the eventual invasion, then believed to be a practical possibility in 1943; the objective chosen was the French port of Dieppe. The opportunity was to be taken to test the enemy's reaction to such a landing in force, particularly in the air, and a major object was to attract the Luftwaffe in France into the air where it was hoped it could be decisively beaten. By mid-1942 it was hoped to be able to deploy as many as 60 fighter and fighter-bomber squadrons plus 10 reconnaissance and light bomber squadrons in the area of the landings, to counter the estimated German force of 250 fighters and 220 bombers based in France and the Low Countries. More important, it was hoped to field a dozen squadrons of the new 400-mph (644-km/h) Typhoons and Spitfire Mk IXs which were calculated to be more than a match for the new German Fw 190A. Command of the air operations was in the hands of Air Vice Marshal Leigh-Mallory.

From the outset matters went wrong with the British plans. After a couple of postponements (which are thought to have given the Germans an inkling of a pending attack), the operation was finally launched at first light on 19 August. The large number of Spitfire Mk V fighter squadrons took off before dawn to cover the landing areas and indeed provided powerful cover for the troops on the beaches as the Blenheims and Bostons attacked targets in and around Dieppe itself, and laid smokescreens over the beaches. Further afield Defiants with jamming equipment attempted to blind enemy radar as American B-17s carried out a raid on the important German fighter base at Abbeville.

At first the Luftwaffe reacted with only single *Staffeln* of Bf 109Fs and Fw 190As, and these were heavily engaged by the patrolling Spitfires. By mid-morning, however, enemy air activity was quickly increasing with the appearance of formations of Do 217 bombers and a number of low-level bombing attacks by Fw 190A-4s which managed to penetrate beneath the RAF fighter cover and escape unscathed.

On the ground the Canadian and commando forces proved unable to capture vital enemy positions overlooking Dieppe, while the Churchill tanks were inadequately armed to knock out enemy strongpoints as they floundered up and down the shingle beaches.

Garbled communications suggested that the Canadians were well established in the town so that support by the Hurricane fighter-bombers was called off at a critical point in the battle, resulting in heavy casualties among these troops.

There is no doubt that the huge armada of covering fighters prevented the German bombers from carrying out their attacks accurately on the ships, and only two vessels were hit by enemy bombs. However, while the Spitfire Mk V pilots had been briefed not to continue combat too far from Dieppe, the Spitfire Mk IXs and Typhoons were allowed free rein. Unfortunately persistent development trouble with the latter had limited its entry into service and only a single wing was available for action at the time of the Dieppe operation, and even then only with a number of flying restrictions. The only occasion on which Typhoons were in action was when they were accidentally attacked by a squadron of Canadian-flown Spitfire Mk IXs. Two Typhoons were lost when their tail units broke off as their pilots attempted to escape by diving away.

By late afternoon the assault ships were withdrawing across the Channel, still covered by the Spitfire Mk V squadrons. At first it was thought, by examination of the RAF pilots' combat reports, that the RAF had indeed won a signal victory. Early estimates suggested that more than 100 German aircraft had been shot down, compared with the loss in combat of 106 RAF aircraft in addition to 32 others written off at base. German records later revealed that the Luftwaffe aircraft losses totalled no more than 48.

The tactical lessons learned at Dieppe were indeed sobering. Ground support by the fighter-bombers and light bombers had been wholly inadequate, and there had been little or no effective communication between the landing forces and the supporting pilots. Overall the ratio of fighters to support aircraft had been far too great, and the supposed superiority of the latest RAF aircraft proved illusory, while control of the fighters had been conducted at land-based radar stations too remote from the actual battle.

Ironically the value of the Dieppe landing lay in one vital piece of information: that the Allied forces, their tactics, equipment and training in 1942 fell far short of the standard obviously required for a successful invasion of Europe. There was, alas, no means of persuading the Soviet Union (which had been pressing the UK to open a 'second front' without delay) of this unpalatable fact.

The Hawker Typhoon got its first real taste of action during the doomed Dieppe raid. These early aircraft tried desperately to hold off the Luftwaffe bombers and to some extent succeeded, but other air cover for the landings was insufficient. The Typhoon had a particularly hard time, with two aircraft shedding their tails while trying to escape from an attack by Canadian Spitfires.

CROSS-CHANNEL OPERATIONS 1941-43

When viewed against events elsewhere, the operations conducted by the Luftwaffe and RAF across the English Channel after the end of the Battle of Britain, their scale and objectives were minor indeed; the principal difference lay in the fact that the British (and later the American) attacks were continuous and increasing in tempo, whereas those of the Germans were sporadic and, in general, of strictly limited effort.

The RAF's aims were threefold: to deny access by enemy coastal shipping to ports along the French coast; to disrupt all military (but particularly air) operations in northern France; and to defeat the relatively small German air force in France and the Low Countries in the air. To do this Fighter Command set about increasing its strength in 1941 by introducing the excellent Supermarine Spitfire Mk V, a version that eventually equipped no fewer than 71 squadrons, the Spitfire Mk VC variant being capable of carrying up to 500 lb (227 kg) of bombs. Hawker Hurricane Mk IIs, of which the four-cannon Hurricane Mk IIC fighter-bomber was the outstanding version, equipped a further 42 squadrons; they eventually carried up to 1,000 lb (454 kg) of bombs.

From the outset of the light bombers of No. 2 Group (Bristol Blenheims and Douglas Bostons) were tasked with Operation 'Channel Stop', a constant offensive against enemy coastal shipping in the Channel but, with the arrival of the fighter-bomber Hurricanes this task was taken over by Fighter Command on 30 October 1941, while the light bombers concentrated on land targets under heavy Spitfire protection. The Spitfires themselves had initiated the first of the offensive sweeps, known as 'Rhubarbs', as early as 20 December 1940, and these continued to grow in scope until by 1942 as many as 500 aircraft would sweep along the French coast, trailing their coat in an effort to lure the Luftwaffe into the sky. Occasionally (and particularly when German radar reported British light bombers approaching key fighter airfields) the Messerschmitt Bf 109Fs of JG 2 and JG 26 would come up to intercept, and heavy air fighting would ensue; by and large, however, air combats tended to involve only the smaller formations.

This pattern changed dramatically with the introduction of the German Focke-Wulf Fw 190A, a superlative fighter that quickly proved superior to the Spitfire Mk V; fortunately for Fighter Command not more than about 60 of these aircraft were operational by February 1942 and, although losses among British aircraft began to increase, there was a breathing space in which to find a remedy.

As told elsewhere, the Hawker Typhoon was introduced into service before all its problems had been solved and, together with the Spitfire Mk IX, was entering service by the time of the Dieppe operation of August 1942. By then, though, the Fw 190A-3 fighter-bomber, capable of carrying a 1,102-lb (500-kg) bomb, was serving with JG 2 in France, 30 of these aircraft launching a vicious attack on Canterbury, Kent, on 30 October. Moreover, misled into believing that the Fw 190A-3 was the latest variant in service when an example landed intact in south Wales on 23 June 1942, the British received an unpleasant surprise when confronted by the more powerful Fw 190A-4 which could outrun both the Spitfire Mk IX and Typhoon (the latter beset with restrictions).

When, during the winter of 1942-3, the newly-formed Schnell-kampfgeschwader 10 (SKG 10) fighter-bomber wing began a series of daylight hit-and-run attacks with Fw 190A-4s, the RAF was forced to deploy disproportionately large forces of fighters to counter the threat. Heavy damage was inflicted in a raid on London on 20 January 1943; in March SKG 10 struck Ashford, Eastbourne and Hastings, and the following month returned to Eastbourne and destroyed a ball-bearing factory at Chelmsford in Essex.

Excellent though the stopgap Spitfire Mk IX was, its performance at low altitude was inadequate to match that of the Fw 190A-3 and Fw 190A-4 fighter-bombers, and a new variant was hurriedly introduced, the Spitfire Mk XII with Griffon engine and clipped wings. Together with the Typhoon, whose snags had been largely cured and which was fast and adequately reliable at low level, the Spitfires gradually got the measure of the snap raids and, by late spring 1943, these had tailed off. In any case, with pressure mounting on other fronts, most Fw 190 fighter-bombers were being moved elsewhere.

By mid-1943 the Americans had arrived in the UK in sufficient numbers for the fighters and fighter-bombers of the US Army Air Force to make a significant contribution to the cross-Channel air offensive; on 13 April the Republic P-47s of the 56th Fighter Group entered combat for the first time with a sweep in the St Omer area, being followed into action in later months by the 55th, 78th, 353rd 358th, 359th and 361st Fighter Groups of the 66th Fighter Wing, VIII Fighter Command. By the end of the year the Allies had at their disposal more than 2,200 Spitfires, Hurricanes, Typhoons, P-47 Thunderbolts, Lockheed P-38 Lightnings and North American P-51 Mustangs based in the UK, their operations being divided between cross-Channel sweeps and escort missions with the British and American medium and heavy bombers which were by then mounting a devastating offensive against German-occupied Europe.

At low levels the Spitfire Mk VB with single-stage low-blown Merlin 45, 46 or 50 was as good as a Mk IX, especially in LF.Mk VB form with clipped wings which provided for a greater rate of roll. BL479 was one of a batch of 1,000 from Castle Bromwich. It served with No. 316 (Polish) Squadron.

The de Havilland Mosquito's high performance and heavy armament made it a good night intruder, and it was used for many low-level missions over France and the Low Countries.

Douglas Boston light bombers are seen attacking Eindhoven in 1942. Such attacks were invariably opposed by fighter defences, which often took a large toll on the attackers.

Temporarily painted matt black, an Fw 190 A-5/U8 of I Gruppe, Schnellkampfgeschwader (SKG) 10, with centreline bomb rack and wing drop tanks, during the Jabo attacks on southern England during summer 1943. Based at Poix, France, this unit virtually obliterated all national insignia in the interests of camouflage.

This fast Ju 88S-1 three-seat bomber was finished in standard 1944 night camouflage and operated from Dedelsdorf in the final months of the war on lone missions against Britain. S-1s flew *Y-Gerät* pathfinder missions at the end of the *Steinbock* reprisal raids.

The early versions of Douglas Boston and Havoc had Twin Wasp engines and a tapered vertical tail, in contrast to the main production which had the more powerful Double Cyclone and broader tail. This Boston I was converted in 1940 as a Havoc Mk I for No. 23 Squadron.

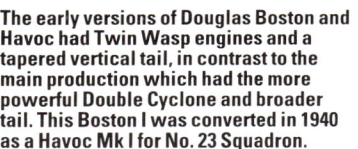

A Typhoon of No. 175 Squadron is readied for a 'Rhubarb' sortie with two short-tail 500-lb (227-kg) bombs; it shows that even by the EJ/EK serial range the bubble canopy had not been introduced.

BRITISH NIGHT BOMBING 1941-42

As the German night Blitz reached its climax at the beginning of 1941, RAF Bomber Command was beginning the long process of building a force of truly heavy bombers with which to carry the war back to the German people. The first landmarks in this process were reached when four-engine Short Stirlings of No. 7 Squadron bombed Rotterdam in The Netherlands on 10/11 February, Avro Manchesters of No. 207 Squadron attacked Brest on 24/25 February, and Handley Page Halifaxes of No. 35 Squadron raided Le Havre on the French coast on 10/11 March; two nights later Manchesters and Halifaxes made their first attack on German soil with a raid on Hamburg. It was, however, the twin-engine Vickers Wellington that dropped the RAF's first 4,000-lb (1814-kg) bombs when aircraft of Nos 9 and 149 Squadrons attacked Emden on the last night of March. Emden was again attacked on 27 April, this time in daylight by the Stirlings of No. 7 Squadron. On the night of 8/9 May Bomber Command assembled the largest force to date for raids on Germany when 360 aircraft of all types attacked Bremen and Hamburg.

By the end of 1941 Bomber Command possessed three operational squadrons of Stirlings, three of Manchesters and three of Halifaxes, in addition to 21 Wellington squadrons, seven of Handley Page Hampdens and five of Armstrong Whitworth Whitleys, a total of about 420 aircraft (excluding Bristol Blenheim and Douglas Boston light bombers), of which fewer than 50 were four-engine bombers. However, the first examples of a new bomber had been delivered to No. 44 Squadron, this Avro Lancaster being a four-engine development of the Manchester which, because of persistent engine problems, was soon discontinued and withdrawn.

1942 thus became the single most formative year for Bomber Command during the war. On 22 February Air Marshal Arthur Harris assumed the leadership of the command, a position he was to occupy with spectacular achievement for the remainder of the war. Disturbed at the continuing inaccuracy of bombing attacks, not to mention the slow delivery of four-engine bombers, Harris at once ordered maximum priority for the introduction of new navigation and bombing aids (the rudimentary 'Gee' had been in limited service for about six months, and a short-range bombing aid, 'Trinity', had proved disappointing). He also gave orders for new tactics to be employed in efforts to increase bombing accuracy and effect, and the first of these (the concentration of bombers in space and time over the target) was used with good results in a raid by 223 aircraft against the Renault factory near Paris on the night of 3/4 March.

On the same night that the Renault works were being bombed, the great Lancaster bomber was making its operational debut, a mining sortie; its first bombing mission, a raid by No. 44 Squadron on Essen, was flown on 10/11 March. Exactly one month later the RAF's first 8,000-lb (3629-kg) bomb was dropped by a No. 76 Squadron Halifax on the same target.

April saw the first of the Lancaster's spectacular 'set piece' attacks with a daylight low-level raid by 20 aircraft of Nos 44 and 97 Squadrons against the MAN plant at Augsburg on 17 April; seven aircraft were lost, but the leader, Squadron Leader John Nettleton, was awarded the Victoria Cross.

On the night of 30/31 May Harris launched his first '1,000-bomber' raid, undertaken as much as a propaganda coup as an attempt to swamp the German defences and thereby reduce the loss rate. A total of 1,046 bombers, culled from every Bomber Command squadron, as well as the operational training units, set out to attack Cologne in Operation 'Millennium'; 40 aircraft were lost out of the 898 that were believed to have bombed their target. At dawn the following day Bomber Command de Havilland Mosquito photo-reconnaissance and bomber aircraft of No. 105 Squadron were over the city to observe the results of the raid in their first operational mission. Two nights later, on 1/2 June, 956 bombers attacked Essen for the loss of 31 aircraft, and on 25/26 June 1,006 aircraft were sent against Bremen, losing 44 of their number; the latter raid was the last operational mission flown by the Manchester.

Harris' three '1,000-bomber' raids provided an enormous filip to the nation's morale, not least to Bomber Command itself. Yet Harris was himself aware that they severely disrupted the training of new bomber crews, while the loss of over 100 aircraft in only three raids was more than the command could afford. But Lancaster deliveries were now accelerating fast, and their second spectacular raid by 94 such aircraft (from Nos 9, 44, 49, 50, 57, 61, 97, 106 and 207 Squadrons) against the Schneider factories at Le Creusot (in Operation 'Robinson' at dusk on 17 October) emphasized the growing availability of these magnificent aeroplanes, only one of which was lost. Already the Hampden, Whitley and Blenheim had flown their last bombing sorties over northern Europe.

August 1942 saw the creation of the Pathfinder Force (under the command of Group Captain D.C.T. Bennett), a number of squadrons tasked with leading major raids and marking the target with easily identifiable coloured bomb bursts. The PFF flew its first mission against Flensburg on the night of 18/19 August. Before the year was out a new navigation and bombing aid, 'Oboe', was first used in a raid by specially-equipped Mosquitoes of No. 109 Squadron on Lutterade on the night of 20/21 December. In the first 10 months of Harris' command the UK's bomber force had more than trebled its striking power, and could now begin to deliver its punches where they were intended to land.

Handley Page Halifax B.Mk II Srs I of No. 35 (Madras Presidency) Squadron, operating from Linton-on-Ouse (Yorks) in May 1942. Note the bulbous Boulton Paul turret that induced much drag.

The Short Stirling Mk I flew predominantly with No. 3 Group, Bomber Command, from 1940-43. This aircraft flew with No. 149 Squadron from Mildenhall.

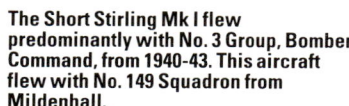

In RAF Fighter Command markings (note sky tailbands and yellow leading edges), this de Havilland Mosquito B.Mk IV Srs II light bomber served with the Marham-based No. 105 Squadron in the summer of 1942.

Plagued with problems, the Avro Manchester entered service with No. 207 Squadron at Waddington in late 1940. This is one of these early aircraft.

Lancaster B.Mk I PO-S of No. 467 Squadron (Australian) was one of the most famous in RAF Bomber Command. Its first mission was flown with No. 38 Squadron on 8/9 July 1942, and it was transferred to No. 467 Squadron in November 1943. Its 100th mission was flown on 11/12 May 1944 and the last, her 137th, on 23 April 1945.

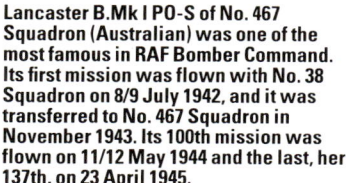

Though British pilots found the tricycle landing gear (and other features) unfamiliar, the powerful Boston Mk III was then the best high-speed bomber in the RAF.

This colour shot gives a good impression of the size of the Short Stirling, at first so awesome to its crews.

THE NIGHT FIGHTER WAR 1939-45

In 1939 neither the RAF nor the Luftwaffe possessed in service a force of night-fighters capable of countering significantly the threat of the night bomber, both air forces depending almost exclusively upon *ad hoc* use of day fighters working in collaboration with searchlights and broadcast instructions from ground controllers. True, RAF Fighter Command was experimenting with a handful of Bristol Blenheims of No. 25 Squadron equipped with rudimentary airborne radar (AI.Mk III), but it was not until the night of 21/22 July 1940 that the first German bomber fell to the guns of a radar-equipped Blenheim.

In September 1940 the RAF began receiving its first purpose-designed night-fighter, the Bristol Beaufighter with AI.Mk IV, and by early 1941 (during the latter stages of the German Blitz) the British night-fighters were beginning to take a substantial toll of the night raiders. The Luftwaffe had recognized the threat posed by the RAF's night bomber force in 1940 and had created the first of its night-fighter wings, Nachtjagdgeschwader 1 (NJG 1), with Messerschmitt Bf 110s, in July of that year. For most of 1940 the German night-fighter crews attacked visually with the aid of searchlights, but by early the following year, under Oberst Josef Kammhuber, a chain of radar stations ('Giant Würzburg' sets) had been established from Denmark to the Swiss border to form the *Himmelbett* system. By June 1941 five night-fighter *Gruppen* were operational with Bf 110, Dornier Do 17 and Junkers Ju 88 night-fighters. After early trials with an infrared-sensing device (Spanner Anlage) had been abandoned, early German airborne radar gave promising results and late in 1941 the Telefunken company was producing the Lichtenstein BC radar which had a range of about 2½ miles (4 km); by the following summer most Luftwaffe night-fighters were equipped with this or the simplified Lichtenstein C-1 version.

Meanwhile the RAF had standardized with the Beaufighter Mks IF and IIF, equipped with metric AI.Mk IV (with a range of about 4 miles/6.4 km under ideal conditions) and by May 1941 some 200 aircraft were in service. At this time British ground control of night-fighters was far superior to the German, introduction in January 1941 of the plan position indicator (PPI) enabling a single controller to distinguish fighter and target on a single display, whereas the Germans employed two operators (one for each aircraft) at separate sets.

Early in 1942 the centimetric AI.Mk VII was introduced in the Beaufighter Mk VIF with Nos 68 and 604 Squadrons, followed by AI.Mk VIII, the new equipment providing better definition, although the pilot-display radar proved unpopular. Another night-fighting tactic, the use of airborne searchlights (Turbinlites) in Douglas Havoc aircraft to illuminate enemy bombers so that accompanying Hawker Hurricanes could close for the kill, was tried by 10 RAF squadrons during 1942-3, but met with little success and was abandoned. Havocs were also fitted with AI radar.

The finest of all British night-fighters was unquestionably the de Havilland Mosquito, of which the Mosquito Mk II version entered service in May 1942; fitted successively with AI.Mks IV, V, VIII, IX and the American Mk X, the Mosquito continued in service until the end of the war, gradually replacing the Beaufighter and ultimately serving with 24 squadrons of the RAF, performing night defence,

intruder and bomber support operations.

In the Luftwaffe relatively little effort could be spared for offensive night-fighter operations, the pressing need being for night defence against the increasing attacks by RAF Bomber Command which, by 1943, were assuming a devastating scale. At the end of 1942 the German night-fighter force comprised a total of 389 operational aircraft, of which 300 were Bf 110s; Kammhuber's defences had destroyed a total of 1,291 British bombers during the year, about two-thirds of them having fallen to his fighters. A serious setback, however, occurred on the night of 24/25 July 1943 when Harris' bombers first dropped large quantities of 'Window' jamming strips during their great raid on Hamburg. At a stroke the Würzburg and Lichtenstein screens of the *Himmelbett* system were rendered useless, and this immediately prompted the introduction of new night-fighting tactics, codenamed *Wilde Sau* and *Zahme Sau* (respectively Wild and Tame Sow). The former involved the use of free-lancing day fighters which, being without radar, were unaffected by the 'Window' jamming. The latter tactic employed a master commentary from the ground which enabled night-fighters to locate and enter the bomber stream where they could attack visually.

It was also during the second half of 1943 that the Germans introduced upward-firing cannon (schräge Musik) into their night fighters; stalking the British heavy bombers from astern, the German pilots positioned themselves below their target and opened fire. Being thus attacked from a blind spot, the British remained unaware of this new tactic and literally hundreds of bombers were thus shot down. By mid-1944 the best of all German night-fighters, the Heinkel He 219, had re-equipped I/NJG 1; some versions of this superb aircraft were armed with as many as eight cannon (including schräge Musik), its most successful exponent being Major Heinz-Wolfgang Schnauffer (121 victories); on one occasion he shot down seven Avro Lancasters in the space of 17 minutes.

The night-fighter war was a constant battle of measures and countermeasures, of jamming, feints and deception. Although the Allies sustained technical superiority throughout the war, German ingenuity produced expedients that enabled the Lutwaffe to take an enormous toll of the night bombers over the Reich.

The Dornier Do 217 was a good platform for airborne radar but its size rendered it rather cumbersome for fighting. It often operated in concert with groups of Messerschmitt Bf 110s.

A Beaufighter Mk II of No. 307 (Lwow) Squadron. Based at Exeter for home defence duties between April 1941 and April 1943, this was the only Polish night fighter squadron in the RAF and for much of this period the unit was commanded by the well-known pilot, Wing Commander Michalowski.

Messerschmitt Bf 110G-4b/R3 of 7.Staffel III/NJG 4, Luftflotte Reich based in north west Germany in 1943-44. Equipped with FuG 220b *Lichtenstein SN-2* radar, FuG 16zY fighter director and flame dampers, this was the final G-series production model. Night-fighter colour schemes varied at this stage of the war.

This Junkers Ju 88G-7a of IV/NJG 6 had its fin painted to represent the less capable Ju 88C version.

One of the first production Mosquito F.Mk II fighters, delivered in the first week of 1942, W4082 served with No. 157 Squadron based at Castle Camps in mid-1942.

The Bristol Beaufighter Mk VI was an accomplished night fighter once the crew had become familiar with the AI radar installation. Beaufighters provided the mainstay of RAF night defences until 1943.

The excellent de Havilland Mosquito was a winner in every role, and in night fighting it excelled. The type began replacing the Beaufighter in 1942 and by the end of the war was the most important RAF night fighter.

While the RAF converted Bostons into Havoc night intruders, the Luftwaffe converted Do 17Z-2 day bombers into Do 17Z-10 Kauz (Screech Owl) night intruders. This Kauz was painted black overall, and served with 1/NJG 2, one of the first of the Luftwaffe's night fighter units, based at Gilze-Rijen.

A Junkers Ju 88G has its compass set. This aircraft, more than any other symbolized the nightly tangle between the Luftwaffe and the RAF bombers. The Ju 88, like the Mosquito, performed well in every role and was the Luftwaffe's main night fighter.

Designed from the outset as a night fighter, the Heinkel He 219 was the best of this specialized breed of aircraft to see service during the war. Only small numbers reached service, but they were devastating against bombers.

This Heinkel He 219A Uhu was based at Munster-Handorf in the autumn of 1944. Its unit was 1. Staffel/ Nachtjagdgeschwader 1. The Heinkel He 219 had claimed five bombers in one night on its debut sortie.

This pale grey Fw 190A-6/R11 of 1./NJG 10 was flown by Oberleutnant Hans Krause from Werneuchen in August 1944. The pilot's insignia consisted of his nickname 'Illo' beneath the *Wilde Sau* emblem. Note *Neptun* radar arrays and two-shade grey on upper wing surface. Krause was awarded the Knight's Cross.

FROM DEMYANSK TO STALINGRAD 1941-43

Throughout the first five months of Hitler's invasion of the Soviet Union the Germans enjoyed almost unrelenting success in their drive eastwards, only just (but disastrously) failing in their bid to capture Moscow before the onset of that first Russian winter. Having halted the German advance in front of their capital, the Soviet armies, better prepared for warfare in the savage cold, opened their counteroffensives early in December 1941 on the Leningrad, Moscow and Kharkov fronts. Almost entirely paralysed by the weather conditions, the Luftwaffe decided to remove much of its strength from the East, redeploying V Fliegerkorps to Belgium, and five *Gruppen* of its latest Messerschmitt Bf 109F fighters to the Mediterranean, thereby reducing its strength from about 2,400 aircraft to 1,700 on the 2,000-mile (3200-km) Eastern Front. And despite a desperate lack of modern aircraft (as well as the loss of some 5,000 sustained since 'Barbarossa' opened the previous summer), the Soviets were able to force the German armies back as much as 200 miles (320 km) in some areas.

In the course of this violent reversal of fortunes for the German army, the Soviets pierced the German front line between the Army Groups 'Centre' and 'North' and, early in February 1942, succeeded in isolating the whole of X Corps at Demyansk. Realizing that the loss of some 100,000 men in a crumbling front could mean disaster for the entire German army in the north, the Luftwaffe collected every available transport aircraft (the Ju 52/3m alone was scarcely affected by the winter conditions, having air-cooled engines) and started a massive supply operation to the Demyansk pocket. Between mid-February and mid-May, when the Germans were able to open up a land corridor to the trapped army, about 400 aircraft airlifted 24,000 tons of supplies and 15,500 troops into the pocket, and evacuated 20,000 casualties. Losses amounted to 262 aircraft, and the increasing toll being taken by the Soviet 20-mm and 37-mm

AA guns brought realization to the Germans of the impossibility of sustaining major air operations in more than one theatre simultaneously; indeed, the losses at Demyansk was never completely made good and many of the Luftwaffe's most experienced transport pilots were lost. Moreover, after a disastrous period of reduced Soviet aircraft production during the latter half of 1941, while aircraft plants had been moved out of danger east of the Urals, production began to make spectacular recovery in 1942, particularly with improved aircraft such as the Yak-1 and LaGG-3 fighters and, soon after, the two-seat Il-2m3 *Shturmovik* close-support aircraft.

While ferocious fighting raged around Demyansk to the north, the Germans went over to the offensive in the south, and in April 1942 Army Group 'South' attacked in the southern Ukraine and the Crimean peninsula, supported by VIII Fliegerkorps and the newly-formed 1.Fliegerdivision. Sevastopol fell on 4 July after a prodigious air assault in which VIII Fliegerkorps had flown 23,750 sorties and its He 111s, Ju 87s and 88s had dropped 20,530 tons of bombs on the fortress town. With the reduction of the Barvenko pocket, the Soviet armies lost half a million men killed and as prisoners in just over three weeks, and the way was now clear for Hitler's major summer offensive eastwards towards Voronezh and into the Caucasus to capture the Maikop oilfields.

Considerable efforts had strengthened the Luftwaffe in the east to 2,750 aircraft, and new types (the Ju 87D-1 and Henschel Hs 129B-1/R2 anti-tank aircraft and Fw 190A fighters) were now entering service. The advance stormed forward and achieved considerable success until, after intervention by Hitler who, in this moment of assumed victory, assumed personal command, the 11th Army was switched from the Caucasus to the Leningrad front, and the 6th Army, under General von Paulus, was ordered against Stalingrad.

To the Soviets the city of Stalingrad was a patriotic symbol and the Soviet armies were ordered to stand firm, if necessary defending it to the last man. As von Paulus split his 6th Army to create two fronts, the Soviets hastily assembled a new army group and set about the destruction of the Axis forces piecemeal. On 23 November the Soviets closed their pincers to the west of the city just as the dreaded winter set in.

The Soviet air strength in the area was not particularly great, with no more than about 600 Pe-2s, Yak-1s, LaGG-3s, Il-4s and a few of the new La-5s. When ultimately the Luftwaffe attempted once more to sustain an encircled army from the air, by assembling transport aircraft from every corner of Europe, they failed to repeat their earlier successes, for the Soviet armies quickly dominated with artillery every available landing ground round Stalingrad. By the end of November heavy snow was falling and temperatures plummeting. One by one the landing grounds were overrun, until by mid-January 1943 only Gumrak remained available. When that also fell, only the dropping of supplies by parachute was possible. The last supply sortie was flown on 3 February, but the German 6th Army was already finished, shot, frozen to death or captured.

An interesting concept put into practice on the Eastern Front was two heavily-armed Polikarpov I-16s being carried under the wings of a Tupolev TB-3 in order to carry out accurate long-range bombing attacks.

In roughly the same class as the Heinkel He 111, the Ilyushin Il-4 was the principal medium bomber used by the Soviets. This type was used for raids on Berlin, and some were adapted for torpedo attacks against German shipping in the Baltic.

Early in 1942 the 4./KG 76 converted on to Junkers Ju 88C-6 fighters at Wöllersdorf instead of remaining on bomber operations. The snow-camouflaged standard Ju 88C-6 of 4.Staffel operated from Taganrog under IV Fliegerkorps in late 1942. Note painted simulation of a transparent nose to confuse the enemy.

The German version of the Shturmovik was the Henschel Hs 129. This was heavily armed and could absorb much battle damage in its role of destroying enemy tanks. Later versions appeared with massive anti-armour cannon carried under the central fuselage.

The Yakovlev Yak-1 was the first operational member of the successful family of single-seat fighters. These began to turn the tide of air warfare in the East, and in later versions was to make a great impact upon the air war. This aircraft was flown by the well-known female pilot, Lydia Litvak.

Gotha Go 242 gliders, towed behind Junkers Ju 52s, were employed in a tactical role on the Eastern Front. These proved easy meat for Soviet fighters and were relegated to duties behind the front.

The Mikoyan-Gurevich MiG-3 continued to play a major part during the defence of the Soviet Union. The type's main attribute was its speed, and this helped it to several victories over the far more manoeuvrable Bf 109.

The Petlyakov Pe-2 was in many ways the Soviet equivalent of the Mosquito as it was employed in many diverse roles.

During the desperate last days at Stalingrad Junkers Ju 52s kept the ground troops supplied, as their landing strips were slowly wiped out by Soviet artillery. However, winter had set in with a vengeance and the troops were never to leave this bloody battleground.

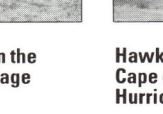

Lavochkin LaGG-3s of the Black Sea Fleet line up for the camera. Conditions in the south were better than in the snowy wastes in the north, and summer camouflage could be worn all year.

Hawker Hurricanes of the Royal Air Force arrived in the Soviet Union via the North Cape convoy route and were soon flying alongside the fighter regiments. The Hurricane was hardy and fared well in the harsh conditions of the Russian winter.

ALAMEIN AND 'TORCH' 1942-43

The redeployment of important elements of the RAF from North Africa to the Balkans in 1941 had left the British fatally exposed following Wavell's brilliant advance into Libya, and with the arrival of the Afrika Korps, supported by Luftwaffe fighters and dive-bombers, the British army in the Western Desert was forced back almost to the Egyptian frontier once more. This was in turn followed by an offensive, Operation 'Crusader', commanded by General Auchinleck which relieved Tobruk and carried the 8th Army west once more to beyond Benghazi. Throughout this advance Hurricanes, Tomahawks and Blenheims of the RAF, RCAF, RAAF and SAAF were constantly in action, as were Wellingtons and Baltimores against enemy ports and airfields, maintaining a marginal but vital degree of air superiority over the less numerous aircraft of the Luftwaffe and Regia Aeronautica.

Auchinleck made a fatal error, however, preferring to concentrate on mopping up enemy resistance and strengthening his positions rather than striking forward at El Agheila before the enemy could counterattack. And it was Rommel who, with shorter supply lines, struck first and quickly forced the 8th Army back once more, this time beyond the Egyptian border. However, as a result of gallant delaying actions, notably by the South Africans at Tobruk and the Free French at Bir Hakim (where the new Hurricane Mk IID 'tank buster' was first used to good effect against enemy armour) in May 1942, vital time was gained in which to establish a 'last defence line' before Cairo at El Alamein.

And so it was that after two years of advance and retreat in North Africa the famous 8th Army found itself with its back to the Suez Canal while the victorious Afrika Korps seemed poised for the final thrust. However, by prodigious efforts the Allied forces had accomplished a massive build-up by the time the Axis forces were brought to a halt at Alamein. In the 18 months since Tedder had assumed command in the Middle East his air force had undergone transformation, now comprising 96 squadrons, of which 60 were British, 13 American, 13 South African, five Australian, two Greek, and one each of Rhodesian, French and Yugoslav, for a total of 1,500 first-line aircraft, of which 1,200 were deployed in the Western Desert. Among his modern aircraft were Spitfire Mk Vs, Kittyhawks, Beaufighters, Beauforts, Marauders and Halifaxes, as well as 10 squadrons of Wellingtons and five Liberator squadrons. Against them were deployed some 3,000 Axis aircraft, of which only about 700 were based in North Africa, and only half of these were serviceable.

On the ground General Bernard Montgomery concentrated a vastly superior army, outnumbering the Axis forces by almost two to one in men, tanks and guns. On 23 October 1942 he was ready to strike at El Alamein, preparing his attack with a massive artillery bombardment of German and Italian positions as six squadrons of Wellingtons bombed them from the air. The next day the fighter-bombers joined in and the RAF and SAAF Hurricane Mk IID tank-busters went for the enemy armoured vehicles. For a week the great battle raged as German Ju 87s joined in attempts to halt the British armoured thrusts, but were almost invariably caught by covering British and American Kittyhawks. On 4 November the 1st Armoured Division broke through the enemy line and at once the Axis began a long westward retreat. At sea Axis supply ships, desperately trying to bring supplies to the Cyrenaican ports, were subjected to incessant air attack, no fewer than 18 vessels heavily laden with guns, fuel and food being either sunk or forced to return to Italy or Greece on account of damage. Almost symbolic of the Luftwaffe's misfortunes at this time was the loss in an accident of Hauptmann Hans-Joachim Marseille, the widely-respected fighter pilot and highest-scoring pilot in the West; after attaining the extraordinary total of 158 victories he was killed baling out of his Bf 109 after engine failure.

As the victorious 8th Army swept eastwards for the last time, British fighters landed at Gazala, 100 miles (160 km) inside Cyrenaica on 17 November; two days later they were at Matruba, 50 miles (80 km) farther on. Two Hurricane squadrons even landed behind the enemy forces, so swiftly were the Allied fighters accompanying the advance.

It was at this moment that, as the Axis forces were desperately preparing to stand firm in Tripolitania, the Allies launched their master stroke when, on 8 November, American and British forces, sailed from the west, put ashore in considerable strength in Morocco and Algeria under cover of carrierborne aircraft and others operating from Gibraltar. These landings, Operation 'Torch', immediately threatened the whole Axis position in North Africa. Straightaway Tunisia was occupied by the Germans as air reinforcements from Italy and Sicily landed at airfields in the north. RAF and USAAF fighters and bombers (Spitfires, Mosquitoes, Beaufighters, P-38s, P-39s, P-40s, B-17s, B-24s, B-25s and B-26s), as well as troop-carrying C-47s, poured ashore at Algerian airfields.

The Luftwaffe made numerous raids but Allied air superiority was such that little vital damage was suffered. In the south the 8th Army, after being held at Mareth, broke through the enemy lines in March 1943 with constant air support from RAF and USAAF fighters and fighter-bombers. By 1 May only a small perimeter in the north east of Tunisia held out and, despite considerable efforts to sustain this by air from Sicily, the Axis forces in North Africa finally surrendered to the Allies under General Alexander on 12 May.

Amid the dust and sand of the Western Desert, which not only reduced visibility but caused severe wear to aircraft engines, these Hurricane Mk IID anti-tank fighters of No. 6 Squadron taxi out for take-off at Sidi bu Amud in January 1943 during the rout of the Afrika Korps following the 2nd Battle of Alamein.

Junkers Ju 88A-10 of II/LG 1, Luftwaffe, based at Heraklion (Crete) in October 1942 for anti-shipping strikes. The aircraft still has desert camouflage from its earlier tour of duty in North Africa, where it had not proved to be a success. It was found far more effective in attacks on British shipping.

As the Germans retreated into Tunisia an ingenious plan was hatched to attack them from the rear. Supported by Lockheed Hudson transports and armoured cars, Hawker Hurricanes operated from landing strips in the desert behind enemy lines, from where they could launch surprise attacks on the enemy's supply lines which were supporting the front line.

The Martin Baltimore was used by British forces in the desert and was a useful light bomber. It had good performance, but suffered from poor defensive armament (to some extent rectified by the addition of a gun turret in later versions) and tricky landing qualities.

The US Navy's first major intervention in the war occurred during the 1942 'Torch' invasion of North West Africa. This Grumman F4F-4 Wildcat of VGF-29 from USS *Santee* was among the carrier aircraft supporting the landings. Yellow circles were added to the national insignia to aid recognition and to avoid confusion with Commonwealth aircraft.

One of the most widely used aircraft in the desert was the Messerschmitt Bf 110. This Bf 110E of 8./ZG 26 based at Berca in late 1942 carries a MK 101 30-mm cannon for anti-armour duties.

Sporting highly effective camouflage is a Messerschmitt Bf 109E-4/Trop of JG 27. When I/JG 27 came to North Africa in the early summer of 1941 its Bf 109s turned the tables on the British.

THE CONDOR THREAT 1940-43

From the moment German forces reached the Atlantic coast of France the threat to the UK's vital lifelines in the Atlantic (from surface raiders, submarines and aircraft) took on an infinitely more menacing character. Yet the Luftwaffe had not envisaged long-range maritime air operations to the same extent as the RAF, its flying-boats and seaplanes (the Dornier Do 18 and Heinkel He 59) being more suited to short-range coastal work in the North Sea.

Instead work was hurriedly undertaken to adapt the one proven long-range aircraft possessed by Germany, the commercial Focke-Wulf Fw 200 Condor, to embark on land-based maritime operations over the Atlantic now that suitable bases existed in Norway and western France. The four-engine Fw 200 had originated in 1936 and in the two years immediately before the war had flown a number of spectacular long-distance flights. Stemming from a Japanese order for a maritime reconnaissance version (which was not completed), the manufacturers continued the adaptation to meet Luftwaffe requirements, and six development aircraft were delivered to I/KG 40 in Denmark in April 1940. Two months later, equipped with Fw 200Cs, this unit moved to Bordeaux-Mérignac to start operations against British shipping, flying patrols from France over the Western Approaches and landing at Trondheim or Stavanger in Norway.

Under the command of Oberstleutnant Geisse, I/KG 40's 15 Fw 200Cs sank 90,000 tons of Allied shipping in August and September and, on 26 October, an aircraft flown by Hauptmann Bernhard Jope attacked and crippled the 44,348-ton liner *Empress of Britain* off the Irish coast, the ship being sunk by a U-boat while under tow two days later.

By the end of 1940 a total of 26 Fw 200s had been completed, and such was the threat they posed to British convoys beyond the protection of land-based fighters that drastic steps were being taken by the British to protect their ships. The first of these involved the erection of catapults on merchant ships from which Sea Hurricane fighters could be launched on the appearance of a Condor. There being no possibility of providing aircraft carriers for convoy escort at that stage of the war the Hurricane pilots, once launched against a raider, had either to ditch in the path of the convoy in the hope of being rescued or try to reach land. The first CAM-ship, SS *Michael E*, set sail on 27 May 1941 but was torpedoed before launching her Hurricane; on 3 August, however, a Condor was shot down by a Sea Hurricane Mk IA flown by Lieutenant R.W.H. Everett, RNVR, after launching from the *Maplin*, a converted naval escort.

The next expedient was to provide merchantmen with flight decks (MAC-ships, or merchant aircraft carriers) and a substantial conversion programme started to prepare large numbers of Sea Hurricanes to enable them to operate from catapults and flight decks.

With the appearance of fighters over the Atlantic convoys the tactics of the Condors changed, the raiders preferring to retire, only returning once the Hurricane had ditched; occasionally the big aircraft stayed to fight it out, their defensive armament undergoing progressive increase until by the end of 1941 they carried three heavy machine-guns, two light machine-guns and a 20-mm cannon. Airframe strengthening and increased engine power allowed progressively heavier bombloads, but early in 1942 the employment of Fw 200s changed again, the aircraft being used to shadow and report the position of convoys to allow U-boats to close in for their attacks. Also in 1942 the Fw 200C-4 appeared with FuG 200 Hohentweil and Rostock shipping search radar.

The sailing of the first North Cape convoys to the USSR resulted in about half the in-service Condors being moved to Norway early in 1942, others later being transferred to southern Italy to operate against the Malta convoys. This dilution of the German raiders in the West was further exacerbated by the removal of 18 aircraft to assist in transport operations at Stalingrad at the beginning of 1943, and it was not until the middle of that year that KG 40 was able to reassemble about 40 Fw 200Cs in western France.

By then a new weapon had appeared in the German anti-shipping arsenal, the radio-controlled, rocket-powered Hs 293A missile, two of which could be carried under the outboard engine nacelles of the Fw 200C-6 and Fw 200C-8 versions. On the first occasion the new weapons were flown operationally by III/KG 40 however, on 28 December 1943, the missile-carrying Condor was forced down by a patrolling Sunderland before the Hs 293s could be launched.

Any account of German maritime air operations should include mention of the Heinkel He 177 four-engine bomber which also engaged in anti-shipping work, both as a carrier of the Hs 293A missiles, LT 50 torpedoes and FX 1400 Fritz X guided bomb and as a maritime reconnaissance aircraft also serving with KG 40. In 1944, however, the relentless pressure by the Allies and loss by the Germans of their air bases in the Mediterranean and Western France led to the withdrawal of the maritime units to Germany where they joined in the crucial work of transportation as the Allies closed the ring on the Reich, and maritime warfare by aircraft over the Atlantic drew to an end.

During the first half of 1941 the Fw 200 Condors of Stab and I/Kampfgeschwader 40 reaped a grim harvest of British merchant shipping in the North Atlantic and off Ireland. Its combination of long range and endurance gained it the title 'Scourge of the Atlantic' from the UK Prime Minister, Winston Churchill.

The Focke-Wulf Fw 200 Condor started life as a long-range airliner for the German national airline Deutsche Lufthansa. A number of long-range record-breaking flights were accomplished before the war, and the military potential of this aircraft was obvious to the Luftwaffe. The first military Condors were used as transports, but the Fw 200C aircraft were dedicated maritime patrol aircraft. About 280 aircraft were completed, and despite this small number they provided the British with enormous problems throughout the war. Some Condors were used on the Eastern Front as last-ditch transports but most served with KG 40 in France. This is one of those aircraft, seen being refuelled at Bordeaux's Merignac airfield.

Wearing improvised winter camouflage for operations from Sorreisa, near Tromsö in Norway, this Heinkel He 115C-1 served with 1./KuFlGr 406 in 1942. This unit, alongside 1./KuFlGr 906, made the first torpedo attacks on the ill-fated PQ-17. The He 115C-1 version mounted a 15-mm (0.59-in) MG 151 cannon under the nose.

Below: Dramatic dusk launch of a Sea Hurricane Mk IA from the catapult of a merchant ship. Introduced to provide Allied convoys with fighter defence against enemy aircraft, the catapult Sea Hurricanes enjoyed limited success in 1941; with nowhere to go, the pilot had to bale out or ditch and hope to be picked up.

The Heinkel He 115 was a handy addition to the coastal fleet. It was used for all coastal duties, including patrol, anti-shipping and minelaying. This overhead view of an aircraft taxiing to take-off shows the typical Heinkel planform, derived from the pre-war He 70 mailplane.

By summer 1943 the Condor-equipped *Staffeln* of KG 40 became concerned solely with shipping attack, for which role a pair of Henschel Hs 293A missiles were mounted beneath the outboard engine nacelles. This aircraft is an Fw 200C-6, one of several Fw 200C-3/U1 and U2 models converted to carry the missiles.

Known as the 'flying clog', the Blohm und Voss Bv 138 was an armed patrol boat. These saw a lot of service around Norwegian coasts, and this Bv 138C-1 flew with 2. Staffel/Küstenfliegergruppe 406 in this theatre in 1942.

THE MIGHTY EIGHTH ARRIVES 1942-43

The Pearl Harbor debacle of December 1941 not only found the United States ill-prepared for war against Japan but ill-equipped to undertake participation in a war in Europe, and it was to be many months before a sizeable air force could be assembled for an assault on Germany, an assembly that would be diluted by attempts to create an expeditionary air force to support the Allied landings in North Africa which would materialize in November 1942.

The first administration elements of the US VIII Bomber Command under Major General Carl A. Spaatz arrived in the UK on 22 February 1942 (the same day that Harris took over the leadership of RAF Bomber Command); it was not until May that year, however, that combat units began arriving with Boeing B-17s and Consolidated B-24s (of the 44th, 91st, 92nd, 93rd, 97th and 301st Heavy Bomb Groups) at Shipdham, Kimbolton, Bovingdon, Alconbury and Polebrook. Their first operation, by a token force of a dozen 97th Group B-17Es, was flown against Rouen under heavy RAF Spitfire protection on 17 August; two days later a similar raid by 24 aircraft against Abbeville was flown in support of the Dieppe landings.

The provision of fighter escorts for these raids ran counter to American bomber tactics advocated at this time and was intended to allow the bomber crews to achieve a measure of operational experience before being called on to fly unescorted raids. The whole philosophy of the US Army Air Corps and US Army Air Force had for a decade centred on daylight bombing by formations of heavily-armed bombers capable of defending themselves by mutual gun protection. With the arrival in service of the high-flying B-17, altitude had added a further element to their supposed immunity from fighter interception.

Already a number of B-17Cs (without tail guns) had been supplied to the RAF in 1941, but British experience on operations with these aircraft in unescorted daylight raids had not been satisfactory, as a result principally of tactical misuse. Undeterred, the Americans continued to fly more and more B-17Es to the UK, and for the remainder of 1942 contented themselves with relatively short-range operations against such targets as Amiens, Rotterdam and Wevelghem, all with heavy Spitfire escort and all without combat loss. The Luftwaffe drew first blood when, on 6 September during a raid by the 92nd, 97th and 301st Groups on St Omer, Messerschmitt Bf 109Gs of JG 2 and JG 26 shot down two B-17s. The following day a raid on Rotterdam escaped without loss despite a vicious fight with Focke-Wulf Fw 190s of JG 1.

Gradually, as the B-17s began raiding further afield, the British fighters had to turn back partway to the target leaving the bomber crews to prove their ability to defend themselves. On 9 October 108 B-17Es and B-24Ds raided Lille and on their return flight were attacked by the fighters of JG 2 and JG 26. A measure of the savage battle that followed may be judged by the fact that the American gunners claimed to have destroyed 56 enemy fighters when in fact only one, an Fw 190A-4 of JG 26, was shot down.

Already the German fighter pilots were evolving tactics to combat the big American bombers; they had learned that closing from astern and abeam subjected them to withering and prolonged cross-fire from the massed 0.5-in (12.7-mm) heavy machine-guns of the bombers. They discovered that the frontal attack was the most deadly (as had been demonstrated by RAF Fighter Command during the Battle of Britain), both the B-17E and B-24D being armed with only single hand-held guns in the nose. The head-on attack demanded great skill and nerve, allowing no more than a snap burst; however it usually required no more than one or two cannon shells in the pilots' cockpit of a B-17 to bring about the bomber's end. In a raid by five groups on St Nazaire ('Ramrod' No. 38) on 23 November, four B-17s were shot down in frontal attacks. The biggest air battle to date, on 20 December, involved 101 B-17s and B-24s and nearly 200 Fw 190s during a raid on an aircraft park near Paris, too far from British bases for the Spitfires to provide continuous escort. Six B-17s were lost (each with a 10-man crew), and six Fw 190s were shot down by the American gunners.

The New Year brought the Americans' first raid on German territory when 91 heavy bombers attacked Wilhelmshaven on 27 January 1943, the raiders now flying more compact box formations to give increased mutual gun protection. Poor weather then restricted the VIII Bomber Command's attacks to relatively short-range targets until the late spring that year, by which time its strength had risen to 10 groups (despite the move by some units to North Africa to bolster the creation of the US 12th Air Force).

May 1943 marked a turning point for the American heavy bomber offensive. A raid on 1 May by 79 B-17s on St Nazaire found the bombers flying the last few miles to the target with their escorting Spitfires, losing seven of their number to the fighters of III/JG 2. On 4 May a raid by the newly-introduced B-17Fs, some with increased nose armament, attacked Antwerp, their escort of RAF Spitfires being joined by US VIII Fighter Command Republic P-47Ds for the first time; despite interception by upwards of 70 enemy fighters no bombers were lost. The philosophy of unescorted daylight raids by the Americans (like those by the RAF three years earlier) had been shown to be fallacious.

This P-51B Mustang was the mount of Don Gentile, one of the most famed fighter pilots of the war and credited with 21 victories.

Last one home, as a Boeing B-17F Fortress touches down at its base in England after a raid over enemy territory. Trips could last up to six hours in the summer of 1943, with crews frozen by −40°C winds at high altitudes. Ten men per aircraft endured bitter cold, and frostbite was a common complaint.

Above: The USAAF bombers were active over most of Europe, and this example is seen releasing fragmentation bombs.

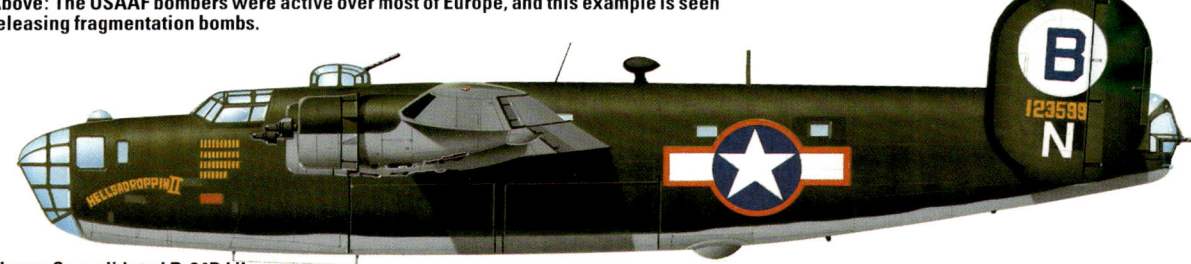

Above: Consolidated B-24D Liberator, operating from Hardwick in 2nd Bomb Division livery in September 1942. Both Liberator groups (44th and 93rd) were absent from the UK in summer 1943, being operated in North Africa, and both took part in the Ploesti mission on 1 August.

Below: One of the hallmarks of the USAAF bombing raids were the vapour trail patterns produced by the bombers at high altitude. Formation flying was immaculate; it had to be, as the formations were designed so as to offer maximum fire protection against fighter attacks.

Below: Boeing B-17F-10 BO of 322nd Squadron, 91st Bomb Group, Bassingbourn, Cambs, under the 1st Bombardment Wing. No group was more famous than the 91st, which claimed the highest number of enemy destroyed and suffered the heaviest losses.

THE U-BOAT WAR 1942-43

The Battle of the Atlantic was essentially a campaign against the German U-boat, a struggle that lasted from the first day of the war to the last. There were other facets such as the German surface raiders, which could be and were dealt with by the Royal Navy on the high seas, and by RAF Bomber Command while in port; and the Luftwaffe's maritime aircraft which, by and large, were the eyes of the U-boats themselves. And it was at the moment in 1940 when the German army occupied the French Atlantic ports (Brest, St Nazaire and Lorient), that the Battle of the Atlantic took an ominous turn for the UK. As soon as the U-boats could find haven in those western ports (and those in northern Norway) the Western Approaches to British ports became the hunting grounds for German submarines. RAF Coastal Command, with its limited numbers of long-range aircraft, the Sunderlands and Hudsons, had its work cut out to escort the inbound convoys, let alone perform long and systematic sea patrols.

By February 1941, after a winter which not only restricted flying by the British aircraft but also the activities of the U-boats, shipping losses began to rise alarmingly, and in March 530,000 tons of shipping went to the bottom, followed by 644,000 tons in April. Moreover, at this time the Germans began introducing ocean-going submarines whose depredations now extended far beyond the range of any British flying-boat.

By mid-1941 more than half of Coastal Command's aircraft, which now included ex-Bomber Command aircraft, such as the Whitley, had been equipped with ASV (air-to-surface vessel) radar which was capable of locating a surfaced U-boat in the dark or bad weather and, although this equipment seldom yet produced successful submarine 'kills', the threat of unheralded attack from the air certainly discouraged U-boat captains from passing through the Bay of Biscay on the surface, and thereby reduced by a small margin the submarine's cruising range. Other expedients were attempted to reduce the U-boat threat, in particular attacks by Bomber Command on factories engaged in submarine production, but these were regarded by that command as superfluous to the bomber's main tasks, and in any case had little lasting effect on account of poor navigation and bombing efficiency. Another task, undertaken jointly by Bomber and Coastal Commands, was the widespread mining of waters outside German ports in the North Sea and Baltic in attempts to prevent U-boats from being sailed from the naval yards into the Atlantic.

Though all these efforts collectively produced some results, it soon became all too clear that Admiral Karl Dönitz was fast acquiring a very large fleet of submarines, and when the United States entered the war against Germany he was able to order a sizable force of U-boats to operate off the American coast where, within six months, they sank an enormous number of unescorted ships.

By then, however, many improvements in tactics, weapons and aircraft were being introduced, not least the magnificent American Catalina flying-boat. Depth charges had been considerably improved, and the range of ASV (now fitted throughout Coastal Command) increased. And the Leigh Light, an airborne searchlight, was in use, causing submerged travel by U-boats in transit to be further increased. There remained, however, a large gap in mid-Atlantic which could be covered neither by Catalinas from the UK nor by those in the USA, Canada and Iceland, and only a handful of the very-long-range (VLR) Liberator Mk Is were in service. The answer therefore lay in the use of escort-carriers, small converted merchantmen capable of carrying half a dozen Swordfish aircraft equipped with ASV and depth charges.

To exploit the existence of the Greenland Gap, Dönitz introduced 'wolf pack' tactics in August 1942 which, until the creation of hunter-killer groups of corvettes and frigates, decimated the convoys. When Coastal Command made greater efforts to attack U-boats in transit through the Bay of Biscay, the Luftwaffe responded by operating increased patrols by Junkers Ju 88s and Focke-Wulf Fw 190 fighters, and the numbers of air combats with RAF Sunderlands, Wellingtons and Beaufighters increased sharply before the end of 1942.

Gradually the number of VLR Liberators increased, and with the securing of the West African seaboard following the 'Torch' landings (which were themselves achieved with very little interference from U-boats), the sinkings by enemy submarines were slowly reduced from the peak monthly total of 814,000 tons in November 1942 to an average of 130,000 tons a month during the last six months of 1943. The greater figures had been largely accounted for by the Americans' reluctance to adopt the convoy system in the western areas of the Atlantic, particularly off the Brazilian coast and in the Caribbean, a decision reversed during the latter half of 1943, by which time the Greenland Gap had been closed. With Catalinas, Sunderlands, Wellingtons and Liberators operating from Iceland in the north to Ascension Island in the south, the U-boat was reduced from a predatory wolf to a hunted dog.

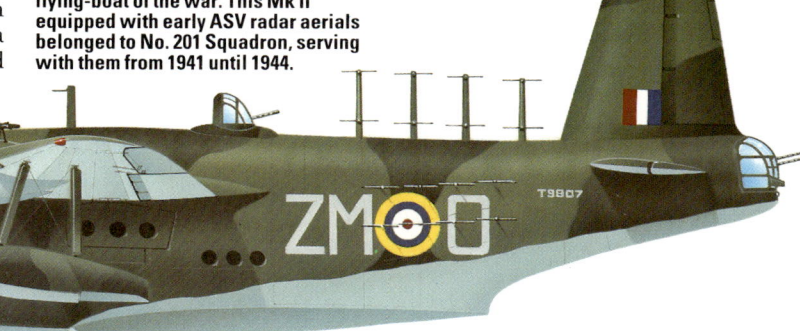

The Short Sunderland was the ubiquitous flying-boat of the war. This Mk II equipped with early ASV radar aerials belonged to No. 201 Squadron, serving with them from 1941 until 1944.

One of the most important jobs for Coastal Command was protecting the convoys sailing regularly to and from Britain. The transatlantic inbound convoys were the principal target for U-boats, and the presence of a depth-charge-armed Sunderland would deter any attack.

Right: Nineteen Boeing B-17F bombers were loaned to RAF Coastal Command and operated as Fortress GR.Mk II maritime patrol aircraft by the Command in 1942-3. Illustrated is one of 45 GR.Mk IIAs issued, in this case operated by No. 220 Squadron, Coastal Command, at Ballykelly from late 1942 onwards.

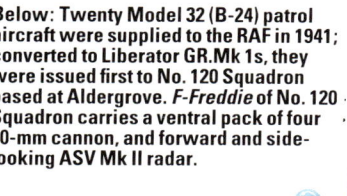

Below: Twenty Model 32 (B-24) patrol aircraft were supplied to the RAF in 1941; converted to Liberator GR.Mk 1s, they were issued first to No. 120 Squadron based at Aldergrove. *F-Freddie* of No. 120 Squadron carries a ventral pack of four 20-mm cannon, and forward and side-looking ASV Mk II radar.

A Vickers Wellington Mk XIV in the markings of No. 304 (Polish) Squadron. Transferring to Coastal Command on 7 May 1942, the squadron operated in the ASW role. Leigh Light-equipped aircraft (as illustrated) began extensive ASW operations in late 1943, with an average of two U-boat attacks per month.

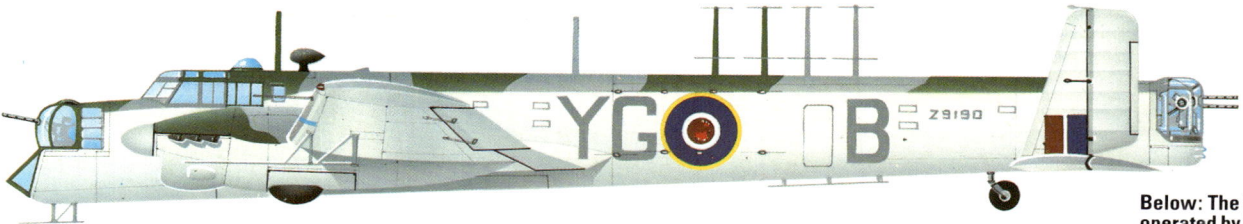

Below: The US Navy employed blimps to patrol the American coastline, their slow speed and long endurance enabling them to track submarines for many hours. This example was involved in the capture of this U-boat.

Above: Whitley Mk VII of No. 502 Squadron, RAF Coastal Command, in the colours adopted after the middle of 1942. Equipped with ASV Mk II radar, this elderly warplane gave valuable service on patrols over the Bay of Biscay. The sinking of the *U-206* on 30 November 1941 was the first confirmed kill achieved by ASV Mk II.

Below: The Consolidated Catalina was operated by Coastal Command on long-endurance patrols in the Atlantic and Bay of Biscay. When a submarine was found, the Catalina could depth-charge the boat and, hopefully, sink it. This aircraft releases a charge on to featureless water, hoping to cripple the metal monster hiding beneath the waves.

SICILY AND ITALY 1943

Throughout the final campaign which led to the destruction of Axis forces in northern Tunisia, the Allies had been assembling considerable strength at sea, on land and in the air with which to assault continental Europe from the south. It remained essential to keep the enemy guessing where that assault would be made: Sicily, Sardinia, the south of France or the Italian mainland.

In the event the blow fell on Sicily on 10 July 1943, by which date the Allied Air Forces in the Mediterranean (Mediterranean Air Command, commanded by Air Chief Marshal Sir Arthur Tedder) had grown to huge proportions, with 104 squadrons of fighters (Spitfires, Hurricanes, Beaufighters, Mosquitoes, P-38s, P-39s and P-51s), 95 squadrons of bombers (Mosquitoes, Bostons, Baltimores, Mitchells, Wellingtons, Marauders, Blenheims, Halifaxes, B-17s and B-24s) and 29 squadrons of transport aircraft (Halifaxes, Albemarles and Dakotas), as well as 43 other squadrons (reconnaissance, maritime patrol, torpedo bombers, meteorological, air-sea rescue and so on).

Supported by fighters and bombers flying from Tunisia, Algeria and Malta, the main landings were carried out in southern Sicily, the British Eighth Army being put ashore from landing craft in the Gulf of Noto and the US Seventh Army in the Gulf of Geta. A major feature of the operation was to be the landing of airborne forces near the Ponte Grande bridge in the British sector and at Gela in the American. Unfortunately owing to bad weather and inexperience among the American transport crews these airborne forces became widely scattered and 69 out of 137 Horsa and Hadrian gliders released fell in the sea. Nevertheless the scattering of the forces did serve to panic the Italian defenders, and by the 12th a bridgehead 20 miles (32 km) deep and about 50 miles (80 km) wide had been secured. Already a number of airfields had been overrun and airstrips constructed, and by the 15th more than a dozen fighter squadrons of the RAF, SAAF and USAAF were operating from Sicilian territory. From the outset the Allies possessed mastery of the air, although in the early stages of the invasion the Luftwaffe (notably Luftflotte II under Generalfeldmarschall Wolfram von Richthofen) and to a much lesser extent the Regia Aeronautica, attempted to mount air attacks against the invaders, using bombers based in Italy and Focke-Wulf Fw 190 fighter-bombers at makeshift airfields at Palermo, Castelvetrano and near Catania. Intruder Beaufighters and Mosquitoes operated with considerable success by night as British and American fighters sought out and destroyed enemy

aircraft in the air and on the ground by day. Within a week the German and Italian air forces were scarcely able to put up any worthwhile resistance in the air. When B-17s and B-24s appeared over the Strait of Messina such enemy fighters that attempted to intercept them had had to fly from Sardinia and central Italy.

By 5 August the entire western part of Sicily had been overrun and the Axis forces had been squeezed into an area in the north east of the island, with desperate efforts being made to protect the likely escape route through Messina. And all the time, as the Axis tried to send supplies and fresh forces south to bolster the defences in the 'toe' of Italy, RAF Wellingtons and Mitchells joined the American heavy bombers in attacks on communications centres at Battipaglia, Foggia and Salerno, as well as the airfields at Crotone, Grottaglie, Leverano and Vibo Valentia.

Yet for all the efforts by the Allied air forces, the Axis commanders with great skill extricated the bulk of their land forces out of Sicily. But in the five weeks of fighting the German and Italian air forces had lost some 1,850 aircraft, compared with the loss of fewer than 400 British and American aircraft.

The stepping stone to Europe had been secured, yet the Allies paused less than three weeks before moving against the Italian mainland. Haste was essential as many of the enemy airfields in southern Italy had not been destroyed in recent attacks by Tedder's bombers, and delay would simply allow their repair. The Allied plan was to land the British 8th Army on the toe of Italy, assault the Taranto naval base in the 'heel' with the 1st Airborne Division and then put ashore the US 5th Army in the Gulf of Salerno, some 200 miles (320 km) to the north.

The first landings across the Strait of Messina by the 8th Army were carried out on 3 September (Operation 'Baytown') and continued for five days, meeting relatively little resistance thanks to an unrelenting air offensive against the enemy supply route down the full length of Italy by medium and heavy bombers of the RAF and USAAF. On 11 September the 8th Army reached a line from Belvedere to Crotone.

Two days earlier the US 5th Army had gone ashore at Salerno. On the eve of those landings, however, the Italian government had announced the nation's surrender.

The North American A-36A Invader was an attack version of the well-known P-51 fighter. This served with distinction over the beach-head at Salerno and during the invasion of Sicily. This aircraft was based on Corsica.

Winter in sunny Italy was not all vino and sunlight: the weather was often abominable. Here a Consolidated B-24D Liberator of the US 376th Group breasts floodwaters at San Pancrazio airfield.

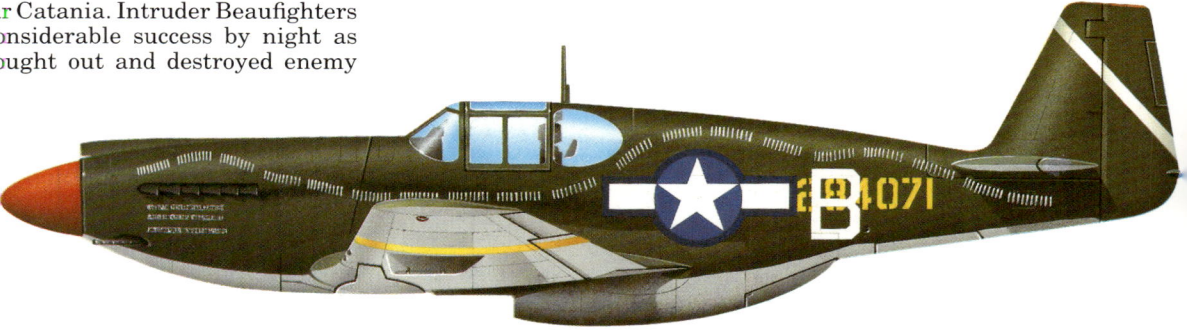

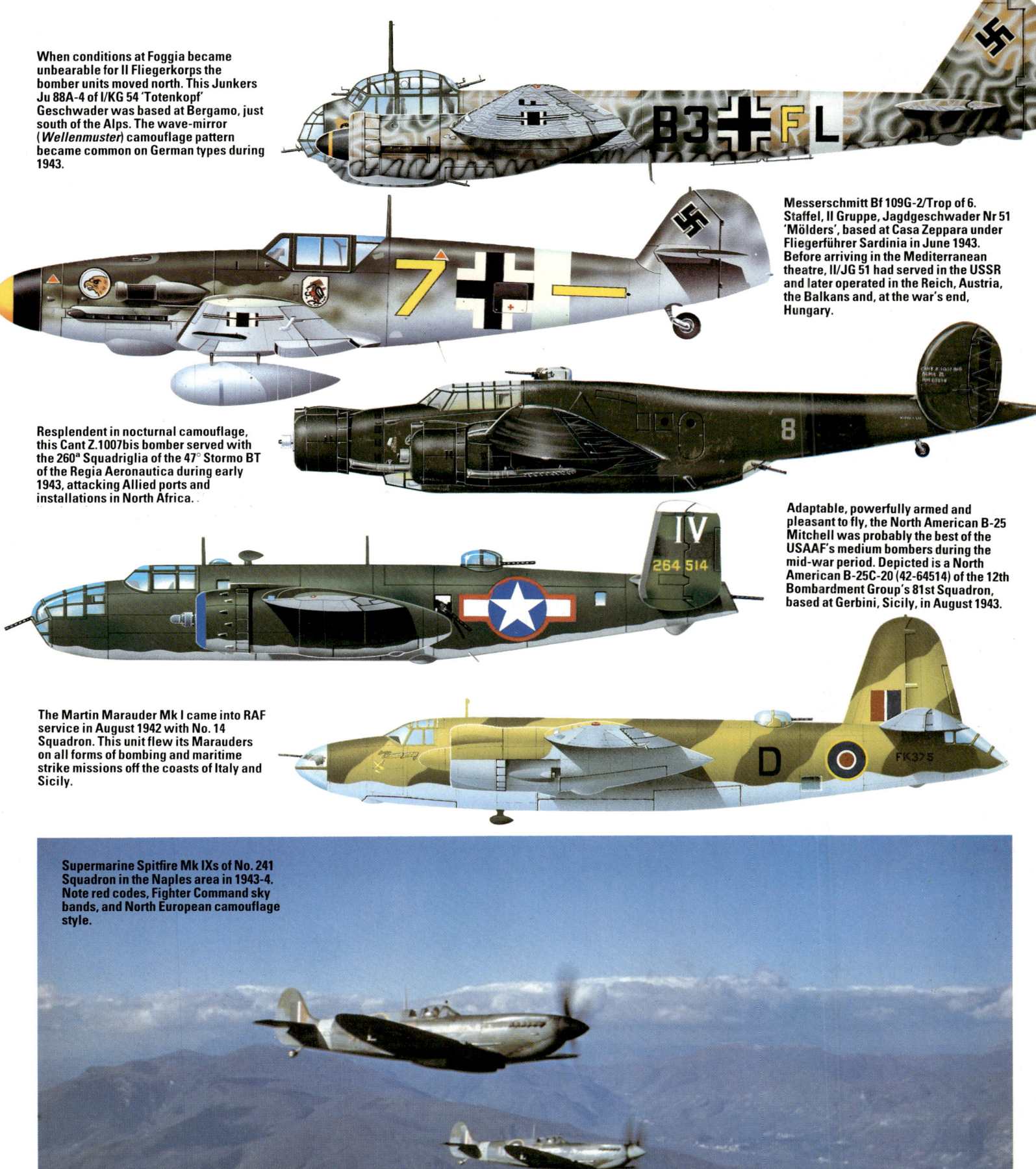

When conditions at Foggia became unbearable for II Fliegerkorps the bomber units moved north. This Junkers Ju 88A-4 of I/KG 54 'Totenkopf' Geschwader was based at Bergamo, just south of the Alps. The wave-mirror (*Wellenmuster*) camouflage pattern became common on German types during 1943.

Messerschmitt Bf 109G-2/Trop of 6. Staffel, II Gruppe, Jagdgeschwader Nr 51 'Mölders', based at Casa Zeppara under Fliegerführer Sardinia in June 1943. Before arriving in the Mediterranean theatre, II/JG 51 had served in the USSR and later operated in the Reich, Austria, the Balkans and, at the war's end, Hungary.

Resplendent in nocturnal camouflage, this Cant Z.1007bis bomber served with the 260ª Squadriglia of the 47° Stormo BT of the Regia Aeronautica during early 1943, attacking Allied ports and installations in North Africa.

Adaptable, powerfully armed and pleasant to fly, the North American B-25 Mitchell was probably the best of the USAAF's medium bombers during the mid-war period. Depicted is a North American B-25C-20 (42-64514) of the 12th Bombardment Group's 81st Squadron, based at Gerbini, Sicily, in August 1943.

The Martin Marauder Mk I came into RAF service in August 1942 with No. 14 Squadron. This unit flew its Marauders on all forms of bombing and maritime strike missions off the coasts of Italy and Sicily.

Supermarine Spitfire Mk IXs of No. 241 Squadron in the Naples area in 1943-4. Note red codes, Fighter Command sky bands, and North European camouflage style.

ADVENTURES IN ITALY 1943-44

The surrender by the Italian government effectively deprived Germany of significant participation by the Regia Aeronautica in the defence of Italy against the Allies, and although some elements elected to fight on alongside the Luftwaffe, the majority either melted away to their homes or joined the Allies. The defection by their ally, as the Germans saw it, only served to stiffen their resolve to fight every yard of the way back through the Italian peninsula.

In attempts to leapfrog northwards and hasten their advance, the Allies planned two major seaborne landings behind the enemy lines, the first at Salerno on 9 September 1943 and another, rather later, at Anzio, which eventually took place in the following January.

As already stated, the landing by the US 5th Army at Salerno was in effect part of the planned invasion of Italy and, by diverting enemy forces from the 8th Army in the extreme south was intended to ease the establishment of a substantial beach-head. In this it was signally successful, but resistance by the Germans at Salerno was unexpectedly stiff. Against the troops that landed on the beaches the Luftwaffe used about four *Staffeln* of Fw 190 fighter-bombers, whose pilots had to contend not only with patrolling Spitfires and Lightnings but also barrage balloons brought ashore by RAF parties. The Luftwaffe was, however, able to score one significant success when a Do 217-launched Hs 293 guided missile scored a direct hit on the British battleship *Warspite*, which had been supporting the landings, and put her out of commission for six months.

The success of the landings remained in the balance for three days as the Germans counterattacked strongly on the ground, and although the airfield at Monte Corvino had been captured at the outset it was unusable so long as it was dominated by German guns. By 15 September four landing strips constructed by Allied airfield engineers were in operation, one of them having been in use by Lightnings since 11 September. Within a week of the landings several squadrons of Seafires and Spitfires were ashore, and these joined the battle to blunt the enemy counterattacks; while the Royal Navy put ashore reinforcements of armour, the American 505th and 509th Airborne Regiments were dropped on 14 and 15 September in areas where the front line was most threatened. By the evening of 15 September enemy efforts to contain the beach-head were spent, thanks to the combined efforts of the British and American land, sea and air forces. On the following day units of the US VI Corps broke out from the perimeter in the south to link up with the advancing 8th Army at Vallo di Lucania.

Thereafter the Allied advance northwards in Italy continued apace until by 1 January 1944 it was being held by the Germans on a line running from the mouth of the River Garigliano in the south west to Ortona on the Adriatic coast. When it became clear that the Germans were standing on a prepared line, and would be difficult to dislodge, the Allies once more launched a seaborne landing further north at Anzio, in the hope of turning the German right flank; at the same time it was hoped to draw the enemy air force into the air to protect that flank where it could be destroyed by the vastly superior numbers of Allied aircraft. A prelude to the landing, which took place on 22 January, was an all-out air attack on the Italian airfields in central Italy, carried out to such good effect that not one enemy reconnaissance sortie was successful in detecting the landing force, and 50,000 British and American troops arrived unscathed on the enemy beaches. Here the Allied commander, Major General Lucas, made an error of judgement, preferring to consolidate his beach-head rather than to strike hard inland, a move that would unquestionably have severed the enemy supply routes to the south. As it was, the Germans had time to mount heavy armoured counterattacks which, though only just failing to break through to the beaches, succeeded in containing the landing areas and forcing the invaders on to the defensive. In the air the Luftwaffe switched two *Gruppen* of Ju 88s to Italy from Greece and Crete, and one of Do 217s equipped with Hs 293 missiles to the south of France; these air reinforcements proved unsuitable for support of the land battle at Anzio and many of the Ju 88s were destroyed by air attacks on their airfields. In the event the enemy air force was unable to support the powerful German ground forces in the area; but equally the Allied ground forces were unable to break out of their beach-head, despite the overwhelming air superiority of the RAF and USAAF.

On 15 March the Allied air forces attempted to breach the main line in the south by reducing the great monastery at Monte Cassino. In four hours wave after wave of medium bombers dropped over 1,000 tons of bombs, pounding the ancient building to rubble. Yet still the line held, and it was not until May that the Allies were finally able to pierce the defences and resume their advance northwards. The Anzio pocket was reached and relieved, and on 4 June the Allies at last entered Rome.

Republic P-47D-25 of the 57th Fighter Group (64th Squadron) under US XII Fighter Command's 87th Fighter Wing taxis out for a mission on the northern Italian front in the autumn of 1944. Aircraft of the 64th Squadron sported red cowlings and their dark grey scorpion motif.

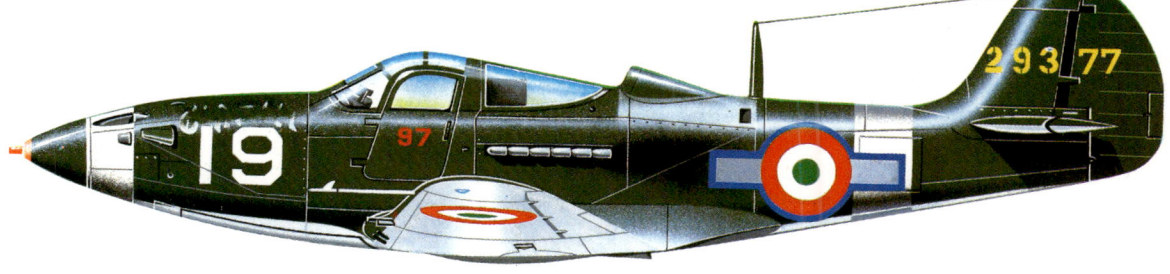

Bell P-39N-1 Airacobra of the Italian Co-Belligerent Air Force's 4° Stormo (Caccia Terrestre), based at Canne, Italy for Balkan missions. This group operated on reconnaissance and air support missions over the Adriatic, and escorted Douglas C-47 supply-drops to Tito's partisans in Yugoslavia in 1944.

Waiting for a call to action, this Messerschmitt Bf 109F pilot keeps himself out of the Italian sunshine with an umbrella. The starting handle is ready in the engine for an immediate departure should the need arise.

Night operations were successful over Italy against pockets of resistance. Lockheed P-38 Lightnings were widely employed in these operations and this P-38L of the 94th Fighter Group is seen being loaded with bombs before take-off.

MC.205V Veltro of the 351ª Squadriglia, 155° Gruppo, 51° Stormo, at Monserrato, June 1943. The aircraft depicted is an early example with two 7.7-mm (0.303-in) guns in the wings. The 'cat and mice' badge was a development of the traditional *Sorci verdi* theme of the old 12° Stormo BT.

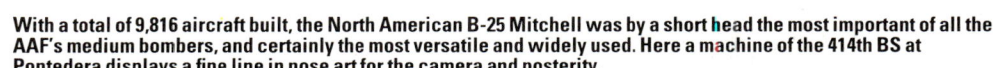

Messerschmitt Me 410A Hornisse aircraft were used in Italy on a variety of Zerstörer missions and for high speed reconnaissance. This aircraft served with 9. Staffel/Zerstörergeschwader 1 from Gerbini.

A pilot of the US 455th Bombardment Group, Lieutenant Bill Disbrow, poses in front of a visiting Lockheed P-38L Lightning. It has seen much service, with dirt and smoke-stains on the nose around the cannon and gun armament.

With a total of 9,816 aircraft built, the North American B-25 Mitchell was by a short head the most important of all the AAF's medium bombers, and certainly the most versatile and widely used. Here a machine of the 414th BS at Pontedera displays a fine line in nose art for the camera and posterity.

HAMBURG, THE RUHR AND BERLIN 1942-45

Shortly after the 'Torch' landings in North Africa, the British and American leaders conferred at Casablanca to determine the future course of the war. One result was a directive, put before Air Marshal Harris, setting out his bombing priorities, which were 'the progressive destruction ... of the German military, industrial and economic system, and the undermining of the morale of the German people to a point where their capacity for armed resistance is fatally weakened'. To begin to achieve this objective RAF Bomber Command was now fairly well-equipped, possessing on 4 March 1943 a total of 18 Lancaster squadrons, 11 of Halifaxes, six of Stirlings and 15 of Wellingtons, all operational at night, for a total of 321 Lancasters, 220 Halifaxes, 141 Stirlings and 268 Wellingtons.

The first manifestation of the great night bombing offensive that now broke over Germany and lasted until the end of the war was what came to be known as the Battle of the Ruhr. This started on the night of 5/6 March 1943 with a raid by 442 aircraft against Essen, the first full-scale operation in which the navigation and bombing aid 'Oboe' was successfully used.

Six weeks later Bomber Command carried out one of its most famous raids of all time, the attack (Operation 'Chastise') on 16/17 May by 19 Lancasters of No. 617 Squadron, led by Wing Commander Guy Gibson, against the Möhne, Eder, Sorpe and Schwelme dams, whose hydro-electric stations supplied power to the industrial Ruhr. Dropping special 9,250-lb (4196-kg) 'bouncing' mines, the Lancasters breached the Möhne and Eder dams for the loss of eight aircraft; Gibson survived to be awarded the Victoria Cross for his leadership on the raid.

The Battle of the Ruhr continued until June, and was considered highly successful for the widespread damage caused, being made possible principally on account of the radio aids available which were efficient at the relatively short ranges involved in flights to the Ruhr.

As new Lancaster and Halifax squadrons continued to join Bomber Command, Harris now determined on the destruction of a single vital city in Germany and on the night of 24/25 July launched 791 heavy bombers against Hamburg, the first of four massive raids on the city in 10 days (Operation 'Gomorrah'), carried out in concert with the heavy bombers of the USAAF which attacked the city during daylight hours. Hamburg was chosen not only on account of its importance as an industrial city but for the manner in which the great port could be distinguished on H_2S radar, a blind bombing and navigation aid that had been in use by Bomber Command for some six months. ('Oboe' could not be used because of Hamburg's distance from the UK). Vital ingredient in the raids on Hamburg was the first significant use of 'Window', vast clouds of tinfoil strips dropped by the bombers to saturate enemy radar screens with spurious signals.

In the four Bomber Command raids 2,630 bombers attacked Hamburg, dropping 8,621 tons of bombs which destroyed more than 6,000 acres of the port, killed more than 41,800 inhabitants and injured over 37,000. The loss of 87 aircraft represented less than three per cent of the aircraft despatched and was well within sustainable limits.

The devastating Battle of Hamburg encouraged Harris to open his last great setpiece assault, this time on Berlin itself (although numerous other targets continued to be attacked before, during and after the attacks on the German capital). On the night of 18/19 November 1943 Bomber Command sent 444 bombers, of which 402 attacked the city, losing nine aircraft, while a simultaneous attack was carried out by 325 bombers on Mannheim, the first occasion on which two heavy raids were launched on a single night.

The offensive against Berlin continued through the winter of 1943-4, almost invariably in bad weather but, despite the employment of Bomber Command's specialist Pathfinder Group, No. 8, commanded by Air Commodore D.C.T. Bennett, and the use of sophisticated marking and radio countermeasures techniques, the concentration of damage and accuracy of bombing fell far short of expectations. A total of 16 major raids was launched before the 'battle' ended on 24/25 March 1944, involving 9,111 bomber sorties. The raids cost the command a total of 587 aircraft and more than 3,500 aircrew killed or missing, an unsustainable loss rate of 6.4 per cent. The damage and casualties inflicted were considerably less than at Hamburg, and the Battle of Berlin failed in its purpose of breaking the spirit of the German people.

One other major raid was launched by Bomber Command at this time (before it was switched to attacks in support of the coming Normandy landings) 795 four-engine bombers being sent to Nuremberg on 30/31 March 1944. On account of inaccurate weather forecasting, inefficient pathfinding and poor raid planning, the bomber stream disintegrated and suffered heavily from German night-fighter attacks; more than 100 bombers were lost. Worse, Nuremberg was scarcely hit by the bombers.

During the final eight months of the war, Bomber Command returned to Germany in greater strength than ever (it ended the war with 56 Lancaster squadrons, 17 of Halifaxes and 18 of Mosquitoes, for a total of 2,370 aircraft). Its last target priority was the German oil industry, an industry so completely devastated that it was to be the chronic lack of aviation fuel that finally grounded the once-formidable Luftwaffe.

The Avro Lancaster was the premier heavy bomber of the Royal Air Force from 1942 onwards, and racked up an impressive record of achievements throughout the rest of the war. This example flew with No. 50 Squadron.

Night bombing and bombing through overcast conditions were greatly helped by the radar and radio navigation aids developed by the 'boffins'. Amongst the most helpful was H$_2$S, which enabled bombers to find targets more easily.

This 'Airborne Cigar'-equipped No. 101 Squadron Lancaster drops incendiary bombs in a daylight raid in 1944. Many hundreds of incendiary sticks could be carried in the capacious bomb bay of the aircraft.

The serial ED912/G means a special aircraft to be kept under armed guard on the ground. It was one of the Mk III (Special) aircraft modified to drop the spinning-drum 'Upkeep' device to destroy the German dams, and was taken into action by No. 617 Squadron under Wing Commander Guy Gibson on the night of 17/18 May 1943.

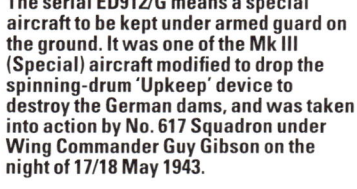

Handley Page Halifax B.Mk III of No. 462 Squadron, RAAF, flying from RAF Foulsham on special radio transmission jamming sorties equipped with 'Airborne Cigar' aerials for this task. Also carried would be large amounts of metal strips known as 'Window' for jamming enemy radar screens.

De Havilland Mosquito B.Mk IX of No. 105 Squadron (1944) in pathfinder camouflage. These aircraft carried Oboe Mk I, a 2,000-lb (907-kg) bombload, and had an operational ceiling of about 36,000 ft (10975 m). Virtually immune to German night fighters, the unit dispensed with flame dampers on many of its aircraft.

Handley Page Halifax B.Mk II Srs IA of No. 78 Squadron. Merlin 22 or 24 engines were standard on this much-modified variant: the squared fin and rudder was intended to cure the vice of rudder stalling; a glazed nose was fitted with a 0.303-in (7.7-mm) Vickers K gun; and the Boulton Paul dorsal turret had four guns.

This Halifax B.Mk III served with No. 462 Squadron, RAAF, from August 1944. Most of the Commonwealth air forces contributed complete squadrons to operations from Britain, as well as many thousands of aircrew to serve with the RAF.

Avro Lancasters were the only aircraft available to the RAF to carry the 12,000-lb (5443-kg) 'Tallboy' (illustrated) and 22,000-lb (9979-kg) 'Grand Slam' earthquake bombs. This Lancaster was used to bomb the *Tirpitz* with 'Tallboys'.

KURSK AND THE UKRAINE 1943-44

With the German army's surge eastwards thwarted at Stalingrad during the winter of 1942-3, the German high command decided on a major offensive on the central sector of the Eastern Front to eliminate the large Soviet salient around Kursk in June 1943; but because of German fears of an Allied invasion of Europe in the Mediterranean the great attack, Operation 'Zitadelle', was delayed until 5 July.

Both sides desperately needed a major victory, the Germans to break a deteriorating stalemate south of Moscow, the Soviets to convince themselves that they could smash the German army in the summer (and not merely in the mud and snow of winter). Deployed on the central front were 4,600 aircraft of the 1st, 2nd, 15th and 16th Air Armies of the Soviet air force, plus 2,750 of the 5th and 17th Air Armies held in reserve, comprising huge numbers of Il-2s and Il-2m3 *Shturmovik* close-support aircraft armed with improved guns and other anti-tank weapons, and like numbers of La-5FNs, Yak-9s and P-39Q Airacobras. Against them the Luftwaffe could muster some 2,100 first-line aircraft, out of a total of about 2,500 deployed on the entire Eastern Front; principal German aircraft included the Fw 190A, Ju 87D, Bf 109G, He 111, Ju 88 and Hs 129. The Luftwaffe, however, was to suffer acute fuel shortages during that desperate summer, largely as the result of the activities of Soviet partisans who destroyed large numbers of supply trains and severely damaged the German communications network, particularly in the key Minsk-Smolensk sector.

Operation 'Zitadelle' opened during the afternoon of 5 July as crack *Panzer* divisions with the new Panther and Tiger tanks were hurled into a typical *Blitzkreig* wedge assault against superior numbers of Soviet tanks in the greatest, most ferocious armoured battle in history. In support the German armies flew formations of Hs 129 anti-tank aircraft armed with 37-mm guns and hollow-charge armour-piercing bombs, as well as large numbers of Ju 87D bombers. The Luftwaffe's support aircraft did enormous damage

among the massed Soviet tanks and, after a week's desperate fighting on the flat grasslands (involving more than 3,000 tanks not to mention the Soviets' 20,000 artillery pieces) it seemed that the Germans were on the point of breakthrough; then the Soviet commander-in-chief, General Georgi K. Zhukov, ordered into action a completely fresh tank army supported by swarms of Il-2s. Manstein, fearing annihilation of his armour, urged the supreme command to allow a withdrawal of German forces to the heavily-defended line on the Duiepr river, but was peremptorily overruled by Hitler who ordered a fighting stand to be made, during which the Soviet air force took a heavy toll of the vital German transport vehicles. The Soviets went on to widen the Kursk salient, and then launched a sustained attack northwards toward Orel.

Much of the blame for the defeat at Kursk was laid at the door of the Luftwaffe, whose commanders had determined on a policy of absolute priority in the East, allied with the sustaining of air superiority by fighter aircraft, a superiority which now rapidly evaporated. With a German loss of more than 900 aircraft during the week-long battle of Kursk (compared with some 600 Soviet aircraft lost), the tide had indeed turned in the air war. Coming close on the heels of the destruction of the Luftwaffe in Sicily, the priority in the East was now abolished, many fighters and all *Zerstörer* units being withdrawn for 'defence of the Reich'. The ground attack (*Schlacht*) units of the Luftwaffe underwent fundamental reorganization, the Fw 190F and Fw 190G gradually replacing the aged Ju 87D; at the same time the *Nachtschlachtgruppen* (night strike groups) were upgraded in importance, their operations being widened to embrace a concerted campaign against the Soviet railway network.

The widespread withdrawal of German fighters from the East gave the Soviets the opportunity to exploit their growing strength in the air. Their own fighters were now able, on account of considerable numerical superiority, if not to dominate the front, at least to provide powerful protection for the Soviet bombers and Il-2s.

In January 1944 the 2nd Soviet Shock Army secured the relief of Leningrad, with the support of 1,200 aircraft, including those of the Red Banner Baltic Fleet. By that time the Yak-9 and La-5FN were able to overwhelm the German fighters, and many of the Luftwaffe's most experienced, high-scoring pilots (men like Heinz Schmidt with 173 victories and Max Stotz with 189) were killed.

Meanwhile in the south, following a Soviet offensive in the Kiev region, at the end of 1943 the Soviets opened their crushing winter campaign in the Ukraine. As their 1st Guards Army and 1st Tank Army smashed their way west towards Zhitomir, supported by General Krasovsky's 2nd Air Army, in January 1944 they trapped some 60,000 Axis troops in the Cherkassy pocket from which, by dint of air supplies dropped to them by Luftwaffe transport aircraft, roughly half managed to escape during the following month. In May the last German aircraft left the isolated Crimea, where 26,000 Germans fell into Soviet hands after the loss of almost 300 Luftwaffe aircraft.

The Yakovlev Yak-3 was introduced to front line units late in 1944 and started an illustrious career as a low-level dogfighter *par excellence*. The type was distinguished from other Yak fighters by the lack of an oil cooler intake under the nose.

Junkers Ju 87D-3 of a Romanian unit, the 6th dive-bomber group of the Corpul 1 Aerien operating over the Kursk salient under VIII Fliegerkorps during the summer of 1943. The spatted wheel covers of the Ju 87 were often removed, as shown here, to prevent them from becoming fouled by mud or snow.

Although disliked by some air forces, the Bell P-39 Airacobra found favour with the V-VS on account of its strength and good performance at low altitudes; 4,924 went under Lend-Lease to the USSR.

This Lavochkin La-5FN was flown by the 1 Czechoslovak IAP in the Ukraine in 1944. Several Czech units were formed within the Red Air Force.

Wearing the yellow horizontal bar and the green heart emblem of II Gruppe, JG 54 'Grunherz', this Focke-Wulf Fw 190A-5 flew from Petseri, Estonia, in the spring of 1944. Then, the rapidly increasing production of Fw 190s led to resumption of Eastern Front *Schlachtflieger* re-equipment with the type.

Many American and British aircraft were supplied through Lend-Lease terms to the Soviet Union. Among the most effective of these were the Douglas A-20 light bombers.

Right: The Focke-Wulf Fw 189 Uhu was a short-range reconnaissance platform which was used to gain battlefield information. The type's good low speed handling and agility gave it a measure of defence from roving Soviet fighters.

Above: The Messerschmitt Bf 109 remained the major Luftwaffe fighter on the Eastern Front throughout the conflict. This Bf 109G wears the white-blue-red spinner which distinguishes it as a Slovakian aircraft.

The Lavochkin La-5 rectified many of the problems of the earlier LaGG-3, the Shvetsov radial providing more than enough power to make this fighter competitive.

Proving to be an extremely versatile light bomber, the Petlyakov Pe-2 first showed this during the battles for the Kursk salient in 1943. Although later overshadowed by the Tupolev Tu-2, the Pe-2 performed sterling work until the end of the war.

The USSR's national insignia had many forms, including stars with circles in the centre or borders if on a dark ground. This Il-2m3 at Stalingrad in early 1943 had stars with borders.

This Messerschmitt Bf 109G was operated by Jagdgeschwader 54 'Grünherz'. It wears a typical Luftwaffe winter scheme and was operational on the northern sector of the Russian front.

DAYLIGHT HEAVIES TRIUMPH 1943-45

Just as the Casablanca Directive was issued by the Allied Chiefs of Staff on 21 January 1943, setting out the objectives of the British and American bomber offensive, the first American Republic P-47 unit (the 56th Fighter Group) was reaching operational status in England; two months later the 4th Fighter Group (formed out of volunteer-manned squadrons of the RAF) converted from Supermarine Spitfires to P-47s. These groups, together with the 78th, joined the RAF's Spitfires in escorting the American daylight raids over Europe in May. Unfortunately the P-47 had not been conceived as an escort fighter and, until long-range drop tanks could be produced for it, its radius of action remained much the same as that of the Spitfire Mks V and IX at about 150 miles (240 km).

This was an uncomfortable period for Major General Ira C. Eaker, commanding the US 8th Air Force. The Americans were under political pressure to extend their bombing operations further afield, but their early Boeing B-17Es and B-17Fs and Consolidated B-24Ds were demonstrably unable to fend for themselves in the face of fast-increasing fighter opposition over France and the Low Countries. VIII Fighter Command was transferred from British to American control in an effort to co-ordinate better escort tactics by the P-47s as the first efficient drop tanks were issued to the fighter groups; these still enabled the P-47s to fly only 50 miles (80 km) farther, however. On 26 June some 250 B-17s attacked Villacoublay, only the P-47s remaining with the bombers all the way. As soon as the Spitfires turned back, the Americans were attacked by the Messerschmitt Bf 109Gs and Focke-Wulf Fw 190As of JG 2, which quickly shot down five B-17s while JG 26 destroyed four P-47s.

Gradually the American fighter pilots worked out their own tactics, mastered the tricky fuel handling of the P-47 and, by the late summer of 1943, were beginning to take an increasing toll of German fighters. Thus encouraged, the 8th Air Force launched its first long-distance raid against Schweinfurt and Regensburg deep inside Germany on 17 August, it being intended that fighters would cover the bombers as far as the German border, return for fuel and then meet the raiders on their way home. Unfortunately the presence of fog at some of the bomber bases caused the timing of the two raids to go wrong, thereby enabling the enemy fighters to make two interception attacks after the escort had turned for home. Of the 376 aircraft despatched, some 60 were shot down. A second mission to the ball-bearing plant at Schweinfurt was flown by 291 B-17s on 14 October but, still without fighter protection for more than half the flight, 60 more bombers were shot down; five others crashed in England and 133 were badly damaged.

The remedy for these catastrophic losses was already at hand, however, with the arrival in England during that autumn of the 354th Fighter Group, the first to fly the superb North American P-51 Mustang, a long-range fighter that was to remain unrivalled

for the remainder of the war. When a third attack by 238 B-17s of the USAAF's 1st Bombardment Division returned to Schweinfurt on 24 February 1944 the fighter escort accompanied the entire raid and bomber losses were held to 11 aircraft.

Throughout 1944 the Americans continued to build up their bomber strength, the B-17G, the B-24G and the B-24H being introduced with twin-gun nose turrets to counter the deadly head-on attacks by German fighters. In the latter half of February a concerted day and night assault by RAF and US bombers (Operation 'Argument', otherwise known as 'Big Week') was launched, in which a total of 16,500 tons of bombs was dropped in five days and nights, the Germans losing more than 150 fighters. On 4 March the Americans carried out their first daylight raid on Berlin (complementing RAF Bomber Command's night Battle of Berlin, then at its height), 609 B-17s and B-24s with P-47, Lockheed P-38 and P-51 escort achieving considerable damage for the loss of 68 bombers and 13 fighters.

Like those of RAF Bomber Command, the heavy bombers of the US 8th Air Force were largely withdrawn from strategic operations in preparation for the coming Normandy invasion, switching to attacks on German airfields and transportation targets in France and the Low Countries.

In August the American bombers began heavy attacks on the German oil industry, synthetic oil plants at Gelsenkirchen and Ludwigshafen being attacked by British-based bombers on 16, 24 and 26 August, and the Ploesti oil plants by Italian-based B-24s of the 15th Air Force on 17 and 18 August. In September the B-17s and B-24s raided Bremen, Koblenz, Frankfurt, Hamm, Karlsruhe, Kassel, Magdeburg, Mainz, Munster, Osnabruck and Stuttgart. And so the toll of German cities and industries devastated by bomb and fire continued to rise.

As the German army was forced back within the boundaries of the Reich so the ferocity of air fighting increased as the German fighter pilots struggled to defend their homeland. The Messerschmitt Me 163 rocket interceptor and Messerschmitt Me 262 jet fighter appeared and began to take a serious toll of the bombers but, as the perimeter contracted from the west, east and south, as Allied bombers 'shuttled' to bases in the Soviet Union, as the Allied long-range fighters maintained constant attacks on the German airfields, and as enemy oil stocks dwindled, so the British and American heavy bombers continued to pound Hitler's Germany into rubble. By late April 1945 the 8th Air Force bombers had little left to attack but targets in southern German, Austria and Czechoslovakia. Their last major raid was on the Skoda works at Pilsen on 25 April 1945.

Elimination of paint from the B-17 gave a measurable gain in speed or reduced fuel consumption (since cruising speed was preset at a figure all aircraft could easily maintain at full load). These B-17Gs, built by Douglas, were of the 381st Bomb Group (VE code 532nd BS; VP code 533rd BS). Home base was Ridgewell.

A classic shot of Mustangs in flight over north west Europe: serial numbers 413926, 413410 and 413568 are all North American-built P-51Ds (the first having the small dorsal fin added just after production had begun), and 2106811 is a P-51B with the earlier pattern framed canopy and deep rear fuselage.

Below: This brightly coloured B-17G served with the 447th Bomb Group from Rattlesden in Norfolk in early 1945. Paint was deleted from the greater part of the aircraft as a weight-saving measure while the yellow and green aided recognition in the formation.

Below: Smoke markers fill the sky as an 8th Air Force B-24 arrives over its target in Germany. B-24s amply supplemented the B-17 in daylight raids.

Below: A P-47D (Evansville-built) of the 82nd Fighter Squadron, 78th Fighter Group on a mission over Europe. The picture is after D-Day as in addition to the famed black/white check cowl the aircraft has black/white 'invasion stripes'.

Specially painted Liberators were employed to 'round up' the vast formations before they headed out to Germany. The polka dots made these aircraft difficult to miss. They did not take part in the mission, returning to base when the formation was on its way.

BACK INTO FRANCE 1944

Almost exactly four years after the British Expeditionary Force had staged its near-miraculous evacuation from Dunkirk, the Allies once more set foot in strength on French soil when on 6 June 1944, under the supreme command of General Eisenhower, British, American and Canadian forces landed in Normandy. And they did so with complete mastery of the air.

For some months past the RAF and USAAF had been preparing the way for the invasion, British and American heavy bombers striking at key points in the French road and rail system to prevent the movement of reinforcements once the invading forces had landed. To this task was added the offensive against the flying bomb sites in the Pas de Calais, while the fighter-bombers and light bombers of the 2nd Tactical Air Force struck at coastal targets (the E-boat bases, radar stations, airfields and coastal gun batteries) along the French coast. On the eve of the landings themselves the Allied Expeditionary Air Force comprised 173 squadrons of fighters and fighter-bombers, 59 squadrons of light and medium bombers, and 70 squadrons of transport aircraft, in addition to some 50 other support squadrons, there was also the might of RAF Bomber Command and the US 8th Air Force. In all, the Allies could count on close to 12,000 aircraft with which to support the invasion.

The assault on the French coast was indeed a highly co-ordinated effort by the land, sea and air forces. As 145,000 men went ashore from the sea on the first day, considerable use was made of airborne forces, the US IX Troop Carrier Command's C-47s dropping large numbers of paratroops behind the American beach-head area, their task being to consolidate an area from which an advance could be made up the Cotentin peninsula to capture the port of Cherbourg. In the event the American airborne operations were not wholly successful, the 81st and 101st Airborne Divisions being scattered over too wide an area to be fully effective. In the eastern sector, behind the British and Canadian beaches, the Stirlings, Albemarles, Halifaxes and Dakotas of the RAF's Nos 38 and 46 Groups dropped 4,310 paratroops and towed about 100 gliders to secure vital objectives such as coastal batteries, river bridges and road junctions.

As part of the elaborate deception plans undertaken to conceal the true location of the assault area during the night of 5/6 June a squadron of Lancasters (No. 617) had flooded the skies over the Channel far to the north east with 'Window' in a slow-moving cloud designed to suggest on enemy radar an approaching invasion fleet; a similar operation was carried out by Halifaxes and Stirlings off Boulogne. And these feints certainly played their part in discouraging the Germans from committing their reinforcements until the real landings had gained a powerful foothold in Normandy.

Throughout that first day, as more and more men and vehicles stormed ashore, the Allied air forces put up an enormous umbrella of protective fighters to keep watch for the Luftwaffe. Indeed the German air force reacted slowly and sluggishly with the relatively small number of aircraft available (a total of around 500 serviceable aircraft in the whole of Luftflotte III's assigned area). Only a small number of enemy air attacks developed and the damage caused by them was negligible. The Allies, on the other hand, recorded a total of 14,674 operational sorties on that first day, for the loss (mainly to flak) of 113 aircraft.

The initial assault phase ended with the delivery of 256 gliders to the inland dropping zones, carrying reinforcements to the men of the British 6th Airborne Division. Heavy tank-carrying Hamilcar gliders were now used for the first time to bring the Tetrarch tank into action.

For four days after D-Day the Allies were content to consolidate their beach-head as the tactical support Typhoons, Spitfires, Mustangs, Lightnings and Thunderbolts ranged over northern France, attacking road convoys and trains struggling to deliver German reinforcements to the battle area. Within 10 days more than half a million men had been landed on the Normandy beaches, scarcely troubled on their voyage from the UK by the Luftwaffe, thanks to the continuing efforts of the 2nd Tactical Air Force to pin the German aircraft to their bases. By 10 June (after only three days' work by the airfield engineers) the first landing strip on French soil had been completed and thereafter RAF Spitfires and Typhoons were able to operate close up behind the land battle, the Typhoons in particular proving deadly with their rocket armament.

The Americans were the first to break out of the beach-head, striking north towards Cherbourg before the end of June, and west and south during July. By the middle of August the British 2nd Army and the Canadian 1st Army had advanced south from Caen so that some 16 German divisions faced encirclement and annihilation at Falaise. After a week of pounding from the air and ground the bulk of the German 7th Army was decimated, and the remainder in flight across France; and all the while it was harried by the rocket-firing Typhoons, the Thunderbolts and Lightnings by day, and the Mosquitoes of the RAF's No. 2 Group by night. On 25 August Paris was liberated by its own citizenry and on 3 September the Welsh Guards swept into Brussels.

DeeFeater, a Martin B-26B-55MA Marauder of 598th Bomb Squadron, 397th Bomb Group, of the US 9th Air Force, carries 26 mission tally marks on its nose.

North American P-51 Mustang Mk III of No. 19 Squadron, No. 122 Wing. The six squadrons of RAF Mustangs were among the most successful of 2nd TAF's fighter units, netting many Bf 109Gs and Fw 190s in the Dreux-St Andre-Evreux sector.

Rocket stores at the forward bases in France did brisk business during the first days of the campaign. Here a crew prepare rockets destined for a Typhoon squadron.

A 9th Air Force A-20 heads over the invasion fleet as it heads inland to strike at German targets. Such 'softening up' raids were vital to the success of the Allied landings.

Below: Mosquito PR.Mk XVIs of the US 8th Air Force sported various colour schemes; those on weather reconnaissance, like this aircraft of No. 653 Bomb Squadron (Light), with crimson rudder and elevators from 16 August 1944 and complete crimson tail units from 23 September. No. 653 operated from Watton, Norfolk, a unit of the 25th Bomb Group.

An important job for the air force was laying smoke across the beach-head. Here Douglas Bostons taxi out at Hartford Bridge with special smokelaying gear under the fuselage.

BRITISH FLAT-TOPS 1940-45

The British, American and Japanese navies made considerable use of aircraft-carriers throughout World War II; indeed the survival of the three US fleet carriers of the Pacific Fleet at the time of the attack on Pearl Harbor was counted as of major importance in America's ability to countenance a successful war against Japan. And it was the US Navy and that of Japan which fought the great set-piece naval battles involving the aircraft-carrier in the role of capital ship.

The UK, on the other hand, after desultory and generally costly use of carriers in isolation on anti-submarine work and in support of land operations, lost both the old *Glorious* and *Courageous* in the first nine months of the war, neither as a direct result of air action. In due course the Royal Navy came to employ the much smaller escort carriers and the hybrid merchant aircraft carriers in the role of anti-submarine convoy escort, their complements of but a dozen or so aircraft being deemed adequate for the strictly limited-range patrols. By the end of 1940 the Royal Navy possessed a total of seven fleet carriers, comprising the veteran *Argus, Furious, Eagle* and *Hermes*, and the modern *Ark Royal, Illustrious* and *Formidable*; to these were to be added the *Victorious* and *Indomitable* in 1941, and the *Implacable* and *Indefatigable* (all of 23,000 tons) in 1944.

One of the first vital tasks undertaken by the British carriers was the reinforcement of Malta and the Middle East with the transporting of crated aircraft to Takoradi in West Africa after Italy's entry into the war in 1940; the frequent sailing of carriers with fighters for Malta involved no fewer than 25 operations before the end of 1942, the *Argus* making five voyages, the *Ark Royal* 12, the *Furious* seven, the *Victorious* one and the *Eagle* nine (as well as two by the American *Wasp*), delivering a total of 718 aircraft.

The first outstanding action by carrierborne aircraft of the Royal Navy was the brilliantly executed night attack by 21 Swordfish led by Lieutenant Commander Kenneth Williamson from the *Illustrious* on 11/12 November 1940 against the Italian fleet at Taranto harbour. Three of Italy's six battleships were sunk or crippled for a cost of two aircraft, an action that restored the balance of naval power in the Mediterranean following the elimination of the French fleet at Dakar.

In the famous naval action in the North Atlantic which finally brought about destruction of the German battleship *Bismarck*, Swordfish from the *Ark Royal* on 26 May 1941 scored two vital torpedo hits on the enemy ship, slowing her and destroying her steering, thereby allowing the British heavy ships to close their quarry. On 13 November that year *Ark Royal* was torpedoed by a U-boat in the Mediterranean and sank on the following day while under tow.

The air war in the Mediterranean involved British carriers in their most hazardous and spectacular fighting, particularly while protecting the Malta convoys. A total of 13 such convoys was sailed either from Gibraltar or Alexandria between August 1940 and January 1943, eight of them including carriers in their escort. Most of their sailings provoked enemy air action, and of the 80 merchant ships which set out 24 were sunk. The bitterest convoy action involving carriers was that of August 1942 when, in Operation 'Pedestal', 14 merchantmen were accompanied by no fewer than four carriers, two battleships, seven cruisers and 24 destroyers. The convoy had to run the gauntlet of mines, E-boats and U-boats, as well as more than 200 German and Italian bombers and torpedo bombers and, despite all the efforts of the pilots of the carrierborne Sea Hurricanes and Wildcats (as well as up to 200 aircraft based on Malta itself), casualties were heavy, the carrier *Eagle* being sunk by a U-boat and the *Indomitable* and *Victorious* being damaged; two cruisers, a destroyer and nine merchantmen were also sunk, and two cruisers and five merchantmen damaged.

For the most part the convoys sailed to the Soviet Union past the North Cape from Iceland were protected by the small escort-carriers, as were the merchant convoys which sailed into British ports from the Atlantic, their aircraft being mainly tasked with anti-submarine duties, although on some occasions they were launched to intercept shadowing enemy aircraft. Use of fleet carriers in the Atlantic was confined to covering the passage of important troop convoys, fleet carriers only occasionally being deployed against U-boats.

In the Far East the UK suffered an early loss when the *Hermes*, one of the oldest carriers afloat and the first to be designed as such from the outset, was sunk by Japanese carrierborne dive bombers off Ceylon on 9 April 1942 without having taken any significant part in the war in the Far East. In the last year of the war the *Illustrious, Indefatigable, Indomitable* and *Victorious* formed the carrier element of Task Force 57, taking part in the operations off the Ryukus with strikes by Corsairs, Hellcats and Avengers. The *Formidable* relieved *Illustrious*, and on 1 April 1945 *Indefatigable* was hit by a Japanese suicide aircraft, only her armoured deck preventing fatal damage. Both *Victorious* and *Formidable* were later hit by these weapons, and both were similarly saved from destruction.

A Fairey Swordfish Mk II of the main Blackburn-built production batch of 400 completed between June 1942 and May 1943. Carrying a smoke float under the starboard wing, this aircraft would probably have been from a carrier-based squadron (chevrons were discarded at the beginning of World War II).

The Hawker Sea Hurricane brought true fighter capability to the fleet's carriers. It was a conversion of the land based fighter and suffered the penalties of not being designed for carrier operations.

An attempt to replace the venerable Swordfish, the Fairey Albacore was always overshadowed by its illustrious forebear. The aircraft was not liked, despite its enclosed cockpit, but it performed usefully, especially in the Mediterranean.

A total of 402 Grumman TBF-1Bs (Avenger Mk Is) was acquired by the Royal Navy, with No. 832 Squadron being the first to equip, in January 1943. They operated initially from escort carriers or shore bases on anti-submarine patrols. This aircraft served with No. 846 Squadron at Macrahanish in western Scotland.

Seen from the flight deck of *Victorious*, HMS *Indomitable* launches an Albacore while Grumman Martlets wait their turn. Sea Hurricanes are positioned in front of the bridge. HMS *Eagle* is the carrier in the background.

The Fairey Barracuda was used extensively during the last two years of the war. It suffered from a weak undercarriage but performed well, particularly during the attacks on the German battleship *Tirpitz*.

The excellent Vought Corsair had been adopted by both the US and Royal Navies as their standard fighter. This example served with No. 1850 Squadron on HMS *Vengeance* off Japan in the summer of 1945. The US Navy's high-gloss midnight blue finish was retained, along with US style national markings.

This Grumman Martlet Mk II served with No. 888 Squadron aboard HMS *Formidable*. US-style markings were adopted for participation in the 'Torch' landings in 1942.

RACE TO THE REICH 1944-45

The destruction of German Forces south of Caen in mid-August 1944 was followed by the collapse of organized resistance throughout northern France as the Canadian 1st, British 2nd, and US 1st and 3rd Armies sped eastwards during the latter part of that month, Paris being liberated (from within) on 25 August. The British reached Brussels on 3 September, and Antwerp on the following day. The US 3rd Army reached Verdun on 1 September, sweeping on to Metz and linking up with the US 7th Army as it advanced northwards having landed in the south of France on 15 August.

During this great onrush the Allied air forces were constantly in action, as their ground echelons strove to establish and re-establish fresh bases close up behind the advancing armies. Before the crossing of the Seine, Mosquitoes, Mitchells, Mustangs, Bostons, Spitfires and Wellingtons of No. 2 Group attacked the ferries and barges at Rouen and elsewhere as German fighters attempted to interfere; these were engaged by No. 83 Group's Spitfires and the US 9th Air Force's P-47s and P-51s, which together claimed more than 100 of the enemy destroyed during the last week in August.

As RAF Bomber Command joined in attacks on German coastal garrisons from St Nazaire to Dunkirk, which had been bypassed by the advancing armies, the Dakotas, Stirlings and Halifaxes of RAF Transport Command were called on to mount the British airborne assault at Arnhem, while the C-47s of the US IX Troop Carrier Command delivered the 82nd and 101st Airborne Division against targets on the Maas and Waal rivers. Unfortunately there were insufficient RAF aircraft available to carry the entire British 1st Airborne Division (and the Polish Parachute Brigade) in one journey and, while the American forces duly secured their targets, the British attack at Arnhem failed despite the constant delivery by air of supplies. Unfortunately, as a result of recurring administrative problems, the 2nd Tactical Air Force was not brought fully into action to support the Arnhem action, and Nos 38 and 46 Groups lost 55 transport aircraft shot down and 320 others damaged by *Flak*.

Elsewhere the Germans kept up attacks on the vital Nijmegen bridge over the Waal, now in British hands, sending among other aircraft the *Mistel* weapon; this comprised an unmanned Ju 88 bomber packed with explosives with a piloted fighter mounted on top, the pilot at the last minute releasing the bomber and guiding it towards its target. These attacks failed to hit the bridge and, during the last week in September the Spitfires of No. 83 Group claimed the destruction of 46 German aircraft.

The airborne attacks in the north had been part of an Allied plan to cross the lower Rhine in force, liberate the Netherlands and outflank the Ruhr. Farther south, however, the Americans were meeting with stiff resistance and by 18 November had reached a line running roughly along the German borders with Belgium, Luxem-

bourg and France. Meanwhile the RAF had been engaged in supporting a major operation to clear the island of Walcheren at the entrance to the Scheldt, thereby opening up the great sea port of Antwerp. In attacks which lasted from 3 October to 8 November Bomber Command attacked gun batteries and dykes, dropping almost 9,000 tons of bombs as the 2nd Tactical Air Force flew some 10,000 sorties, dropped 1,500 tons of bombs and fired 11,600 rockets.

On 16 December the 5th and 6th Panzer Armies, assisted by bad weather and the element of surprise, attacked in the Ardennes between the US 9th and 7th Armies, and within a week had penetrated some 60 miles (96 km). The poor weather prevented large-scale air action, and it was without significant air support that the Americans were eventually able to counterattack and crush the German attack. Among the enemy aircraft that did appear were some of the new bomber versions of the Me 262 jets.

The bad weather that had dogged Allied air operations during the Ardennes attack improved gradually during the last few days of 1944, and Allied offensive action by the 2nd Tactical Air Force was resumed. However, unsuspected by British and American intelligence, the Luftwaffe had for some weeks been planning a great set-piece operation against the RAF and USAAF bases in northern Europe, the OKL believing that sufficient destruction could be caused to severely disrupt Allied operations to buy time to re-organize the defence of Germany. After assembling some 800 fighters and fighter-bombers of all types (including Me 262 and Ar 234 jets) from units all over the Reich the attack, Operation 'Bodenplatte' (Baseplate), was launched soon after first light on New Year's Day 1945, JG 1, 3, 6, 26, 27 and 77 attacking bases at Volkel, Gilze-Rijen, Eindhoven, Brussels, Ursel, Antwerp and Woensdrecht, JG 2, 4 and 11 the bases at Asch, St Trond and Le Culot, and JG 53 the base at Metz-Frescaty. Surprise was almost universal as the attacks came in soon after 09.00. Considerable damage was caused and about 500 Allied aircraft were destroyed or later scrapped but, after the defences had recovered from the shock, about 300 German aircraft were shot down or crashed on the way home. But whereas the Allies were able to replace their losses within a few days (relatively few aircrew were killed), the German losses, which included some 230 airmen, were little short of disastrous. Indeed the folly of the operation was voiced by many senior German commanders, but they were confronting Nazi leaders fanatically blind to the realities of unquenchable Allied air supremacy and the inevitable grounding of the Luftwaffe through lack of fuel, just four months away.

Major Glen Eagleston of the 354th Fighter Group taxis his P-47D-25RE, 44-20473, through the slush of Rosières-en-Haye in December 1944. Paintwork includes yellow cowl, black skull-and-crossbones and a bald eagle.

One of the hardest ways of hitting Germany was by putting out communications. Typhoons were used widely for this purpose, and here one launches a rocket at a German train.

Mass paradrops of troops were employed as the Allies inched through France and Belgium, the most famous occasion being at Arnhem. Douglas C-47s were the favoured type, whilst Stirlings and Halifaxes were used for glider towing.

Main German fighter of Operation 'Bodenplatte' was the Focke-Wulf Fw 190. This example is an Fw 190D of II/JG 26, which originated at Nordhorn. During the mission the unit attacked Brussels-Evère, enjoying almost 45 minutes of uninterrupted strafing, but destroying only 11 Spitfires and a few transports.

No. 74 Squadron RAF was employed on ground-attack duties during 1945, flying Supermarine Spitfire Mk XVIs. These mostly featured clipped wings for low level manoeuvrability.

Douglas A-26B-15-DT (43-22369) *Stinky* of 552nd Bomb Squadron, 386th Bomb Group, US 9th Air Force, based at Beaumont-sur-Oise, France in April 1945. Heavily armed and armoured and able to carry up to 4,000-lb (1814-kg) of bombs, a maximum speed of 355 mph (571 km/h) made the A-26 a formidable weapon.

Typical of last-ditch measures employed by the Germans, the Mistel composites were Junkers Ju 88 bombers carrying a large warhead in place of the cockpit and controlled by a fighter mounted above the fuselage. This left the bomber after it was aimed and returned to base.

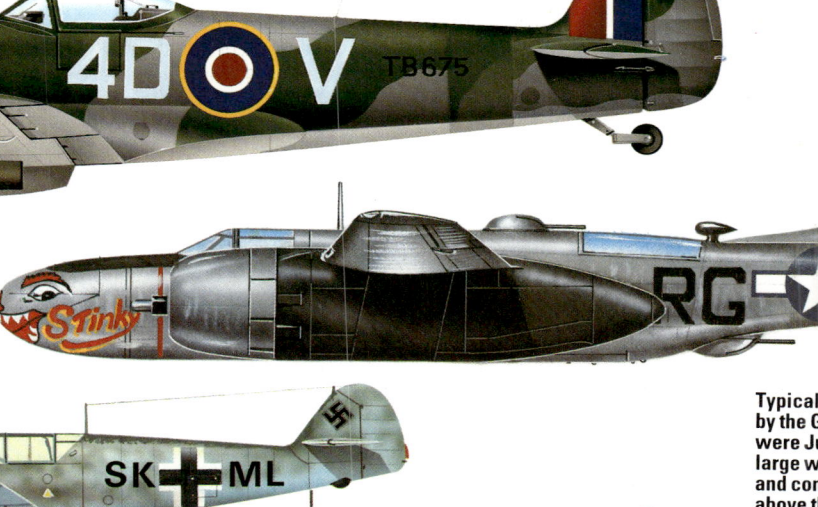

Capable of a speed of 435 mph (700 km/h) at operating height, the Hawker Tempest Mk V was one of the few Allied fighters fast enough to catch the fleeting German V-1s. Depicted is a Mk V (NV706) of No. 486 Squadron RNZAF, which turned to anti-V-1 duties soon after D-Day, claiming no less than 223½ kills.

FINAL YEAR IN THE EAST 1944-45

As the Soviet spring offensive of 1944 gained momentum in the Ukraine, the Luftwaffe faced an increasingly desperate task of attempting to cover the German army in its fighting withdrawals eastwards. To do so the *Jagdverband* could field a daily average in March that year of about 330 serviceable fighters along the entire 1,800-mile (2897-km) front from northern Finland to the Black Sea. Opposing them were around 3,000 first-line Soviet aircraft, of which roughly half were modern fighters. The balance was to some extent redressed by the superlative quality and experience of many of the German pilots, but even among these the losses were very heavy. Nevertheless on 23 March 1944 JG 54 was the second Luftwaffe fighter wing to destroy its 7,000th enemy aircraft (a milestone already reached by JG 51 Mölders in the previous September).

By that month the Soviet armies had overrun all but the eastern quarter of the Ukraine and were attacking through a gap between the 1st and 4th Panzer Armies. In the north on 10 June the Soviets attacked the Finns and invaded the Karalian isthmus with the 21st and 23rd Armies, supported by 750 aircraft of the 13th Air Army. Bolstered by a tiny detachment of Luftwaffe pilots and aircraft, the Ilmavoimat (Finnish air force) maintained a stout resistance with about 350 aircraft but, 10 days later, the key city-port of Viborg fell to the Soviets and on 4 September a ceasefire ended the campaign in Finland.

A measure of the scale of operations on the Eastern Front in mid-1944 may be gained by the fact that, compared with 54 divisions deployed against the Allies in France and Belgium, Germany had massed 164 divisions against the Soviets; yet compared with about 2,600 Luftwaffe aircraft in the East the Soviet air force now mustered a total of 13,000 first-line aircraft. Astonishingly the Luftwaffe was able to display its traditional skill and when, in June 1944, the US 8th and 15th Air Forces began their shuttle bombing flights to Soviet bases, about 180 He 111s of KG 4, 27 and 55 caught the American B-17s on the ground at Poltava on 22 June, destroying 47 of them as well as the base's fuel dump.

The city of Vilna fell to the Soviet armies on 9 July, completing the recapture of Belorussia and opening the way for an advance into north eastern Poland while, farther south, Marshal Konev's forces reached the Vistula 130 miles (210 km) south of Warsaw. At this point German resistance on the central front stiffened and the swift advance by the Soviet armies temporarily overextended their supply lines. The Soviets therefore switched the focus of their great offensive to the Balkans, and on 20 August two Soviet army groups, supported by more than 1,700 aircraft of the 5th and 17th Air Armies, launched an offensive on the Odessa front against

Romania, where the puppet Axis government was overthrown three days later. Bulgaria capitulated on 8 September, but despite the loss of almost 20 German divisions and the capture of the Ploesti oilfields, the surviving Axis air forces in the Balkans (largely comprising the Luftwaffe's Luftflotten II and IV – the former redeployed from France in August – and the small Hungarian air force) continued to fight desperately against the huge Soviet air forces.

By December 1944 the Eastern Front extended from the mouth of the Niemen river on the Baltic coast to Warsaw and on to Budapest. During the previous six months the German army had suffered the loss of more than 800,000 men in the East and almost 400,000 in the West and South. The Soviets now fielded 55 armies and six tank armies, while their first-line aircraft strength had increased to more than 15,500, against which Germany could muster fewer than 2,000.

Following requests by the Americans, who had suffered some 40,000 casualties during the Ardennes offensive late in December 1944 and sought relief from German pressure, the Soviets started their final winter offensive earlier than originally planned. On 13 January 1945 the drive opened in East Prussia but met with stubborn resistance at the fortress town of Königsberg, efforts by the Soviet air force to assist being hampered by bad weather. On 17 January Warsaw was finally captured, and a fortnight later the 5th Shock Army and 2nd Guards Army crossed the frozen Oder river at Küstrin, only about 50 miles (80 km) east of Berlin; to the south east Soviet armies reached and invested Breslau.

The final three months of the war were characterized by increased savagery in the air as the shrinking perimeter of Hitler's Reich eased the problems of defence. The Luftwaffe even switched a large proportion of its surviving fighter forces (including JG 1, JG 3, JG 6, JG 11 and JG 77) from the West and South to the East, believing that their pilots would stand a better chance of countering the Soviet air force despite the overwhelming odds. The German air force resorted to desperate measures to halt the advancing Soviets, employing the extraordinary *Mistel* composite aircraft in widespread attacks on the Soviet bridges and bridgeheads over the Oder and Vistula, and achieving a considerable measure of success.

As the Soviet armies fought their way through Berlin's streets early in May, the once-vaunted Luftwaffe lay scattered on its few remaining airfields, finally grounded without fuel and at the mercy of Allied bombers.

The Lavochkin La-7 in which top-scoring V-VS pilot Ivan N. Kozhedub claimed the last of his 62 'kills', on 19 April 1945. Flying with the 176 (formerly 19) 'Guards' IAP, Kozhedub destroyed in one day (15 February 1945) a remarkable total of 12 enemy aircraft, this number including an Me 262 jet fighter.

Messerschmitt Bf 109s were used throughout the entire Russian campaign. By 1944, the Bf 109G-10 was in action and these proved a handful for Soviet pilots if flown well. This G-10 was flown by a Croatian squadron, as denoted by the different cross.

Yakovlev Yak-9 of the 2ᵉ Escadrille of the 'Normandie' regiment operating from Sloboda in October 1943. This was manned by French volunteers and had been formed on 28 November 1942. The 'Normandie' regiment fought well over Belorussia and Lithuania in 1944, when the title 'Niemen' was added to the unit's name.

A wartime Tupolev Tu-2S, with typical handpainted individual number and a tail stripe of the standard diagonal form, possibly indicating a regiment on the Kalinin front. The three rear portholes on each side were replaced at about the end of the war by a single large window, and there were other minor changes.

Yak-9s on patrol. This type did more than any other to turn the tide against the Luftwaffe, with more than 16,000 aircraft delivered.

Below: Evolved from the Yak-1M series, the Yak-3 was an incredibly agile low-level fighter. Luftwaffe pilots were warned by their superiors to stay away from this aircraft. Luckily for them it was easy to distinguish from the less capable Yak-9, as it lacked the oil cooler intake under the nose.

Below: The Ilyushin Il-2 continued to pave the phenomenal advance of the Red Army. The type packed an enormous punch and was available in huge numbers.

The ugly Arado Ar 232B-0 was a four-engine development of the twin-engine Ar 232A (of which only two prototypes were built). Nicknamed *Tausendfüssler* (millipede), a small number served on the Eastern Front in 1944.

Above: Along with the Yak-3, the Lavochkin La-7 was the best low-level fighter of the war, being extremely manoeuvrable and very fast. These two types swept all German aircraft before them, all the way to Berlin.

A Heinkel He 177A-5/R6 Greif operated by II Gruppe, KG 1 'Hindenburg' in May 1944. Led by Oberstleutnant Horst von Riesen, KG 1 assembled some 90 He 177s for attacks on Allied communications and military concentrations.

THE JET GOES TO WAR 1944-45

Among the closely guarded secrets of the early part of the war was the work being done both in the UK and Germany on the gas turbine as a powerplant for aircraft. In particular, British intelligence was unaware that Germany had successfully flown a small research jet aeroplane, the Heinkel He 178, as early as 27 August 1939, five days before the outbreak of World War II. For years parallel work had been carried out by Frank Whittle in the UK but, because of lack of official interest, his work had been slow and underfinanced. It was not until May 1941 that the first British research jet, the Gloster E.28/39, powered by a Whittle engine, was first flown.

In the belief that the war would be short-lived, work on the development of an operational jet aircraft in Germany went ahead relatively slowly until 1940, the Heinkel company pushing on with development of its pioneer HeS 3b and HeS 6 turbojets. Discouraged by the problems with single-engine installation, however, the company ventured to produce a twin-jet fighter, the He 280, the first prototype of which, powered by two 1,102-lb (500-kg) thrust HeS 8 (109-006) turbojets, was flown on 2 April 1941. This design was not adopted by RLM for production and is of interest if only to illustrate the weight of interest by the German aircraft industry in jet power, while the UK was still only taking its first faltering steps in the concept.

Meanwhile the Messerschmitt company had also opted for a twin-jet layout for a fighter. This turbojet fighter, the Me 262, was designed about a pair of Junkers 109-004A turbojets, of which the first example was bench-run in November 1940. Because flight engines were not available in time, the first Me 262 prototype was flown under piston engine power on 18 April 1941, and it was not until 15 March 1942 that a Messerschmitt Me 262 was flown under all-jet power, being fitted with a pair of 1,852-lb (840-kg) thrust Junkers 109-004A-0 turbojets. By October that year 60 Me 262s had been ordered for use as development aircraft. From the fifth aircraft onwards a nosewheel landing gear arrangement was adopted in place of the tailwheel type previously used.

It was not until November 1943 that any urgency was afforded to the Me 262 programme, and it was Hitler himself who, despite protests from the Luftwaffe, insisted that the aircraft should go ahead, but only as a bomber which he assumed to be capable of carrying a 1,102-lb (500-kg) bomb to England. Nevertheless Messerschmitt continued also to press ahead with a fighter version armed with four 30-mm cannon, and during the summer of 1944 the first pre-production Me 262A-0s were delivered to Erprobungsstelle Rechlin for service trials, the fighter version being named the Schwalbe (swallow) and the bomber the Sturmvogel (stormbird). The first operational fighter unit, Kommando Nowotny (led by the fighter ace Major Walter Nowotny), was formed at Achmer and Hesepe on 3 October 1944 with about 20 Me 262A fighters for defence against the American daylight heavy bombers. Although the appearance of the new jets caused consternation among the American crews, the early jets achieved poor results because of their sluggish acceleration after pilots had been cruising slowly to increase patrol time. When Nowotny was killed on 8 November a new unit, JG 7, came into being, and early in 1945 another unit, Jagdverband 44 commanded by General Adolf Galland and crewed by some of the Luftwaffe's top fighter pilots (including Barkhorn, Steinhoff, Lützow and Späte) was formed. Although lack of fuel and poor serviceability reduced the average airworthy strength of this unit to no more than about six aircraft, JV 44 destroyed more than 40 Allied aircraft in about a month.

Before the end of the war Me 262 fighters equipped about half a dozen *Gruppen*, including some night-fighter *Staffeln* whose two-seat radar-equipped Me 262B-1a/U-1 aircraft were used in the night defence of Berlin in the last weeks of the war. Bomber versions of the Me 262 also entered service alongside another German jet bomber, the Arado Ar 234, an exceptionally 'clean' twin-jet aircraft which was also used to fly reconnaissance missions at up to 40,200 ft (12250 m) over the UK and Italy without any fear of interception by Allied fighters.

Although the appearance of these German jet aircraft (as well as the rocket-powered Messerschmitt Me 163 Komet, whose development had been equally protracted but which also entered service on a limited scale) undoubtedly caused some concern to the Allies on account of their very high speed and heavy armament, Hitler's interference certainly prevented their widespread use which could have threatened the continuation of the heavy American daylight bomber offensive in the last year of the war. They were not immune to attack from Allied fighters, particularly in the hands of experienced pilots, and there were occasions when Tempest and P-51 pilots succeeded in downing the enemy jets. And, despite its late start, the RAF introduced its own Meteor Mk I twin-jet fighter into service (with No. 616 Squadron) in July 1944, before the first Luftwaffe jet fighter unit was formed. There never occurred a jet-versus-jet combat in World War II.

A Messerschmitt Me 262B-1a/U1, which had been captured by the British, is under test with USAAF coding FE-610 (Foreign Evaluation) at Wright Field in 1946.

Arado Ar 234s were used for high speed bombing attacks and reconnaissance flights over Britain and Italy. Its speed rendered it uncatchable.

Messerschmitt Me 262A-2a/U1 fighter-bomber of Erprobungskommando Schenk in the summer of 1944. This was the first Luftwaffe unit to take the Me 262 fighter-bomber into action. Normal bomb load was two SC250 (250-kg/551-lb) bombs, but to attack troop positions the Me 262 carried two AB250 containers.

In an effort to improve maximum take-off weight, Arado fitted Walter rocket engines outboard of the jet nacelles, which allowed the aircraft to carry bombs. The rockets were jettisoned after their fuel had been burned.

Ground operations of the Messerschmitt Me 163 were extremely dangerous due to the highly inflammable fuel used in the rocket motor. Contact between the two constituents of this fuel was extremely explosive and accidents usually had fatal results.

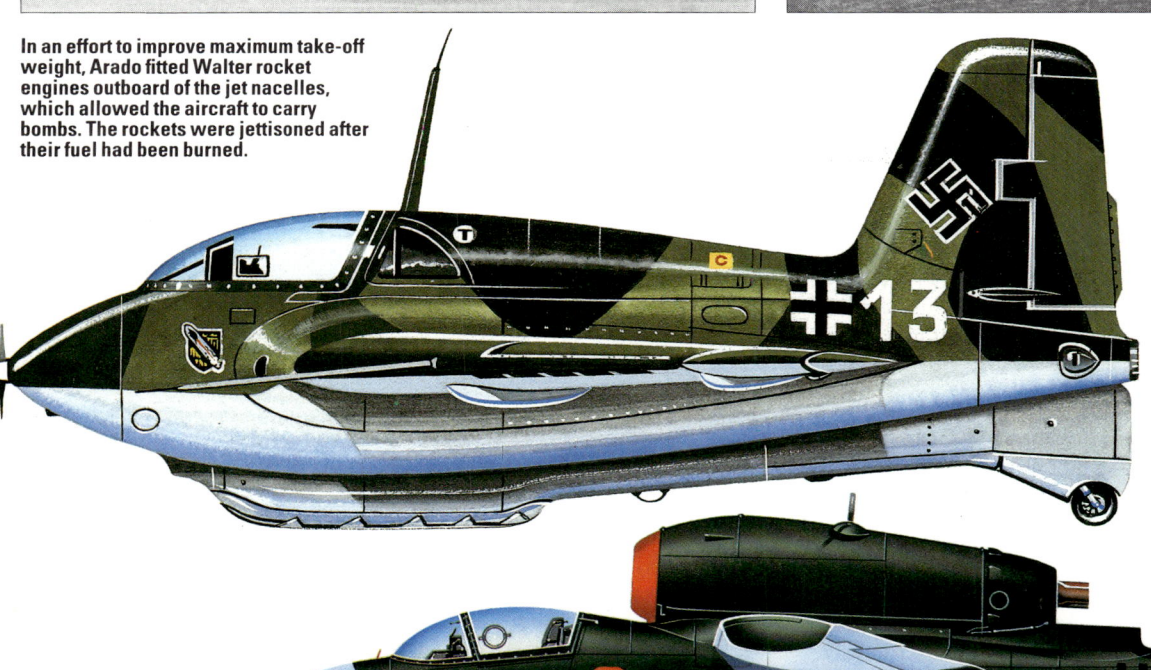

This Messerschmitt Me 163 Komet was in regular service with JG 400 at Brandis, and carried the famed badge 'Wie ein floh – aber Oh-ho' (only a flea, but Oh-ho). Cannon magazines were arranged in tandem in the top of the fuselage, between the filling points for the highly reactive *T-Stoff* and *C-Stoff*.

The Heinkel He 162 was an attempt to provide a mass-produced jet fighter which could be flown by hastily trained men with little more than glider experience. Only a few reached operational units in Schleswig-Holstein, and most of these were captured by the Allies before they could be used.

No. 616 Squadron RAF introduced Gloster Meteors in 1944. These were primarily employed against V-1 flying-bombs as their high speeds enabled them to catch the V-1s easily. In the last weeks of the war, No. 616 went to Belgium to test the aircraft on ground attack duties.

PEARL HARBOR 1941

The Japanese air attack on the American naval base at Pearl Harbor, Hawaii, was the manifestation of militarist expansionism that had gained expression in the Tokyo government as the result of a decade of successful adventures on the Chinese mainland, which had witnessed unremitting strengthening of Japan's army and navy. It was acknowledged that such territorial expansion in the Pacific would inevitably provoke war with the United States, and to have any chance of defeating the industrial might of that nation it was essential to open hostilities sooner rather than later, so as to take advantage of the USA's unpreparedness. The Roosevelt administration, on the other hand, after years of preoccupation with events in Europe, began backing its traditional friends, the UK and France, against Germany, with the supply of war materials; it woke up to the Japanese threat in the Pacific during 1941, but could do little but make token efforts to strengthen American outposts on Wake and Midway islands.

Even as Japanese and American diplomats met in Washington in attempts to reduce acrimony between the two nations and so to avert war, a large Japanese naval task force was at sea on course for Pearl Harbor. This force was not in fact the principal Japanese thrust, but was intended to prevent the US Pacific Fleet from interfering with their major assault in the south against the East Indies, whose oil and rubber resources were so vital to Japan's long-term strategic plans.

The strike force which made for Pearl Harbor comprised the six attack carriers, *Akagi, Hiryu, Kaga, Shokaku, Soryu* and *Zuikaku*, supported by two battleships, two heavy cruisers, one light cruiser, nine destroyers and three submarines. Anchored in Pearl Harbor were eight battleships, eight cruisers, 29 destroyers, five submarines and 44 other naval vessels. Fortunately for the Americans the Pacific Fleet's three aircraft-carriers, *Enterprise, Lexington* and *Saratoga*, whose survival was to be crucial in the subsequent Pacific war, were at sea or on the west coast of the USA.

Led by Commander Mitsuo Fuchida, the first wave of the Japanese air strike, comprising 51 Aichi D3A1 dive-bombers, 49 Nakajima B5N2 level bombers, 40 B5N2 torpedo-bombers and 43 Mitsubishi A6M2 Zero fighters, started launching from their carriers at 06.00 on 7 December 1941; 75 minutes later a second wave of 78 D3A1s, 54 B5N2s and 35 A6M2s, led by Lieutenant Commander Shigekazu Shimazaki, took off and set course for the American base.

The first bomb to strike home in the devastating attack fell at 07.55 on the naval air station on Ford Island, destroying six PBY flying-boats and putting out of action an entire patrol squadron. The attack achieved total surprise. Expecting to find five carriers anchored in Pearl Harbor, the Japanese pilots were quickly ordered to concentrate their attention on the battleships, neatly moored along Ford Island. The battleship *Nevada*, at the head of the row, was hit by a single torpedo before her crew cast off and the ship took a couple of direct hits by bombs; as she made for the open sea she was again hit by bombs and had to be beached with 50 dead aboard. Next in line, the *Arizona* was hit by several torpedoes as well as eight bombs before her shattered hulk sank to the shallow bottom, taking 1,103 crewmen with her. The *West Virginia* received half a dozen torpedo hits and settled to the bottom with 105 dead. Next, the *Oklahoma* was hit by five torpedoes and capsized, trapping 415 men. The last ship in 'battleship row' was the *California*, struck by two torpedoes; with unsecured watertight compartments she eventually foundered three nights later having lost 98 of her crew.

Elsewhere numerous other naval vessels were sunk or severely damaged as the Japanese pilots turned their attention to the airfields and naval air stations. At Kaneohe Field 27 of the 33 PBY flying-boats were destroyed and the remaining six damaged. At Ewa Field there were 49 US Marine Corps fighters and scout bombers; after the Japanese attacks 33 had been destroyed, and none of the remainder could be flown. The story was much the same at the US Army's Hickham Field, where the aircraft were lined up in neat rows; at Wheeler Field 42 US Army aircraft were also destroyed.

Total cost to the Japanese raiding formations amounted to nine A6M2 fighters, 15 D3A1 dive-bombers and five B5N2s, plus one of the latter which ditched near its carrier. Five midget submarines were also lost without achieving any damage. The air attack had gained spectacular results, killing 2,335 American personnel, leaving four battleships sunk or sinking, damaging four others, sinking three destroyers and a minelayer, and severely damaging two cruisers and a repair ship. In all, 188 aircraft had been destroyed in the air and on the ground, and almost every other aircraft (including several which arrived over Pearl Harbor at the height of the raid having flown from *Enterprise* in ignorance of the attack) was damaged to some extent.

The last of the Japanese aircraft had been recovered aboard their carriers by 13.00 on 7 December. By then the United States was finally at war.

Ford Island, Pearl Harbor, is under attack: bombs can be seen exploding on the far side of the island ('Battleship Row'), and Aichi D3A 'Val' dive-bombers can be seen turning over the harbour.

Typical of the early A6M2 Reisens that administered a paralysing shock to the Allied aircraft in the Pacific in the first half of 1942, this example served aboard the carrier *Hiryu* with the 2nd Sentai (two blue bands) of the 1st Koku Kantai (air fleet). Ruling colour was sky grey with matt black engine cowling.

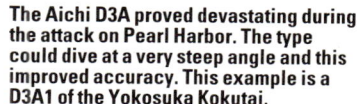

The Aichi D3A proved devastating during the attack on Pearl Harbor. The type could dive at a very steep angle and this improved accuracy. This example is a D3A1 of the Yokosuka Kokutai.

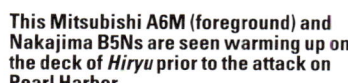

This Mitsubishi A6M (foreground) and Nakajima B5Ns are seen warming up on the deck of *Hiryu* prior to the attack on Pearl Harbor.

The Japanese raided airfields and other installations as well as the main anchorage at Ford Island. This Boeing B-17 force-landed at Bellows Field while under attack.

The attack on Pearl Harbor on that fine Sunday morning of December 1941 was by far the greatest military shock ever suffered by the United States in its entire history. Here Ford Island is under attack; ships burn and flak dots the sky while the Japanese bombers press home their relentless attack.

MALAYA AND BURMA 1941-42

If the Japanese gained total tactical surprise in their attack on Pearl Harbor, strategic surprise was no less complete against the British in South East Asia. Token forces had been spared for the defence of the Malayan peninsula for some years, particularly for the British naval base at Singapore. By December 1941 the British air forces in the whole of the Far East fielded 362 aircraft, of which 233 were serviceable. In Malaya there were four RAF squadrons of Blenheims (Nos 27, 34, 60 and 62), two squadrons (Nos 36 and 100) of anti-quated Vildebeest torpedo biplanes, two RAAF squadrons of Hudsons (Nos 1 and 8) and three Catalina flying-boats of No. 230 Squadron. Fighter defence rested upon 52 Buffaloes of No. 243 Squadron, RAF, No. 488 Squadron, RNZAF, and Nos 21 and 453 Squadrons, RAAF. Ranged against this force was the Imperial Japanese Army's 3rd Hikoshidan comprising 11 *sentais* and four independent *chutais*. Powerful elements of the Japanese fleet were also available, although in the early stages of the Malayan campaign most of its aircraft were shore-based, including at least two *sentais* of the excellent Mitsubishi A6M fighter.

On 7 December 1941 Japanese forces moved against northern Malaya and were soon ashore at Kota Bharu. The RAF's initial task was to locate and report the whereabouts of Japanese invasion convoys; the Blenheims, Hudsons and Vildebeests were soon in action but were able to do little to hinder the landings. On the following morning Singapore experienced the first of many air raids, and it soon became clear that the Buffaloes were quite inadequate to match the modern Japanese aircraft. Elsewhere at Alor Star a Japanese raid destroyed all but two of No. 62 Squadron's Blenheims. By the evening of 8 December only 50 RAF aircraft remained serviceable.

Meanwhile reinforcements had been ordered to Singapore, the battleship *Prince of Wales* and the battle-cruiser *Repulse* having arrived on 2 December. On 8 December these ships set sail to find and attack the Japanese invasion fleets in the north, but within 48 hours had been spotted by the Japanese who despatched 60 Mitsubishi G3M2 and 26 G4M1 bombers to attack. Devoid of fighter protection, the British warships were quickly sunk, with heavy loss of life.

The other reinforcements (51 Hurricanes shipped by sea) took much longer to arrive and were not ready for action until 20 January 1942, by which time the Japanese army had advanced to within 100 miles (160 km) of Singapore. On that day 27 unescorted Japanese bombers were caught by the Hurricanes whose pilots destroyed eight of the raiders. The next day the bombers returned with an escort of A6M fighters which in turn shot down five Hurricanes without loss. Within a week only 21 Hurricanes were airworthy; by the time the Japanese opened their direct assault on Singapore island only 10 Hurricanes and a handful of Buffaloes and Vildebeests were available at any one time, and these continued to fight as best they could throughout the fortnight-long evacuation, despite their landing strip at Kallang being under constant Japanese fire. On 15 February the island fortress surrendered.

Long before the fall of Singapore the Japanese had embarked on the conquest of Burma to safeguard their right flank in South East Asia. Emulating the German pattern of terror raids, Japanese bombers attacked Rangoon on 23 December 1941, showering the densely-packed market places with fragmentation bombs, killing 2,000 civilians in this raid and 5,000 more in a Christmas Day attack. However, whereas most of the Far Eastern air force, such as it was, had been deployed for the defence of Singapore, Burma was of less obvious strategic value and accordingly merited much weaker air defences. In all, these comprised just 16 Buffaloes of No. 67 Squadron, RAF, and 21 P-40s of the American Volunteer Group (AVG). For the attack on Burma the Japanese brought up no fewer than 40 aircraft.

Despite the presence of Ki-27 and Ki-43 escort fighters, the Buffaloes and P-40s claimed the destruction of 36 of the Christmas Day raiders, and continued to dispute air superiority over Rangoon for more than a month; however, although reinforced by 30 Hurricanes and a squadron of Blenheims, they could not halt the Japanese advance in southern Burma and on 30 January 1941 the important British airfield at Moulmein was overrun. Threatened by an encircling thrust from the north east, the great port of Rangoon was evacuated early in March and the surviving components of the RAF began the long retreat northwards. Using such makeshift airstrips that existed in the dense jungle, the squadrons of 'Burwing' (Blenheim Mk IVs of No. 45 Squadron, No. 67 Squadron with some aged Hurricanes and a few Hudsons of No. 139 Squadron) carried out sporadic attacks on the invaders; their last significant attack was made on Japanese aircraft at Mingaladon airfield on 21 March, the destruction of 27 enemy aircraft being claimed.

By mid-1941 the Japanese had overrun almost the whole of Burma. In the final stages of the campaign the Dakotas of No. 31 Squadron, RAF, and the C-47s of the 2nd Troop Carrier Squadron, USAAF, evacuated 8,616 men, women and children from Magwe, Myitkyina and Shwebo. It was only the onset of the monsoon season that brought the invaders to a halt on the border with India, within easy bombing range of the vital port of Calcutta.

Above: The Nakajima Ki-43 Hayabusa was the most widely-used fighter in the war against the British in Burma and Malaya. It had extremely good manoeuvrability but suffered from poor armament and low speed.

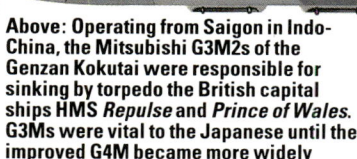

Above: Operating from Saigon in Indo-China, the Mitsubishi G3M2s of the Genzan Kokutai were responsible for sinking by torpedo the British capital ships HMS *Repulse* and *Prince of Wales*. G3Ms were vital to the Japanese until the improved G4M became more widely available.

Brewster Buffaloes were hastily bought from the US following the start of the war, but were sent to the Far East as their performance was found to be lacking against German fighters. In the Far East they were pretty useless too, although they put up a desperate defence of Singapore. This example served with No. 453 Squadron.

No. 60 Squadron flew its Blenheim Mk Is from Mingaladon, Burma and Kuantan, Malaya. When the Japanese began their march south the Blenheims put up a brave defence, but were no match for the Japanese fighters and the squadron's personnel were forced to retire to India to reform with new aircraft.

Mitsubishi Ki-21s were used as level bombers throughout the invasion of Burma and Malaya. First appearing during the air wars over China and Manchuria in the late 1930s, this type was obsolete by the outbreak of hostilities in the Pacific and was only used in areas where fighter opposition was weak.

The Nakajima Ki-43 was a clean design which had been produced to retain the manoeuvrability of earlier fighters, but with better performance and retractable undercarriage. The result was disappointing, but it continued in service until the war's end.

Hurricanes became the most important Allied type in India and Burma as the war progressed, performing many roles. These aircraft were tropicalized by the addition of a dust filter. The crew is seen relaxing on a Mk IIC.

Forerunner of the Ki-43, the Nakajima Ki-27 was used in Burma and Indo-China and was probably the most manoeuvrable fighter to be used in this theatre. This Ki-27b of the 3rd Chutai, 64th Sentai at Chiangmai in northern Thailand, March 1942.

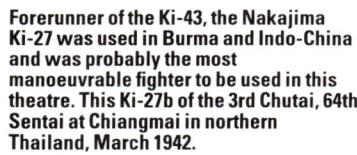

A Nakajima Ki-43-I-Hei flown by the 64th Sentai during the initial Japanese attempts to cut off China from Allied forces in India and Burma. The tail marking colours identified the *Chutais* within the *Sentai*; blue used normally for the HQ Chutai, white for the 1st, red for the 2nd and yellow for the 3rd.

In February 1942 No. 30 Squadron was withdrawn from the Western Desert fighting and embarked on HMS *Indomitable*, landing at Ratmalana (Ceylon) in March. It flew Hawker Hurricanes, at first in the defence of Ceylon and later in the campaign in Burma.

LOSS OF THE EAST INDIES 1941-42

As if to emphasize the vital importance to Japan of concluding a swift and successful war in the Pacific, the capture of the Philippines, Marianas, Carolinas, East Indies and New Guinea was virtually completed within the space of four months.

Just three days after the attack on Pearl Harbor the Japanese overran the garrison on Guam in the Marianas on 10 December 1941, but 500 US Marines on Wake Island, attacked the following day, held out until 23 December, blasted from the air and sea despite all the handful of F4F Wildcats could do against the raiding Japanese bombers, flying from Kwajalein in the Marshall Islands; in all, some 21 Japanese aircraft were shot down.

By the time Wake Island fell the Japanese were already making rapid progress in their Philippine invasion where heavy raids on the fateful 7 December had destroyed 12 of the 35 B-17s in the theatre, and went on to knock out the others in the following days; this force had been regarded as second only in importance to the American Pacific Fleet. As the Americans retreated in Luzon towards the Bataan peninsula, General MacArthur attempted to save Manilla from needless damage and casualties by declaring it an 'open city'; he might have saved himself the trouble for on 27 December the Japanese subjected it to a series of savage air attacks. As MacArthur prepared to make a stand on the Bataan peninsula following the Japanese capture of Cavite on 2 January 1942, other enemy forces were embarking in large convoys for landings in New Guinea and the Solomon Islands, where they duly arrived on 23 January.

Meanwhile, as the British and Commonwealth forces in Malaya failed to stem the Japanese advance towards Singapore, efforts were being made to rush RAF reinforcements of fighters to the Far East, and although some Hurricanes did arrive during January to assist in the defence of the great port, it was the same story everywhere: too little and too late. A regrouping of Japanese carriers in mid-February allowed four of them, the *Hiryu*, *Soryu*, *Akagi* and *Kaga*, to steam through the East Indies and launch nearly 200 aircraft for a very heavy raid on the Australian port of Darwin, sinking a dozen ships and causing immense damage in the town.

February had begun with the first significant American offensive air action when, on 1 February carrier aircraft attacked the Japanese base at Kwajalein; this was a minor triumph amidst a chapter of disasters, and several ships (mostly troop transports) were either sunk or damaged. But nothing could deflect the Japanese from their next prize, the rich island of Java, defended by some 120,000 Allied troops with scarcely any air cover. As Sumatra was effectively abandoned to the Japanese – for its few small airfields were capable only of supporting small numbers of fighters (some

Hurricanes having arrived by sea only to be quickly overwhelmed) – the Americans accordingly sailed the veteran carrier *Langley* from Freemantle in Australia, with 32 P-40Es aboard and orders to land them at Tjilatjap on the south coast of Java; also sailed at the same time was the freighter *Seawitch* with 27 other fighters in crates. The *Langley* was discovered by Japanese aircraft when only 70 miles (113 km) from her destination and sunk with the loss of all her aircraft; the *Seawitch* arrived a day or so later but was unable to unload her cargo which was then dumped overboard. On that day, 28 February, a large Japanese fleet put ashore its invasion force on Java's north coast. Without any effective air cover the fate of the island and its defenders was sealed. With little cohesive action by ships of the British, Dutch, Australian and American navies, the Japanese carrier aircraft were able to sink the Allied naval vessels piecemeal, while the Battle of the Java Sea cost them the loss of 14 out of 19 ships and delayed the invasion of Java by no more than a single day. On 9 March the defenders of Java surrendered and 98,000 British, American and Dutch troops passed into captivity. Two days later General MacArthur was ordered to leave Corregidor island in Manila Bay to establish new headquarters in Australia, leaving an embattled garrison to slog it out until it was finally forced to surrender on 9 April. Of the 76,000 taken prisoner, 10,000 were to die in captivity.

These shattering Allied losses had involved giving up virtually every island between continental Asia and Australia to the Japanese. The cost in men and matériel had been prodigious, yet one factor alone perhaps saved American strategy in the Pacific: the survival of the three big carriers, *Enterprise*, *Saratoga* and *Lexington*. When a fourth carrier, the *Yorktown*, was transferred from the Atlantic to the Pacific the effective number of carriers remained at three when *Saratoga* was damaged by a submarine's torpedo and put out of action for five months.

It was to be the *Yorktown* that was to stage a morale-boosting operation on 18 April 1941 when, accompanied by the *Enterprise*, she steamed to within 620 miles (1000 km) of Japan and launched 16 US Army B-25 Mitchells, led by Lieutenant Colonel James Doolittle, in a raid on Tokyo. Little material damage was caused, and all the aircraft were lost after force landing in China (their crews being repatriated later); but the raid's effect on the morale of the American nation was enormous, coming as it did after four months of unremitting defeat and disaster.

The Vought OS2U Kingfisher (illustrated) was used alongside the Curtiss SOC Seagull as a 'slingshot' aircraft, being launched from the catapults aboard battleships for artillery spotting and general reconnaissance duties.

Developed as a light bomber, the Mitsubishi Ki-30 was allocated the codename 'Ann'. It was not widely encountered as its performance did not allow entanglement with enemy fighters. It was used on a small scale during the lightning advance through the South Pacific.

Fresh from its success at Pearl Harbor, the Nakajima B5N continued on its victorious way through 1942, sinking many Allied ships. However, things became tougher when the Japanese turned their attention to the US Navy's carrier fleet.

A hangover from Colonial days, this Dutch Martin 139WH2 was operated by the Royal Netherlands Indies Army Air Corps in 1941. Such aircraft would put up a brave but futile defence against the Japanese aggressors.

Below: Early victims of the Japanese campaign were the Boeing B-17Ds of the 14th Squadron, 19th Bomb Group, based at Clark Field, Luzon, Philippines. These were mostly wiped out before the end of December 1941.

One of Colonel James Doolittle's B-25As takes off from the deck of USS *Hornet* (CVA-8) for the famous raid on Tokyo on 18 April 1942. Heavily laden with fuel to a gross weight of 31,000 lb (14061 kg), these aircraft were probably the heaviest that had ever taken off from an aircraft carrier.

CHENNAULT'S FLYING TIGERS 1941-44

As the call 'Remember Pearl Harbor' reverberated throughout the United States in 1942, a force of American airmen and aircraft was carrying the war to the Japanese in China and, despite virtual isolation by distance and relative inaccessibility, did much to slow their advance in South East Asia.

As long ago as 1936 a retired USAAC major, Claire Lee Chennault, had been invited by the Chinese to create a fighter defence system against the Japanese by instructing young pilots in modern fighting tactics and improvising with the few aircraft available. In due course the Chinese government negotiated to obtain 100 P-40Bs from the USA under Lend-Lease terms (of these 90 arrived at Kyedaw in 1941), Chennault having in 1940 recruited 80 ex-USAAC, US Navy and US Marine Corps volunteer pilots and 150 groundcrew members. With scarcely any official backing from Washington, Chennault organized this force into two squadrons operating out of Kunming to protect the vital Burma Road (which carried supplies to the Chinese) and a third at Mingaladon to cover the Burmese port of Rangoon. This had all been achieved by the time the Japanese entered the war in December 1941.

The Americans were quickly in action against the Japanese, shooting down six of a formation of 10 enemy bombers which attacked Kunming on 20 December, but fared less well when the Japanese attacked Rangoon on 23 December, losing two pilots. Thereafter the American Volunteer Group (AVG), as it became known, contributed substantially to the defence of Burma but, despite extraordinary ingenuity to keep the aircraft serviceable (as spares were available only by cannibalization) the American losses mounted rapidly. The American pilots were credited with 286 victories over Burma and southern China within four months (the true figure was probably nearer 150) and by March, when Rangoon fell to the Japanese, only six P-40s and six Hurricanes (which had been provided by the RAF as reinforcements) remained airworthy on the squadron in the south; 14 others were still flying from Kunming.

As the Japanese army advanced inexorably north through Burma the AVG continued to retain its identity under its indefatigable condottiere, fighting alongside the Buffaloes (and later Hurricanes) of No. 67 (Fighter) Squadron RAF, and striving to operate in appalling conditions from hastily prepared strips hacked out of the Burmese jungle. By May 1942 the beaten Allied army in Burma had retreated as far as Imphal, capital of the Indian state of Manipur, as the survivors of the AVG made their way back into China.

Despite constant opposition to the existence of the AVG by the American ground commander in China, Lieutenant General J.W. ('Vinegar Joe') Stilwell, who saw the 'Flying Tigers' only as a bunch of barely-disciplined mercenaries intent on diverting supplies from his own troops (rather than a vital protection of his own supplies), the American government came to accept the importance of the AVG in China, and forthwith despatched a number of the improved, six-gun P-40E, of which 30 reached Chennault's command. Chennault himself was reinstated in the active list of the USAAF and promoted major general, while the AVG was renamed the China Air Task Force as President Roosevelt personally directed Stilwell to ensure it received all possible assistance and supplies.

Largely through the continuing efforts of Chennault's pilots, the Japanese failed to reach and capture Kunming, although the Burma Road ceased to be of use with the Japanese in possession of almost all Burma. On 4 July 1942 the China Air Task Force was formally integrated into the USAAF (later as a component of the 14th Air Force) as the 23rd Pursuit Group, its three component squadrons becoming the 74th, 75th and 76th Pursuit Squadrons.

During the following year these were in constant action against the Japanese, intercepting raids on Allied airfields and strafing enemy airfields, river craft, troop concentrations and railways; they also flew escort for American bombers attacking Canton, Shanghai and Hong Kong. They operated against the Japanese during the enemy offensives towards Changsha and Chungking, and in the Tungting Hu region. They remained at Kunming until September 1943 when they moved to Kweilin in the north to provide air defence of the Chinese terminus of the 'Hump' air route for supplies from India to China. In due course the Flying Tigers gave up their P-40s in favour of the P-51D, and it was with these aircraft that they were in action against the Japanese forces which advanced down the Hsiang Valley in June 1944, earning a Distinguished Unit Citation. The following spring they helped to rout the enemy and then harrassed the Japanese during their final retreat in China. Chennault himself was appointed to command the US 14th Air Force from its inception until the end of the Pacific War.

Right: The Mitsubishi Ki-46-II 'Dinah' was allowed almost free rein over the skies of China in late 1941 and early 1942. The opposing Curtiss fighters did not have the performance to catch it at its operating height. This example served with the 51st Dokuritsu Dai Shijugo Chutai (Independent Squadron).

Left: Most of the American fighters deployed in China were Curtiss P-40s, but a few North American P-51B Mustangs were received by the 14th Air Force. Like that of the P-40, the colour scheme was non-standard and appears to have the British style 'dark green, dark earth' upper sides, with grey below.

The American Volunteer Group in China blossomed into the 23rd Fighter Group, and here men of one of its constituent squadrons, the 74th Fighter Squadron, pose on one of their P-40 aircraft.

The predecessor of the Curtiss P-40 was the Hawk 75, and this flew alongside the P-40 in the colours of the Chinese Nationalist air force from Kunming. These fighters were not as capable as the P-40 and gave the Japanese little trouble.

Flown by Charles Older of the 3rd Squadron 'Hell's Angels' of the American Volunteer Group commanded by Brigadier General Claire I. Chennault, this Curtiss Hawk 81A-2 (P-8268) was based at Kunming, China, in the spring of 1942. Among its distinctive markings are 10 victory symbols below the windscreen.

The 'Flying Tigers' (more formally known as the American Volunteer Group), operated in China under Claire Chennault with Curtiss Hawk 81A-2s, and scored many famous victories over what were much superior Japanese aircraft.

Sergeant Elmer J. Pence adds, with the help of his pet monkey, another Rising Sun to a Curtiss P-40E of the 26th Fighter Squadron, 51st Fighter Group which was operating in China in 1944 as part of the 14th Air Force.

THE BATTLE OF THE CORAL SEA 1942

Pursuing their drive southwards towards Australia early in 1942 the Japanese mounted what they termed Operation 'MO' to capture Port Moresby in New Guinea, thereby eliminating Allied air attacks on their bases at Kavieng and Rabaul in the Solomons, and laying open the coast of Australia for attacks by their own land-based bombers. To do this a number of naval groups and invasion fleets were assembled, totalling 70 ships of which two were large carriers (the *Shokaku* and *Zuikaku*) and one a small carrier (the *Shoho*); between them these ships embarked 51 B5N 'Kate' torpedo-bombers, 42 D3A 'Val' dive-bombers and 54 A6M Zero fighters. The US task force in the area (Task Force 17 under Rear Admiral Frank Fletcher) included the carriers *Lexington* and *Yorktown*, whose air strength comprised 25 TBD Devastator torpedo-bombers, 74 SBD Dauntless dive-bombers and 44 F4F Wildcat fighters. In addition the Japanese could call on about 120 aircraft land-based at Rabaul.

As the result of code-breaking, American intelligence learned that a Japanese fleet would enter the Coral Sea early in May, so that Admiral Fletcher, guessing that Port Moresby was its destination, was able to scout the area around Guadalcanal. Finding a small Japanese force off Tulagi on 4 May, Fletcher launched three strikes from the *Yorktown*, dropping 76 bombs and 22 torpedoes and sinking a destroyer and three minesweepers for the loss of one TBD and two F4Fs. The *Lexington* meanwhile was still far to the south.

On the night of 5/6 May the two large Japanese carriers entered the Coral Sea but, despite land- and carrier-based patrols by both sides, neither fleet was detected for many hours, although the Japanese aircraft found and sank the detached American destroyer *Sims* and the oiler *Neosho*. Early in the morning of 7 May a *Yorktown* aircraft apparently reported two Japanese carriers and four heavy cruisers 225 miles (360 km) north west of the American task force (now joined up), and within two hours 93 aircraft had been launched to the attack; unfortunately the sighting report had been decoded incorrectly and the force detected was of no importance and comprised no carriers. The American strike did, however, come up with the Japanese covering group consisting of the light carrier *Shoho* and her escorting ships. Despite the presence of a few enemy fighters, the 53 SBDs and 22 TBDs went into the attack, sinking the *Shoho* with 13 bombs and seven torpedoes; it was after this attack that Lieutenant Commander Robert Dixon radioed back to *Lexington* his famous signal 'Scratch one flattop'. That evening the Japanese commander, Admiral Takagi, launched a search/strike by

27 aircraft, these being intercepted by American Wildcats whose pilots claimed nine aircraft shot down. The survivors had a difficult flight back to the Japanese carriers and only seven succeeded in landing on.

Early on 8 May Japanese air patrols found the American carriers and, just as a strike by 69 D3As and B5Ns was approaching the *Lexington* and *Yorktown*, a force of 82 American aircraft was making for the Japanese carriers, whose position had just been reported 175 miles (280 km) to the north west. At 11.15 the Japanese attack started, and five minutes later two torpedoes and five bombs struck the *Lexington*, and one bomb hit the *Yorktown*. The former was badly damaged but, as the Japanese aircraft made off, the crew of the big carrier appeared to be controlling the raging fires. An hour later, however, her aviation fuel tanks exploded and at about 20.00 in that evening the *Lexington* was abandoned to be sunk by American torpedoes, the first American carrier to be lost in World War II.

The American strike aircraft had meanwhile spotted the Japanese carriers, aircraft from the *Yorktown* attacking the *Shokaku* an hour before noon; but all their torpedoes missed or failed to explode, and only two bombs found their mark. Although damaged and unable to launch or recover aircraft, the *Shokaku* remained afloat, while the *Zuikaku* recovered all the surviving strike aircraft.

Both sides now withdrew, the Japanese having lost one small carrier sunk and a large carrier badly damaged. Admiral Takagi had lost more than 100 of his aircraft and, with no more than 39 survivors able to fly, decided to postpone the invasion of Port Moresby for two months. More important was the loss of many of the best and most experienced Japanese naval airmen, a loss that would be keenly felt in the great battles to come.

The sinking of the *Lexington* was a considerable blow to the Americans who, now that the *Yorktown* was also damaged, had only the *Enterprise* and *Hornet* operational in the Pacific. Yet despite the adverse ship loss tally, and the fact that Japan could still count five large carriers operational in the Pacific, the Battle of the Coral Sea (the first in history to be fought by opposing warships that never saw nor fired on each other, and the first fought entirely by aircraft) was generally regarded as an American victory. Admiral Fletcher had succeeded in his purpose of frustrating a Japanese invasion of Port Moresby.

The Douglas TBD Devastator equipped the US Navy's torpedo squadrons in the early part of the war and these scored a victory over the carrier *Shoho* at Coral Sea. The Devastator was severely lacking in performance and was cut down by the experienced Japanese fighter pilots. This example is a TBD-1 of VT-6 aboard USS *Enterprise*.

Grumman F4F Wildcats and Douglas TBD Devastators are prepared for launch from the deck of USS *Enterprise*. The 'Big E' was to go on through the war to compile the most impressive record of any ship in recent times, seeing action in virtually all the battles of the Pacific.

The Grumman F4F Wildcat was the principal fighter available to the US Navy until 1943. At Coral Sea the Wildcats were hard put to contain the superior Mitsubishi A6M Reisen, but succeeded to some extent thanks to the bravery and training of their pilots. These F4Fs are lined up on *Lexington* during her last days.

THE TIDE TURNS AT MIDWAY 1942

The Japanese strategic plan in the Pacific was to establish by conquest an outer defence perimeter from Kiska in the Aleutians to Port Moresby, passing through Midway, Wake, the Marshalls and the Gilberts. Key bastion of this line of defence would lie at Midway, whose capture would extend the homeland warning network and serve as a base for the future capture of Pearl Harbor. Moreover the Japanese naval commander-in-chief, Admiral Yamamoto, believed that any battle to defeat the US Pacific Fleet must be fought and won in 1942 before the vast American naval building programme bore fruit, and correctly assumed that an attack on Midway would bring about such a battle.

For the assault on Midway Yamamoto assembled four fleets, of which one was an invasion force and three were heavy support forces; in all, these forces included five large carriers (the *Akagi, Kaga, Hiryu, Soryu* and *Junyo*), three light carriers, 11 battleships and 100 other naval vessels. Of the large carriers, the first four embarked a force of 81 B5N 'Kate' torpedo bombers, 72 D3A 'Val' dive-bombers and 72 A6M Zero fighters. The American fleet covering Midway was divided between two task forces under Rear Admiral Fletcher and included the carriers *Enterprise, Hornet* and *Yorktown* (the latter having completed speedy repairs since sustaining damage in the Battle of Coral Sea a month earlier); the American ships carried 42 TBD Devastator torpedo bombers, 82 SBD Dauntless dive-bombers and 79 F4F Wildcat fighters. There were also valuable American PBY patrol flying-boats and some of the new TBF Avenger torpedo aircraft based at Midway, as well as some older aircraft.

It was a PBY flying-boat that first spotted the Japanese invasion fleet on 3 June, and early in the following morning the *Akagi, Kaga, Hiryu* and *Soryu* launched the first strike against Midway by 108 aircraft at almost the same moment that another PBY was reporting the enemy fleet's position. The six TBFs were ordered off from Midway to attack the Japanese carriers, but they were intercepted by Japanese fighters and all but one shot down.

As yet the Japanese were not aware that any American task force was in the area of Midway, and only after a number of incomplete sighting reports had been received did suspicion dawn that American carriers were nearby. All through 3 June the American aircraft based on Midway carried out attacks on the Japanese fleet, inflicting little damage but forcing the carriers to keep launching their fighters for defence. This in turn prevented the Japanese from launching strikes against the American naval force, now known to include at least one carrier.

Early on 4 June a PBY reported the positions of two Japanese carriers but, suspecting that at least two other carriers were also in the area, Admiral Fletcher launched only two limited strikes, one of which (from the *Hornet*) failed to locate its target, some of its aircraft running out of fuel and landing in the sea, the remainder having to land on Midway. The other strike, composed of 15 TBDs of Torpedo Squadron Eight, found and attacked the *Kaga*; every one was shot down. This was followed by 14 TBDs of Torpedo Six from the *Enterprise*; only four survived. Last came 12 TBDs of Torpedo Three from the *Yorktown*, all of which were shot down. And not a single torpedo found its mark.

By now the *Akagi, Kaga, Soryu* and *Hiryu* were fairly close together, and their position was known. At 09.55 the first SBDs came in to the attack and within 30 minutes the first three of these carriers had been heavily damaged by direct bomb hits. Thus far the American losses among the carrier aircraft amounted to 37 TBDs, 16 SBDs and 14 F4Fs.

At 10.40 on 4 June the surviving Japanese carrier *Hiryu* launched a strike by 18 dive-bombers whose pilots discreetly followed the departing SBDs back to their carrier, the *Yorktown*, and carried out a highly courageous attack. All but five of the Japanese aircraft were shot down, but the heavy damage inflicted caused the carrier to sink three days later. Ironically, just as the attack on the *Yorktown* started, 10 of her SBDs attacked the *Hiryu*, scoring four direct hits.

The final stages of the Battle of Midway involved isolated attacks by American shore-based aircraft against the Japanese fleet, but little further damage was done. The *Soryu* eventually sank during the evening of 4 June with 718 men; five minutes later the *Kaga* blew up and sank with 800 of her crew. The *Akagi* and *Hiryu* both remained afloat until 5 June, both being abandoned to be torpedoed by Japanese destroyers, the *Hiryu* taking 416 of her crew to the bottom. As the Japanese fleet withdrew, now without air cover, a strike by 57 SBDs from *Enterprise* and *Hornet* found the Japanese cruisers *Mikuma* and *Mogami*, sinking the former and badly damaging the latter.

Midway may be regarded as one of history's decisive battles. It ended Japan's carrier domination of the Pacific, without which the American fleet could at last begin to contain the forward momentum of the Japanese advance. That advance would continue for many months, but with the cumulative losses among her best naval airmen at Coral Sea and Midway the Imperial Japanese Navy would no longer operate in safety from the air. Midway confirmed the carrier as the major warship in the Pacific; within a month the USA would have a further 131 carriers in construction or on order.

Before the storm: the crews of torpedo squadron VT-6 board their Douglas TBD-1 Devastators prior to launch for the Battle of Midway. Flying from USS *Enterprise*, only four of these aircraft were to return to the carrier.

Douglas SBD Dauntless aircraft make a second attack on a Japanese ship burning during the Battle of Midway.

Douglas SBD Dauntlesses from USS *Enterprise* were instrumental in the American victory at Midway, participating in the sinking of four Japanese carriers. At the time of the battle of Midway, the Dauntless had removed the earlier red and white markings carried on the tail.

AFTER MIDWAY: THE SOLOMONS 1940-43

The loss of four Japanese carriers at Midway gave the Americans the chance of seizing the initiative, if only for a short time, before the Japanese reorganized their fleets. It was therefore decided to mount a series of operations whose ultimate object was to recapture Rabaul in the north of New Britain. To do this it was necessary to secure the Solomon Islands which stretched away to the south east for 600 miles (960 km), and particularly the large jungle-clad island of Guadalcanal with its half-completed airfield (later named Henderson Field), as well as the island of Tulagi where the Japanese had established a seaplane base.

On 6 August 1942 Task Force 61, under Vice Admiral Fletcher, with the carriers *Enterprise, Saratoga* and *Wasp*, a battleship, 14 cruisers, 31 destroyers and 23 transports, entered the Solomon Sea. Aboard these ships were 99 F4F Wildcat fighters, 103 SBD Dauntless dive-bombers and 41 TBF Avenger torpedo bombers, plus 19,000 US Marines. Early the following day the US Marines went ashore on Tulagi and Guadalcanal, and within 24 hours the Japanese local defences had been overwhelmed, prompting immediate reaction by the Japanese commander at Rabaul who sent a raid by 27 G4M bombers, escorted by 18 A6M Zero fighters against the invasion force. Among the Japanese fighter pilots was Saburo Sakae, a veteran who had already amassed a score of 57 victories; after claiming his 58th victim (an SBD) he was hit by crossfire from a formation of TBFs. His aircraft was badly damaged but, despite injuries to both eyes and being paralysed down his left side, he managed to fly his aircraft the 640 miles (1030 km) back to Rabaul after a flight of more than six hours. (He later rejoined combat operations to gain a total victory tally of 64, including an aircraft shot down on the last day of the war.)

After a second air strike, which cost the Japanese 15 aircraft, a night attack by enemy surface forces caught part of the American invasion force unawares between Tulagi and Guadalcanal, sinking four heavy cruisers with the loss of 1,000 lives in the Battle of Savo Island. Worried by the presence of a large land-based air force, and with his cruiser escort seriously depleted, Fletcher obtained sanction to withdraw his carriers from the area. Throughout the following week the US Marines toiled to complete the airstrip on Guadalcanal and, despite constant attacks by Japanese aircraft, 19 US Marine Wildcats and 12 SBDs landed on the new airfield from the escort carrier *Long Island*.

Events now followed rapidly. The Japanese despatched a carrier-escorted invasion force with the carriers *Ryujo, Shokaku* and *Zuikaku* (with 168 aircraft) to land 1,500 troops for the recapture of Guadalcanal. On 24 August, after the Japanese force had been sighted by PBYs, the American carriers hastily returned, their SBDs and TBFs sinking the *Ryujo* that afternoon. But shortly afterwards, as both sides launched strikes against the opposing carriers, a big air battle developed. The *Enterprise* was hit by three bombs, but despite severe damage, remained in action. By the end of the day the Battle of the East Solomons had cost the Japanese the loss of a light carrier and 61 aircraft, and the Americans withdrew the *Enterprise* for repairs, her SBDs landing on Guadalcanal to help the US Marines. Following an attack by land-based B-17s which sank a Japanese destroyer and damaged another, the Japanese temporarily abandoned their attack on the island.

Japanese submarines then took up the hunt, torpedoing the *Saratoga* on 31 August (the carrier being withdrawn once more for repairs), and sinking the *Wasp* on 15 September.

One further major battle was fought in the Solomon Islands campaign, the Battle of Santa Cruz Islands, fought at the end of October. By then the Americans could deploy but two carriers, the *Enterprise* and *Hornet* with a total of 70 Wildcats, 72 SBDs and 29 TBFs. Against them Yamamoto sent a force which included the *Shokaku* and *Zuikaku* once more, and the *Junyo* and *Zuiho* with a total of 222 aircraft. On 26 October the *Enterprise* launched a search/strike by 16 SBDs which found and scored two hits on the *Zuiho*. On the same day a 62-aircraft strike attacked the American carriers, hitting the *Hornet* (which sank later), while at the same moment American SBDs attacked the Japanese carriers, hitting the *Shokaku* with at least three bombs. The Japanese launched a further strike whose pilots were able to concentrate on the *Enterprise* which was hit by three more bombs but which, by skilful manoeuvring, avoided nine torpedoes.

The Battle of Santa Cruz Islands ended the Solomon campaign at sea; it was a tactical victory for the Japanese despite damage to two carriers and the loss of 90 aircraft. The Americans, who lost 74 aircraft, were now down to one operational carrier in the Pacific, the *Enterprise* returning to sea after hasty repairs. Desperate fighting went on in Guadalcanal itself for seven months until in February 1943 the Japanese evacuated 11,000 survivors, leaving 21,000 dead on the island; by that time the battle had cost them 900 aircraft, two battleships and the *Ryujo* sunk, as well as 21 other naval vessels. Not until the Battle for the Marianas in June 1944 would major units of the Japanese navy again engage their counterparts in the US Pacific Fleet.

The Corsair was the leading front-line fighter of the Royal New Zealand Air Force in the Pacific in 1944-5, with 13 squadrons operating from land bases. They included F4U-1s and F4U-1Ds, in all cases without carrier equipment. This F4U-1A has the unusual insignia of No. 18 Squadron at Bougainville, Solomon Islands.

Much of the Japanese bombing of this period was handled by Mitsubishi G4M1s flying from Rabaul in New Britain. These suffered heavy losses at the hands of the US Navy F4F Wildcat pilots.

Sporting a disruptive 'snake-weave' camouflage, this Nakajima Ki-49-IIa was serving with the 1st Chutai, 7th Sentai, in 1943. This aircraft failed to live up to early expectations, soon proving in action that it was too slow to escape interception. The motif on the tail of this aircraft represents Mount Fuji.

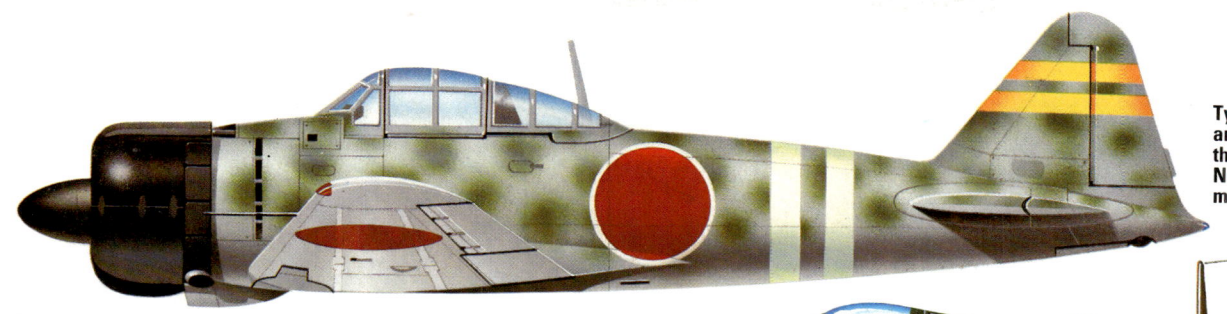

Typical of 'Zeros' operating from carrier and land bases in the Pacific theatre is this A6M2 of the 6th Kokutai at Rabaul, New Britain in late 1942, and later seeing much action over Rabaul.

Originally part of a British order and repossessed by the USAAF under the designation P-400, this Bell Airacobra flew with the 67th Fighter Squadron, 35th Fighter Group based in New Caledonia in 1942. The type proved much better at ground attack than at its intended role of interceptor.

The Solomons played host to the Vought F4U-1 Corsairs of the Marine Corps. These excellent aircraft were soon found to be highly capable at ground attack and were used widely in this role, supplementing the Douglas SBD in ground support.

Following the capture of the Solomons, these islands were used as base for many US and New Zealand aircraft. These Marine Corps Grumman TBF Avenger torpedo bombers are typical of the aircraft utilizing these islands. The airfield is on Bougainville.

A Yokosuka D4Y3 Suisei Model 33 of the 601st Kokutai. Later versions of the D4Y were frequently equipped with three solid-fuel RATOG units under the rear fuselage to enable them to lift heavier loads from the decks of the smaller Japanese aircraft carriers.

The decisive aircraft of the early years in the Pacific was the Douglas SBD Dauntless; this aircraft was responsible for sinking more enemy tonnage than any other Allied aircraft. This trio wears typical mid-war camouflage.

ISLAND-HOPPING 1943-44

Fortified and garrisoned by the Japanese during the 1930s, the Marshalls, Carolines and Marianas formed a defence perimeter across the Pacific which interrupted the direct routes from the USA and Pearl Harbor to south east Asia, the East Indies and Australia. Following Japan's attack on Pearl Harbor the British colonies in the area, the Gilbert and Ellice islands, were captured and incorporated into the Japanese defence perimeter. And it was the tiny atolls of Tarawa and Makin that were to be recaptured first by the Americans, their airfields providing the key bases from which further island-hopping operations would be covered.

Operation 'Galvanic,' the assault on the Gilberts, involved the newly-organized Task Force 50 under Rear Admiral Charles A. Pownall, the largest assembly of carriers hitherto concentrated: six fleet and five light carriers supported by six fast battleships, six cruisers and 21 destroyers. Split into four task groups, these carriers opened their attacks on 19 November 1943 with raids on Jaluit and Mili in the Marshalls to prevent Japanese aircraft based there from interfering over the Gilberts, keeping up their attacks for five days as the US Army went ashore on Makin on 20 November, supported by aircraft from the *Essex, Enterprise* and *Bunker Hill* fleet carriers and the *Belleau Wood, Monterey* and *Independence* light carriers. Meanwhile another carrier task group with the *Saratoga* and *Princeton* under Rear Admiral Frederick Sherman had been hitting airfields on Bougainville in the Solomons, where the carrier aircraft destroyed 33 Japanese aircraft and sank nine supply ships and 11 lesser vessels for the loss of three aircraft. And in a major air strike on Rabaul, American carrier aircraft damaged four Japanese heavy cruisers, while the crews of 97 Hellcats, Dauntless and Avengers claimed the destruction of about 25 enemy aircraft.

In yet another task group of Task Force 50, the escort carrier *Liscome Bay*, which was about to launch a strike over the Gilberts on the morning of 23 November, was struck by a torpedo from the Japanese submarine *I-175*. On board were almost 200 bombs of weights up to 2,000 lb (907 kg), and the torpedo evidently struck the bomb store. There was a colossal explosion which blasted the vessel apart and killed 643 crew members including Rear Admiral Henry M. Mullinnix, the task group commander. This was the only US warship lost during this phase of the American drive across the Central Pacific.

The successful assault on Tarawa was accomplished in three days. It also marked a new air fighting tactic by naval aircraft, that of radar-guided night-fighting. A radar-equipped TBF Avenger,

accompanied by a pair of F6F Hellcats, would be launched, and the TBF would vector the F6Fs into visual range of the target. In the first operational sortie, on 26/27 November, the F6Fs were slow in closing up to the TBF and it was left to the latter's pilot, Commander John Phillips, to shoot down the first target, a G4M 'Betty', with his two wing machine-guns; later in the same sortie, as the F6Fs closed up, the TBF's turret gunner opened fire at what he assumed to be a Japanese bomber but was in fact the fighter flown by Commander Butch O'Hare, the US Navy's first fighter ace and holder of the Medal of Honor. He was never seen again.

The next phase of the American offensive involved the assault of Kwajalein and Namur islands in the Marshalls, Operation 'Flintlock', on 31 January 1944. In support was Task Force 58, reconstituted under Rear Admiral Mark A. Mitscher from TF 50, now with six fleet and six light carriers. Among their aircraft were the first F4U-2 Corsair and F6F-3N Hellcat radar night-fighters. During the six-day operations to capture the key Marshall islands, American carrier aircraft destroyed some 150 Japanese aircraft (mostly on the ground), for the cost of 49 of their own number.

Following the capture of Kwajalein, Sherman's carrier task group descended upon Eniwetok atoll, 300 miles (480 km) to the west and almost mid-way between the Marshalls and the next archipelago, the Carolines. Eleven days after the fall of Kwajalein the amphibious forces of the US 5th Fleet went ashore and eliminated the Japanese garrison at Eniwetok.

The climax of the American destruction of Japan's central Pacific defence perimeter arrived with the assault on Truk atoll, capital of the Carolines, 650 miles (1050 km) north of Rabaul in New Britain. The first air strikes on Truk (apart from pre-emptive attacks launched during previous assaults elsewhere) were flown at dawn on D-day, 17 February 1944. On the airstrips the US Navy pilots found 365 Japanese aircraft parked nose to tail, destroyed at least 125 of them and sank 30 merchant vessels, a cruiser, three destroyers and a sub-chaser. The success of the devastating air strikes deprived the Japanese of effective air cover when the amphibious forces assaulted the islands, and in contrast to the 2,677 Japanese defenders who died the US casualties totalled 399.

Reduction of the Japanese garrisons in the large archipelagoes, successfully accomplished between November 1943 and February 1944, was followed by a temporary withdrawal of the American carrier forces to re-group for the next phase, the great thrust into the south west Pacific.

The Lockheed P-38 Lightning provided the American forces with true long-range fighter cover until late in the war, when the P-51D arrived in numbers. This example is a P-38J serving with the 432nd Fighter Squadron, 475th Fighter Group based on New Guinea in late 1943.

The Nakajima Ki-49-I was found to be underpowered, and so more powerful engines were introduced on the Ki-49-II, exemplified here by an aircraft of the 3rd Chutai, 61st Sentai. Performance was insufficiently improved, and the type was easy meat for the Allied fighters which encountered it over the islands and atolls of the South Pacific.

The Vought F4U Corsair entered the Pacific war with US Marine Corps units stationed in the Solomons. Corsairs were also flown by the USMC from Roi island in the Kwajalein group. This F4U-2 was one of these aircraft, being assigned to VMF(N)-532.

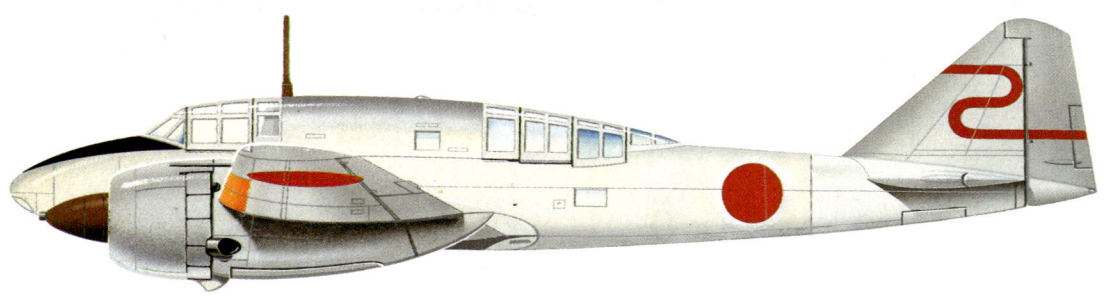

Of the many new types encountered by the Allies over the Solomons, the Mitsubishi Ki-46 was one of the most effective. These were used originally as fast reconnaissance aircraft, but were soon employed in an offensive role. This Ki-46-II flew with the 76th Dokuritsu Hikochutai, East Indies, 1943.

USAAF long-range bombers were quickly moved up behind the advancing Allied forces to bases where they could continue to strike the Japanese forces. This Boeing B-17E was stationed on New Guinea in 1943, and had carried General MacArthur to the New Guinea battle zone.

The most widely employed Japanese land bomber was the Mitsubishi G4M, better known as the 'Betty'. This had paved the way for the lightning advance through the Pacific in 1942, but on the arrival of more capable Allied fighters were found seriously lacking. Nicknames for the 'Betty' were the 'Zippo' and the 'One-shot lighter'.

A fine flying-boat from the Kawanishi stable was the H6K 'Mavis', which was widely employed on both reconnaissance and anti-shipping duties. The general vulnerabilities of the flying-boat soon drove the H6K to areas away from fighter opposition.

NZ4017 was one of a batch of Boeing-built PB2B-1 Catalinas, approximately equivalent to the PBY-5, which were supplied under the Lend-Lease Act to the Royal New Zealand Air Force in 1943-4. Equipped with ASV radar transmitters on the wings, it served in the South West Pacific theatre until after VJ-Day.

During the raid on Kwajalein in the Marshalls, this Nakajima B5N was winged by *Yorktown* gunners as it attempted a torpedo run on the carrier. The defensive fire that was put up by the large American ships was virtually a wall of hot metal, but several Japanese aircraft managed to get through.

A dramatic action picture of two Douglas A-20Gs as they sweep across the harbour at Karas in Dutch New Guinea. This scene was to be repeated many times throughout the remainder of the Pacific war as American light bombers pounded Japanese defences. The right-hand aircraft has been hit by enemy flak.

SAIPAN AND GUAM 1944

Key to the US Navy's success in the Gilberts, Marshalls and Carolines had been the inability of the Japanese to bring into action any significant numbers of naval aircraft to contest air superiority over the landings. Indeed, following earlier heavy losses, the Japanese had been hard at work reorganizing their depleted carrier forces. By mid-May the Japanese fleet at Tawi Tawi off the coast of Borneo included the surviving veterans *Zuiho*, *Shokaku* and *Zuikaku*, the new *Taiho*, the *Hiyo* and *Junyo*, and the light carriers *Chitose*, *Chiyoda* and *Ryuho*. These nine vessels constituted the largest force of carriers ever assembled under a Japanese task force commander. Yet although a new generation of aircraft, such as the improved A6M5 fighter-bomber, the D4Y3 'Judy' and the B6N1 'Jill' torpedo/attack bombers, were joining the fleet in growing numbers in 1944, the real weakness lay in a chronic shortage of experienced fliers. Two years of heavy fighting had taken a huge toll of Japan's naval airmen, and the replacements would now be pitted against vastly improved US aircraft, notably the F6F Hellcat and F4U Corsair.

Furthermore, following the assault on Truk in February 1944, the American carriers withdrew to reorganize, re-equip and re-crew. By June Task Force 58 had grown to five task groups with 15 carriers, the fleet carriers *Bunker Hill*, *Enterprise*, *Essex*, *Hornet*, *Lexington*, *Wasp* and *Yorktown*, and the light carriers *Bataan*, *Belleau Wood*, *Cabot*, *Cowpens*, *Langley*, *Monterey*, *Princeton* and *San Jacinto*; between them they embarked no fewer than 480 Hellcat day and night fighters, 199 Avengers, 222 Helldiver and Dauntless dive-bombers and three Corsair night-fighters.

Recognizing that the American operations in the Central Pacific were but a prelude to a major and sustained thrust either westwards or south-westwards, and that such a thrust would pose a serious threat to their forces in New Guinea and the East Indies, the newly-appointed Japanese commander-in-chief, Admiral Soemu Toyoda, decided on a plan, Operation 'A-Go', to seek a decisive battle with the US 5th Fleet, his own forces being spearheaded by his carriers. It was to be close to the fuel source of the Borneo oil fields that Toyoda chose to base his fleet at Tawi Tawi (accepting the risk of using their characteristically highly volatile fuel in his ships).

As soon as US reconnaissance aircraft exposed the Japanese naval concentration at Tawi Tawi, US Navy submarines flocked to the area and, by mid-June had torpedoed four oilers and five destroyers. The presence of these submarines prevented the Japanese from going to sea for training, so that many new aircrews had to remain without adequate experience of operations with the fleet. The Americans on the other hand, while failing to entice the Japanese out of Tawi Tawi, sailed for Marcus and Wake in order to gain 'controlled' combat experience for their new airmen, flying strikes during the last 10 days of May with relatively light losses.

The US plans now included the capture of Saipan and Guam, respectively at the north and south ends of the Mariana chain, and the stage was now being set for what was to be the greatest-ever carrier battle, the Battle of the Philippine Sea, in which the once-vaunted Japanese carrier force would be crushingly defeated and suffer huge losses in aircraft.

The preliminary actions of Operation 'Forager' against Saipan and Guam opened on 11 June as the American carriers launched strikes against Saipan and Tinian with 208 Hellcats and eight Avengers, destroying about 36 enemy aircraft on the ground; on the following day a small Japanese convoy was attacked from the air as it sailed from Saipan, losing 10 merchant ships, a torpedo boat and three sub-chasers. On 15 June US Marines landed on Saipan.

Two days earlier, however, now warned of the presence of the American 5th Fleet, the Japanese navy sortied from Tawi Tawi, a sailing immediately reported by the submarine *Redfin* to Admiral Spruance. This admiral then made one of the few major controversial decisions of the American naval campaign in the Pacific. He cancelled the imminent invasion of Guam and ordered most of the assault and supply ships off Saipan to disperse; he also ordered all five task groups of TF 58 to concentrate to meet the Japanese threat. It has been argued that he should have allowed the fast battleships of Task Group 58.7 under Vice Admiral Willis Lee to remain independent; with the subsequent decimation of the Japanese carrier forces, in which the battleships would take little or no part during the Battle of the Philippine Sea, such a powerful force of capital ships could have been deployed in readiness to destroy the remaining Japanese fleet without fear of attack from the air. While the gruesome naval battle was being fought out, the island of Saipan eventually fell on 9 July after 14,000 Americans had fallen dead or wounded; Japanese dead totalled some 30,000 from a garrison of 32,000.

Never was an aircraft more welcome than the Grumman TBF Avenger when it arrived in service. The earlier TBD Devastator had been outclassed by the Japanese carrier-based aircraft, and the Avenger more than met all of its predecessors shortcomings. These TBF-1s of VT-5 are about to launch from USS *Yorktown*.

The Curtiss SB2C was disliked by pilots and ground crew alike, but went on to compile a useful war record. It played a large part in the raids on Truk, Saipan, Tinian and Guam.

Pushed rapidly into production, the Kawanishi N1K2-J Shiden suffered from the speed of development and its unreliable Nakajima NK9H Homare 21 engine. Despite this, the aircraft managed to give a good account of itself in combat with American fighters.

Below left: One of the best flying-boats of the war was the Kawanishi H8K, known to the Allies as 'Emily'. This had good performance, excellent rough water characteristics and heavy armament.

Below: Throughout the war in the Pacific the Nakajima B5N took its toll of Allied shipping. This excellent torpedo-bomber figured in all the naval engagements from Pearl Harbor until its place was taken on board the Japanese carriers by the same company's B6N.

Above: Built by Nakajima, the A6M2-N was a Mitsubishi A6M mounted on floats. These fighters lost most of the performance associated with the 'Zero' and were only successful away from Allied fighters.

Above: This dramatic view shows a Japanese bomber after being shot down as it attempted to attack the USS Kitkun Bay (CVE-71). Once a Japanese aircraft had got through the fighter cover it faced a wall of anti-aircraft fire from the American carriers.

Replacing the B5N, the Nakajima B6N Tenzan saw intensive action throughout the last two years of the war in both the torpedo carrying and kamikaze roles.

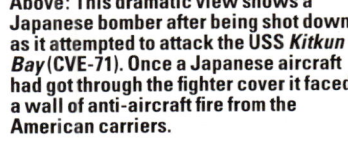

Long-range reconnaissance for the Japanese was handled by the Mitsubishi Ki-46; this was virtually immune to interception due to its high speed and good ceiling. The Ki-46-III, here exemplified by an aircraft of the 3rd Chutai, 81st Sentai based on Java, was the most capable version and was later converted into a high-altitude fighter for attacks on bombers.

THE MARIANAS TURKEY SHOOT 1944

June 1944 found the American forces heavily committed in their 'island-hopping' advance through the central Pacific, and the US forces were by that time far inside the original empire defence perimeter declared by the Japanese some two years previously. The success that attended this bloody advance was rendered possible by the steady build-up of powerful American naval forces, not least in carriers, in the Pacific. On 15 June 20,000 US Marines, supported by US carrier aircraft and a heavy naval bombardment, went ashore on Saipan.

As soon as the Japanese supreme command learned of this landing, it ordered the 'destruction' of the US Pacific Fleet by the Japanese Mobile Fleet. In effect the American force then located in the Philippine Sea comprised Task Force 58, commanded by Vice Admiral Marc A. Mitscher, with seven fleet carriers (the *Bunker Hill, Enterprise, Essex, Hornet, Lexington, Wasp* and *Yorktown*), eight light carriers, seven fast battleships, eight heavy cruisers, 12 other cruisers and 66 destroyers. Embarked in the carriers were 199 TBF/TBM Avenger torpedo bombers, 222 SB2C Helldiver and SBD Dauntless divebombers and 483 F6F Hellcat fighters. Against them the Japanese Mobile Fleet, under Vice Admiral Jisaburo Ozawa, consisted of five fleet carriers (the *Hiyo, Junyo, Shokaku, Taiho* and *Zuikaku*), four light carriers, five battleships, seven heavy cruisers, two light cruisers and 23 destroyers; embarked were 99 B5N and B6N torpedo bombers, 206 dive-bombers and 145 A6M Zero fighters.

After sightings of the units of the Japanese fleet by US submarines, Admiral Spruance, commanding the American 5th Fleet, ordered Task Force 58 to assemble on 18 June, when it was located by a Japanese carrier search aircraft. That night the Mobile Fleet also assembled for battle and was spotted on radar by a PBM Mariner patrol flying-boat. By early on 19 June Task Force 58 was some 100 miles (160 km) west of Guam in the Marianas, the Japanese Mobile Fleet about 200 miles (320 km) farther west. Sporadic air fighting occurred around dawn as Hellcats were launched to investigate radar reports of enemy aircraft; these proved to be search aircraft from the Japanese battleships and cruisers. Soon afterwards the first powerful strikes were launched by the Japanese carriers, and just after the *Taiho* had flown off 42 aircraft the carrier was struck by a torpedo from the US submarine *Albacore* (a second torpedo would have hit had its track not been spotted by a Japanese pilot who dived his aircraft on to the missile and exploded it).

Warned by radar of the approaching strike, the American carriers launched every available fighter. The US Navy and US Marine pilots destroying 42 of the 69 attacking aircraft. Apart from a single bomb hit on the battleship *South Dakota*, little damage was done and the raiders failed to reach the carriers. Shortly after 11.00 a second strike by 109 aircraft was spotted on radar. Again the Hellcats were launched and this time only about 15 of the raiders returned to their carriers. A third strike by 47 aircraft followed, and this time about half of them failed to find the American ships; of the others, seven were shot down. Yet one more strike, by 82 aircraft, was launched before mid-day on 19 June, no fewer than 73 of them being destroyed, many of them by the ships' guns as well as some caught by Hellcats as they tried to land on Guam.

Meanwhile the *Taiho*, whose seaworthiness had been little affected by the *Albacore*'s torpedo hit, was in trouble as her crew fought to get the fires under control; these efforts were succeeding when the ship's ventilating system was opened to dissipate the fumes of leaking fuel; suddenly in mid-afternoon a tremendous explosion occurred in the big carrier and she eventually capsized, Ozawa and his staff having been transferred to a destroyer; 13 aircraft went down with her.

Disaster had overtaken another Japanese carrier, this time the Pearl Harbor and Coral Sea veteran *Shokaku* being hit by three torpedoes from the American submarine *Cavallo* soon after midday. Once more volatile gases spread through the ship from ruptured fuel tanks and three hours later she blew up and sank, taking with her 1,263 men and nine more aircraft.

It was now the turn of the Americans to launch strikes against the Japanese fleet. Starting at 18.40 a total of 216 aircraft was flown off, split into half a dozen groups, one of which sank two Japanese fleet oilers. Another attacked the Japanese 2nd Carrier Division, two torpedo hits being made on the *Hiyo*, which later sank; the *Junyo* was hit by two bombs but escaped. Elsewhere the *Zuikaku* was struck by one bomb, as was the light carrier *Chiyoda*. Although the Japanese fighters reacted strongly and shot down about 20 of the American aircraft, far more were destroyed in accidents as their pilots tried to land back on their carriers in the darkness and short of fuel. A total of 130 American aircraft was lost during the day, compared with three Japanese carriers, two oilers and 346 aircraft.

Little wonder the Battle of the Philippine Sea earned the gruesome nickname among the US Navy of 'the Great Marianas Turkey Shoot'. By 10 August Saipan had been captured.

No aircraft was to turn the tide against the Japanese more effectively than the Grumman F6F Hellcat. The type provided the backbone of the US Navy's fighter defences throughout the offensive stages of the war. This example is seen on board USS *Yorktown* just prior to engine start for an operational sortie.

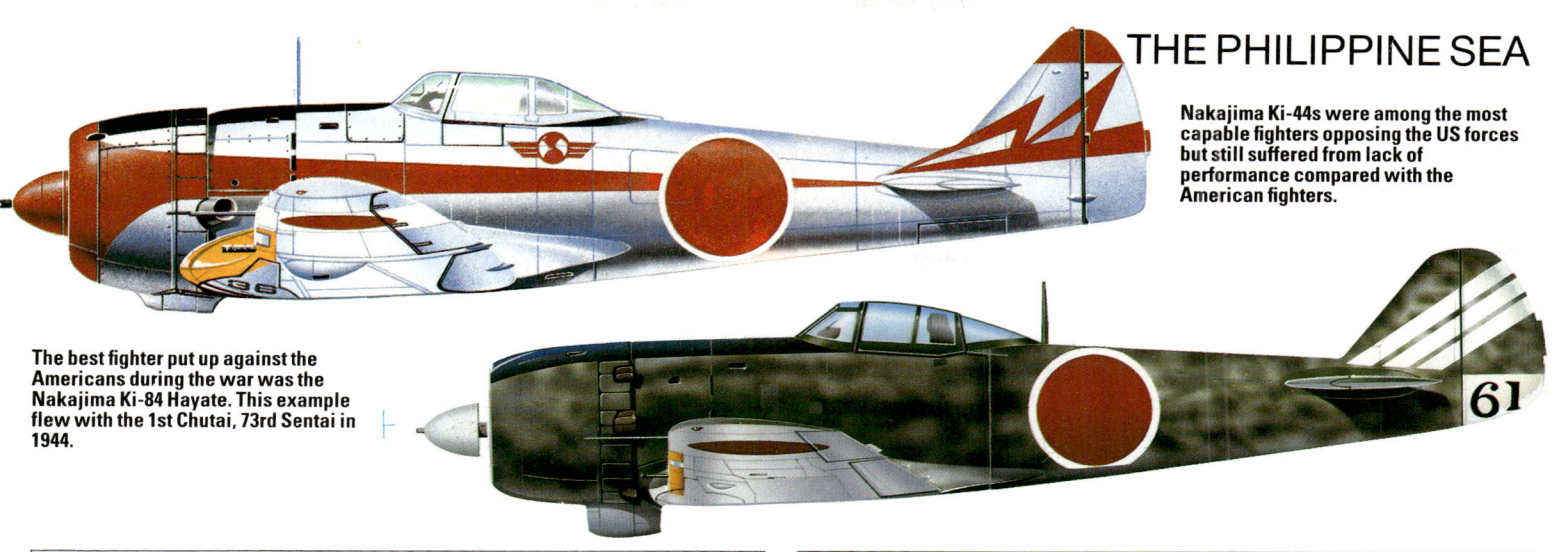

Nakajima Ki-44s were among the most capable fighters opposing the US forces but still suffered from lack of performance compared with the American fighters.

The best fighter put up against the Americans during the war was the Nakajima Ki-84 Hayate. This example flew with the 1st Chutai, 73rd Sentai in 1944.

The Nakajima Ki-49, codenamed 'Helen', was a less than capable bomber which suffered considerably from the attentions of the Grumman Hellcat.

Right: Principal torpedo bomber for the US Navy throughout the war was the Grumman TBF Avenger. These replaced the Douglas TBD and fought hard throughout the Pacific, scoring several hits during the Battle of the Philippine Sea.

Below right: The capture of the Marianas allowed bombers to hit Japan, and the USAAF soon moved its fleets in. This Consolidated B-24 is typical of many operating from Saipan, Tinian and Guam until the end of the war.

The islands of the Pacific were littered with crashed aircraft. This Mitsubishi A6M is symbolic of the devastation wrought upon the Japanese air forces by the Grumman F6F Hellcat.

Following a raid over the Marianas, this Hellcat has its wings manually folded by deck crew before it taxis forward. The Hellcat was by far the most successful fighter during the Marianas campaign.

PHILIPPINE LANDINGS 1944

After the great carrier battle of the Marianas, American forces went on to complete the capture of Saipan, thereby providing an important base for subsequent B-29 attacks on Japan. They landed on Guam on 21 July, and on Tinian four days later. The final capture of Guam on 10 August marked the end of the American campaign in the Central Pacific and the end of organized Japanese carrier warfare. The *Hiyo* had been sunk by air action, and the *Taiho* and *Shokaku* had been sunk by US submarines, while no fewer than 1,223 Japanese naval aircraft had been destroyed in the two-month campaign.

Four further Japanese carriers, the *Zuikaku, Chitose, Chiyoda* and *Zuiho*, went to the bottom during the battles of Leyte Gulf. On 30 November, only 11 days after her commissioning, the huge ex-battleship aircraft-carrier *Shinano* (68,060 tons) was sunk by the submarine USS *Archerfish* in Tokyo Bay. Before the end of the year the carriers *Unryu, Shinyo, Taiyo, Chuyo* and *Unyo* had been sunk and the *Junyo* was permanently crippled. During the same period the US Navy lost but one carrier, the light carrier *Princeton*.

Although the initial landings on Leyte marked the start of the Philippines campaign, the invasion of the main island, Luzon, did not take place until 9 January 1945, four divisions being put ashore in Lingayen Gulf. Already Task Force 38 had to contend with a powerful new enemy: atrocious weather. On 18 December a fully-fledged typhoon struck the fleet; three destroyers capsized with the loss of more than 800 men; aircraft tore loose in the carriers, starting fires as they ripped up electric cabling; the *Cowpens, Monterey* and *San Jacinto* between them lost 33 aircraft, 19 others were swept off the battleships and cruisers, and the smaller escort carriers lost a further 94. Such losses and the search for survivors in the mountainous seas delayed the ultimate assault on Luzon.

As pre-emptive strikes against Japanese air bases on Formosa were being flown by the carriers of TF 38 in the first week of 1945, the Lingayen Gulf assault force, carried by the US 7th Fleet under Vice Admiral Thomas C. Kinkaid, came under heavy Japanese suicide attacks as it approached the landing area. The escort carrier *Ommaney Bay* was hit and sunk on 4 January, and the following day the *Manila Bay* was damaged and suffered more than 70 casualties; on 8 January both the *Kitkun Bay* and the *Kadashan Bay* were badly damaged and had to retire from the battle.

On 9 January, as the American forces went ashore in Lingayen Gulf, Admiral William F. Halsey's 3rd Fleet (including TF 38), with eight fleet carriers, five light carriers, two escort carriers, six battleships, 11 cruisers and 61 destroyers, entered the South China Sea, its main task being to locate and destroy the two battleship-carriers, *Hyuga* and *Ise*, and also to prevent the Japanese from sending reinforcements to Luzon. Although the giant carriers were not found, the American carrier aircraft flew wide-ranging strikes over French Indo-China, China proper and Formosa; few targets were found.

Suicide attacks around Luzon continued to increase, the Australian cruiser *Australia* being hit five times. Fighting on the ground grew fiercer and, despite an order from General Yamashita to evacuate Manila, a Japanese admiral organized resistance by 20,000 men in the naval base. Bataan fell on 16 February, and Corregidor (in Manila Bay) on 28 February. By then, however, the bulk of the American carrier forces had moved on to prepare for the invasion of Iwo Jima. Indeed, with the steady but bloody advance through Luzon, and the overrunning or building of airstrips on the island, it now fell to the fighter and fighter-bomber squadrons of the USAAF and US Marine Corps to provide cover over the battlefield, and to the guns of the fleet to create a curtain of fire against the suicide attacks.

On 4 March 1945, after 173 days ashore on Luzon, American forces finally captured the shattered city of Manila, having lost more than 40,000 in dead and wounded, and more than 360 aircraft. Ten days later Iwo Jima also fell to the Americans. The US 10th Army, and the 16 carriers of Task Force 58 in support, were poised for assault on the last stepping stone to Japan: Okinawa.

Curtiss SB2C Helldiver is flagged off on a mission from USS *Hancock* (CV-19). The destination was Manila Bay, and the date 25 November 1944.

View from the deck as a Yokosuka D4Y dive-bomber heads for a US ship after being hit by flak. Such attacks caused a great deal of damage to the Allied fleet.

The Nakajima Ki-44 handled more like a Western aircraft than any other Japanese fighter. It fought bravely over the Philippines.

Air support was provided for the ground troops by Vought F4U Corsairs of the Marine Corps. These aircraft are carrying bombs on the centre section.

THE BATTLE OF LEYTE GULF 1944

Mid-1944 found the US forces in the Pacific engaged in two main offensives towards the Philippines, one under the direction of Admiral William F. Halsey north west from Guadalcanal along the northern coast of New Guinea, the other through the Gilberts, Marshalls and Marianas led by Admiral Raymond A. Spruance's 5th Fleet. Between the two thrusts Task Force 38 with 16 carriers struck the major Japanese bases in the Palaus and at Yap early in September, expecting to encounter heavy Japanese resistance in the air. In the event opposition was very light and the American ships and aircraft went on the rampage, destroying 58 aircraft and sinking 15 supply ships.

Surprised by the relatively weak defences, Halsey changed his plans and initiated air attacks on the central Philippines, the islands of Bohol, Cebu, Leyte, Negros, Panay and Samar. In two days the American carrier aircraft destroyed 478 aircraft and sank some 60 small ships, all for the loss of nine aircraft. Moving his sights up, Halsey now attacked the main island of Luzon and on 22 September his carrier aircraft destroyed 300 more Japanese aircraft. He went further, putting forward a proposal for the invasion of Leyte two months earlier than planned. As General MacArthur was at sea and observing radio silence the proposal went before Roosevelt and Churchill, who were in conference at Quebec, and approval for the plan was given without any delay. By the time Halsey had been forced by bad weather to leave Luzon waters on 24 September his pilots had destroyed more than 1,000 aircraft and about 150 ocean-going ships for the loss of 72 aircraft.

At the time of these preliminaries to the invasion of the Philippines, the Japanese still possessed eight completed carriers with a total theoretical complement of 400 aircraft; however, neither the pilots nor aircraft existed to equip them fully. Recognizing that the naval and air forces remaining in the Philippines stood no chance of withstanding the combined strength of Task Force 38 and Task Group 77.4 under Rear Admiral Thomas L. Sprague with 18 escort carriers and 500 aircraft, the Japanese decided to assemble the Combined Fleet with four of their carriers and two battleship carriers (the *Ise* and *Hyuga*).

On 17 October US Army Rangers began going ashore on the islands in the mouth of Leyte Gulf, covered by Task Group 77.4. Meanwhile, uncertain of the ultimate invasion point, the Japanese Combined Fleet had split into three groups, two diversion attack forces being despatched to the Lingga Roads and the Ryukyu Islands, 400 and 300 miles (640 and 480 km) respectively to the west

of Leyte. As reports came in of the American landings the main Japanese naval force sailed from Formosa.

The first battle involved Task Force 38, whose northernmost carrier group, with the carriers *Essex, Lexington, Langley* and *Princeton*, was attacked by about 160 land-based aircraft (hurriedly moved from Formosa to the Philippines) on 23 October. When seven F6F Hellcats intercepted the attackers one American pilot, Commander David McCampbell, shot down at least nine within one hour. The *Princeton* was hit by two bombs and after internal explosions had reduced her to a hulk she was sent to the bottom by American torpedoes. Following the location of the first Japanese diversion attack force, 259 American carrier aircraft took off to attack the enemy ships which now included the 18.1-in (460-mm) gunned battleships *Musashi* and *Yamato*. The former was hit by no fewer than 19 torpedoes and about 10 bombs before the 64,000-ton ship sank, taking with her more than 1,000 of her crew. In another battle, this time involving Vice Admiral Nishimura's force of two battleships, a heavy cruiser and four destroyers, Vice Admiral Kinkaid's force sank both the Japanese capital ships and two destroyers in history's last battleship-versus-battleship engagement, in Surigao Strait.

The next phase opened when carrier aircraft from TF 38 spotted the Japanese carriers approaching on 25 October. Strikes were sent off, hitting and sinking the *Chitose*, and damaging the *Zuiho* and *Zuikaku*; later that day another strike sank the *Zuiho*. In another action involving the American escort carriers 200 miles (320 km) to the south west, the US ships were less fortunate when four Japanese heavy cruisers engaged them, damaging the *Kalinin Bay, Fanshaw Bay* and *White Plains*, and sinking the *Gambier Bay*.

It was at this point that the Japanese first introduced their *kamikaze* (suicide) aircraft, the first to achieve success being a Zero pilot who struck and damaged the escort carrier USS *Santee*; another damaged the *Suwannee*, and then the *St Lô* was hit and sunk, the first American warship to be sunk by suicide aircraft.

The Battles of Leyte Gulf marked the end of the Imperial Japanese Fleet as a powerful and balanced fighting force, its losses of four carriers, three battleships, nine cruisers and eight destroyers comparing with the American loss of three carriers and two destroyers. The fighting on Leyte continued until the spring of 1945 but, with Japanese naval power virtually eliminated, the final outcome was never in any doubt.

The Mitsubishi A6M Reisen was still providing the main fighter assets of the Japanese navy at the time of Leyte Gulf. This aircraft was land-based at Clark Field, Manila, for many years an American base.

The Battle of Leyte Gulf saw the first wide-scale use of *kamikaze* aircraft. Here a Japanese pilot is cheered off by ground crew as he sets off on a *kamikaze* mission in his bomb-laden Mitsubishi A6M.

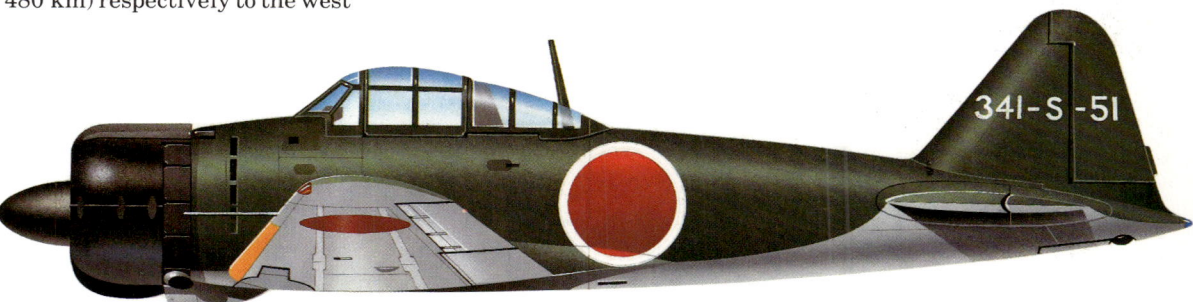

The Curtiss SB2C Helldiver was well established in the navy bombing squadrons on the larger carriers. These Helldivers are returning to USS *Hornet* (CV-12) following strikes over the Philippines.

BURMA AND CHINA

After months of limited advance and counteroffensive in northern Burma, the Japanese embarked on their last major offensive in March 1944, thrusting towards Assam in the north west. Now re-formed as Long-Range Penetration Groups (LRPs), the Chindits were parachuted into the jungle behind enemy lines at Indaw on 5 March and, after overland reinforcement, began construction of a number of landing strips (of which 'Broadway' was the most important); within a week 9,000 Allied troops had been flown deep into enemy-held territory. However, when the Japanese launched an attack against the airfields being used to fly supplies over 'the Hump' into China, they also destroyed 'Broadway', together with most of the RAF fighters based there.

In the course of the Japanese advance the defended towns of Kohima and Imphal were surrounded and besieged. By June it seemed that Imphal would be forced into surrender but, in the nick of time, General Slim's 14th Army managed to reach and break through the Japanese perimeter and within days the withdrawal of the enemy had turned to rout, as RAF, SAAF and USAAF fighters and fighter-bombers now began a year-long operation to destroy the Japanese forces in Burma.

By that time (July 1944), Air Command, South East Asia, commanded by Air Chief Marshal Sir Richard Peirse, had grown to a total of 90 squadrons, of which 26 were American (flying P-38s, P-40s, P-51s, B-24s, B-25s and C-47s), four were Indian (flying Hurricanes), one a Canadian squadron with Catalinas and one a South African squadron with Venturas. The remaining 58 were of the RAF, flying Spitfires, Thunderbolts, Hurricanes, Beaufighters, Mosquitoes, Wellingtons, Liberators, Sunderlands and Catalinas.

As the new advance (somewhat cautious at first) began, and the Allied forces found abundant evidence that the Japanese army was far from invincible, a new morale gripped the Allied aircrews. Combat procedures and weapons, hitherto confined to the European war, gained adoption. The dreadful napalm weapon, found so effective in the jungle, came into use, as did Air Support Signals Units for the control of 'cab ranks', the patrols by fighters over the battlefield.

When the 1944 monsoon season arrived in July all effective operations by the Japanese air force in Burma ceased. by then the Allies were closing up to the Irrawaddy and their air forces, particularly the long-range Liberators, concentrated on the enemy supply lines to prevent a build-up of reinforcements. By the end of the rains in

November when the advance southwards resumed, the Japanese could muster no more than 125 aircraft in the entire theatre. In the North Shan States efforts were made to open the Burma Road from Mandalay to China as a Chinese Expeditionary Force fell on and captured Wangting on 21 January 1945, supported by aircraft of the USAAF in China. Exactly two months later the northern capital of Mandalay fell to the 14th Army as the Chinese fought their way southwards through Lashio and Hsipaw. Throughout this campaign the needs of more than 350,000 fighting men were supplied by the Dakotas of the Combat Cargo Task Force, an achievement which, having regard to the harsh weather conditions, hazardous terrain and a desperate enemy, was acknowledged by Slim as the vital component of the 14th Army's victory. Even when a sudden Japanese thrust menaced Kunming in distant China, the Dakotas were quickly switched to fly 25,000 Chinese troops, their guns and pack animals across the 'Hump' to meet the threat.

The advance southwards from Mandalay was double-pronged along the great rivers, the Irrawaddy and the Sittang, while XV Corps advanced down the coast, leapfrogging islands until Taungup was reached and captured on 28 April. Occasionally Ki-43 fighters tried to interfere, but these were always quickly overwhelmed by the ever-present Spitfires, Hurricanes and Thunderbolts. Soon there was no remaining usable base or airstrip available to the Japanese aircraft and all air opposition evaporated.

The great seaport of Rangoon was itself captured after a landing by XV Corps from the sea on 2 May, and four days later a link-up was achieved with IV Corps advancing down the Sittang. Now trapped in the Burmese hinterland lay some 20,000 Japanese troops, sick and hungry yet fanatically determined to break eastwards across the Sittang into the mountains of Indo-China. In 10 days' concerted action by Allied tactical aircraft, the RAF alone flew more than 3,000 sorties and dropped 1,500,000 lb (680400 kg) of bombs and napalm, killing 10,000 of the enemy. By the end of July the Japanese had been defeated throughout Burma. Plans were already in hand to mount Operation 'Zipper', the invasion of Malaya and the capture of Singapore. It was never put into action. On 9 August the second atomic bomb, which fell on the city of Nagasaki, persuaded the Japanese to acknowledge final defeat.

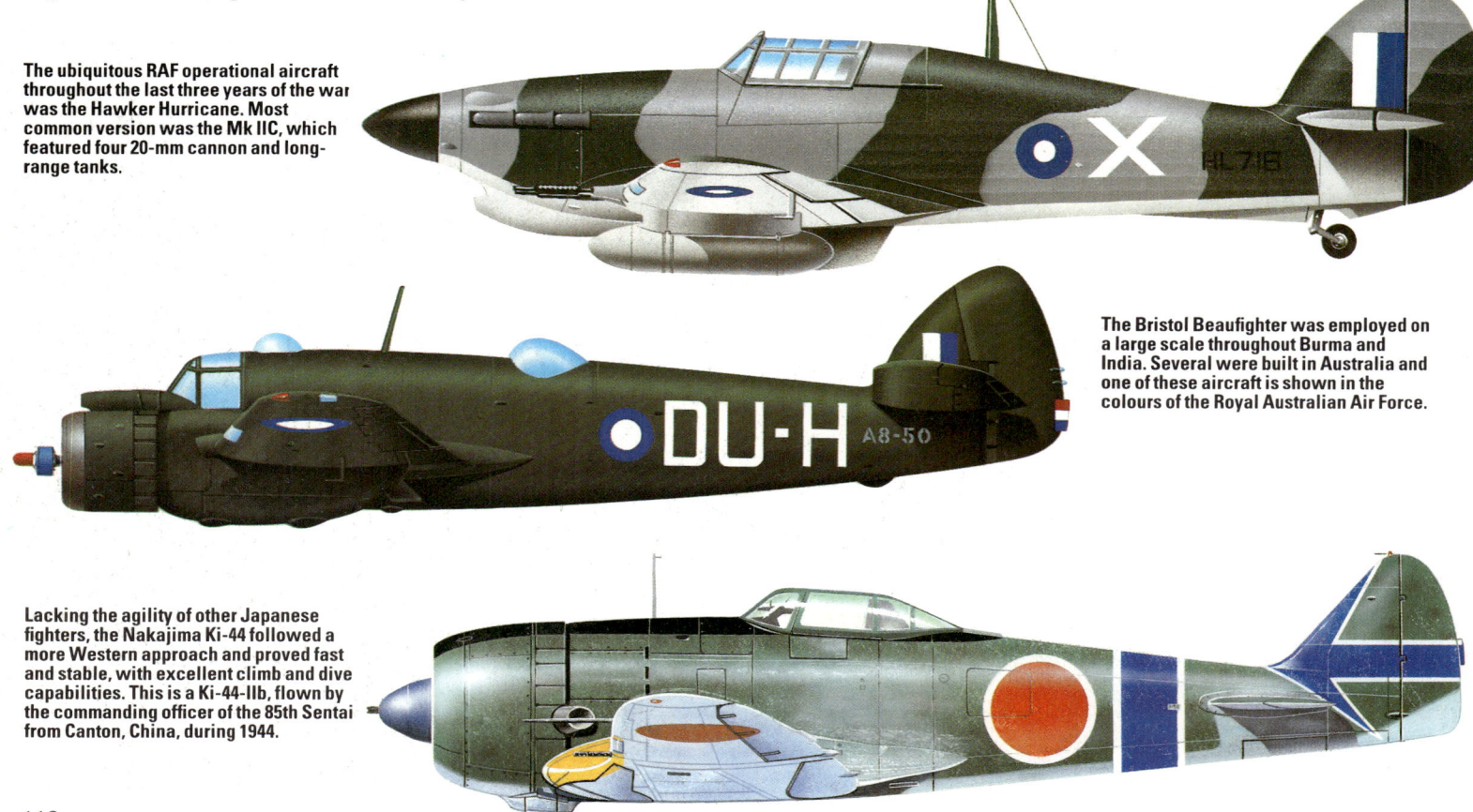

The ubiquitous RAF operational aircraft throughout the last three years of the war was the Hawker Hurricane. Most common version was the Mk IIC, which featured four 20-mm cannon and long-range tanks.

The Bristol Beaufighter was employed on a large scale throughout Burma and India. Several were built in Australia and one of these aircraft is shown in the colours of the Royal Australian Air Force.

Lacking the agility of other Japanese fighters, the Nakajima Ki-44 followed a more Western approach and proved fast and stable, with excellent climb and dive capabilities. This is a Ki-44-IIb, flown by the commanding officer of the 85th Sentai from Canton, China, during 1944.

The P-51A was the original USAAF version of the Mustang, with only four 0.5-in (12.7-mm) wing guns and underwing provision for bombs or other stores. This example, with a direction-finding loop antenna on the rear fuselage, was flown by the 1st Air Commando's CO, Colonel Philip Cochran, in Burma in 1944.

The Handley Page Halifax arrived later on in the Far East, but would have been used in large numbers had the war gone on longer. No. 1341 Flight was the first recipient in this theatre and operated this Mk IIIA as part of its equipment.

The RAF and USAAF combined in India to provide a massive airlift support to all the forces in the area. Both Douglas C-47 Dakotas (landing) and Curtiss C-46 Commandos (taxiing) were used on tactical support and, more importantly, on the 'Hump' route, flying supplies over the mountains into China.

The monsoon brought special problems to RAF squadrons, both in the air and in the shape of abysmal conditions at the primitive bases. Standard fighter in the closing months was the Spitfire Mk VIII, aircraft of No. 607 Squadron seen here.

Undoubtedly the nicest of all 'Spits' to fly or fight with, the Mk VIII got into the war late because of the prolonged output of the 'interim' Mk IX. This Mk VIII belonged to Wing Commander Glenn Cooper, CO of No. 457 Squadron RAAF based at Darwin and, from December 1944, at Morotai in the Moluccas.

A colourful Ki-43-IIb, the main production model of this nimble IJA fighter, in markings of the leader of the HQ Chutai, 77th Sentai, during operations in Burma in winter 1943-4. The unit was then escorting bombers flown sporadically against British installations in India.

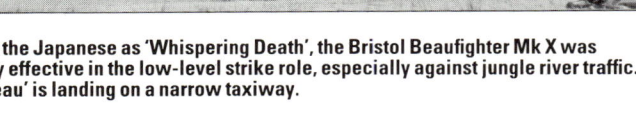

Known by the Japanese as 'Whispering Death', the Bristol Beaufighter Mk X was supremely effective in the low-level strike role, especially against jungle river traffic. Here a 'Beau' is landing on a narrow taxiway.

Seen with the aircraft it replaced, the Hawker Hurricane, these No. 5 Squadron Republic Thunderbolts taxi out at an airfield in Burma. Eight 0.5-in (12.7-mm) machine-guns and long-range tanks enabled them to provide fighter support for bombing raids far into Japanese territory.

THE ALEUTIANS AND KURILES 1941-45

Among the lesser-known war theatres in the war against Japan was the North Pacific, an ill-defined geographical area that embraced the chain of Aleutian Islands which extend westwards from Alaska, and the Kurile Islands that run north east from Japan towards the Kamchatka peninsula.

At the time of Pearl Harbor the air defence of Alaska and the northern Pacific was vested in the USAAC's 28th Composite Group which had recently been trained to operate in Arctic conditions, and had its headquarters at Elmendorf, Alaska. It possessed two pursuit squadrons, the 18th and 34th with P-40Bs, plus the 36th, 37th and 73rd Squadrons with a miscellany of aircraft, including a small number of bombers. However, it was beyond the scope of this group to perform long-range reconnaissance, and although the Japanese task force which attacked Pearl Harbor from the north had sailed from Hittokappu Bay in the Kuriles it was not detected by the American air force.

It was part of the Japanese overall war strategy to create an outer defence perimeter stretching from Kiska in the Aleutians southwards through Midway, and the capture of the islands of Attu, Adak and Kiska were intended to divert American attention from the major attack on Midway. This part of the plan did not succeed and the American commander, Rear Admiral Frank Fletcher, concentrated his naval forces (including all his available carriers) to win the great Battle of Midway; by so doing he was forced to leave the Aleutians exposed to attack from the air and sea. By June 1942 American air forces in the immediate area of the Aleutians comprised some 100 USAAF P-40s, 12 B-17s, 24 B-26s and 20 US Navy PBY flying-boats.

The Japanese launched a strike/invasion force which included the carrier *Junyo* and *Ryujo* with 30 Mitsubishi A6M fighters, 24 dive-bombers and 20 torpedo bombers. As carrier strikes were launched against Dutch Harbor in the eastern island of Unalaska, 2,500 troops would land and seize the three western islands. The air strike on Dutch Harbor was duly carried out on 3 June and achieved the destruction of three PBY flying-boats for the loss of four aircraft. One of these was an A6M which force landed on Akutan Island, the first such aircraft to fall into American hands in a repairable state; its recovery and subsequent testing by the USAAF was to prove of inestimable value to the Allies.

The following day the Japanese launched a further strike against Dutch Harbor, causing considerable damage to shore installations, losing five further aircraft. The B-17s located and attacked the Japanese carriers but failed to hit them, and lost one of their own number. Meanwhile the invasion of the western islands was postponed while Admiral Yamamoto sent the carrier *Zuiho* (and later the *Zuikaku*) north as reinforcements lest the Americans should now attempt to reinforce the Aleutians by diverting carriers. No such carriers could be spared and the Japanese duly went ashore on Kiska and Attu, to find them occupied by just 10 unarmed men. To have attempted to defend and sustain these islands at that stage of the Pacific war would have overtaxed the USA's air and naval forces beyond their strength. As it was the Japanese retained their toe-hold on a tiny part of the American continent (sic) for just one year.

Meanwhile the 28th Composite Group was joined in Alaska by the newly constituted 343rd Fighter Group whose 11th, 18th, 54th and 344th Fighter Squadrons were equipped with P-38s and P-40s, initially at Elmendorf and Fort Glenn in Alaska, and later at Adak. It was largely this move forward by these squadrons that prompted the Japanese to withdraw hurriedly from Kiska, only just before a joint US-Canadian assault force landed. Both this island and Attu were reoccupied by the Americans in July and August 1943, aircraft of the 28th and 343rd Groups moving into bases there almost immediately.

In particular the 28th Group's B-24s flew long range reconnaissance and bombing missions over the Kuriles, latterly 'trailing their coat' to attract Japanese fighters and thereby weaken their forces in the south, a strategy that earned the Group a Distinguished Unit Citation. The 343rd Group, which had been heavily engaged in strafing attacks on Kiska prior to the American re-occupation, flew no further combat missions after October 1943.

The presence of some 50 B-24s, which flew sporadic raids over the Kuriles during the last 16 months of the war, caused the Japanese to divert two *sentais* of Ki-45 'Nick' heavy fighters to the north of the Japanese homeland, a force of some 40 aircraft that would otherwise have been a useful element in the defence against the disastrous raids by the American B-29s.

This rare colour shot taken in the Aleutian Islands illustrates the principal long- and medium-range patrol aircraft used by the US Navy in 1942. In the foreground is a Consolidated PBY-5 Catalina, with a Lockheed PV-1 Ventura behind. These operated on patrol out over the Pacific Ocean.

Displaying distinctive 'tiger's head' cowling markings, this P-40E of the 11th Fighter Squadron, 343rd Fighter Group, was based at Fort Glenn, Alaska in late 1942. The unit saw action in the Aleutian Islands during 1943-5 with frequent detachments to Amchitka.

A welcome sight to any crew were the Consolidated PBY Catalinas operating throughout the Pacific on anti-submarine, anti-shipping and rescue missions. The Aleutians were a major base for these flying-boats.

IWO JIMA 1945

By January 1945 US fleet dispositions were being made for an assault on and capture of the island of Iwo Jima, just 760 miles (1223 km) south of Tokyo itself, and roughly the same distance north of Saipan. Principal covering naval force under Vice Admiral Mitscher was Task Force 58 (the Fast Carrier Force) comprising five task groups sailing a total of 11 fleet carriers and five light carriers plus 100 battleships, cruisers and destroyers. The assault force destined for Iwo Jima itself, a force of more than 1,000 ships, included Rear Admiral Durgin's Task Group 52.2 with 12 escort carriers, embarking a total of 226 F4F Wildcats and 138 TBM Avengers, some of whose pilots were trained in gunnery spotting.

The importance of Iwo Jima lay in its location almost directly in the path of B-29 Superfortress heavy bombers flying from Saipan on raids over Japan, enabling the Japanese observation posts to alert interceptor fighters both on Iwo Jima and in the homeland. Once captured the island could be used by the USAAF as a base for fighters to escort the B-29s.

To cover the approach by Task Group 52.2, Task Force 58 sailed to within 60 miles (97 km) of Tokyo and launched a number of strikes in the area of the Japanese capital, attracting some 100 enemy aircraft into the air and shooting down about 40. On the following day, 17 February, Mitscher carried out searches for Japanese shipping and, failing to find any, turned the great fleet south for Iwo Jima.

On 19 February the Fast Carrier Force struck the island with both big-gun bombardment from two of the eight battleships and strikes by Helldivers, Avengers and Corsairs. Meanwhile, evidently believing the US fleet still to be close to Tokyo, the home-based Japanese aircraft did not interfere with the invasion force off Iwo Jima until the evening of 19 February, by which time no fewer than 40,000 US Marines had gone ashore under cover of fighters from the carriers *Enterprise* and *Saratoga*. When the Japanese aircraft did arrive they failed to get through to the invasion transports and were heavily engaged by the naval fighters which, with gunfire from the fleet joining in, shot down a dozen of the attackers. On 21 February the *Saratoga* was detached from Task Force 58 with three destroyers to cover the amphibious forces, and at about 17.00 that afternoon was attacked by six Japanese aircraft manned, as it transpired, by

suicide pilots. Two were hit by the carrier's guns but struck the ship's side where their bombs exploded; the bomb from a third aircraft struck the forward end of the flight deck, a fourth also struck the flight deck and a fifth hit the starboard side of the ship; the sixth aircraft was shot down. Two hours later the *Saratoga* was again attacked, this time by five suicide aircraft, one of which struck the flight deck but bounced overboard, its bomb causing further damage. Yet the old carrier survived; with 123 dead or missing and 192 injured, and 42 of her aircraft destroyed or jettisoned, she was ordered to retire from the area, returning to active duty after only two months under repair.

Later in that same evening the escort-carrier *Bismarck Sea* was hit by two suicide aircraft, and soon afterwards became a raging inferno; her captain ordered her to be abandoned and just as the survivors got clear a torpedo hit blew the carrier apart. She went down with 218 of her crew, 19 Wildcats and 15 Avengers.

In an effort to prevent further attacks by suicide aircraft, the Fast Carrier Force was detached north towards Japan once more on 23 February, but poor weather curtailed the carrier strikes and few combats ensued; instead Mitscher turned his attention against Okinawa to the west but, apart from securing useful reconnaissance of the island, found little in the way of targets. Within a fortnight the capture of Iwo Jima had been completed, no further significant air attacks having troubled the land or naval forces, while aircraft from the escort-carrier *Anzio* had sunk two Japanese submarines on 26 and 27 February.

During the Iwo Jima operations the guns and pilots of the Fast Carrier Force and Task Group 52.2 were estimated to have destroyed 393 enemy aircraft in the air, and a further 200 on the ground. Task Force 58 had, however, lost 95 aircrew and 143 aircraft. Far more significant, a key base had been secured within fighter range of Japanese airspace, and without any irreplaceable losses among the vital American carrier task forces.

Following the capture of Iwo Jima, the US Army Air Force moved in to take over the airfield left behind by the Japanese. Curtiss C-46 transports moved in men and matériel while the first tactical aircraft to arrive was the North American P-51D Mustang. Capturing Iwo Jima allowed the fighters to escort bombers to Japan.

OKINAWA 1945

The invasion of Okinawa, an island which lies almost midway between Formosa and the southernmost point in the Japanese homeland, involved an assault and support force second only in size to that thrown against the Normandy coast in Europe 10 months previously, but far exceeded that great operation in the distances and logistics involved. If the American naval forces had been fortunate to escape serious losses in the Iwo Jima assault, the Japanese were about to react with the utmost force and ferocity at Okinawa. Once more the 5th Fleet Task Force 58 would provide the naval muscle in the assault and its protection.

Before the fleet sailed from Ulithi to the south west of the Marianas, the fleet carrier *Randolph* was hit by a suicide aircraft flying from Minami Iwo, and put out of action with 27 men killed. On 14 March 1945 Task Force 58 sailed north to attack airfields in Japan where the majority of suicide units were thought to be based; warned of the Americans' approach many of the Japanese aircraft were withdrawn out of range of the carrier aircraft. Fifty aircraft did take-off to attack the Task Force, however, but only caused superficial damage. Meanwhile the carrier aircraft had found and attacked Japanese warships in their home waters, causing some damage, particularly to the light carrier *Ryuho*. Pre-occupation with these attacks on the Japanese naval vessels allowed a number of Japanese bombing raids to take off, the aircraft making for Task Group 52.2, whose *Wasp* was hit and badly damaged; 102 men were killed and 269 injured, but her crew managed to extinguish the fires and within an hour she was recovering her aircraft. Almost simultaneously the fleet carrier *Franklin* suffered two bomb hits which started massive fires in her hangar and set off explosions that continued to rock the ship for hours. In an epic of sea rescue only 55 miles (90 km) from Japan, the carrier was saved, although 832 of her crew perished. In attacks over Japan the Task Force pilots claimed the destruction of 432 enemy aircraft during 18-19 March, and the following day the American ships withdrew as further attacks, now by suicide pilots, were aimed at the carriers, causing some damage to the *Enterprise*. Two days later the *Franklin, Enterprise* and *Wasp* left the combat area for repairs.

On 23 March the assault on Okinawa opened with air strikes by TF 58's carrier aircraft and a bombardment by 10 battleships, which lasted a week. The invasion was to be supported by the 13 remaining fast carriers, by six light carriers and by no fewer than 18 escort-carriers, between them embarking more than 1,000 aircraft. A further 10 escort carriers were loaded with replacement aircraft and the US Marine fighters which would be based on Okinawa.

When the landing assault on Okinawa was launched on 1 April the Japanese responded by ordering the opening of Operation 'Ten-Go', a concerted suicide assault by surface and air forces. No fewer than 4,500 aircraft would be involved in suicide and conventional attacks on the Americans. Of all the extraordinary elements of this operation was the sailing of the super-battleship *Yamato* (64,000 tons) from Japan on 6 April, it being intended to penetrate right to the Okinawa invasion beaches and destroy as many transport ships

as possible before being overwhelmed by American bombs and guns. Fortunately the huge ship was detected on her departure from home waters, shadowed by Mariner flying-boats and ultimately attacked by a strike of 280 carrier aircraft from Task Force 58, including 98 Avenger torpedo aircraft. Inevitably the *Yamato* succumbed, but only after being hit by 10 torpedoes and five bombs, taking to the bottom 2,498 of her crew; with her went an accompanying light cruiser with almost 450 men, hit by seven torpedoes and 12 bombs.

The reduction of Okinawa itself occupied three months and involved one of the greatest naval/air campaigns ever fought. The early part of April was marked by sustained conventional and suicide attack. On the same day that the *Yamato* was sunk the American carrier *Hancock* was badly damaged by a suicide aircraft; on 11 April the *Enterprise* (recently rejoined after repairs) was again hit, as was the carrier *Essex*. On 11 May the fast carrier *Bunker Hill* (Mitscher's flagship) was hit by bombs and suicide aircraft, but was saved after losing 389 of her crew.

When the Okinawa campaign was officially declared ended on 2 July 1945, it was calculated that the Japanese had launched some 34,000 sorties by 6,000 aircraft, many of them suicide attacks. US pilots and gunners claimed 2,336 shot down, losing a total of 790 aircraft. American naval losses amounted to 33 ships sunk (including 13 destroyers) and 119 severely damaged, including nine fleet carriers, one light carrier and three escort carriers, nine battleships and 37 destroyers. Obviously the Japanese suicide attacks posed a serious threat in all the operations of 1945, but such were the enormous reserves and resources now available to the Americans that the losses, grievous though they were, could be shrugged aside, and never in fact endangered the success of the campaign.

The load of Hellcats on board USS *Sangamon* were lucky to be missed by the *kamikaze* dive of this Kawasaki Ki-61.

Right and below: From the 4,100th F4U-1 and 2,602nd FG-1 zero-length launchers were added under the outer wings for eight 5-in (127-mm) rockets. This important extra firepower was added to many Corsairs already delivered, and was widely used during the attack on Okinawa.

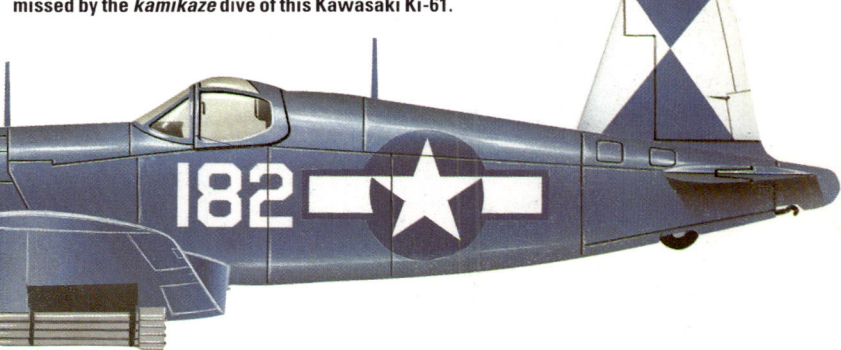

THE BOMBERS FINISH JAPAN

If controversy still rages about the effect of bombing on Germany in World War II, there is no questioning the effect of the American Superfortress campaign in the Far East. The USAAF's B-29s literally burned and blasted the heart out of Japan. The cost in dollars was prodigious, yet without the big bombers the cost in American lives, in an invasion of the Japanese homeland, would have been horrifying.

Plans to produce a 'super bomber' had been laid in January 1940, long before the USA entered the war, calling for a 400-mph (644-km/h) aircraft capable of delivering 2,000 lb (907 kg) of bombs over a range of 5,300 miles (8530 km). Initial development was leisurely by later standards, and only after Pearl Harbor was the utmost priority afforded to the new aircraft, and on 21 September 1942 the first XB-29 was flown. By that time orders for 1,664 production examples had been placed.

On 1 June 1943 the 58th (Very Heavy) Bombardment Wing was activated in the USA for initial service trials and B-29 crew training. The future pattern of the war in the Pacific had been decided and, with fortunes running in the Allies' favour in Europe, the big bomber was henceforth only considered in the context of the war against Japan. With four 2,200-hp (1641-kW) engines the service version, with a span of 141 ft 3 in (43.05 m), had a speed of 358 mph (576 km/h) at 25,000 ft (7620 m), a maximum range of 4,100 miles (6600 km) and a maximum bombload of 20,000 lb (9072 kg). In every respect it eclipsed all other in-service aeroplanes anywhere in the world; in an unparalleled feat of engineering enterprise a total of 3,970 of these very large bombers was built by Boeing, Bell and Martin in just three years.

The first B-29s to arrive in the Far East were those of the US 20th Air Force which landed at Kwanghan in China on 24 April 1944. No fewer than nine huge bases had been constructed by 700,000 Chinese labourers in India and China to accommodate the new bomber force. It flew its first raid on 5 June, attacking Bangkok in Thailand, and on 15 June 50 aircraft were sent against Yawata in Japan, the first American raid on the Japanese mainland since Doolittle's B-25 raid back in April 1942.

The great distances from the Indian and Chinese bases to Japan severely limited the bombloads of the B-29s, while bad weather rendered such raids of only limited effect. However, the capture of the Marianas in mid-1944 was followed by another marathon feat as American service engineers built five vast new bases (two on Guam, two on Tinian and one on Saipan), each capable of handling 180 B-29s. On 24 November 111 B-29s, led by General Emmett O'Donnell, took off to raid the Nakajima engine works at Musashi; however, only 24 bombers found their target.

On 20 January 1945 Major General Curtis E. LeMay assumed command of XXI Bomber Command, USAAF, and at once announced a radical change of bombing policy and tactics by the B-29s. Henceforth the bombers would attack with incendiary bombs by night, individually and from below 10,000 ft (3050 m), and with reduced defensive armament in the interests of increased bomb-loads.

The first such attack was made on 9/10 March by 302 aircraft against Yawata and Tokyo; for the loss of 14 aircraft over 16 sq miles (41.4 km^2) of the Japanese capital were reduced to ashes. In 10 days five raids on Tokyo, Yawata, Nagoya, Osaka and Kobe 29 sq miles (75.1 km^2) of Japan's main industrial centres were destroyed by 10,100 tons of bombs. On 25/26 May the bitterest-fought raid was flown when 464 B-29s, led by pathfinders, attacked Tokyo, destroying 18.9 sq miles (48.95 km^2) of the city for the loss of 26 aircraft. In these great fire raids (and others, including a raid on Yokohama where 85 per cent of the city was gutted) well over half a million Japanese civilians were killed and 13 million others rendered homeless.

Many historians have averred that continuation of the B-29 fire raids could by themselves have smashed the Japanese nation into surrender. It fell, however, to the delivery of two atomic bombs against Hiroshima and Nagasaki by the B-29s *Enola Gay* and *Bock's Car* of the USAAF's 509th Composite Group on 6 and 9 August 1945 respectively to convince the Japanese of the futility of continuing the war. Apart from special training and the strictest security, the delivery of these awesome weapons posed no major operational problems and the bombs duly detonated above the doomed Japanese cities, killing more than 100,000 persons instantly; thousands were to die the next day, and the next...

The B-29s' atomic bombs ended the war, quickly and surgically. As already suggested they may well have been superfluous having regard to the systematic destruction being achieved by the 'conventional' fire raids on Japanese cities and industry. Apart from almost certainly avoiding even greater carnage and destruction that would have accompanied such raids, the demonstration of those diabolical weapons was the convincing prelude to the post-war policy of 'peace by deterrent', and the deterrent to world war was to be the threat of nuclear weapons. Had Hiroshima and Nagasaki not been sacrificed someone, somewhere, would have attempted a more horrifying demonstration.

Saipan in the Marianas became the home of B-29s in late 1944. In this picture 145 aircraft are waiting to be loaded with food and clothes for drops to PoW camps in Japan. These aerial armadas were remembered some 30 years later when the Marianas played host to hundreds of B-52s during the Vietnam war.

Boeing B-29s pass Mount Fujiyama, the sacred Japanese mountain, on their way to bomb targets. This symbolized the state of the air war in 1945 as the Americans had such air superiority at this stage, despite large-scale attempts by the Japanese to rescue the situation.

Left: The Boeing B-29 Superfortress was a revolutionary design, introducing such high wing loading that many people were surprised that it could fly so well.

This B-29A is typical of many which took part in the raids on Japan. Bombing Through Overcast (BTO) radar enabled the large formations to find their target accurately in all weather and this they unerringly did, day after day, until the two atomic bombs eventually finished Japan off.

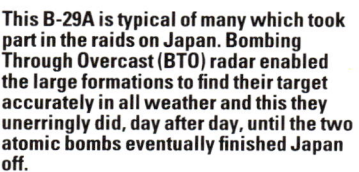

Japan threw everything at its disposal into the final defence of the mainland. The principal targets were the bomber streams that were bringing Japan to her knees and all available fighters were pressed into attacking these aircraft. This Kawasaki Ki-61 is typical of these defenders, this particular example flying in defence of Tokyo.

The conventional and incendiary raids on the metropolitan areas of Tokyo and Yokohama were considerably more devastating than the two atomic bombs and casualties were much higher. These B-29s dropping incendiaries illustrate the weight of bombs dropped during the last days of the war.

While operating from the islands in the Pacific, fighters had to be escorted to Japan by a bomber with electronic navigation equipment. This B-29 leads a unit of North American P-51 Mustangs to the Tokyo area, where the fighters can then protect the bombers attacking the capital.

POST-WAR EUROPE 1945-47

Amidst the destruction and desolation of a ravaged continent, national economic priorities rated the sustaining of armed forces very low as peace dawned over Europe in 1945. As fighting men returned home, thousands of aircraft were scrapped to provide raw materials for the demands of domestic reconstruction. The RAF emerged as the most powerful and modern air force on the continent, a new generation of combat aeroplanes being on the point of entering service when the war ended. The Meteor jet fighter, which had seen limited action in the last nine months of the war, rapidly became established as the RAF's main interceptor for 10 years, setting up world speed records in 1945 and 1946 at more than 600 mph (966 km/h). The little Vampire single-jet fighter first joined No. 247 Squadron in 1946 and served alongside the Meteor well into the 1950s, while the Mosquito night-fighters soldiered on for a number of years. A single-seat development of the Mosquito, the superb Hornet, would have been built in large numbers but for the end of the war, and was then severely curtailed in the light of reduced service demands, equipping only four home-based squadrons. In the field of heavy bombers the Lincoln, of which 800 had been ordered by VJ-Day and which was intended for service in the Far East, gradually replaced the Lancaster and eventually equipped 20 Bomber Command squadrons, first joining No. 57 Squadron before the end of 1945. In the maritime reconnaissance category the Short Seaford flying-boat would have replaced the Sunderland but, in the pervading austerity, only a small number was built and joined No. 201 Squadron only, the Sunderland being retained until finally replaced by land-based maritime reconnaissance bombers.

In short, the RAF suffered massive reduction in strength, its establishment being roughly divided between responsibilities at home, in the Middle and Far East, and in Germany. Squadrons which had been created within the RAF during the war, staffed by 'free personnel' from enemy-occupied countries, now returned home to provide the nuclei of new air forces. France whose own air forces, the Armée de l'Air and Aéronavale, had started to re-establish autonomy as long ago as 1943 and possessed large numbers of British, American, Soviet and German aircraft in service, including Spitfires, Mosquitoes, Dakotas, Marauders, Mustangs, Halifaxes, Junkers Ju 52/3ms and Ju 88s, to which were soon added Vampires ordered from Britain. Indeed there were in service no fewer than 88 different types, an astonishing variety that posed almost impossible problems of maintenance.

The Belgian air force, then termed the Force Aérienne Belge, was recreated on 1 October 1946 around Nos 349 and 350 Squadrons, which ceased to exist in the RAF and re-emerged at home with Spitfires and later Mosquitoes. In the Netherlands progress was much slower, the policy being to resume with flying training (with Tiger Moths, Ansons and Oxfords) and to create an entirely new air force equipped with Spitfires in 1947 and Meteors in 1948. Norway's air force also delayed full autonomy until 1947 negotiating purchase of 50 Spitfires, 23 Mosquitoes, 10 Catalinas, 20 Oxfords and 10 Ansons all for £720,000.

Italy, whose Aeronautica Militare Italiana, had fought alongside the Allies in the last two years of the war, possessed an assortment of British, American and indigenous aircraft in 1945, but then confined its activities largely to training and transportation until the 1947 treaty permitted a strength of 200 fighters and reconnaissance aircraft.

Although to a limited extent staffed by ex-RAF personnel, the post-war Polish and Czech air forces were equipped mainly with Soviet aircraft and, although the 'Iron Curtain' had yet to formalize the political alignments of West and East Europe, these countries were already embraced within the communist bloc.

The Soviet Union itself had attained massive momentum in the modernization of its armed forces during the last two years of the war and sustained this impetus into the years of 'peace', benefiting greatly from the sequestration of German technology. At VE-Day the Soviet air forces possessed some 17,500 aircraft, of which about one-third could be regarded as fairly modern. However, it was not until April 1946 that the first truly indigenous Soviet jet fighters intended for service, the Yak-15 and MiG-9, were first flown. Thereafter, with expatriate German assistance, as well as ill-advised export of Rolls-Royce Derwent and Nene turbojets, sanctioned by the socialist government of the UK, technological progress was swift.

With a contribution of some 350 P-47s, P-51s, B-25s, B-17s, B-24s and C-47s of a rapidly diminishing USAAF left in Europe, the Western nations seemed well matched on paper for any threat posed by the emerging communist bloc. Such strength however that existed among the heterogeneous air forces was belied by a lack of command cohesion, however, and such a cohesion would result only from the military unification afforded by the creation of NATO.

Following the end of hostilities, most aircraft continued in service for a few months and several types were developed pending the delivery of new jet fighters. The Spitfire received a facelift in the form of the Mk 20 series. Here, two Mk 22s and one Mk 21 are flying from Supermarine's test airfield at High Post.

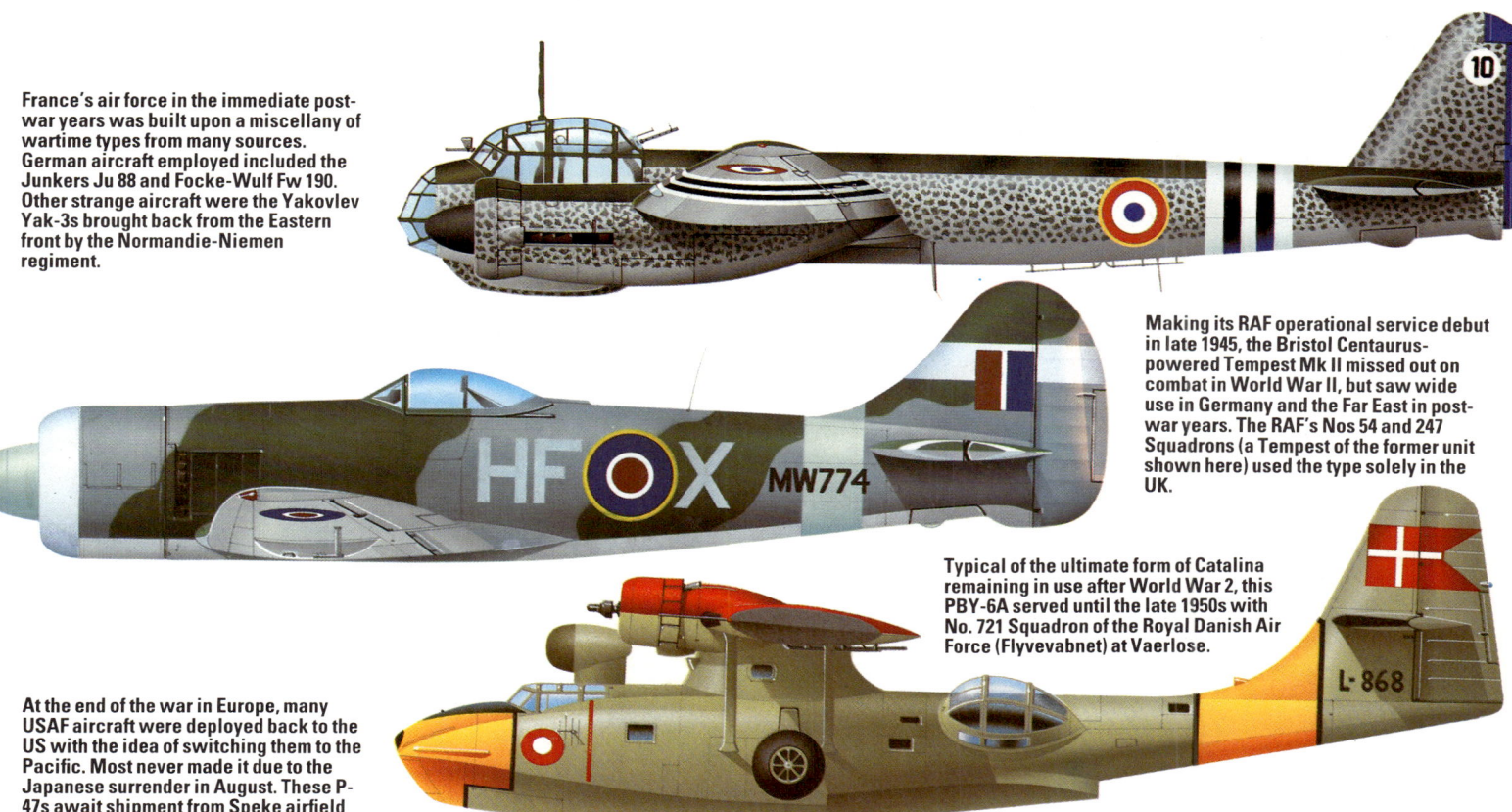

France's air force in the immediate post-war years was built upon a miscellany of wartime types from many sources. German aircraft employed included the Junkers Ju 88 and Focke-Wulf Fw 190. Other strange aircraft were the Yakovlev Yak-3s brought back from the Eastern front by the Normandie-Niemen regiment.

Making its RAF operational service debut in late 1945, the Bristol Centaurus-powered Tempest Mk II missed out on combat in World War II, but saw wide use in Germany and the Far East in post-war years. The RAF's Nos 54 and 247 Squadrons (a Tempest of the former unit shown here) used the type solely in the UK.

Typical of the ultimate form of Catalina remaining in use after World War 2, this PBY-6A served until the late 1950s with No. 721 Squadron of the Royal Danish Air Force (Flyvevabnet) at Vaerlose.

At the end of the war in Europe, many USAF aircraft were deployed back to the US with the idea of switching them to the Pacific. Most never made it due to the Japanese surrender in August. These P-47s await shipment from Speke airfield near Liverpool.

West Raynham was typical of many RAF airfields where both wartime and post-war aircraft rubbed shoulders. Visible are the Tempest, Spitfire, Meteor, Mosquito, Hornet and Firefly.

Soviet equipment formed the basis of many Eastern European countries. This Tupolev Tu-2 was a training variant produced with engines of less power than the full tactical versions.

Hungary used its Ilyushin Il-10s until the mid 1950s. Piston-engined types hung around much longer in Eastern bloc air forces than in Western air arms.

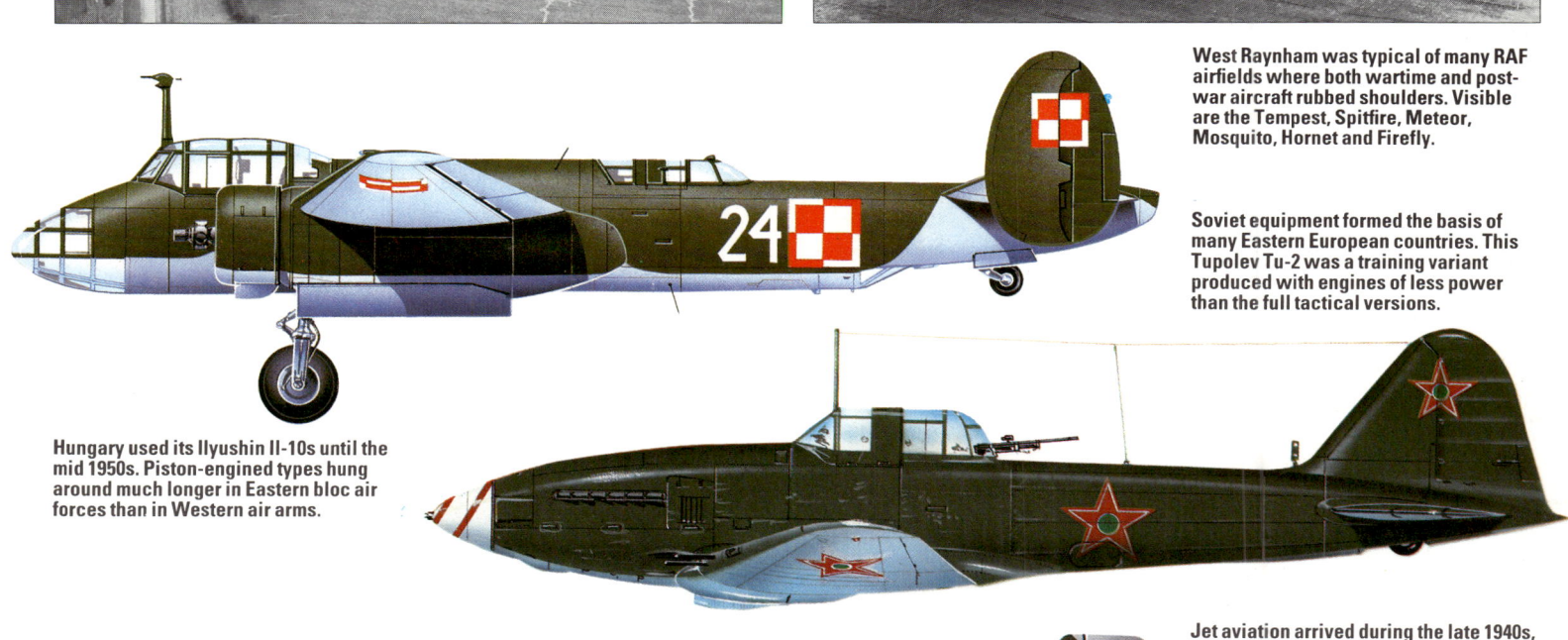

Jet aviation arrived during the late 1940s, and many RAF squadrons began re-equipment with the de Havilland Vampire. This aircraft belonged to No. 247 Squadron at Odiham.

DAWN OF THE COLD WAR 1948-55

Reflecting the bitterness and hatred by the wartime Allies towards Nazi Germany, World War II left the German nation geographically and politically divided along a roughly north-south border, western Germany being occupied by the forces of the UK, France and the United States, and eastern Germany by those of the Soviet Union. The devastated capital, Berlin, although lying to the east of this border, was also partitioned between the occupying forces, traffic from the city to the west following agreed roads, railways, rivers and air lanes.

It was not long, however, before friction occurred between the Soviet authorities and the West over the administration of the Berlin sectors; on 20 March 1948 Marshal Sokolovsky, Soviet military governor in Berlin, walked out of the Allied Control Council complaining that a recent Allied conference on Germany had been held without reference to the Soviet Union. In the following month all rail passenger traffic between Berlin and West Germany was suspended, and on 5 April a Soviet fighter collided with a British Viking airliner in an agreed commercial air corridor, killing 15 people. On 20 April the Soviets stopped barge traffic on the Elbe, and on 24 June suspended all supplies of food to Berlin by road, rail and river. Two days later the USAF, using C-47s, inaugurated an airlift from West Germany into Tempelhof Airport, Berlin, carrying 80 tons of food to the capital in the first day. RAF Transport Command joined the airlift on 28 June.

During the following six months the Berlin Airlift was steadily increased, the airports of the capital (Tempelhof in the American sector, and Gatow in the British) being joined by Tegel in the French sector on 15 November. On 23 July the US Military Air Transport Service established an Air Lift Task Force of eight squadrons of 72 C-54 Skymasters, and a week later British commercial aircraft, comprising Tudors, Lancastrians, Yorks and Haltons, joined the Airlift. On 15 October the RAF and USAF efforts were merged to form a Combined Air Lift Task Force, and by the end of November transport aircraft of the South African Air Force and Royal New Zealand Air Force were also participating.

On 9 May 1949 General Chuikov, the Soviet military governor who had succeeded Sokolovsky, announced that the Berlin blockade would be lifted at midnight on 11/12 May. However, to assist in building up fuel and food stocks for the winter, the airlift continued until October. In the first year of the Berlin Airlift a total of two million tons of coal, liquid fuel and food was transported to the city in a fleet of aircraft that never simultaneously numbered more than 300 in number.

The constant sabre-rattling (if nothing worse) by the Soviet Union, and the obvious fragility of peace in a political atmosphere charged with tension as East and West sought to extend their ideologies within their respective spheres of influence, could have but one inevitable result: the creation of mutual defence alliances. Already a Western European Union, following the Brussels Treaty of March 1948, had been created between the UK, France, Belgium, the Netherlands and Luxembourg, to provide mutual assistance in the event of attack, but following the ravages of war in Europe there existed neither the finance nor industry to create the military might necessary to withstand an attack by the Soviet Union.

Accordingly, following the Vandenburg resolution of May 1948, the United States expressed its readiness to strengthen the Western European Union with the creation of a new organization by the signature of the North Atlantic Treaty on 4 April 1949. The original signatories were Belgium, Canada, Denmark, France, Iceland, Italy, Luxembourg, the Netherlands, Norway, Portugal, the United Kingdom and the United States. NATO air forces were originally almost exclusively equipped with British and American aircraft, but in recent years aircraft of French, Italian and German manufacture have increasingly contributed.

Although the creation of NATO was patently a mutual defensive structure, neither motivated nor equipped to perform first-strike war operations, its existence was inevitably seen by the Soviet Union as a potentially subversive threat to the communist bloc whose member nations from time to time displayed open hostility to Soviet constrictive influence. Following Stalin's death in 1953, and West Germany's inclusion in NATO in 1954, Moscow decided to put the USSR and its satellite countries on a more contractual basis, and on 14 May 1955 the Eastern European Mutual Assistance Treaty (the so-called Warsaw Pact) was signed by Albania, Bulgaria, Czechoslovakia, East Germany, Hungary, Poland, Romania and the Soviet Union.

In reality, although both NATO and 'Warpac' were established to provide mutual defence between the nations of Eastern and Western Europe, the United States and the Soviet Union have come to regard continental Europe as the 'no man's land' of a future war, a convenient buffer zone capable of sustaining no more than a war of conventional (non-nuclear) weapons. As such the viability of NATO (and, by implication, Warpac) has been increasingly questioned in recent years, although ostensibly justified by the moderating influence capable of being imposed upon the superpowers.

Douglas C-54 Skymasters stand ready for yet another sortie to carry food and essential supplies to help relieve besieged Berliners. But more than this, they symbolized the West's – and especially the USA's – resolve to stand firm against the prospect of Soviet aggression in Europe.

Runway maintenance crew watch as two Handley Page Hastings taxi in with another load for Berlin.

France began to receive modern aircraft with the arrival of the Republic F-84 Thunderjet. These represented a dramatic upgrading of capabilities as they replaced Spitfires and Thunderbolts.

Representative of the enormous aid from the US to NATO countries in the 1950s were the Republic RF-84F Thunderflashes supplied to Belgium. These aircraft were used for many years.

Many civilian aircraft were impressed into service for the Berlin run. This is an Avro Lancaster 'civilianized' by the deletion of gun turrets.

Based around the VK-1 engine which had been copied from the British Rolls-Royce Nene turbojet supplied (controversially) to the Soviet Union after the war, the Ilyushin Il-28 served as the primary bomber of the Eastern European nations. Czechoslovakia was one of the major operators of the type.

Types flown after the war by non-Soviet Warsaw Pact countries included this Petlyakov Pe-2 of the Polish air force; three Tu-2s fly over a Pe-2UT trainer.

Left: Gloster Meteor F.Mk 4 of the Netherlands air force. The Netherlands received a mix of British-built and Fokker licence-built aircraft under MDAP arrangements.

In an attempt to replace the elderly Lavochkin La-7s and Yakovlev Yak-9s in service with the Eastern European air arms after the war, the Soviet Union supplied the first-generation jet fighter, the Yakovlev Yak-23, while its own air force was flying the very advanced Mikoyan-Gurevich MiG-15.

FRENCH INDO-CHINA 1945-54

The return of French government to Indo-China after the ending of Japanese occupation during World War II was followed inevitably by increasing tension created by the Viet Minh who attempted but failed to wrest control of Hanoi and other cities from the French. However, although the French took the initiative, they never managed to crush the Vietnamese partisans, whose strength steadly increased.

As early as August 1945 the French government had ordered the embarkation of Armée de l'Air units for the Far East and, after the blocking by the USA of use of P-47 Thunderbolts in South East Asia, France acquired from the UK a number of Spitfire Mk IXs which arrived at Saigon to join some Spitfire Mk VIIIs (transferred after the departure of No. 273 Squadron RAF from Tan Son Nhut in January 1946) and a few Nakajima Ki-43 'Oscar' fighters seized from the Japanese after the Pacific war.

The French air forces in Indo-China were employed exclusively in the ground supply and support roles as the Viet Minh possessed no combat aircraft. On the other hand, supplied increasingly and almost exclusively by communist China in the north, the guerrillas became highly proficient in the use of light flak guns of 20-, 23- and 37-mm calibres, weapons that were to take a mounting toll of French aircraft.

The Armée de L'Air in Indo-China was initially organized into two tactical groupes, TFIN in Tonkin and northern Amman, and TFIS in Cochin-China and southern Amman. In 1950 these were re-deployed as three groupes, GATAC North for Tonkin, GATAC Central for Amman, and GATAC South for Cochin-China. During the first half of 1947 the French flew a number of Mosquito Mk VI fighter-bombers in the theatre but, although they were able to reach further over guerrilla-held territory, they were plagued by poor serviceability, their wooden construction proving quite unsuitable for prolonged service in the hot, humid conditions.

As the nature of the anti-guerrilla operations underwent change during 1948-9, and the Viet Minh tended to concentrate their forces closer to the distant borders with China, the French made renewed efforts to persuade the Americans to permit the use of US aircraft, at just the moment when the communists were gaining spectacular victories over the Western-aligned Chinese nationalists. As a result of these overtures the French were able to send about 50 Bell F-63C Kingcobras to Indo-China, aircraft which proved well suited to the conditions and demands of the campaign and, indeed, were superior to the relatively short-range Spitfires. These two aircraft types were in turn joined and eventually replaced by Grumman F8F Bearcats which, although still possessing a disappointing radius of action, were fast and capable of delivering a wide range of ground-support weapons.

Before 1951 the French did not employ bombers as such (other than fighter-bombers with relatively modest loads), simply because the dispersal of the guerrilla forces rendered them almost immune to set-piece bombing. However during November that year, despite pre-occupation with the war in Korea, the USA supplied sufficient B-26 Invaders to equip two groupes, and these aircraft undertook vital and successful bombing and reconnaissance work right up to

the end of the campaign.

Air transport played a vital, albeit inconspicuous part in the French operations, the World War II Junkers Ju 52/3m (dubbed the Toucan in the Armée de l'Air) and the C-47 later being joined by a few Bristol Type 170 Freighters and Fairchild C-119s, whose operations were limited to the small number of well-paved air bases. For the evacuation of casualties and movement of prisoners in the forward areas, the French possessd 17 Hiller UH-12 and H-23 light helicopters and 25 Westland-Sikorsky S-51 and S-55 medium helicopters.

Throughout the war in Indo-China French naval aircraft were active, some ex-US Navy PBY Catalinas and Japanese Aichi E13A1s being joined by British Sea Otters and American SBD-5 Dauntless aircraft in 1947. After the lifting of the embargo on the use of American aircraft Hellcats and Helldivers arrived in Far Eastern waters aboard the carrier *Arromanches* in time for the final tragic events at Dien Bien Phu.

This last chapter followed a change in French tactics by Général Henri Navarre based on the concentration of well-supplied 'honeypot' garrisons within Viet Minh-dominated territory in the north, intended to draw the guerrilla forces into open battle. After a number of limited successes by these garrisons, the forces at Dien Bien Phu were totally surrounded by considerable communist formations, and although constantly reinforced, supported and supplied from the air the French garrison was finally overrun in May 1954. This crushing psychological blow, coming as it did less than 10 years after France had emerged battered from World War II, lent impetus to peace negotiations which were then about to open in Geneva. A ceasefire, which in fact acknowledged defeat of the French throughout Indo-China, was agreed on 20 July that year.

Until the arrival of the Douglas C-47, air transport assets rested on the Junkers Ju 52, licence-built in France as the Amiot AAC.1 Toucan. Paradrops were a speciality of this aircraft.

In southern Indo-China the French Armée de l'Air obtained several Spitfires from British forces, and also gained permission to use some Nakajima Ki-43-11-Kai 'Oscar' fighters seized from the Japanese. This aircraft was based at Phnom Penh, Cambodia, during the late 1940s.

Also aboard the *Arromanches* was Flotille 1F, Aéronavale, with Grumman F6F-5 Hellcats. Though the Bearcat got most of the publicity in Indo-China, the proven and effective Hellcat delivered from US Navy surplus stores played an important part through the war, operating from both land and carrier bases.

Designed primarily as an interceptor fighter, the Grumman F8F Bearcat was used widely in Indo-China for ground attack, a role in which French pilots found the aircraft with inadequate ventilation and limited downward view.

Curtiss SB2C-5 Helldiver of Flotille 3F, Aéronavale, based aboard the carrier *Arromanches* for operations in Indo-China during 1954. Though obsolescent with the US Navy, Helldivers were acquired by the Aéronavale for dive-bombing attacks in the undefended skies of Indo-China, and these carried a useful war load.

A pair of Supermarine Spitfire Mk IXs, carrying bombs and looking distinctly war-weary, patrol over Indo-China. They equipped GC I/4 'Dauphine' which arrived with its sister-unit II/4 'La Fayette' during September 1947.

The carrier *Arromanches* was used extensively throughout the campaign, its aircraft providing useful air support for ground forces. Here it carries Grumman F6F Hellcats and Curtiss SB2C Helldivers.

One of the most effective aircraft used by the French was the Vought Corsair. This F4U-7 of Flotille 12 was one of the last Corsairs built when production ended in 1953.

OPERATION 'FIREDOG' 1948-60

There had been an anti-British guerrilla movement in Malaya before the Japanese occupation of 1942, but the British administration then supported this Chinese-led organization as the only element able to harass and spy on the mutual enemy, Japan. Thus, at the end of the war the British found themselves with a depleted infrastructure of their own but facing a well organized and equipped guerrilla force. Under pressure, but otherwise reluctant to grant independence, the British attempted to shepherd the diverse sultanates and states into a federation under the British flag. The communist-inspired guerrillas now took on the mantle of freedom fighters and unified all independence seeking groups behind them against the UK. So started the campaign, generally known as the Malayan Emergency, which lasted until 1962. The military operation in Malaya was known as Operation 'Firedog'.

When the state of emergency was declared in 1948, the RAF deployed a total of eight squadrons of Spitfires, Mosquitoes, Beaufighters and Dakotas at Changi, Seletar and Tengah on Singapore Island, and at Kuala Lumpur in the north. The tropical climate played havoc with the wooden Mosquitoes and these aircraft had quickly to be replaced along with the Spitfires, the more recently deployed Tempests which could not carry sufficient stores, and the Beaufighter which was becoming obsolete. In came the Bristol Brigand flown by No. 45 Squadron, and although these could put up impressive displays of attacks with guns, bombs and rockets, it was soon discovered that such techniques had little effect on the loose bands of guerrillas operating 'somewhere' under the triple-canopy rain forest below. Only when Lincolns were deployed from the UK to carry out area bombing was it that an impression began to be made. Such deployments were sporadic as these bombers could not be easily spared from their other duties, but the Royal Australian Air Force contributed Lincolns on a more permanent basis from 1950 onwards. The Brigands ran into serviceability and safety problems and were supplanted by de Havilland Hornets, which were very manoeuvrable and could attack with precision in conditions of bad weather and tricky terrain.

By 1953, jet aircraft began to arrive in the form of Vampires and Meteors and, a little later, Venoms and Canberras. Once again, these were found to be unsuitable with poor serviceability, range and payload, plus an inherent inability to operate slowly at low level. The tangible results of all this offensive air support was minimal, but it probably helped by keeping the insurgents under pressure and on the move.

Of greater importance was the transport effort. Malaya was devoid of good roads and it was a very slow business for the ground troops to make headway through the jungle and plantations. Resupply from the air was often a necessity, and Dakotas, Valettas and later Hastings paradropped essential supplies to the forces in the field while Yorks ferried material around the peninsula. Paratrooping itself was not often employed since the dropping zones were seldom hospitable, but Malaya saw the world's first extensive use of helicopters and these soon transformed the tactics of the security forces.

Introduced in 1950, the Sikorsky S-51 Dragonfly began to take on casualty evacuation duties, which improved both efficiency and morale. By the mid-1950s, Bristol Sycamores and Westland Whirlwinds arrived to undertake assault as well as evacuation sorties. Able to insert up to nine troops into remote areas, they introduced mobility into an otherwise tough, debilitating and painfully slow-moving action. Alongside the helicopters, Auster lightplanes were used to support the observation posts and jungle forts essential to maintaining local security. The Auster AOP.Mk 6 and the later AOP.Mk 9 were able to land and take off in 150 m (165 yards) and proved very useful. Later came the tough Scottish Aviation Pioneer which could carry four passengers instead of the Auster's one and could operate out of airstrips only half the length of those required by the Auster.

Perhaps the most essential air task of all fell to a single squadron which performed superbly throughout 'Firedog'. There was hardly any good mapping of Malaya at the start of the operation and it was impossible to fight the war without this and other vital information. No. 81 Squadron was tasked with photographic reconnaissance of the entire peninsula. Flying a variety of aircraft (Spitfire PR.Mk 19, Mosquito PR.Mk 34, Meteor PR.Mk 10, Pembroke C(PR).Mk 1 and Canberra PR.Mk 7) the squadron unstintingly persevered in its mission and provided vital information for both air strikes and ground operations. It also incidentally flew the last operational sorties of the RAF's Spitfire and Mosquito.

The UK eventually moved towards the grant of independence, fostering the indigenous Malays as the new ruling element. The conflict then took on a racial dimension with the Chinese isolated against the now unified Malays and British. 'Divide and rule' succeeded and the insurgents fought a losing battle. 'Firedog' was always a war fought on the ground, but air support in the offensive, transport and reconnaissance roles played a valuable and, maybe, a vital part in the success of the operation.

In 1955 English Electric Canberras were assigned to replace the Lincolns, but proved a poor substitute. They carried half the bomb load, their cruising speed was too high, and their bombing height needed unavailable navigation aids.

Helicopters introduced into Malaya in 1953 immediately transformed the war. They made possible unannounced strikes against terrorist positions, and here an S-51 Dragonfly of No. 194 Squadron evacuates an injured soldier out of the jungle.

The old and new side-by-side in Malaya: a No. 60 Squadron Vampire is parked alongside a No. 81 Squadron Mosquito PR.Mk 34. No. 81 Squadron flew the last combat sortie of RAF Mosquitoes, and claimed the same distinction for the Supermarine Spitfire. Both types were employed on reconnaissance duties.

Bristol Brigand B.Mk 1 of No. 84 Squadron. The Brigand replaced the Beaufighter in Malaya in 1949-50, serving with both Nos 45 and 84 squadrons. The Brigand was ideal for pinpoint attack, but the jungles of Malaya did not provide such clearly defined permanent targets and the Brigand was not cost-effective.

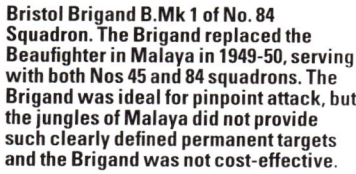

Supermarine Spitfire PR.Mk 19, operated by No. 81 Squadron, RAF at Seletar, Singapore, circa 1950. The Malayan emergency provided the last operational theatre for the Spitfire, from where it bowed out after being engaged in photographing vast expanses of jungle for signs of terrorist activity.

De Havilland Hornet F.Mk 3 of No. 33 Squadron, RAF, based at Tengah but detached to Butterworth in the early 1950s. Carrying underwing rockets, the squadron's aircraft made numerous sorties against terrorists, but such was the nature of the jungle cover that they achieved only minimal results.

This de Havilland Venom FB.Mk 4 of No. 60 Squadron was based at Tengah between May 1955 and October 1959. Unfortunately, the Venom was totally unsuited to that theatre, being too fast, too delicate and too complicated. It lacked essential range and weapons load and had very low serviceability.

British ground forces had made several forts deep in the jungle, and these could only effectively and safely be supplied from the air. For this job the tough Scottish Aviation (Prestwick) Pioneer was to prove ideal.

RAF and RAAF Lincolns (aircraft of No. 1 Squadron RAAF illustrated) proved most effective in the Malayan campaign. Flying in a close 'vic' formation of five aircraft, they could deliver a high concentration of bombs by day or night.

ISRAEL'S BIRTH PANGS 1948-49

Following the termination on 15 May 1948 of the UK's mandate in Palestine, it was almost inevitable that open strife would erupt between Jew and Arab, a situation that had been aggravated by Jewish opposition to a British plan for the partition of the country and by the support by neighbouring Arab states for ever-growing numbers of Palestinian 'refugees' whose means of livelihood and land fell into Jewish hands. Faced with the constant threat by these neighbours (in particular Egypt, but also Iraq and Jordan) to the creation of a Jewish state, the Zionists had in November 1947 already started to assemble an air arm, Shin Aleph, of the Jewish 'underground' army, Haganah, the operations of this small citizens' air force, with its collection of light aircraft, being initially confined to ground support during the civil war between the Palestinian Arabs and the Jewish immigrants. Towards the end of April 1948 the Haganah took control by force of the Arab town of Jaffa, despite the efforts of two RAF Spitfire squadrons, still based in Palestine.

On 15 May the state of Israel came into being, the remaining RAF units being given orders to start dispersing to Habbaniyah in Iraq or to the Suez Canal Zone. However, the Royal Egyptian air force (REAF) possessed an expeditionary force based at El Arish in Sinai to support the Palestinians, a force that comprised a squadron of Spitfire Mk 9s, five C-47s (adapted as bombers) and a flight of Westland Lysanders. The moment the state of Israel was proclaimed it became the aim of the REAF to prevent the creation of an effective Israeli air force. Believing the airfield at Ramat David to be in hostile hands, the Egyptian pilots carried out a strafing attack, only to find that RAF squadrons based there had not yet left. Four RAF Spitfires promptly took off and shot down two of the attackers. Elsewhere better success attended the REAF raids and about half the Israeli strength of 50-odd and obsolete aircraft were put out of action at Sde Dov and elsewhere. On 18 May the C-47 bombers hit the Israeli fuel depot at Tel Aviv.

Meanwhile frantic efforts were being made by Israel in Europe to obtain more effective combat aircraft, in the knowledge that the UK was already established as a major arms supplier to the Arab states. In the face of almost complete air superiority by the REAF, it was essential first to acquire interceptor fighters to buy time in which to create an organized air force. The first such aircraft, Avia S.199s (a Junkers Jumo-powered development of the Messerschmitt Bf 109G) arrived from Czechoslovakia on 20 May and were first in action nine days later. On 31 May the Israeli air force (Heyl Ha'Avir) was officially established. On 3 June the S.199s forced down two Egyptian C-47s.

While the Israelis were gaining these minor successes in the south, they were suffering setbacks in the north and east where Syrian and Iraqi forces, modestly supported by their tiny air forces, launched attacks at Jenin, Degania and Semakh. No one welcomed the UN-instigated truce between 11 June and 9 July more than the Israelis, who put the respite to good use as aircraft from Europe and elsewhere began flooding in, together with Mahal volunteers.

In the second phase of fighting, which persisted from 9 July only until 18 July, Israel took the initiative, bombing Lydda and Ramleh (both occupied by Palestinian forces) on the first day. On 14 July three Israeli B-17 Fortresses bombed Cairo in the stated retaliation for an attack on Old Jerusalem; however, the B-17s had been loaded with bombs in Czechoslovakia, where they had flown for the Cairo raid before the alleged attack on Jerusalem.

The second truce, which remained intact until 15 October, enabled Israel greatly to strengthen its air force, so that when fighting resumed it possessed five Beaufighters, three B-17s, five C-47s, six C-46s, 20 S.199s, four F-51 Mustangs, six Norduyn Norsemans, three Lockheed Constellations, two Hudsons and one Mosquito. To these would soon be added nearly 50 ex-Czech air force Spitfire Mk 9s and Mk 16s.

While this considerable Israeli build-up was taking place, the Syrian and Iraqi governments began to voice reluctance to continue involvement in the war, so enabling Israel to bring the great majority of its forces to bear on the Egyptian front. By December, despite being reinforced by a second Spitfire squadron at El Arish, the strength of the REAF's force in eastern Sinai had dropped so drastically that it faced odds of almost four to one. To the north a force of 5,000 Egyptian troops was cut off at Faluja, and was only sustained by supplies dropped from the air. Four Egyptian Stirlings, intended as transports, were pressed into use as bombers, making a number of daylight attacks on an Israeli force threatening El Arish from the south; this vital forward Egyptian base fell on 29 December.

In the confused fighting that accompanied the final armistice of 6/7 January 1949, whose terms included British insistence that Israeli forces withdraw from Egyptian territory, IAF Spitfires shot down four RAF Spitfires and a Tempest whose pilots were under orders to reconnoitre the compliance with the armistice. In little more than six months the neo-nationalist state of Israel had become a powerful force to be reckoned with in the Middle East. With the Egyptian monarchy fast becoming discredited, the scene was set for a disturbing realignment of a republican Egypt with the communist bloc.

One of the immediate problems faced by the RAF was the steady stream of Jewish immigrants entering Palestine. No. 38 Squadron, based at Ein Shemer, flew maritime reconnaissance patrols using Avro Lancaster GR.Mk 3s and B.Mk 7s left over from the Tiger Force squadron.

One of the remaining RAF units in the Middle East was No. 32 Squadron. Based at Ein Shemer in the Suez Canal zone during 1947-8, the unit's Spitfire FR.Mk 18s kept an eye on the crisis in Palestine. Note the 'hunting horn' emblem of the squadron beneath the windscreen, and the camera port aft of the cockpit.

Egypt's almost desperate need for effective strike power was amply illustrated by the commandeering of Hawker's prototype Fury F.2/43 while on a demonstration tour in Egypt. Fitted with guns from a Spitfire, the aircraft was flown in action by Egypt's most skilful pilot, Squadron Leader Abu Said.

Westland Lysanders were employed by the Egyptian air force on spotting and liaison duties.

Supplementing the rebuilt RAF machines in Israeli air force service were a batch of 50 Spitfire LF.Mk 9Es, operated previously by Czech pilots of the RAF. The first of the aircraft were flown out to Israel in September 1948 to join two captured Egyptian air force Spitfire LF.Mk 9s.

Just as Israel put surplus RAF equipment to use, so Egypt took advantage of RAF operations in the Italian and Central Mediterranean sectors by acquiring surplus Spitfire LF.Mk 9s in 1946. The aircraft were operated by Nos 2 and 6 Squadrons and provided the REAF with its front-line attack capability.

Israel acquired 25 Avia S.199 fighters from May 1948 to equip No. 101 Squadron. Based on the Messerschmitt Bf 109G airframe, the Czech aircraft had a Junkers Jumo 211F engine and is shown here with its original sideways-hinged 'Galland' canopy. The Avias and Spitfires formed Israel's first line of defence.

Israel acquired aircraft by many devious methods throughout its development, and the exact history of the Mosquitoes is unknown. These were potent aircraft which caused the Egyptians a great deal of trouble. They were later employed during the Suez campaign.

One of the aircraft types equipping Israel's fledgling air force was the Supermarine Spitfire, many assembled from scrapped machines or spare parts. Here two LF.Mk 9Es buzz a UN aircraft carrying Muslim pilgrims in early 1949.

THE SUEZ CRISIS 1956

Precipitated by Israeli-Egyptian hostility and continuing Egyptian commando raids into Israel, by Anglo-French fears of the Nasserite threat to Western interests in the Middle East, and by the Egyptian nationalization of the Suez Canal (itself provoked by American refusal to finance the Aswan Dam project), the Suez campaign of October-November 1956 reflected precious little credit on the diplomacy of the West, least of all on that of the USA whose volte-face at a critical moment in the military operations was to destroy all Western credibility in the Middle East for two decades.

After an initial military plan (originally created in August 1956) by the UK and France to secure the Suez Canal had been modified and delayed to accommodate an attack through Sinai by Israel, which opened on 29 October, an Anglo-French ultimatum was issued demanding the withdrawal of Egyptian and Israeli forces to the west and east banks of the Suez Canal respectively, a seemingly meaningless demand as the Israelis had failed in any case to reach the canal from the east. With the issue of the ultimatum, an Anglo-French carrier task force sailed from the Central Mediterranean eastwards to the war zone.

At the start of hostilities the Egyptian air force could field two squadrons of 30 Soviet MiG-15s, 12 Il-28 jet bombers, 15 Vampires, 12 Meteor day and night fighters, 60 transport aircraft of various types and about 80 other obsolete aircraft a total of some 210 aircraft of all types. Against them were ranged about 180 Israeli Meteors, Ouragans, Mustangs, Mosquitoes, C-47s and B-17 Fortress bombers, to which were added three French squadrons of Mystères, Republic F-84s and Noratlas transports. In addition to these forces the French deployed 100 aircraft at Akrotiri (F-84s and RF-84s) and 50 carrierborne Corsairs and Hellcats embarked in the carrier *Arromanches*. By far the most modern air forces deployed were those of the UK, whose Royal Air Force moved four Valiant squadrons to Luqa, Malta, together with six squadrons of Canberras and Hunters to Cyprus, and some 120 carrierborne Sea Venoms, Sea Hawks, Skyraiders and Wyverns embarked in the carriers *Eagle*, *Albion* and *Bulwark*, and army and naval Whirlwind and Sycamore helicopters in the assault carriers *Theseus* and *Ocean*.

During the first two days the Israelis and Egyptians were heavily committed, the Israelis attacking the Mitla Pass in Sinai, with paratroops dropped from C-47s and sustained by supplies dropped by the Noratlas transports, and covered by Meteors and Mystères. At dawn on 30 October four Canberras attempted to reconnoitre Egyptian forces in the Canal Zone, but all were intercepted by Egyptian MiGs, one of the RAF aircraft being damaged. In the same afternoon the Egyptian MiGs engaged Israeli Mystères over the Mitla Pass while Meteors attacked the paratroops on the ground,

causing heavy casualties. On the following day the Israelis suffered their only serious setback on the ground when the Egyptians were able to repulse a series of attacks on Abu Ageila, and the situation might have become critical had not Israel fighter-bombers been able to delay the arrival of Egyptian reinforcements.

On the night of 1/2 November the RAF launched an attack by Canberras and Valiants from Malta and Cyprus against the Egyptian air bases at Abu Sueir, Almaza, Cairo International, Inchas and Kabrit and, though their task was relatively simple owing to the absence of any blackout in the nearby towns, the bombers failed to cause any significant damage, most of the Egyptian Il-28 bombers having been moved to the relative safety of Luxor in the south. During daylight on 2 November the air attacks on Egyptian airfields were kept up by the Canberras from Cyprus, escorted by Hunter Mk 5s and joined by the British naval fighter-bombers from the Task Force. The French *Arromanches* was herself attacked by two Egyptian destroyers which had to retire under smoke when set on by the carrier's Corsairs.

The gradual attrition within the Egyptian air force allowed the Israelis to commit their limited armour to the battle in Sinai on 5 November as, simultaneously, British and French paratroops and helicopter-borne forces landed on the outskirts of Port Said and Port Fuad respectively. These actions were fought successfully under cover of the carrier aircraft, the small number shot down being lost to Egyptian ground fire. However, a subsequent swift advance south along the east bank of the canal was abruptly halted when a ceasefire was peremptorily ordered as the result of opposition by the American government to the operation motivated by an underestimation of Soviet influence throughout the Middle East.

Combat losses in the week-long Suez operation amounted to four British and one French aircraft (plus nine and two others, respectively, in accidents), compared with 48 Egyptian and other Arab-flown aircraft, including 18 MiG and seven Il-28s. The Israelis admitted the loss of about 20 aircraft.

Both politically and militarily the entire Suez operation was a fruitless venture. Despite fears for the continued freedom of passage through the canal, it remained open until eventually closed as a result of the 1967 Six-Day War. If anything, the disarray created in the Western bloc by misplaced American intransigence merely served to commit Nasserite Egypt (and therefore Arab influence in the Middle East) more firmly than ever to the Soviet Union.

Built as the US Navy AD-4W no. 124111, this airborne early-warning Skyraider was transferred to the Fleet Air Arm as WV178 and duly became no. 424 of No. 849 Squadron's 'C' flight. The yellow and black stripes (which were a parody on those used on June 1944) were for the Suez campaign of November 1956.

Along with 1ᵉ and 33ᵉ Escadre de Chasse, the 3ᵉ Escadre at Rheims deployed its Republic RF-84F Thunderflashes to Akrotiri for two months in late 1956. This aircraft flew with the 3 'Ardennes' Escadrille, as indicated by the boar's-head emblem beneath the cockpit and its yellow wingtips.

By various methods, some of them legal, the infant Israeli air force acquired real offensive muscle with Mosquito Mks IV, VI and NF.36. This colourful FB.Mk 6 (post-war designation) was one of a batch bought at a knock-down price from the French Armée de l'Air. After 1952 many of them came unglued in the air.

Four squadrons of Vickers Valiants were moved to Luqa, Malta, during the crisis, and together with Canberras took part in several bombing raids on Egyptian airfields. These were largely ineffective as the Egyptians had moved their aircraft to other bases.

To augment the massive airlift supporting the Suez campaign, Avro Shackletons were used to shuttle troops and equipment to Cyprus from the UK. After the landings in Egypt, these aircraft flew direct to the Suez region.

Armstrong Whitworth Sea Hawk FB.Mk 3s were used on rocket attacks against Egyptian installations. This example flew with No. 802 Squadron from HMS *Albion*. British carrier aircraft were aided by Vought Corsairs from the French carrier *Arromanches*.

One of the six ex-RAF tropicalized Gloster Meteor NF.Mk 13s which had been supplied to Egypt during June-August 1955. In the Suez conflict in 1956 at least two of these aircraft were destroyed, one by an aircraft operating from HMS *Bulwark*.

Bearing the yellow and black stripes which typified aircraft of this campaign, this North American P-51D Mustang was one of many which proved excellent in the ground attack role. Principal weaponry was the unguided rocket.

During the Suez crisis of late 1956, an RAF Canberra B.Mk 6 takes off from Malta on a strike against Egyptian airfields and defence positions.

CONFRONTATION IN BORNEO 1962-66

Possibly the least-known of all post-war RAF operational deployments was that of 1962-4 in Borneo, where neighbouring Indonesia held territorial ambitions following the transfer of independence to North Borneo. The campaign in some respects had much in common with that in Malaya which had only just ended, not least in the similarity of terrain for Borneo, like the Malayan peninsula, is covered with dense jungle with few landmarks of use to navigation. Accurate maps were scarce and, on account of frequent and fairly regular tropical rainstorms, flying was impossible except for about six hours daily between mid-morning and mid-afternoon.

In very broad terms the campaign may be divided into three overlapping phases, namely the suppressing of Indonesian-inspired rebellions in Brunei and Sarawak, the subsequent deployment of units of the Far East Air Force (FEAF) to Borneo to counter Indonesian-trained terrorist infiltrators crossing the 1,000-mile (1610 km) border with Kalimantan, and wider-ranging operations to counter Indonesian air sorties across the border and the despatch of Indonesian raiding parties to Malaya itself.

The FEAF had undergone considerable modernization since the signing of the SEAC Defence Treaty of 1954. The RAF component comprised a squadron (No. 20) of Hunter FGA.Mk 9s at Tengah, Singapore, together with Javelin FAW.Mk 9s of No. 60 Squadron and Canberra B.Mk 2s of No. 45 Squadron. Also in Malaya were RAF Canberra PR.Mk 7s, Shackleton MR.Mk 2s and a variety of transport aircraft. At the RAAF base at Butterworth were two CAC Sabre squadrons and No. 2 Squadron RAAF with Canberras, and a Canberra squadron (No. 75) of the RNZAF, also at Tengah. In addition it had become standard RAF training practice to send small detachments of conventionally-armed V-bombers to the Far East for short periods.

Immediately after news of the rebellions in Brunei and Sarawak was received on 8 December 1962, Hastings, Beverleys and Valetta transports began delivering troops to Brunei town, its airfield having been secured from the rebels by Gurkha troops who were landed first. Within a fortnight 3,200 troops had been delivered, together with 113 vehicles and supporting weapons and stores, and the rebellion in Sarawak put down. Joining the airlift had been an RAAF C-130A Hercules and an RNZAF Bristol Freighter, as well as RAF Shackletons of No. 205 Squadron. On arrival in Borneo the troops were moved forward by Beverleys and Pioneers and by Sycamore helicopters; also employed were the big twin-rotor Bristol Belvedere helicopters of No. 66 Squadron.

The rebellion in Brunei was being sustained by neighbouring Indonesia, and to restore the situation in the area British forces were tasked with isolating and mopping up the rebel bands, a task which involved airlifting troops to the oilfield at Seria and the airstrip at Anduki, the former being successfully undertaken by the short-field Twin Pioneers of No. 209 Sqadron and the latter by a single Beverley (which was fired on by the rebels but suffered only negligible damage).

The rebellions having failed, Indonesia began infiltrating guerrilla forces across the border, to counter which the security forces established a number of small strongpoints near to the known crossing points, and these tiny garrisons were to be sustained wholly from the air, a task which caused a number of new squadrons to be deployed to Borneo, in particular Nos 103, 110 and 230 with the new Westland Whirlwind Mk 10 helicopter.

In a general widening of the conflict Indonesia greatly increased its cross-border incursions, even starting to send F-51 Mustangs into Borneo airspace, aircraft that were particularly difficult to counter as they were able to outmanoeuvre the big Javelins and were virtually immune from the RAF's heat-seeking missiles on account of their piston engines. It was at this time that the RAF's V-bombers on detachment to the Far East joined in the bombing of areas suspected of being occupied by the infiltrating guerrillas. In February 1964 an air defence identification zone (ADIZ) was established, after which the Hunters and Javelins, based at Labuan and Kuching, maintained a 24-hour all-weather alert system, their pilots being authorized to engage and destroy any Indonesian aircraft entering the ADIZ.

In August of that year 100 regular Indonesian troops went ashore at three points on the west coast of the Malayan peninsula, and two weeks later an Indonesian C-130 Hercules dropped paratroops in central Johore. Although these forces had been rounded up by mid-October, there were some 40 other landings and it was against these that the Hunters and Canberras of the RAF, RAAF and RNZAF were now deployed, and airborne early warning Gannets from the carrier *Victorious* were employed to patrol Malayan coastal airspace.

That the Indonesian operations eventually petered out without a major escalation of the conflict was considered largely the result of the controlled response by British and Commonwealth ground and air forces, despite what came to represent a major deployment and logistical operation.

Regular deployments of V-bombers from Britain provided the heavy bombing element of the RAF's forces in Borneo. This Handley Page Victor flew with No. 10 Squadron from its base at Tengah.

A Hawker Hunter FGA.Mk 9 of No. 20 Squadron carrying 12 60-lb (27-kg) rockets and two 230-Imp gal (1046-litre) drop tanks patrols the Malaysian coastline during the 1960s. Hunters fulfilled both a ground attack and an interception role, though their deterrent value was perhaps their most effective attribute.

Small garrisons were maintained by helicopter, particularly the Westland Whirlwind Mk 10, flying with Nos 103, 110 and 230 Squadrons. This air support was vital to the ground campaign and continued throughout all weather conditions, including monsoons.

Scottish Aviation Pioneer CC.Mk 1 of No. 209 Squadron based at Seletar, Singapore, but operating throughout Borneo during the period of confrontation. Greatly improving ground force support in the earlier Malayan campaign, this STOL aircraft once again supplied ground troops deep in the jungle.

The key to control of Borneo lay in winning over the hearts and minds of the villagers whose goodwill and co-operation was vital. The large capacity of this Bristol Belvedere of No. 66 Squadron was ideal to carry in supplies to the Ghurkas, much to the evident delight of the village children.

ALGERIA 1954-62

Coming as it did within months of the humiliating defeat in Indo-China, the rebellion in Algeria, a state that was closer to being a *departement* of metropolitan France than a colony, was so profound in its portents that only the authoritarian grasp of President Charles de Gaulle, to whom that nation turned for leadership in 1958, prevented the horror of open revolution at home from becoming a reality.

As in Indo-China, the armed Algerian nationalists, the Armée de Libération Nationale, possessed no air arm but, with intimate familiarity with the local terrain, preferred to conduct guerrilla warfare. Despite the commitment of almost one million troops against them, they proved not only highly proficient but eventually persuaded France that once again no military solution was attainable. And in 1962, despite all that sophisticated weaponry could achieve, Algeria won her independence under the erstwhile nationalist leader Ahmed Ben Bella.

At the beginning of the war in November 1954 the French air force in Algeria comprised a squadron of S.E.535 Mistral jet interceptors (licence-built Vampires) and a training squadron flying aged F-47 Thunderbolts, as well as a hotch-potch of obsolete second-line aircraft and trainers. None of these aircraft was in any way suitable for operations against fleeting and mobile guerrilla forces, whose tactics were based on lightning strikes and instant dispersal. As a matter of expediency, therefore, the local French commanders ordered a host of light aircraft and trainers into operational use, hurriedly modified with machine-guns and light bomb racks. Quite fortuitously they had hit upon an ideal counter-insurgency weapon and one that was to sire a whole new operational philosophy employing dedicated COIN aircraft. Such aircraft as the North American T-6 Texan became synonymous with the world's mounting problem of anti-guerrilla operations.

Thus in 1955, as the regular squadrons of conventional fighters retained their normal air defence tasks, the first *escadrilles d'aviation légère d'appui* (EALA, or light support squadrons) with Morane-Saulnier MS.500s and 733s became operational. The following year they were joined by a *groupe*, GALA 72, of four *escadrilles* with T-6 Texans, and three of SIPA S.111s and 112s (the latter distributed between Tunisia, Morocco and Algeria).

More significantly, however, was the introduction of the Max Holste Broussard, the first aircraft formally customized for the counter-insurgency role and capable of lifting small numbers of troops to remote areas of local trouble. Following de Gaulle's resumption of command of the state in 1958, Général Maurice Challe was given the task of crushing the Algerian rebellion and undertook a complete overhaul and reorganization of the air force. One of his first priorities was to replace the excellent but aged T-6s which had hitherto flown the majority of operations against the rebel forces, and it was an adaptation of the T-28 Trojan, itself a modern derivative of the T-6, that was selected (being named the Fennec in French service).

Major weapons in the counter-insurgency arsenal was, however, to become the helicopter, the Armée de l'Air having formed its first light helicopter squadron in Algeria in 1955 with Bell 47Gs and Sikorsky H-19s (S-55s). Pioneer operations by this *escadrille* had quickly demonstrated the flexibility of the helicopter, as much for casualty evacuation as delivery of troops into combat, and by the end of 1956 the 12-man Sikorsky H-34 was in service in the assault role. Within a year the French forces in Algeria possessed a total of 250 helicopters, of which the army flew 139, the Armée de l'Air 90 and the Aéronavale 18. In due course the French gave some of their helicopters a 'ground-attack' capability by mounting in them guns of 7.5-mm (0.295-in), 12.7-mm (0.5-in) and 20-mm calibre, as well as rockets. Among the army helicopters were such troop-carrying aircraft as the Vertol-Piasecki H-21.

As the war dragged on, and the rebel forces (far from acknowledging defeat) stepped up their operations, so the French brought greater pressure to bear in Algeria, not least in the air. Two medium attack bomber *groupes* with B-26 Invaders were deployed in Algeria, together with a growing number of ex-US Navy AD-4 Skyraiders (of which France had ordered 113 from the USA in 1956). The latter was to prove a highly-effective COIN aircraft, capable of delivering a very heavy punch in the ground-attack role and suppressing ground opposition during helicopter assaults.

Effective as Challe's 'steamroller' campaign was, forcing the rebels to revert to isolated guerrilla tactics by the end of 1960, the mounting cost of the war and the depradations imposed on French society by increasing terrorist activities in metropolitan France combined to sap the enthusiasm for an apparently fruitless continuation of the war, and in 1962 de Gaulle was forced to accept terms for Algerian independence. Militarily, whatever else the war in Algeria demonstrated, it illustrated the impotence of a conventional air force, equipped and organized for air defence, in the environment of concerted guerrilla warfare. The lessons were there for the USA to digest when, just two years later, it faced a similar threat in Vietnam. Ironically it took 10 years for the USA to arrive at no less a humiliating political defeat than had the French in Algeria.

The French air force in Algeria flew a squadron of Mistrals (licence-built de Havilland Vampires), but these lightweight jets proved unequal to the gruelling conditions in the desert.

Large numbers of helicopters were used in Algeria, for the first time in attack and assault roles, proving to be highly effective against the ALN. The Armée de l'Air used hundreds of Sikorsky H-34s (S-58s), S-55s and Aérospatiale Alouettes, but the French army used these Piasecki (Vertol) H-21s.

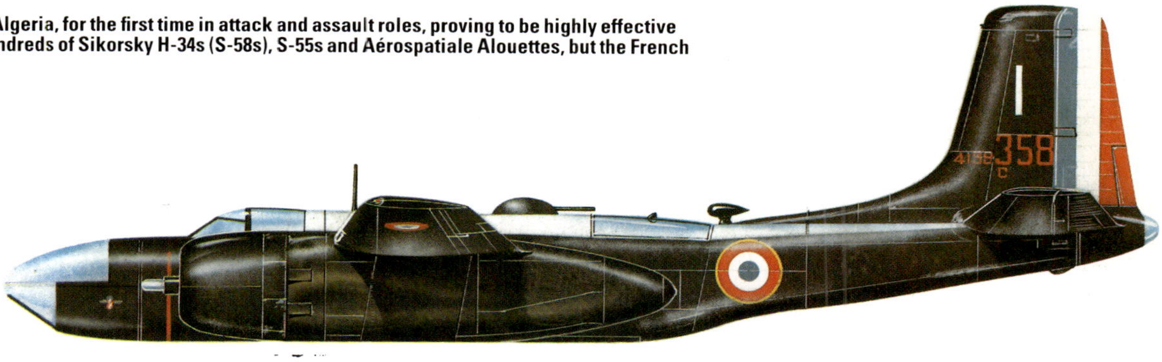

Most formidable of the heterogeneous array of attack aircraft, the Douglas Invader was usually used in B-26C form but some units had the B-26N or camera-equipped RB-26P. This B-26C served with one of the premier bomber units, EB 2/91 'Guyenne', based throughout at Oran. White tops cooled the interior.

A lesser-known type employed by the French in Algeria was the SIPA S.12, a version of the Arado Ar 396 with a French engine. Nosing over in soft sand was common.

By 1960 the North American T-6 equipped 38 front-line squadrons in Algeria, plus the 1/320 light attack training wing. These T-6s were almost certainly from one of 72ᵉ Escadre's 21 squadrons.

STRATEGIC AIR COMMAND 1947-84

The philosophy of deterring aggression by a world power with the threat of immediate and devastating retaliation became a necessary reality the moment the two opposing world political blocs acquired nuclear weapons. From a position of nuclear stalemate that existed in the early 1950s to an apparent proliferation of such weapons the world has moved ever nearer Armageddon, a knife-edge of technological development and counter-development. Throughout the past 40 years the mainstay of the West's airborne nuclear deterrent has been the USAF's Strategic Air Command, a force of long-range strategic bombers constantly deployed between bases throughout the world, of which a proportion are constantly airborne or at take-off alert.

The history of the airborne deterrent may be roughly divided into three chapters covering the eras of the three principal aircraft employed, the Convair B-36 (1950-8), the Boeing B-47 Stratojet (1953-61) and the Boeing B-52 Stratofortress (1956 to date), the chronological overlap being created by production build-up.

The B-36 was an enormous aeroplane originally conceived in the World War II 'super-B-29' philosophy of a self-defending bomber capable of great range and/or heavy bombload. The concept of the airborne nuclear deterrent, evolved between 1947 and 1950, undoubtedly lent urgency to development of the B-36 (whose design origin dated back to 1941), and in 1949 the B-36D, with four turbojets added under the wings to supplement the six big piston engines, was flown; with a maximum bombload of 84,000 lb (38102 kg) and a range of up to 7,500 miles (12070 km), this and the later B-36H and B-36J were adopted as SAC's strategic nuclear bomber with which considerable development work was carried out in creating the system of worldwide deployment of big bombers.

Although the later B-36s were capable of speeds of over 400 mph (644 km/h) and of operating at altitudes near to 40,000 ft (12190 m), it was quickly realised that with conventionally-aimed bombs requiring target overflight they were potentially extremely vulnerable to fighter interception, and before the Korean War was over the first six-jet Mach 0.8 Boeing B-47s were being delivered, and in 1953 the first B-47E (the main production variant) was flown. By 1957 SAC had some 1,800 in service. In 1960 SAC adopted the Reflex system of deployment, in which all B-47 wings were based in the United States but were on constant 21-day 'alert' rotation to bases in the United Kingdom, Spain, North Africa, Alaska and Guam.

While initial trials with stand-off bombs (for example the Bell GAM-63 Rascal) were conducted on the B-47, a more advanced and bigger aircraft was already being designed even as the Stratojet prototypes were being flown for the first time, and on 15 April 1952 the eight-jet YB-52 made its first flight.

From the outset the B-52 was envisaged as a truly multi-mission global bomber with inflight-refuelling capability, and on 21 May 1956 a B-52B was used to drop the first hydrogen bomb in tests at Bikini Atoll in the Pacific. In November that year eight B-52Bs of the 93rd Heavy Bombardment Wing flew a 32-hour, 17,000-mile (27360-km) course round North America and over the North Pole; this was followed three months later by a round-the-world nonstop flight by three aircraft which were refuelled three times by KC-97s during the 45-hour flight.

The multi-mission B-52C, which featured larger underwing tanks and flew in 1956, was followed by the B-52D for long-range bombing only, the B-52E with more advanced bombing and navigation electronics, and the B-52F with more powerful engines. The B-52G first flew at Wichita, Kansas, on 26 October 1958 and featured wing integral fuel tanks (the so-called 'wet wing') which bestowed a greatly increased range; the latter was demonstrated in December 1960 when an aircraft of the 5th Strategic Bombardment Wing flew 10,000 miles (16095 km) in 19 hours 45 minutes without refuelling. The B-52Gs of the 4135th Strategic Bombardment Wing at Elgin AFB were the first to be equipped with GAM-77 Hound Dog ASMs.

The final production version was the B-52H, although subsequent life extension programmes have progressively updated earlier versions. Powered by eight Pratt & Whitney TF-33 turbofans, the B-52H has remained SAC's standard equipment to this day, having originally entered service with the 379th Wing at Wurtsmith AFB on 9 May 1961. The following January a B-52H of the 4136th Wing flew from Okinawa to Spain without inflight-refuelling to establish a new world distance record of 12,519 miles (20147 km).

The B-52H was intended to carry four Douglas GAM-87 Skybolt ASMs, but this weapon system (RS638A) was cancelled. Apart from the 'trucking' missions over Vietnam, in which the big aircraft were required to drench the featureless jungle with huge quantities of 'iron' bombs, B-52Hs continued to carry the Hound Dog missile until 1976, and from 1982 onwards B-52H Wings have become operational with the Boeing AGM-86 air-launched cruise missile, a programme that will continue until 1987.

Convair B-36s were the mainstay of the Strategic Air Command bomber force from 1950 until 1956, when the Boeing B-52 arrived in service. 44-92033 was a Convair B-36B which served in the Arctic, hence the Dayglo fin and wingtips.

Featuring the SAC sash on the nose, this Boeing B-47E Stratojet is typical of the 2,000 such aircraft that served with SAC througout the late 1950s. The 'E' was by far the most important version, amounting to 1,481 aircraft.

An ingenious method of obtaining good reconnaissance was to carry a fighter-reconnaissance (FICON) parasite under a B-36. The aircraft chosen was the Republic GRF-84F slung underneath a GRB-36F. At least 12 bombers were converted as carriers and these equipped the 91st SRS in 1955.

The Boeing B-52C variant possessed multi-mission capability, whereas later aircraft were strictly long-range bombers. The 'C' model reached SAC service in June 1956, followed by the 'D' model in December.

Below: The Boeing B-47B was the first major production version of the Stratojet, entering service in 1951. These had RATO (rocket-assisted take-off) capability, but this was deleted when most aircraft were upgraded to B-47E standard.

Below: A considerable redesign of the Boeing B-29 Superfortress resulted in the Boeing B-50, which provided stop-gap bombing capability until the B-47 arrived in service. The type continued in service until 1965 after conversion into reconnaissance aircraft and tankers.

Above: Inflight-refuelling is an important task for Strategic Air Command, and it not only provides this service for its own bombers and reconnaissance aircraft but also constitutes the refuelling capacity for the entire USAF. Chief aircraft used is the Boeing KC-135A, but this is being supplemented by the KC-10 Extender.

Below: The B-52H, powered by larger TF33 turbofans (derived from the J57) which offered much greater take-off thrust, less noise and much reduced specific fuel consumption. The B-52H carried the Hound Dog missile until 1976.

BRITAIN'S V-FORCE 1951-75

Although not normally privy to the secrets of the American wartime atomic bomb the UK, by the participation of her scientists in the production of the weapon in the USA, was favourably equipped to undertake the development of her own atomic bomb after the war. Although an aircraft such as the Lincoln would have been capable of carrying a 'tailored' atomic bomb (but over much shorter distances than the American B-29), the British Air Staff decided to embark on a programme aimed at equipping Bomber Command with large jet-powered bombers, and issued a number of very advanced requirements shortly after the end of the war. Fortunately the world has been spared any demonstration of the true credibility of these aircraft in their role of nuclear-armed deterrents.

First of the new bomber specifications, B.14/46, which brought forth the Short Sperrin, proved abortive largely through over-estimated bomb dimensions which hopelessly compromised the design. Shortly afterwards a follow-up requirement, B.35/46, proved more promising and, with a new specification issued in 1947, provided the basis on which the UK's nuclear bombing force was to be founded; B.35/46 was updated in 1948 by B.9/48.

The first of the new generation of V-bombers, the Vickers Valiant, was flown on 18 May 1951 and entered service with No. 138 Squadron in February 1955. Meanwhile the UK had detonated her first nuclear device in the Monte Bello Islands off the north western coast of Australia. On 11 October 1956 Valiants of No. 49 Squadron took part in trials at Maralinga, Australia, when an aircraft captained by Squadron Leader E.J.G. Flavell dropped the first British atomic bomb; on 15 May the following year, in Operation 'Grapple', another No. 49 Squadron Valiant dropped the first British hydrogen bomb over Christmas Island in the Pacific. In the meantime Valiants of Nos 138, 148, 207 and 214 Squadrons had been deployed to Luqa, Malta, for operations against Egypt during the Suez campaign, the first V-bombers to drop 'conventional' bombs in anger. In 1965 Valiants were found to be suffering from metal fatigue in the main wing spars and were withdrawn from service, their last duties with Bomber Command including those operated as inflight-refuelling tankers, all members of the V-force being given inflight-refuelling facility.

Next of the V-force trio to fly had been the Avro Vulcan, on 30 August 1952. This, the most impressive of all the bombers, was a large delta-wing aircraft originally powered by Avon and then Sapphire turbojets, but in production by two-spool Olympus engines which eventually produced about 20,000-lb (9072-kg) thrust. Production of the Vulcan was very modest, only 45 Mk 1s and 68 Mk 2s (with bigger wings and elevons) being built. By means of a number of life-extension expedients, however, this force remained in a service for almost 30 years, serving in turn as high- and low-level bombers, stand-off bombers, reconnaissance aircraft and ultimately as tankers. During that period they equipped nine RAF squadrons

at Coningsby, Cottesmore, Finningley, Honington, Scampton and Waddington in the UK, and at Akrotiri in Cyprus between 1969 and 1975. Most of the Vulcan B.Mk 2s were adapted to carry the Avro Blue Steel stand-off nuclear missile, but plans to equip the aircraft with the American Skybolt missile were aborted by cancellation of that programme, and the nuclear deterrent passed to the Polaris submarine force. Despite its great bulk the Vulcan was classed as a medium bomber, capable of carrying up to 21 1,000-lb (454-kg) iron bombs or a 10,000-lb (4536-kg) Blue Steel. Though employed out of context as a global nuclear deterrent, the Vulcan's last operation was the most spectacular when two aircraft were deployed to attack the Falkland Islands in 1982 during the illegal occupation by Argentine forces; in successive sorties from Ascension Island, these aircraft attacked Port Stanley airfield with 1,000-lb (454-kg) bombs and a radar installation with anti-radiation missiles.

Third of the V-bombers was the Handley Page Victor with crescent wing, an aeroplane that took so long to develop that by the time it entered service in 1958 it was already obsolescent in a world of surface-to-air missiles and Mach 2+ interceptors; 55 Mk 1s and Mk 1As were produced, as well as 34 Mk 2s, so small a quantity that their unit cost was considered inordinately high. As with the Vulcan, their vulnerability at altitude resulted in a change of role to low-level bombing, equipped with Blue Steel missiles, while the last eight aircraft were completed as strategic reconnaissance aircraft for service with No. 534 Squadron at Wyton. Although capable of carrying 35 1,000-lb (454-kg) iron bombs (14 more than the Vulcan), the true value of the Victor was to be as a tanker for the other aircraft of the V-force, Nos 55 and 57 Squadrons at Marham (as well as No. 543 Squadron) being the last surviving operational units in existence. Victor bombers served with nine RAF squadrons.

Whether or not a force of V-bombers, of which fewer than 50 were ever combat-available simultaneously, constituted a credible deterrent (to which the independent French *Force de Frappe* might in certain circumstances be added) will for ever remain unknown. Yet while these forces have been combined with the might of American land- sea- and air-based nuclear deterrent, nuclear war has remained a spectre . . . and no more.

The first of the V-bombers to reach service was the Vickers Valiant, in February 1955. This had the shortest career, being withdrawn 10 years later after the discovery of cracks in the wings. Most ended their days as tankers.

'Quick Reaction Alert' (or QRA) was the most important facet of Britain's nuclear deterrent while this position was held by the V-bombers. These Vulcan B.Mk 2s are fuelled and ready to go at the end of the runway, waiting for the call to action.

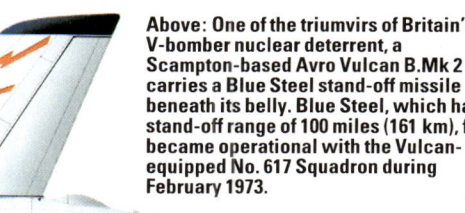

Painted anti-flash white, with pale blue insignia and serial XL321, was one of the first Vulcan B.Mk 2s in service with the Blue Steel missile. A No. 617 (Dambusters) Squadron aircraft, its lightning flash marking is usually in blue.

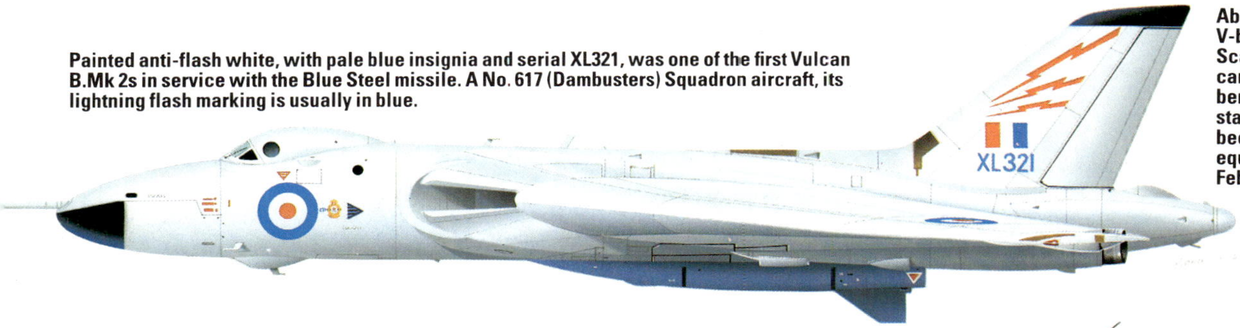

Above: One of the triumvirs of Britain's V-bomber nuclear deterrent, a Scampton-based Avro Vulcan B.Mk 2 carries a Blue Steel stand-off missile beneath its belly. Blue Steel, which had a stand-off range of 100 miles (161 km), first became operational with the Vulcan-equipped No. 617 Squadron during February 1973.

As the V-bombers became more vulnerable at high altitude, they switched to low-level duties and gained tactical camouflage. Principal weapon was the Blue Steel stand-off missile.

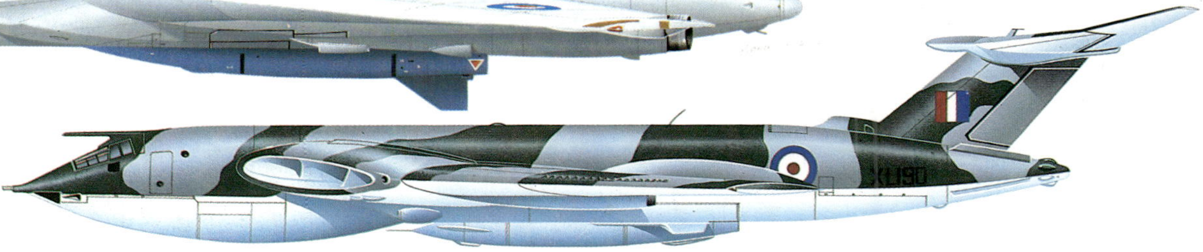

Despite their primary role as nuclear bombers, the V-bombers possessed devastating conventional bombing capability. Here a Victor releases a full load of iron bombs. The Victor had the greatest capacity for conventional weapons.

No. 214 Squadron was a famous user of the Valiant, and was the first to develop inflight-refuelling techniques. This aircraft is a Valiant B(K).Mk 1, shown taxiing past the Bloodhound squadron at Marham.

THE EARLY MONTHS 1950

Following some months of intermittent border 'incidents' along the 38th Parallel, the artificial boundary separating North and South Korea that had been established by the United Nations, all-out hostilities began on 25 June 1950 when eight North Korean (Communist) divisions crossed the border in an attempt to achieve a swift conquest of the Republic of Korea (ROK) and impose reunification of the whole country under a single communist government.

Correctly assessing the almost non-existence of the ROK air force, which comprised no more than 16 unarmed trainers, the North Korean air force (NKAF) possessed a fighter regiment of 70 Yak-9 and La-11s and a ground-attack regiment of 62 Il-10s, all Soviet aircraft of late World War II vintage, but highly effective when no air opposition existed. The North Koreans had not counted, however, on an immediate decision by the UN to resist their aggression by employing all available Western forces under the command of General Douglas MacArthur.

Few modern American combat aircraft had reached the Far East by mid-1950 and, as USAF C-54s hurriedly evacuated American citizens from Seoul, the South Korean capital, the only combat aircraft immediately available in the theatre were a small number of obsolescent F-80C Shooting Star jet fighters and some F-82 Twin Mustang piston-engine fighters. On 27 June, however, occurred the first jet fighter combat by American fighters when four F-80Cs shot down four NKAF Il-10s, while elsewhere F-82Gs destroyed three Yak-9s. The inability of the ROK ground forces to defend their own territory was such that the Communists made swift progress southwards, Seoul and its airfield at Kimpo falling on 28 June as the South Korean army retreated in disarray. Realizing that the immediate need was for ground support from the air, the USAF quickly moved three wings of F-51 Mustangs to the theatre, aircraft which proved excellent in the ground-attack role when armed with rockets and bombs and which equipped South African and Australian volunteer squadrons with the UN forces in Korea. At the same time the F-80s were assigned the air combat role on occasions of interference by the NKAF.

As the UN command frantically assembled ground forces with which to stem the Communist advance, the ROK army having been all but destroyed, USAF strength in the theatre quickly increased, and Japan-based B-26s light and B-29 heavy bombers joined aircraft of the US Navy in frequent raids on North Korean industrial targets as well as the key supply routes to the south. By September all but a

small area around Pusan in the extreme south east had been over-run by the invaders and almost all operations by the UN air forces had to be launched from the US Navy's carriers at sea or from Japan. In the nick of time the advance was halted, as much by exhaustion among the Communist forces as by the relentless air attacks on their supply lines. This exercise of growing UN air superiority was to be the key to the entire war.

On 15 September MacArthur launched a powerful amphibious assault at Inchon, 100 miles (160 km) up the west coast of Korea, gaining (on account of poor Communist intelligence) total surprise. Supported from the air by aircraft from the fast carriers *Philippine Sea, Valley Forge* and *Boxer*, the escort carriers *Bandoeng Strait* and *Sicily* and the Royal Navy's *Triumph*, the landings were co-ordinated with a break-out from the Pusan perimeter, and in a short time the invading Communist army was being systematically decimated. Vought F4U Corsairs, Douglas AD-4 Skyraiders and Grumman F9F-2 Panthers of the US Navy and US Marine Corps, joined by Fleet Air Arm Fireflies and Seafires, let loose a storm of gunfire, rockets and bombs in support of US Marines who went ashore at Wolmi Do; within a couple of days Kimpo airfield had been recaptured, and a US Marine night-fighter squadron of Grumman F7F-2N Tigercats, together with helicopters and spotter aircraft, were operating from shore bases.

By the end of September scarcely any organized Communist forces remained at large south of the 38th Parallel. This return to the *status quo* might well have brought the Korean War to an end after only three months' fighting, together with a return to the negotiating table, had not Communist China intervened with threats of armed intervention in support of the North Koreans; indeed reconnaissance carried out by the Japan-based B-29s confirmed a substantial build-up of Chinese military forces immediately behind the North Korean borders with China and an increase in activity by Chinese MiG-15 jet fighters just north of the Yalu river.

It was at this moment that General MacArthur made clear his intention to occupy the whole of North Korea, in contrast to the UN's stated objective of simply restoring partition of the two states on the 38th Parallel. Thereafter prolongation of the war and active intervention by Communist China became inevitable.

Generally able to look after itself in Korea until the advent of the MiG-15, the Lockheed F-80C progressed from interceptor to fighter-bomber in the first two years of war. Servicing remained a considerable problem.

Hawker Sea Fury FB.Mk 11 from HMS *Triumph* lets fly at a Communist outpost with its underwing rockets. Sea Furies gained at least two kills over MiG-15s.

The Korean War demonstrated the outstanding qualities of two superb naval propeller aircraft, the Douglas AD-1 Skyraider and Vought F4U Corsair.

The United States Marine Corps acquired 41 Fairchild Boxcar assault transports (similar to the USAF's C-119C) under the designation R4Q-1. They equipped Marine Squadrons VMR-252 and VMR-253 (one of the latter's aircraft depicted here), and served in the Korean theatre of operations from 1951 until 1953.

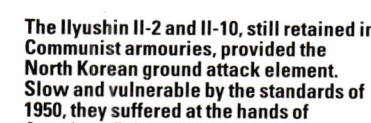

The Ilyushin Il-2 and Il-10, still retained in Communist armouries, provided the North Korean ground attack element. Slow and vulnerable by the standards of 1950, they suffered at the hands of American fighter pilots.

Destined never to see service aboard a carrier, Grumman's F7F Tigercat did see combat with the Marine Corps, mainly as a night fighter.

North American P-51Ds were the most widely used ground attack aircraft in Korea, armed with rockets, bombs and napalm.

CHINA INTERVENES 1950-51

Whatever efforts might have been made by the UN to gainsay MacArthur's hawkish ambitions, the matter was rendered academic when on 1 November 1950 an American F-80C was shot down by Chinese AA guns firing into Korean airspace from across the Yalu river. In another incident the pilots of some UN F-51s reported being fired on by MiG-15s which then made off towards Chinese territory. By now American forces had advanced deep into North Korea, their intention (now sanctioned by the UN) being ostensibly to 'secure peace throughout the Korean peninsula'. The North Korean capital, Pyongyang, had fallen to them on 19 October, and already the USAF had begun to run down its strength in the theatre. At the moment of intervention by the Chinese jets the UN air forces in the Korean theatre comprised three F-51 wings, two of F-80Cs, two of B-26s and three of B-29s.

No further pretence at non-intervention was made by the Chinese as, on 3 November, their forces swarmed across the Yalu. An American division was forced hurriedly to retreat to protect its supply lines as the powerful US Navy Carrier Task Force 77 sailed north to launch heavy strikes against the Chinese crossing the Yalu. At first the MiG-15 pilots simply 'trailed their coat' over Korea in efforts to tempt American aircraft into Chinese airspace, but on 8 November a section of four of the Communist jets ventured too far and were boxed in by four F-80s; in the first all-jet air combat in history Lieutenant Russell J. Brown, USAF, shot down a MiG-15 which crashed just 200 yards (185 m) inside Korean territory. On the following day a US Navy F9F Panther pilot from *Philippine Sea* also downed a Chinese MiG. On 10 November the Chinese jets shot down a B-29 heavy bomber. By the end of the month a quarter of a million Chinese troops were in the field in Korea. The war had certainly entered a new phase.

Forced to accept that the appearance of the modern Soviet-designed MiG-15, which with transonic performance was far superior to the great majority of aircraft with the UN forces, and that the F-80 pilots could not reasonably be expected to match the new enemy fighters, the decision was quickly taken to send to Korea a wing of North American F-86A Sabres, then the latest fighters in service with the USAF, and early in December the 4th Fighter Interceptor Wing, thus equipped, arrived at Kimpo airfield. At about the same time the 27th Fighter-Escort Wing, with Republic F-84D Thunderjets, also arrived in the war theatre. Bearing in mind that many of the newly-arrived American fighter pilots were World War II veterans with considerable flying and combat experience, whereas US intelligence disclosed that the Korean and Chinese pilots were much younger and lacked such experience, it was felt that the remedy was adequate to restore UN air supremacy.

The first brushes with enemy jets were inconclusive, but on 22 December eight F-86s fought 15 MiG-15s and shot down six. Further combats were not immediately possible because of the advance by Communist forces threatening Kimpo, whence the Sabres were moved southwards out of danger; now based far from the MiGs' patrol areas they were unable to stay long enough to enjoy long patrol sorties. By the same token, however, the Communist advance southwards also moved out of range of the MiGs which remained firmly based around Antung beyond the Yalu.

It was this relative difficulty in providing air cover with jet aircraft for the UN forces that lent importance to the work of the carrierborne strike aircraft of the US Navy and Royal Navy (the latter contributing the carriers *Theseus, Glory* and *Ocean*, which took turns on station with the *Sydney* of the Royal Australian Navy). Among the American aircraft that were to prove exceptionally efficient in the strike role were the AD Skyraiders and F4U Corsairs which, being propeller driven, could be flown from the wooden flight decks with which some of the American carriers were still equipped. Indeed a successful attack by torpedo-carrying Skyraiders against the Hwachon dam on 1 May 1951 achieved more than previous raids by B-29 heavy bombers (and a commando-style attack by US Rangers), so depriving the Communists of the ability to adjust river levels to suit their own troop movements during their build-up for their spring offensive.

The preparation for this offensive included considerable strengthening of the Communist air forces, principally with the established Yak-9s, La-11s, Il-10s and Tu-2s from the Soviet Union, but also with a few MiG-9 fighters. Meanwhile the 4th Wing's Sabres, which had been temporarily moved to Japan while the winter rains flooded their Korean airfields, returned to Korea, now to be based at Suwon. They were not, however, on hand to prevent an attack on 1 March by nine MiG-15s whose pilots made a single firing pass against a formation of 18 B-29s, three of which crashlanded at Taegu. The tables were turned on 12 April when some 60 MiGs attacked 48 B-29s, escorted by 36 F-84s and 18 F-86s. Three bombers were shot down, but the Americans destroyed 13 of the enemy jets. Notwithstanding this success, it was already becoming clear that the F-84 was no match for the MiG-15, which itself was superior in some performance aspects to the early F-86A Sabre. Only the quality of the American pilots was able to redress the balance.

Thunderjets – like this F-84G of the 69th Fighter-Bomber Squadron – continued to fly strike missions right up to the end of the Korean War. The majority of their losses were to ground fire, rather than enemy fighters.

No other single factor imposed greater influence on the air war in Korea than appearance of the MiG-15 jet fighter, whose performance remained marginally superior to that of the North American F-86. This improved version with wing fences was introduced to try to match the Sabre's combat manoeuvrability.

Boeing B-29s were employed on long-range bombing attacks flying from Japanese bases. This aircraft was used on clandestine reconnaissance missions, possibly overflying China to keep watch on the military build-up on the Korean border.

Even after introduction of the MiG-15 the North Koreans continued to use piston-engine fighters, including the Yakovlev Yak-9P, often for close escort of Ilyushin Il-10s during ground attack missions. Flown by pilots with less experience than the Americans, they were usually outfought by the UN's F-51Ds.

A Fairey Firefly fighter-bomber of No. 810 Squadron, Fleet Air Arm, which flew sorties from the Royal Navy's carrier HMS *Theseus*. All Fleet Air Arm aircraft carried the distinctive black and white stripes to assist identification by American personnel who were not familiar with British aircraft.

Typical air group composition of late Korea was Grumman F9F Panthers, McDonnell F2H Banshees, Douglas AD Skyraiders and Grumman TBF Avengers.

THE JET DOMINATES 1951-53

The Communist spring offensive of 1951 failed in its objective to overrun South Korea and had all but petered out by the end of May, but nevertheless the Chinese intervention had forced the UN to abandon its original aim of unification of north and south. As both sides now attempted to wring the last ounce of propaganda from the military situation, peace talks aimed at securing a truce opened at Kaesong on 10 July 1951, and dragged on for two years. The hawkish MacArthur was replaced by a slightly more conciliatory General Matthew Ridgeway, but one of the last operations planned before the change of command was an all-out air offensive against the Communists' supply lines which, owing to the vulnerability of the railways, depended almost exclusively on the road network.

All manner of aircraft, from the B-26 and B-29 bombers to the fighter-bomber F-80s and F-84s (now frequently relieved of air combat duties) and aircraft of the US Navy and Fleet Air Arm, the RAAF and SAAF, started a prolonged offensive against roads, bridges, supply depots and ports, and quickly provoked reaction from the Communist MiGs, which remained based beyond the Yalu but which were afforded fairly efficient radar warning of the approach of UN aircraft. Sabre-versus-MiG combats now became commonplace and the Communists quickly became aware that the 4th Fighter Wing was operating out of Suwon, and this prompted a series of nuisance night raids by antiquated Po-2 biplanes against the base. Extremely difficult to counter, these pinprick attacks, with 25-lb (11-kg) fragmentation bombs, caused little damage but their nuisance value was disproportionately high.

The UN bombing offensive, however, did not come up to expectations because of the Communists' ability to repair damage using huge numbers of impressed labourers. Photographic reconnaissance disclosed that the Chinese movement of troops and supplies remained almost undiminished. Furthermore, setpiece bombing attacks on North Korean cities and ports met with intense AA fire and the raids were severely restricted by orders to the crews not to overfly neighbouring Chinese territory. Casualties among the big B-29s were fairly high (in a force that never exceeded 99 aircraft).

Meanwhile development of an improved version of the Sabre, the F-86E, had gone on apace in the USA, and September brought deliveries of this aircraft to the 4th Wing, by now operating from Kimpo. The Communists had also increased their force of MiG-15s by activating a second regiment and this was equipped with improved MiG-15bis. At once the tempo of air combat increased, and formations of 80 enemy jets were frequently sighted. One of the war's biggest single combats was fought on 22 October 1951 as eight B-29s, escorted by 55 F-84s and 34 F-86s, were bombing Namsi;

suddenly 100 MiGs appeared and boxed-in the escort as 50 others made for the bombers, shooting down three and severely damaging four others. Six MiGs were shot down for the loss of an F-84.

Concerned at the large number of MiGs available to the Communists, the USAF now began to withdraw some of the old F-80Cs, replacing them with F-84Es, and a second wing, the 116th, was sent to Korea with F-84s. The night-fighter F-82s of the 347th All-Weather Group were also showing their age (and were of course no match for the MiG-15), and 15 jet all-weather F-94s were despatched to the war; this Starfire proved a disappointment as it lacked an adequate anti-icing system. By the end of 1951 F-86Es were replacing F-80Cs with the 51st Fighter-Interceptor Wing and soon the number of MiGs being destroyed started to rise significantly. At that time the 4th Wing's combat record showed a total of 144 MiG-15s destroyed for the loss in combat of 14 Sabres. The MiG pilots themselves were becoming more aggressive and the improved performance of the opposing fighters resulted in numerous combats taking place above 40,000 ft (12190 m). In March 1952 39 enemy jets were destroyed; the following month the tally rose to 44.

Combat information from Korea had long since filtered through to the Sabre's designers and in June and July 1952 yet further improved Sabres, the F-86F, were joining the 51st Wing. At last the Sabre was superior in all respects to the MiG-15bis. By the spring of 1953 there were four wings of F-86s in Korea, and during the last six months of the war these fighters wholly dominated the skies. In May their pilots destroyed 56 enemy jets, and in June no fewer than 77, losing 11 and 23 respectively of their own number.

The death of the Soviet leader, Joseph Stalin, on 5 March 1953, produced a profound change of attitude by the Chinese delegation at the peace talks and, after reversing their previously intransigent demands on such matters as prisoner repatriation, agreed to a ceasefire on 27 July.

From an air combat viewpoint the Korean War was interesting in that it was the first major conflict in which large numbers of opposing jet fighters engaged each other and, while it is true that a number of high-scoring American Sabre pilots (the 31-year-old Joseph McConnell of the 51st Wing heading the list with 16 MiG-15s to his credit), the fleeting nature of those all-jet combats graphically demonstrated that the age of gun-only armament was over. The era of the air-to-air missile was about to dawn.

Lockheed F-94 Starfires were deployed to the theatre but not committed to battle until late on, as the Americans did not want the radar to fall into the hands of Communist China. When it did enter service it was the most advanced aircraft on either side.

Left: A Sikorsky H-5G (S-51) lifts off on a vital medevac flight. Though only able to carry two stretchers, the casualties were afforded a degree of comfort when inside the streamlined pod, which protected them from wind buffets.

The F-51D was widely used throughout Korea as a fighter bomber by the United States, South Korea, Australia and South Africa. This 18th FBW aircraft is caught in the act of a wheels-up landing.

Apart from the Americans, the South Africans and Australians also flew the F-86 in Korea. This F-86F of No. 2 Squadron, SAAF, was based at K-55 and was attached to the 18th Fighter-Bomber Wing throughout the war. The squadron originally flew in Korea equipped with F-51D fighter-bombers.

When war in Korea started in mid-1950 the South Korean Air Force (ROKAF) had few aircraft of combat value. Large numbers of ex-USAF North American F-51Ds were hurriedly withdrawn from storage for delivery to the ROKAF, starting in August 1950. These operated from K-18 (Kangnung) for the remainder of the war.

Grumman F9F-2 Panthers were the US Navy's main fighter during the war and scored several victories against MiG-15s and Yak-9s.

Colourful F-86E-10 (51-2800) *El Diablo* of the 335th Fighter Squadron at Kimpo (K-14); it displays the squadron's mission and victory tallies.

WAR WITHOUT FRONTIERS 1952-65

In 1957 the United States, in its self-assumed role of bastion against the insidious, creeping advance of world Communism, took over from France the task of training and strengthening the armed forces of South Vietnam, of which the Vietnamese air force (VNAF) was poorly equipped and trained, despite the fact that the American Military Assistance and Advisory Group (MAAG) had been at work in the country since 1950. The aim of the USA, in line with the 1954 Geneva Protocols, was to achieve unification with North Vietnam by means of democratic elections, but this was compromised from the outset by the Communist totalitarian policies of the North, as well as military infiltration of the South.

By the end of the 1950s American 'advisers' in South Vietnam numbered nearly 700, and updating the VNAF accelerated when its F8F Bearcats were replaced by AD-6 Skyraiders. In 1961 the Viet Cong guerrillas staged a show of strength when, by means of increased infiltration, they attacked and cut many of the principal north-south trunk roads. The Kennedy administration, though still loath to involve American forces in formally-declared warfare, in turn redoubled the efforts being made to train the South Vietnamese forces in the skills of counter-insurgency, and the first US Special Forces entered the country; it later emerged that these engaged in active but covert war operations against the North, usually being injected into hostile territory by helicopter for purpose of sabotage and intelligence gathering.

Meanwhile, by use of the newly-opened Ho Chi Minh Trail, large quantities of war matériel were flooding into the North from communist China and the Soviet Union. The USA responded by supplying US Army Piasecki H-21 helicopters to the South, together with pilots to fly them, though not in combat conditions. On 2 May 1964 the American aircraft supply ship *Card* was sunk in Saigon harbour by a Viet Cong underwater demolition team while offloading helicopters. Elsewhere Fairchild C-123 Providers of the USAF were engaged in a defoliation operation (Operation 'Ranch Hand') in South Vietnam, stripping areas of the jungle of foliage by spraying chemicals and thereby depriving enemy infiltrators of their natural camouflage and cover.

On 2 August the same year the American destroyer *Maddox* was attacked in international waters in the Gulf of Tonkin by Soviet-built torpedo boats, and five nights later the destroyer *Turner Joy* was similarly attacked. In the USA President Johnson announced, a 'measured response' to these unprovoked attacks, and US Navy A-1 and A-4 strike aircraft from the carriers *Ticonderoga* and *Constellation* carried out highly successful attacks on the North Vietnamese

bases at Hon Gai and Loc Chao, losing one A-1 and one A-4.

This progressive drift to open conflict was not accompanied by a formal declaration of war, but simply escalated by a series of local incidents of growing scale, followed by righteous indignation and retaliation. A guerrilla attack on Christmas Eve 1964 on a hotel used by US officrs in Saigon was followed by a mortar attack on Pleiku Air Base which killed eight American personnel. The US Navy again retaliated, this time with Operation 'Flaming Dart', sending strike aircraft from the carriers *Ranger, Hancock* and *Coral Sea* of Task Force 77 against north Vietnamese military targets at Dong Hoi and Vit Thuu. Further Viet Cong mortar attacks on American bases, resulting in numerous casualties, were followed by 'Flaming Dart II', this time involving USAF as well as US Navy aircraft in strikes against Chanh Hoa and elsewhere. Open war, involving American ground forces, began on 7 March 1965 when 3,500 US Marines were airlifted by C-130 Hercules transports into Da Nang Air Base for combat against the Viet Cong. Within four months the number of American combat troops in Vietnam had grown to 75,000 men; during the next three years this figure was to reach over half a million.

The war in the air was relatively slow to gain ferocity, although both the USAF and US Navy undertook frequent air strikes against targets in the North. Hitherto, however, the Vietnamese Peoples' Air Force (VPAF) had not counted on this response by modern American combat aircraft, and the pilots of its aged MiG-15bis fighters tended to keep well away from the US Navy Skyhawks and the USAF's F-100s. Such losses that were suffered were the result of Soviet-supplied AA guns, which were quickly and substantially reinforced early in 1965. It was now that large numbers of Chinese-built MiG-17s started arriving in the North, aircraft which, by reason of their different performance and armament emphases rather than any design superiority, were to cause the Americans considerable problems in air combat.

Indeed the nature of the entire war, the absence of a 'front line', the use of guerrilla tactics on a large scale and the underlying ideologies all combined to stretch the endurance of the American fighting men. Worse, these factors were misunderstood by an ill-informed but powerful pacifist lobby back home in the United States.

Martin B-57s bore the brunt of the early tactical bombing missions against the Viet Cong in the South. Bombs were carried in rotating bays and on pylons under the wings. This pair are overflying the Mekong delta.

Cannon-armed F8F-1DB no. 121510 is shown serving with the No. 514 Fighter Squadron (Escadron de Chasse) of the newly-formed Royal Vietnam air force based at Saigon in 1956. The markings of this force were to survive to the end of the Vietnam war, though the F8Fs were withdrawn from front-line service in the 1960s.

Lockheed F-104 Starfighters had a brief and inauspicious career with the USAF, but this did take them to Vietnam, where their high straight-line speed made them useful as bombers against difficult targets. They were, however, inaccurate in this role.

Piasecki H-21s were used in the early days of operations against the VC; most flew with national insignia deleted in the interests of both camouflage. The door gunner of this aircraft can be seen firing on a VC position with his free M60 machine-gun.

Tactical reconnaissance units relied upon the McDonnell RF-101 Voodoo until more capable types such as the RF-4 Phantom arrived. RF-101s suffered heavily from anti-aircraft defences when they overflew Communist territory, but their contribution to the war effort was enormous.

The leafy jungles of Vietnam provided hidden routes for the Viet Cong to infiltrate south with little danger of detection. Under the code-name 'Ranch Hand', jet-boosted C-123Ks were used to spray defoliating chemicals, but this massive and controversial campaign produced limited military benefits.

'ROLLING THUNDER' 1965-72

In March 1965 the air war in Vietnam entered a new phase with the beginning of 'Rolling Thunder', a campaign designed to strike at central Vietnam south of the 19° Parallel. The strikes continued for several months, but were only partially successful because the targets were often hidden beneath the jungle canopy and could not be located: the obvious targets around Hanoi and Haiphong were off-limits to the US forces at the time. Many types were employed throughout the campaign, including the Martin B-57, Republic F-105 Thunderchief, Douglas B-66 Destroyer and Lockheed F-104 Starfighter. The aircraft which stood out was the North American F-100 Super Sabre, which carried the brunt of the 'in-country' war, with over 300,000 sorties flown during the course of the war, more than were flown by the same company's P-51 Mustang in World War II.

The air war continued unabated against Viet Cong guerrillas in the Mekong delta throughout the conflict, with only a limited degree of success. Virtually the entire combat inventory of the US air forces was used, often as training sorties for those units soon to be sent north. Special counter-insurgency aircraft such as the Rockwell OV-10 were employed against the guerrillas, using gun and rocket pods in a massive show of firepower against often empty jungle. The US Navy's carriers sailing at 'Dixie Station' off the Mekong delta flew many strikes into the delta, and used these missions to work up to full strength before moving north to 'Yankee Station' in the Gulf of Tonkin, where the action was much more fierce.

The main strike effort of the US forces was augmented by many supporting missions such as aerial tanking, recovery of ditched aircraft, airborne early warning supplied by Lockheed EC-121 Warning Stars and massive airlift and ferrying involving Lockheed's C-5, C-141 and C-130, the de Havilland Canada C-7 Caribou, Douglas C-47, Boeing C-135 and numerous smaller types. Among the most daring of the supporting roles was that of rescuing downed airmen from enemy-held country, involving the use of Sikorsky HH-3 and HH-53 helicopters under cover of Douglas A-1 Skyraiders. These aircraft, operating under the widely-known call-sign of 'Sandy', flew truly fearless missions in the face of some of the most concentrated and accurate anti-aircraft fire encountered during the war, their job being to draw and then destroy the enemy guns, lay smoke screen and supply suppressive fire while the helicopters

moved in to rescue the airmen. 'Sandy' pilots collected more than their fair share of Purple Hearts, the medal given to killed or injured American servicemen. Many more crews owe their lives to this fearless group of men.

Nakhon Phanom air base in Thailand was the centre of a major operation which was to assume ever increasing importance as the war dragged on. The North Vietnamese supplied the Viet Cong guerrillas operating in the South via the Ho Chi Minh Trail, a series of winding mud tracks running the length of Laos and so bypassing the heavily defended area in the middle of Vietnam. The American forces went to great lengths to cut off the supply of matériel to the South by using all manner of airborne strike-power, from area-bombing by B-52s to attacks by converted light aircraft such as the Cessna O-2. As a result of their low-speed manoeuvrability, the two most successful types were the elderly Douglas A-1 Skyraider and the same company's even older B-26 Invader, both capable of carrying considerable loads and able to deliver them extremely accurately on to the truck targets hidden beneath the jungle. These were controlled by forward-air-controllers (FAC) which located the targets from light aircaft circling above the canopy. Favourite weapons of the attackers were unguided rockets and napalm.

As the trail war grew, the US forces invested more time and money in it and new types such as the General Dynamics F-111 were employed, this type operating with considerable success thanks to its unprecedented accuracy under blind first-pass conditions. In order to monitor the traffic along the trail, ingenious measures were introduced such as 'Igloo White', where seismic sensors were 'sown' across the trail by F-4s, C-130s and specially adapted Lockheed P-2 Neptunes. The signals were processed by EC-121s and positive results of truck movements flashed to the strike aircraft which immediately pressed home the attack. However, despite all the effort thrown in to the Laos war, the Viet Cong received ever more equipment along the mass of almost impassable, almost undetectable tracks, and this was to seal the fate of South Vietnam as much as any other factor.

A splendid picture of a Douglas A-1H (formerly AD-7), final production version of the Skyraider, setting out with full ordnance on a rescue support mission on 1 April 1970. Such roles were ably fulfilled by the A-1, with its useful loiter endurance, low speed and heavy disposable weapons load.

Several Lockheed Neptunes were equipped with low light level TV (LLLTV) and other sensors for night operations over the Trail. Known as AP-2H, these aircraft were operated by the US Navy.

The Grumman OV-1 Mohawk represented the Army's principal battlefield reconnaissance platform. It could carry offensive stores under the wings and also white phosphorus rockets for marking targets. The main sensor was the side-looking airborne radar (SLAR) slung under the fuselage.

Forward air control was an important job in the featureless jungles of Vietnam, and the Cessna O-1 and O-2 were the principal types employed. This is an O-2 armed with minigun pods and white marker rockets.

Below: Seen blasting off into some 'dirty' weather, this North American F-100 Super Sabre is typical of many that bore the brunt of the in-country fighting.

A Douglas AC-26K Invader, rebuilt from a World War 2 vintage B-26, prepares for a hazardous night interdiction mission down the Ho Chi Minh Trail.

AIR POWER STRIKES NORTH 1965-72

The increase in operations against the guerrillas in the South was accompanied by many raids mounted against the North. McDonnell RF-101 Voodoos had been overflying the military installations in North Vietnam since the outbreak of open hostilities (these aircraft being the first jets to arrive in South Vietnam) and there were many targets which the USAF deemed suitable. Among the earliest aircraft to attack the North was the redoubtable Republic F-105 Thunderchief, which could lift eight 750-lb (340-kg) iron bombs and auxiliary fuel tanks. Many carried air-to-air missiles and victories were scored over MiG fighters with both Sidewinder missiles and the internal 20-mm gun. These F-105s usually attacked their targets from medium level on the command of a lead aircraft which was usually a Douglas EB-66 Destroyer, equipped with full electronic countermeasures (ECM) and navigation aids. Inflight-refuelling was often necessary to enable the 'Thuds' to reach their targets.

The arrival in South East Asia of the McDonnell F-4 Phantom heralded a new era as the greater range, load and speed of the aircraft enabled many more targets to be attacked. At first the F-4s were used in the bombing role, with much the same tactics as employed by the F-105s, but losses were beginning to mount to both surface-to-air missiles (SAMs) and North Vietnamese air force MiG-17s and MiG-21s. In order to conquer the latter, Colonel Robin Olds, leader of the 8th Tactical Fighter Wing 'Wolf Pack' devised a mission to draw the MiGs into the air: 80 F-4s configured for the air defence role flew exactly the same pattern as that regularly used by bombing F-105s and F-4s. The MiGs, under the control of excellent ground radar, soon intercepted the force and in the ensuing battle seven were destroyed for the loss of no Phantoms, Olds himself bagging two. Following this action, which was to remain the largest aerial fight of the war, the North Vietnamese were considerably more cuatious with their interceptions, especially as the Americans introduced MIGCAP fighter cover flights equipped with F-4s carrying Sidewinder and Sparrow missiles. Victories continued to be scored, especially when the new F-4E was introduced with internal cannon for the close-in work which was demanded by Washington in the rules for aerial engagement. When bombing rules were relaxed attacks on the North Vietnamese airfields were sanctioned, and the MiG problem stabilized as the war proceeded.

At the same time as the MiGs were being tamed, the SAMs became an ever increasing problem as supplies of the Soviet SA-2 'Guideline' established themselves. To combat the SAMs, the USAF was allowed by Washington to use 'Wild Weasel' F-100s and F-105s equipped with Shrike anti-radiation missiles (ARMs) which homed in on the radar emissions of the 'Fan Song' guiding system for the SA-2. Under the codename 'Iron Hand', the 'Wild Weasels' streaked in ahead of the main attacking force to try to suppress the SAM forces before the main strike. This was partially successful and the war against the SAMs continued throughout the conflict, the Americans continuing to lose aircraft to this often unseen threat.

As the war went on the USAF, despite temporary bombing halts and restrictions, extended its raids to cover the centres of population and installations (although the targets were strictly military) at Hanoi and Haiphong. F-4s and the supporting aircraft such as 'Iron Hand' F-105s, EB-66s and the inevitable tankers started flying as support to the heavy B-52 raids on the north, often used to soften up the SAM defences before the slow, lumbering B-52s arrived over the target. These attacks on Hanoi and its surrounding areas brought up the MiGs again in large numbers and the MIGCAP F-4s were busy again, especially around the B-52s.

Further developments to the strikes against the North involved the introduction of the laser-guided 'smart' bomb, which could be delivered with unerring accuracy. These were carried primarily by Phantoms, which carried a Pave Spike or Pave Knife designator for targeting the bombs. Other weapons employed were conventional bombs, often with 'daisy-cutter' fuse-extenders to make the bomb explode above the ground to cause maximum area damage, Bullpup radio-guided missiles 'flown' from the back seat of the aircraft, and high-drag Snakeye bombs with 'parachutes' which retarded the bomb enabling the low-level attacker to escape the blast of the bomb.

Several of the low-level, small-scale strikes were controlled from a 'fast-mover FAC', an adviser sitting in the back-seat of a two-seat F-100, A-4 or TF-9 Cougar. These aircraft were able to survive the defensive fire by agility and speed, whereas more typical FAC aircraft such as Cessna's O-1 and O-2 were too slow for this hostile environment. Overall control of the battle zone was entrusted to ships sailing in the Gulf of Tonkin and to Lockheed EC-121 Warning Stars circling over the sea. These carried airborne early-warning radar and co-ordinated strikes and interceptions against defending MiGs. Under the code-name 'College Eye', these old-stagers flew for many hours at a time, their crews ever vigilant for impending MiG attacks.

Republic's F-105 Thunderchief, known as the 'Thud', 'Lead Sled' and 'Ultra Hog', was often employed alongside F-4 Phantoms on medium-level bombing whilst other Phantoms flew fighter cover. The Thunderchief proved reliable and durable in the hostile skies over the North.

Bombing F-4s and F-105s were often escorted by Douglas EB-66 Destroyers, which provided accurate navigation and ECM jamming for protection against anti-aircraft missiles.

Airborne early warning and fighter control assets in Vietnam were entrusted to ships in the Tonkin Gulf and the Lockheed EC-121 Warning Star, which patrolled off the coast of Vietnam warning attackers of MiG and SAM activity.

Left: To enable the bombers to reach the North, inflight-refuelling was a necessity. Here a SAC Boeing KC-135A refuels TAC F-4s inbound to North Vietnam. Tanker bases were in Thailand and the Philippines.

Below: North Vietnam operated MiG-17 (illustrated), MiG-19 and MiG-21 aircraft against the attackers. These were flown under strict ground control and gained many victories over US aircraft.

Above: Tactical reconnaissance assets were enhanced by the deployment of the McDonnell FF-4C Phantom. This was far more capable than the earlier RF-101 Voodoo and was less vulnerable to ground fire.

Below: Sterling work was performed by the Douglas EB-66 Destroyer in the electronic countermeasures role. These flew mainly from Thai bases and often escorted the strikes into the North.

Below: Laser guided bombs (LGBs) were introduced into the war and made a dramatic impact, downing many targets that had hitherto been impregnable. These F-4Ds carry Paveway LGBs as well as their air-to-air Sparrow missiles.

The much-loved Thunderchief did more than just drop bombs. Here an F-105 of the 469th TFS, Korat AB, Thailand downs a North Vietnamese MiG-17 west of Hanoi.

HELICOPTER WAR 1965-72

It is perhaps an extraordinary fact that, in terms of aircraft numbers, by the end of the Vietnam War the US Army had become the world's third largest air force after that of the Soviet Union and the USAF. And of all the helicopters used by the US Army, the Bell UH-1 Huey family was produced in larger numbers than any other aircraft in the world except the Soviet An-2 biplane since World War II. The Hueys came to be adopted as the standard transport vehicle of the US Army's Air Cavalry, being capable of carrying, in its early form, up to seven troops, but later 14 or more.

The first US Army helicopters to go to Vietnam in July 1962 were those of the Utility Tactical Helicopter Company (UTHC) which was equipped with UH-1A Iroquois, these being joined later that year by UH-1Bs, and in 1963 the enlarged UH-1D entered service. As already recorded, America started supplying H-21 Workhorse helicopters to Vietnam in 1964, by which time regular units of the US Army, including the 118th Assault Helicopter Company, was operational at Bien Hoa with the UH-1D.

As a result of assessment of experience gained by the UTHC, the US Army quickly adapted to the jungle conditions in Vietnam and numerous helicopter units were activated in the USA for deployment to the theatre. A typical assault mission involving, say, about 100 troops, would require some 16-18 helicopters of which one UH-1 would be equipped as a communications command aircraft carrying the force commander and an air liaison officer whose task would be to call up any USAF support required; another UH-1 would deliver the landing zone (LZ) control party which would land first and guide the assault force in. Fast agile support helicopters (usually Hughes OH-6A Cayuse) armed with Miniguns and/or grenade-launchers would circle the LZ on the lookout for enemy forces, and any seen would be attacked and reported to the assault commander. Medium and light support weapons that were not portable by the assault

helicopters would be brought in by the mortar delivery units or, in large-scale assaults, such weapons as the 105-mm (4.13-in) howitzer would be airlifted by the big CH-53.

Not unnaturally, the development of new assault weapons was accelerated and more and more sophisticated equipment was fitted in the helicopters so as to bring to the battlefield ever-increasing firepower for the US Army's airmobile companies. The AH-1 HueyCobra first entered service in Vietnam in 1967, a fast manoeuvrable helicopter which mounted Miniguns, 20-mm cannon, grenade-launchers and up to 76 high-velocity rockets; later, integrated sensors (such as Smash, a multi-sensor system with IR and MTI which was linked to the weapon-aiming subsystems) were introduced. By 1968 about 50 assault helicopter companies, equipped with between 600 and 700 AH-1G HueyCobras, were based at such locations as Ban Me Thuot, Phuoc Vinh, Pleiku, Bien Hoa, Nha Trang and Tuy Hoa; they included the 135th US-Australian Integrated Assault Helicopter Company based at Vung Tau, Dong Tam and Di An between 1967 and 1972.

Apart from the constant and massive use of assault helicopters by the US Army, other large helicopters were also widely used for numerous heavy-lift tasks, not least of which was the recovery of downed aircraft from otherwise inaccessible locations. It has been stated that during the course of the entire Vietnam war the Boeing Vertol CH-47 Chinook alone recovered no fewer than 11,000 such aircraft, worth a reputed $2.9 billion. The big twin-rotor Chinook, of which more than 680 were produced by the end of the war, equipped numerous units, including those of the 1st Cavalry Division, and could carry up to 44 troops, modest army vehicles, artillery or up to about 28,000 (12700 kg) of stores on external load hooks. The bigger Sikorsky CH-54 Tarhe crane helicopter, which also served with the 1st Cavalry Division (Airmobile), was also used in much smaller numbers in Vietnam and was capable of carrying items such as light armoured vehicles and bulldozers as slung loads; they also recovered 380 downed aircraft. Marginally bigger still was the heavy-lift HH-53 which equipped the 37th Aerospace Rescue and Recovery Squadron at Phu Cat Air Base in Vietnam later in the war. Replacing the earlier Hughes OH-6A as the standard light observation helicopter with the US Army, the Bell OH-58A Kiowa entered service in Vietnam in the early autumn of 1969 with a comprehensive radio fit.

When it was decided to expand the VNAF in 1971 as a self-sufficient air force in the long term, a fast growing number of American helicopters (including CH-47As) were supplied on loan, but in the event the American withdrawal was finally undertaken so hurriedly early in 1974 that the number of Huey-family helicopters left behind and struck off US Army charge exceeded the helicopter strength of any West European air force.

Casualties among American helicopters (and their occupants) were enormous, the relatively slow, lightly-armoured aircraft being easy prey for any weapons from small arms to shoulder-fired ground-to-air missiles; literally thousands were forced down after crew members were wounded or rotors were damaged, and it was these casualties that constituted the bulk of aircraft recovered by the hard-worked Chinooks.

The Sikorsky CH-3C was used extensively in Vietnam, most notably in the rescue role. Here a US Air Force machine hovers over a downed Northrop F-5 prior to airlifting both the pilot and the wrecked aircraft back to a friendly base. There could have been a no more wonderful sight for a pilot in hostile territory.

Hughes OH-6 Cayuse (Loach) pilots earned their fair share of Purple Hearts. These fearless aircrews flew at treetop (and often below) height searching for targets for the Bell AH-1 gunships they were escorting.

Bell UH-1s were the principal helicopters in Vietnam and were used in many roles. This Navy aircraft is flying riverine patrol in the Mekong Delta.

A gunship developed from the successful UH-1B/C serving in Vietnam, the AH-1 had a fuselage only 38 in (0.97 m) wide that housed a gunner in the nose, with his pilot above and behind. Armed with rockets, missiles, grenade-launchers and guns, they escorted troop carriers and provided fire power in landing areas.

Left: Larger units could be moved by the Boeing Vertol Chinook, a tandem-rotor transport helicopter with a payload of 15,000 lb (6804 kg), but ladder descents had to be made quite frequently.

Above: Heavy lift was provided by the Sikorsky CH-54 Tarhe, one of which is seen here being refuelled from rubber fuel bladders.

Below: With loaded side armament and a full complement of troops, a unit of Bell UH-1 assault transports prepares for lift-off and rapid transit to the designated landing zone.

SPECIAL FORCES AND GUNSHIPS 1962-75

Early military campaigns in South East Asia, including the British operations in Burma and Malaya during and after World War II, as well as the French campaigns in Indo-China during the 1940s and 1950s, had demonstrated the need to prepare and support forces specially trained in jungle warfare and long-range infiltration. Tasks would be intelligence gathering, sabotage and destruction of enemy lines of communication, arms depots, fuel dumps, bridges and airfields, etc.

Just as the Viet Cong demonstrated the disproportionate disruption and destruction that relatively small groups of infiltrating guerrillas could cause, so the American Special Forces (modelled along lines similar to those of the British Special Air Service) were active in Vietnam for more than 10 years. At the outset their activities, usually conducted covertly, made considerable use of helicopters for lifting small groups of men to remote jungle sites, sustaining them with food and arms supplies, and retrieving them on completion of their missions. Later, as many more airfields and strips were constructed or extended, the big Lockheed C-130 Hercules came to be widely employed, either dropping the forces by parachute or landing on short stretches of road; numerous new techniques were evolved to supply the Special Forces, including the discharge of stores from the rear of the aircraft as it flew low over prepared clearings. Retrieval of small groups of men (as well as aircrew shot down in enemy territory, and at sea) was sometimes achieved by C-130s equipped with the Fulton recovery gear which literally snatched men from the ground as the aircraft flew overhead. On other occasions Hercules transports delivered vehicles (including tanks) and supply pallets using the low-altitude parachute extraction procedure, the load being dragged off the aircraft's rear ramp by large parachutes.

A novel use of transport aircraft in Vietnam was as 'gunships', in which guns of all calibres were mounted to fire from the side while the aircraft circled an area suspected of occupation by an enemy force. After early use of aged C-47s, the USAF converted a number of C-119K Flying Boxcars (to become the AC-119 Stinger) for the role, but none achieved the success of the AC-130A in the gunship guise. These AC-130As acquired devastating gun batteries which included 7.62-mm (0.3-in) Miniguns, 20-mm cannon, 40-mm Bofors guns and, ultimately a 105-mm (4.13-in) howitzer. These gunships were flown by the 1st Special Operations Wing (as well as by the 8th Tactical Fighter Wing), as much in support of operations by the Special Forces as in self-contained strikes, of which many were flown as far north as the Viet Cong's vital Ho Chi Minh Trail.

C-130s were flown in Vietnam in countless roles. Apart from the routine tasks of airlifting military personnel within the war

theatre, they carried huge loads of equipment required in the extensive programme of constructing and improving airfields in Vietnam. They were employed in electronic countermeasures, gathering information of enemy operating frequencies, and were widely used in the extraordinary 'Igloo White' counter-infiltration project. This involved the discharge of tens of thousands of small seismic sensors through Vietnam, small devices which remained inert on the ground or suspended from trees until activated by the nearby movements of a human being or vehicle; the sensor would then detect and transmit a coded signal denoting the nature of the disturbance, its signals being received by aircraft flying in the vicinity (including reconnaissance drones launched by DC-130As). The signals were automatically relayed to the Infiltration Surveillance Center at Nakhon Phanom Air Base in neighbouring Thailand; information could then be passed to forces alerted for a possible air or ground strike.

Two US Marine Corps squadrons of C-130s were tasked with refuelling US Navy aircraft, VMGR-152 performing much of the support of combat sorties flown by aircraft operating from carriers in the Gulf of Tonkin (as well as USAF aircraft flying up from the south), and VMGR-352 employed in refuelling the large number of US Navy aircraft being flown across the Pacific direct to the war theatre from the USA.

Perhaps one of the most spectacular tasks undertaken by the Hercules was its use of huge charges of explosive to blast clearings in the jungle for use by Army helicopters. Pallets stacked with up to 15,000 lb (6804 kg) of explosive were pushed off the rear ramp of the Hercules, parachuting down to explode just above the ground so as to gain maximum blast without cratering the surface.

Casualties among the Hercules were fairly heavy, but reflect the extent to which they were used in the combat environment; at least 66 were lost through direct enemy action and operational accidents, of which roughly one-third were destroyed on the ground, or during landing and take-off, by Viet Cong attacks on American bases. Of the 26 AC-130 gunships produced, six were lost, four of them in 1972.

C-130s were also used for weather reconnaissance and as battlefield command control centres, and were heavily engaged in the final evacuation of American forces and Vietnamese civilians in April 1974. One such aircraft, whose normal passenger load was about 90, carried a total of 437 evacuees on the last flight out of Saigon.

Lockheed C-130s line up for a resupply mission. The Hercules was used in large numbers for all manner of transport duties and was even used for dropping large bombs to clear landing zones for helicopters.

'Spooky' working out: streams of tracer fill the air above Saigon during the 1968 Tet offensive, fired from a Douglas AC-47 'Spooky' gunship. These were the most welcome sight for a beleaguered ground trooper faced with Viet Cong on his perimeter fence.

Fairchild's C-119 Flying Boxcar was also converted to AC standard, these flying under the call sign 'Shadow'. Armament was four Chain Guns controlled by radar. The AC-119 was not as successful as the AC-47 or AC-130.

Stability in the air, combined with a capacious fuselage, suited the old Douglas C-47 admirably for conversion into the AC-47 Gunship. Orbiting over its target, this AC-47 of the 1st Special Operations Wing could pour a withering hail of fire downwards with its trio of 0.3-in (7.62-mm) Miniguns.

An AC-130 'Spectre' lets fly with its forward Vulcans. The AC-130 was the most impressive of the gunships, in some variants mounting a 105-mm howitzer in the rear fuselage.

A fork-lift truck moves heavy items into the fuselage hold of a Lockheed C-130 Hercules. When all is aboard the sacks of mail in the foreground follow, these usually carried by filling up odd spaces left by more martial stores.

MISSIONS OF THE B-52s 1965-75

Among the most controversial aspects of the war in Vietnam was the degree with which the United States employed its strategic bomber force, the huge Boeing B-52 Stratofortress eight-jet heavy bombers. That they came to be used at all, ostensibly for tactical reasons, was in reality no more nor less than a political ploy and, as such, angered the Communists no less than it fuelled the indignation of the self-styled humanitarian pacifist lobby at home in the USA. What was perhaps more galling to the out-and-out 'hawks' among the military was that the B-52s achieved precious little in tactical or strategic gain, and only served to emphasize America's inability to arrive at a successful military solution to the war.

The aircraft itself was a relic of a 15-year-old design and intended to tote around the world America's airborne nuclear deterrent. That no such ultimate weapon was dropped over Vietnam no one but the most blinkered observer regretted, for such a step would unquestionably have sparked a global war. Nevertheless the fact that the USAF started to assemble B-52s for service over Vietnam as early as February 1965 illustrated the frustration that permeated the USAF at the deteriorating military situation in that country, and this in turn was already clouding political judgement in Washington.

During that month two B-52 wings, the 2nd and 320th, deployed from the USA to the huge Andersen Air Base on Guam in the Marianas. At that time each of the big bombers could lift a total of 27 bombs, each of 825-lb (374-kg) weight, all of them carried in the fuselage bay, but the addition of external racks soon increased the load to 51 such bombs. As a return sortie between Guam and targets in Vietnam involved a round trip of 5,500 miles (8850 km), the aircraft took off with full fuel load and were topped off by KC-135 tankers flying from Okinawa.

Under the codename 'Arc Light', operations by the Buffs (an acronym for Big Ugly Fat Fella) started inauspiciously on 18 June 1965 when 30 B-52Fs set out to bomb supposed Viet Cong bases in Binh Duong province; two of the bombers collided while inflight-refuelling and were destroyed, killing eight crewmen, and 26 aircraft attacked their targets, but without any visible effect on the enemy.

Despite the lack of identifiable aiming points in the featureless jungle, techniques slowly improved and on 15 November of that year 18 B-52s were called on to saturate with bombs an area known to be occupied by North Vietnamese forces attacking the US 1st Air Cavalry Division in the Ia Drang valley. Deemed to be successful, this first 'tactical strike' was followed by others, and it was not long before Viet Cong defectors began to speak of their fear and hatred of the B-52s, whose deluges of bombs would suddenly engulf them,

though the bombers had been neither seen nor heard.

During the normal rotation of units the B-52Fs were relieved by the 28th and 48th Wings equipped with re-engineered B-52Ds, modified for the task of 'trucking explosive' and capable of carrying 90 825-lb (374-kg) bombs, a total load of 74,250 lb (33680 kg). As Andersen became the busiest air base in the world, accommodating up to 200 B-52s, bombing accuracy was being improved by the deployment to Vietnam of mobile bombing-director radar posts which allowed all-radar bombing missions ('Combat Skyspot').

Such was the spectacular effect of the B-52 bombing sorties, demands for such tactical strikes were constant, and the strain on the bomber crews of frequent long distance sorties was alleviated in April 1967 when U-Tapao Air Base in neighbouring Thailand was made available for B-52 operations, thereby cutting sortie times by up to one-third.

In the belief that raids by the B-52s, particularly in the North, had provided the Americans with a powerful argument at proposed peace talks, the US government announced a bombing halt, the threat of its resumption being used as a bargaining weapon. Such a gesture proved fruitless as the communists in turn believed that their own massive build-up of SAM-sites would prove effective in halting the bombers. And certainly, from September 1967 these missiles began to take a heavy toll of American aircraft.

The pause in the B-52 bombing was accompanied by the return of many aircraft and crews to the USA, but in March 1972 a massive North Vietnamese offensive was followed by a rapid reassembly of the bombers, now including the 'wet-wing' B-52G of increased range and with electronic countermeasures equipment. By June that year about 200 B-52Ds and B-52Gs had resumed bombing targets in North Vietnam (in Operation 'Linebacker') and this continued until October when President Nixon ordered a further bombing halt while peace talks were held. The following month the Communists walked out of the negotiations, to be followed by the most intensive of all the B-52s' offensives ('Linebacker II'). In one such raid the Communists loosed off every available SAM at the raiders, destroying no fewer than 15 bombers and severely damaging a further 14. In the face of such opposition the bomber offensive had reached stalemate, and petered out in 1973. By then, however, the USA was already committed to abandon their fruitless peace aims in South East Asia. By the end of April 1974 nothing remained to do but to abandon Vietnam to the unrestrained ravages of the Communists.

A 'Big Belly' B-52D, probably of 43rd BW, parked between missions at Andersen AB, Guam, in 1969. In these harsh trucking missions engines were started with loads some 2,000 lb (907 kg) over the B-52D's safe structural limit.

This aircraft is a Boeing B-52F, wearing the original silver paint scheme carried in the early years. Later B-52s received tactical camouflage.

The most used version of the 'Buff' was the B-52D which received the 'Big Belly' modification to allow it to carry more bombs internally. This B-52D sports the green/tan upper sides and black lower sides particular to this model.

Above: Some 51 general-purpose 750-lb (340-kg) bombs, each weighing around 825 lb (374 kg), rain down from a B-52 towards a suspected Viet Cong position that was, in all probability, not there. With sophisticated navigation equipment, later attacks on North Vietnam's capital caused tremendous destruction.

Above right: B-52Ds taxi out at U-Tapao AFB in Thailand for another mission. Using Thai bases instead of those in Guam cut mission times drastically and reduced crew fatigue.

Right: Smoking exhausts mark the departure of this B-52D from the switchback runway at Guam. Full water-injection was needed to lift the aircraft and its heavy load for the long round trip to Vietnam.

Below: Andersen AFB on Guam became host to the greatest armada of bombers amassed since World War II. Peak numbers were reached in 1972, when a proportion of the force had to be on a mission at any given time as there were no hardstandings for them.

NAVAL INVOLVEMENT 1964-75

Following the retaliatory strikes launched by the *Ticonderoga* and *Constellation*, the US Navy became heavily involved in the struggle in South East Asia. Among its earliest operations was the monitoring and interception of junk traffic carrying war matériel into South Vietnam. Under the name 'Market Time', Lockheed P-2 Neptunes and Martin P-5 Marlins plied the coasts around Vietnam, keeping watch on all movements, including Soviet supply vessels entering Haiphong harbour. These elderly aircraft were supplemented by the Lockheed P-3 Orion in the late 1960s and the maritime patrols lasted throughout the war.

The main operations concerned the carriers sailing at two stations off Vietnam ('Dixie' and 'Yankee'), from where strikes were launched against the enemy. Strikes followed the lines of those of the USAF and were often held in concert with that service. The early ships carried Vought F-8 Crusaders, Douglas A-1 Skyraiders, Douglas A-3 Skywarriors, Douglas A-4 Skyhawks and Grumman E-1 Tracer AEW aircraft. Gradually these aircraft were phased out of service as new types reached the war-zone, the more modern machines including types such as the McDonnell F-4 Phantom II, Grumman A-6 Intruder, Grumman E-2 Hawkeye, North American RA-5 Vigilante and the Vought A-7 Corsair II. The older types continued to serve on the smaller carriers such as *Bon Homme Richard*, *Hancock*, *Intrepid*, *Oriskany* and *Ticonderoga*, while the larger carriers such as *Constellation*, *Forrestal*, *John F. Kennedy*, *Kitty Hawk* and *Midway* re-equipped with the newer types.

All these aircraft were flown on strikes against the North with A-1s, A-4s, A-6s and A-7s, ably assisted by bomb-carrying F-4s providing the teeth of the strike, whilst F-4s and F-8s provided top cover (MIGCAP). Further F-4s and F-8s flew fleet defence missions (BARCAP) and specially adapted A-3s and A-6s were equipped for the inflight-refuelling and ECM roles. The naval fighter pilots were well-trained, and the scores against the North Vietnamese MiGs rose steadily, most falling to F-4s and F-8s, which were highly regarded by their pilots for their manoeuvrability. Further kills were recorded by A-4s, A-7s and, on one historic occasion, two elderly A-1s downed a MiG-17 between them. The Skyraider had started the war as the US Navy's main attack aircraft, already 20 years old and continuing in service until 1968 (a few survived in the electronic warfare role beyond this date). The 'Spad', as it was known, could lift phenomenal loads and absorb massive battle damage and flew many RESCAP missions in support of search-and-rescue Kaman SH-2s and Sikorsky SH-3s, in much the same way as the USAF 'Spads'. The A-4 Skyhawk was another brilliant Douglas design which served on the attack squadrons throughout the war,its agility enabling it to perform attacks on the most heavily defended

targets. Its place was being taken by the A-7 towards the end of the conflict, an aircraft capable of carrying out the same role as the A-4 but also adding extra air-to-air support for the F-4s, as well as being able to carry the Shrike anti-radiation missile in the 'Iron Hand' role. Perhaps the greatest addition to the air wings was the A-6 Intruder, which at the time had the most advanced weapons delivery and navigation system in the world. It was able to deliver low-level first-pass strikes with extraordinary accuracy in weather that often prevented other aircraft from flying. Reconnaissance and battle damage assessment for the fleet was provided by the RA-5 Vigilante and the RF-8 Crusader. These often had to be escorted by F-4s and F-8s over North Vietnam as they carried no defensive armament; additionally, the Vigilante was not particularly manoeuvrable.

The US Marine Corps flew large numbers of aircraft in Vietnam, mainly on short-range attacks from their bases at Chu Lai and Da Nang. Aircraft types involved were A-4, A-6, F-4 and F-8, used almost exclusively as 'mud-movers'. These were controlled from 'fast-mover' FAC aircraft such as TA-4s and TF-9 Cougars, and an element of ECM was provided by modified Douglas EF-10 Skyknights, an elderly jet design. Rockwell OV-10s were later procured to perform light strike and FAC duties.

The US Navy undertook many special operations during the war, often of a reconnaissance and intelligence nature. These included flights over the Ho Chi Minh Trail with Douglas RA-3s equipped with camouflage detection film and real-time video cameras to find the trucks hidden beneath the triple-canopy forest. EA-3s, EA-1s and EA-6s carried out many jamming and electronic intelligence missions around the area and EP-3 Orions took over from the EC-121s in the airborne command post role. Another facet of the US Navy's work was the 'brown-water navy' which plied the endless creeks of the Mekong delta, policing the waterways and searching for Viet Cong guerrillas. The surface vessels were supported in the air by Bell UH-1s and OV-10 Broncos, usually used to destroy guerrilla pockets which had attacked shipping.

Following the peace talks, the last acts of the US Navy were to mine-sweep Haiphong harbour with Sikorsky CH-53s under Operation 'Endsweep', and in 1975 the carriers *Enterprise*, *Midway* and *Coral Sea* provided air cover for the evacuation of Saigon. In the final few panic stricken hours, helicopters were being pushed over the side as soon as they had unloaded to create landing room for further aircraft on the already overcrowded flight deck.

Reconnaissance for the fleet was handled by the North American RA-5 Vigilante (illustrated) and the Vought RF-8 Crusader. Both types were extremely capable in this role but were vulnerable to attack, and usually had to be escorted on missions over North Vietnam by fighters.

Two Vought types which played a large part in the proceedings were the excellent F-8 Crusader fighter and the A-7 Corsair II attack aircraft. Corsair IIs were often employed on 'Iron Hand' anti-radiation missions whilst the Crusaders were normally used as clear-air dogfighters, a role at which they excelled.

The Grumman A-6 Intruder introduced devastating blind first-pass accuracy to the arena. It carried a heavy load and provided the heaviest punch available to the Navy.

Electronic missions and airborne early warning were handled by the Douglas EA-1 Skyraider and the Grumman E-1 Tracer (both illustrated) until the far more capable Grumman E-2 Hawkeye reached service. Both types continued in use on the smaller carriers for several years.

The remarkable Douglas A-3 Skywarrior was used in a large variety of roles including bomber, electronic and photographic reconnaissance, ECM and tanker. This is an RA-3 reconnaissance platform about to trap.

The Douglas A-4 Skyhawk could carry an enormous load for its small size and was the Navy's chief attack aircraft throughout the campaign, although at the end it was being replaced by the Vought A-7. Trials were carried out with tactical camouflage, but this was dropped after complaints from deck crew, especially during night operations.

Perhaps the most famous and colourful aircraft of the war were the F-4 Phantoms of VF-111 'Sundowners'. The Phantom emerged as the Navy's most successful fighter in terms of numbers, although the Vought F-8 returned a much higher kill-loss ratio.

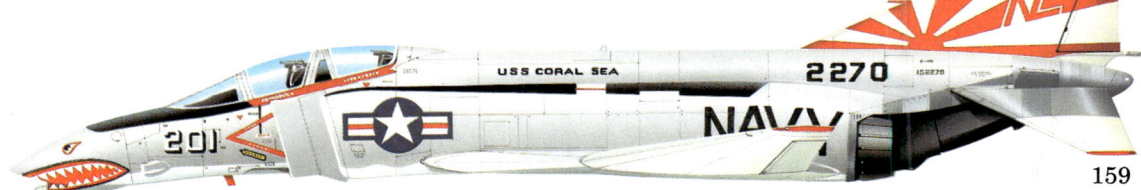

MIDDLE EAST TROUBLES 1956-75

The dominant western influence in the Middle East between the world wars had been that of the UK, whose RAF had been engaged largely in ensuring freedom of passage through the Mediterranean, Suez Canal and Red Sea, policing duties in Iraq, securing oil supply lines and exercizing administration of the mandate in Palestine. To perform this variety of tasks the British had established quite a large number of air bases whose names were to become part of the RAF's lore.

Moreover, resulting from this military influence and further enhanced by operations during World War II, the British had been instrumental in creating national forces whose equipment and weapons were supplied under strict diplomatic control by British industry. As the UK's worldwide responsibilities waned (particularly in the Far East, or 'east of Suez'), however, so the importance of strategic passage through the Middle East diminished, and the economically-motivated decline in Middle and Far Eastern responsibilities coincided with a steadily increasing determination of nationalist factions to be rid of British influence. The fast-growing population of immigrant Jews into, and the ending of the British mandate in Palestine, constituted the first manifestation of declining British interest and influence.

The seeming intransigence of Britain towards settlement of the Palestine problem did much to alienate Arab support and, following the abortive Suez operations of 1956, British prestige in the Middle East reached an all-time low. The British-Transjordan treaty was abrogated and the RAF thus lost access to its former bases at Amman and Mafraq. However, use by the Arab Legion Air Force (and later the Royal Jordanian Air Force) of British aircraft, at least resulted in a measure of RAF presence in the Gulf area for a number of years.

To the east of Jordan, Iraq's post-war history was more turbulent, and it was perhaps unfortunate that Habbaniyah, built by the RAF in 1934, together with Heliopolis in Egypt and Khormaksar at Aden, represented something of a cornerstone of British air power in the Middle East. Denied the use of the other two bases, Khormaksar assumed considerably greater strategic importance, lying as it did at the southern end of the Red Sea as well as being within range of RAF bases in East Africa and those on the southern coast of the Persian Gulf. Faced with an increasing build-up of Soviet-supplied weapons throughout the area, states friendly towards the West,

particularly the Gulf States, looked to the UK to maintain a military presence and at the same time entered defence agreements which embraced British-style training programmes for their own forces.

During the 1950s the RAF deployed in Aden No. 8 Squadron (with Brigands, Vampires, Venoms and Meteors), No. 37 Squadron (with Shackletons) and three squadrons (Nos 37, 78 and 84) of transports, their task being the protection of oil shipping in the Gulf and Red Sea, and intercession between Arab factions when called on to do so. In due course the Aden States and the United Arab Emirates gained autonomy, so that Khormaksar alone remained the UK's foothold in the Arabian peninsula.

The British government's formal declaration in 1967 of its withdrawal of military interest 'east of Suez' coincided with an assumption of power by the National Liberation Front in South Yemen, a familiar pattern of revolutionary opportunism adopted by communist factions the world over. At that time the RAF deployed seven squadrons (Nos 8, 21, 37, 43, 78, 84 and 105) with Hunter FGA.Mk 9s, Twin Pioneers, Andovers, Pembrokes, Shackletons, Argosies, Beverleys and Wessex helicopters. These units were either disbanded or dispersed elsewhere, although British commercial companies remained to undertake the training of a South Yemeni air force.

Stability was maintained by the combined efforts of Iraq, Jordan, Saudi Arabia, Pakistan and India, which supported the tiny state of Oman when it was threatened by Soviet-supported guerrilla operations by the PFLO between 1968 and the mid-1970s. This prolonged confrontation certainly served to demonstrate all too clearly the potential political alignments after the formal departure of the UK's stabilizing influence. Unfortunately the USA, a large proportion of whose oil supplies flowed from the Persian Gulf, chose to prop up a discredited regime in Iran, so that when a new dimension in religious demarcation emerged following the revolution in that country, not only were the previous political influences destroyed but full-scale war between Iraq and Iran broke out, a war that threatened the total destruction of the international economic structure that had evolved in the Middle East during the previous half-century.

The Handley Page Hastings lumbered around the Middle East for many years, proving a useful and reliable transport for men and material.

Yemeni terrorists are about to receive rockets from a Hawker Hunter FGA.Mk 9 of No. 43 Squadron on the border with Aden in the latter days of the British presence in the area. Aden, once the cornerstone of Britain's Middle East 'empire' had, 10 years later, become one of the most revolutionary states in the world.

Operations room for No. 208 Squadron at Amman in Jordan during 1958 was this tent, where sorties for the Hunter F.Mk 6s were planned.

Below: Before receiving Hunters, No. 208 Squadron flew Gloster Meteors, chiefly the FR.Mk 9 version, which could fly both the fighter and the reconnaissance mission.

Below: The de Havilland Vampire, in its FB.Mk 5 and FB.Mk 9 versions, served as the standard fighter and ground-attack aircraft in the Middle East for the first half of the 1950s. This is an FB.Mk 9 in service with No. 32 Squadron, whose blue and white insignia are carried on the tail booms.

Five RAF squadrons (Nos 21, 78, 152, 209 and 230) flew the Scottish Aviation Twin Pioneer CC.Mk 1. No. 21 Squadron was the first to become equipped in 1959, taking them from the UK to Eastleigh, Kenya, and remaining there until moved to Khormaksar in 1965 to support army operations in the Radfan.

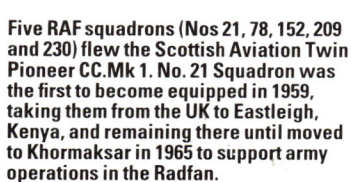

THE INDO-PAKISTAN WARS 1947-71

Following the withdrawal of British rule from India in 1947, the sub-continent underwent partitioning which proved awesome in its realization, having regard to the fragmentation of indigenous administration within the Indian Civil Service and the framework of traditional hereditary rule, not to mention the problems posed by fiercely divided religious interests. The principal bone of contention was to be the state of Kashmir, whose population was overwhelmingly Moslem and which was to be included not in Moslem Pakistan but in predominantly Hindu India.

Partition was not yet a year old when Kashmir was the scene of fighting when tribesmen from Pakistan's border areas threatened the capital Srinagar, a situation only restored by the intervention of Indian airborne forces brought into action by a fleet of Dakotas. At that time the air forces of both India and Pakistan were almost exclusively equipped with ex-RAF or other British aircraft, the former possessing Spitfires, Tempest Mk 2s, Liberator heavy bombers and Dakota transports, and the latter a smaller number of Spitfires, Tempests, Halifaxes and Dakotas.

Following this brief conflict which, despite being put before the United Nations, did not resolve the Kashmiri problem, the UK continued to supply aircraft to Pakistan (Hawker Fury Mk 60s, Supermarine Attacker jet fighters, Halifax bombers and Bristol 170 freighters) as well as Vampire jet fighters to India, until the mid-1950s. However, as if to emphasize their determination to break all former colonial ties, both nations then started negotiations for arms purchase elsewhere, Pakistan acquiring F-86Fs and B-57Bs from the United States, and India obtaining Ouragan and Mystère IVA fighters from France. The UK nevertheless continued to supply large numbers of aircraft, notably the Hunter Mk 56 and Mk 66 fighters and Canberra jet bombers to India.

In August 1965 the Kashmir dispute once more erupted and brought war between India and Pakistan, a vicious 17-day war in which Indian Hunters fought a number of combats with Pakistan's F-86s. The missile-armed Sabres proved superior on most occasions to the gun-armed Hunters, and India's losses in the air were substantially higher than those of Pakistan, although the end of the war brought about the latter nation's virtual isolation from the United States when the USA peremptorily suspended all military supplies to Pakistan.

The suspension of economic aid from the USA prompted Pakistan to commence overtures to communist China, a political expediency rendered no difficult undertaking in view of the poor relations between China and India that had resulted in border clashes since 1962. Accordingly, during the latter half of the 1960s, Pakistan received some 140 twin-jet Shenyang J-6s (Chinese-built MiG-19s) and deployed these at Masroor, Rafiqui and Sargodha, at the same time acquiring 90 Dassault Mirage IIIs from France. The nation's radar network was also modernized with Marconi Condor GCI stations and Plessey AR-1 equipment.

India on the other hand, while continuing to receive Hunters from the UK and negotiating to produce Folland Gnat close-support fighters, turned to the Soviet Union, concluded a treaty of mutual assistance and received MiG-21 interceptors (also licence-built in large numbers) as well as about 100 Sukhoi Su-7B jet aircraft.

A third Indo-Pakistan war broke out in 1971 following India's invasion of East Pakistan, a war in which Pakistan found itself at a considerable disadvantage as the bulk of its forces were located 1,000 miles (1610 km) distant in West Pakistan. Thus, while there was little Pakistan could do to influence the war in the east, the nation attempted to wrest some measure of success by provoking an air war in the west. Such had been the considerable strengthening of the Indian air force since 1965, however, that Pakistan effectively brought defeat upon itself, the elderly F-86s now proving no match for the large numbers of Hunters and Gnats, while the small numbers of Pakistani F-104 Starfighters (supplied by the USA before the suspension of arms supplies) were quickly grounded by a lack of spares. Although the PAF's Mirage IIIs and J-6s proved effective in the air defence and ground-attack roles respectively, fairly large numbers were destroyed by Indian flak and on the ground in raids by IAF Canberras, MiG-21s and Su-7s. The end of the war brought about the creation of the independent state of Bangladesh out of East Pakistan.

More recently the Soviet invasion of neighbouring Afghanistan has brought apprehension to both India and Pakistan, both of whose air forces have embarked on frantic modernization, a task rendered infinitely embarrassing by a need to avoid straining relations with the Soviet Union while attempting to woo sympathy from the West.

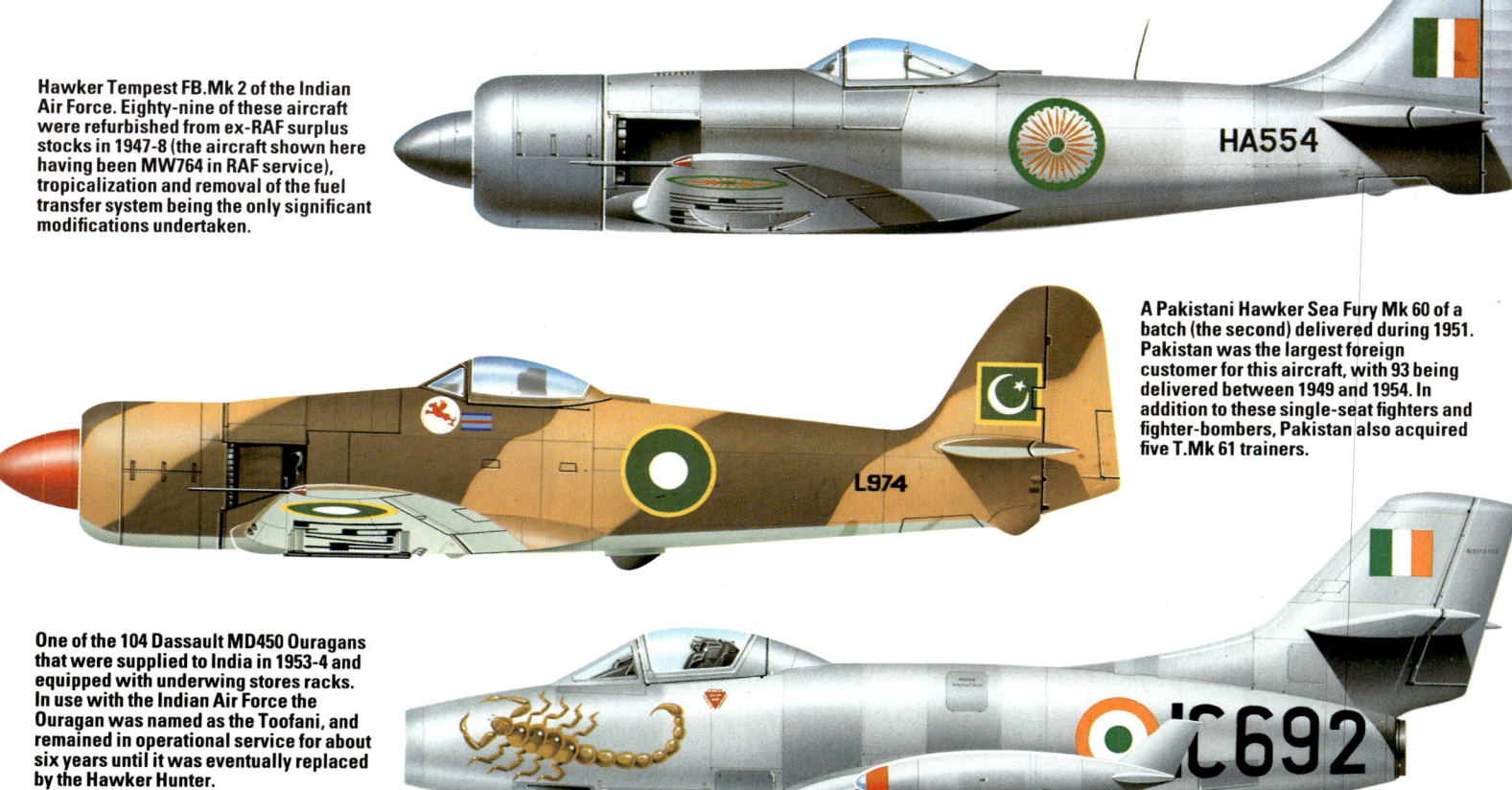

Hawker Tempest FB.Mk 2 of the Indian Air Force. Eighty-nine of these aircraft were refurbished from ex-RAF surplus stocks in 1947-8 (the aircraft shown here having been MW764 in RAF service), tropicalization and removal of the fuel transfer system being the only significant modifications undertaken.

A Pakistani Hawker Sea Fury Mk 60 of a batch (the second) delivered during 1951. Pakistan was the largest foreign customer for this aircraft, with 93 being delivered between 1949 and 1954. In addition to these single-seat fighters and fighter-bombers, Pakistan also acquired five T.Mk 61 trainers.

One of the 104 Dassault MD450 Ouragans that were supplied to India in 1953-4 and equipped with underwing stores racks. In use with the Indian Air Force the Ouragan was named as the Toofani, and remained in operational service for about six years until it was eventually replaced by the Hawker Hunter.

Three Indian HAL Type 77s (basically a licence-built MiG-21FL) in disparate colour schemes wait at dispersal. The MiG-21 has been built in four main versions by Hindustan Aeronautics Ltd, and the company is now manufacturing the MiG-23, which will serve alongside the MiG-21 for many years to come.

Pakistani Canadair Sabres played a large part in the 1971 war. But they soon found themselves outclassed in the air by Indian HAL-built Gnats and Hawker Hunters, were destroyed on the ground by IAF Canberras, MiG-21s and Sukhoi Su-7s, or proved easy targets for defending Indian anti-aircraft fire.

Sukhoi Su-7BM Fitter-A of the Indian Air Force in December 1971. The dark grey/green camouflage was applied in the field, and partly obscured the national insignia. India received about 100 of these aircraft, and towards the end of the 1970s some 75 of them still equipped Nos 26, 32, 221 and 222 Squadrons.

Martin B-57 Canberra bombers were supplied to Pakistan and these played a small part in the wars with India.

A Dassault-Breguet Mirage IIIEP of No. 5 Squadron, Pakistan air force. Equipped with attack radar, this version, which was longer than most Mirage III variants, was based at Sargodha throughout the 1970s.

A Pakistani Shenyang J-6 is caught in the sights. These formed the basis of Pakistani air power alongside the Dassault Mirage III at the time of the 1971 war and proved extremely tough and capable against perhaps better opposition.

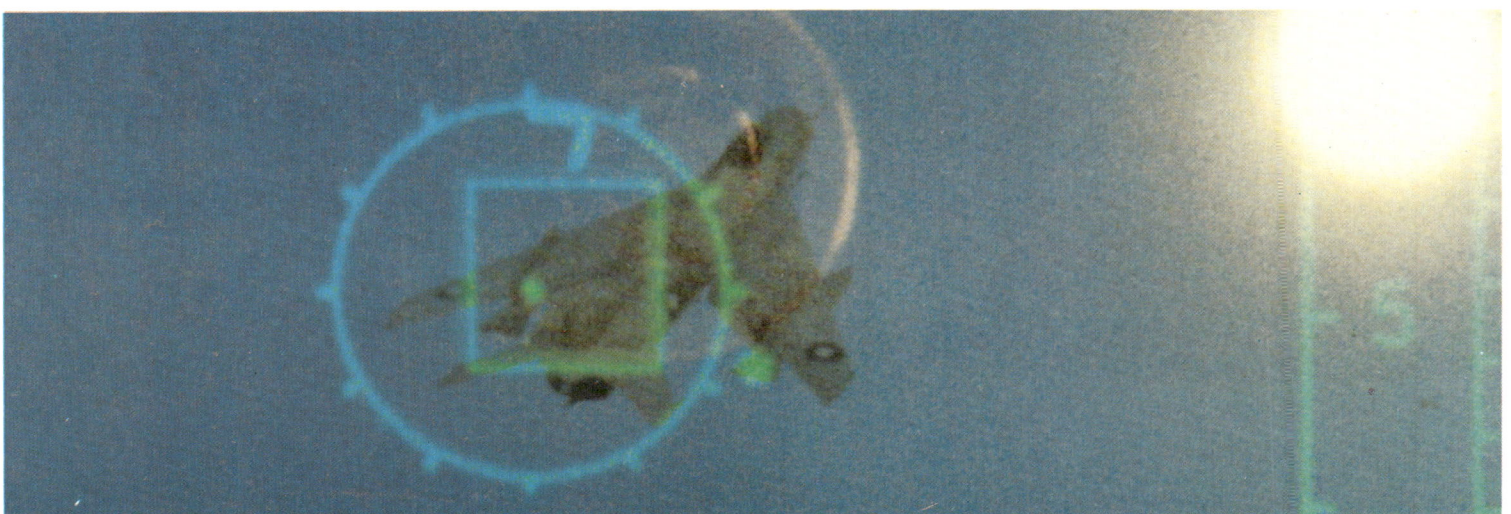

THE SIX-DAY WAR

Antagonism between Israel and her Arab neighbours reached a new level of acerbity following the UN decision to withdraw its peace-keeping forces from the Egypt/Israel border on 17 May 1967, a diplomatic success that encouraged Egypt to close the Gulf of Aqaba to Israeli shipping. Although the Arab military staffs believed this action would provoke Israel into war with Egypt, President Nasser allayed their fears, and on 2 June the Arab forces relaxed their advanced state of alert.

At around dawn on 5 June 40 Israeli air force (IAF) aircraft were spotted on Egyptian coastal radar flying west over the Mediterranean, supposedly on their routine daily training exercise; no action was taken and the Egyptian dawn fighter patrols were stood down. Less than 15 minutes later 10 sections, each of four Mirage IIIs and Super Mystères, struck the Egyptian airfields at Abu Sueir, Beni Sueif, Bir Gifgafa, Bir Thamada, Cairo West, El Arish, Fayid, Inchas, Jebel Libni and Kabrit, bombing and strafing the parked aircraft and cratering the runways. Two more waves followed immediately afterwards as the first returned to base to refuel and rearm before returning to the attack. In three hours the Israeli pre-emptive strikes destroyed more than 300 Egyptian aircraft, almost all of them Soviet-built MiG-17s, -19s and -21, Su-7s, Il-28s and Tu-16s. Of the last (considered to be vital targets because of their ability to carry large stand-off missiles capable of reaching Israeli population centres) the two squadrons extant were wiped out. Nineteen Israeli aircraft were shot down.

Within hours Jordan, Syria, Iraq and Lebanon joined the war, Jordan's artillery cratering the vital runways at Ramat David, and her air force (RJAF) launching an attack by 16 Hunters on Kfar Sirkin and Natanya. The Israeli army had already advanced against Jerusalem by mid-day, however, and now the IAF turned its attention to the RJAF with devastating strikes against its bases at Mafraq and Amman, destroying 17 of its total force of 18 Hunters; with no aircraft for his pilots to fly, King Hussein placed them at the disposal of the Iraqi air force at its base H3. It was Syria's turn to be attacked in the afternoon as IAF aircraft struck bases at Damascus, Dumayr, Marj Rial and Seikal. The final attacks of this first day found the IAF striking the vital Egyptian radar stations in Sinai and along the Suez Canal, followed immediately by airfield strikes on Al Minya, Cairo International Airport and Helwan, as well as Luxor and Ras Banas in the south.

Egyptian defence plans for the Sinai had depended heavily on air support, but with more than three-quarters of the Egyptian air force destroyed on the first day and a successful Israeli Sikorsky S-58 helicopter-mounted commando attack behind the Sinai frontier,

Field Marshal Amer decided to pull his forces back from the border on 6 June. Seeing the enemy in retreat the Israeli army launched two powerful armoured thrusts, which quickly broke through the Egyptian front, to seize the key Giddi and Mitla mountain passes in western Sinai. Succeeding in this, the Israeli army trapped in the east large Egyptian forces which were ruthlessly attacked by Fouga Magisters (previously held back for defence of home skies), Mirage IIIs, Super Mystères and Vautour twin-jet bombers.

As desperate efforts were made by the Egyptians to contain the Israelis' advance in Sinai, their air force strove to make airworthy small numbers of MiG-21s with which to attack the IAF when favourable opportunities accurred. By and large, however, the real casualties had been suffered among Egypt's pilots, of whom not more than about 50 of the most experienced now survived, not to mention the badly damaged runways. Pairs of aircraft were sent into action but, almost invariably, they were overwhelmed.

In the north most of the fighting was in the air. An Iraqi Tu-16 attacked the Nataniya industrial area on 6 June, but was shot down. When the IAF tried to attack Iraqi air bases it was heavily engaged by Hunters whose pilots claimed nine of the raiders. A Lebanese reconnaissance Hunter was shot down over Galilee as frequent air battles continued for the next four days. One of the Jordanian Hunter pilots, Captain Ihsan Shurdom, was credited with the destruction of one Mirage, two Mystères and a Vautour jet bomber.

By 8 June the battle in Sinai was approaching its end, with the Israelis now established on the east bank of the Suez Canal and the Egyptian air force powerless to strike effectively. A UN ceasefire came into effect early on the following day, and this was observed by both Israelis and Egyptians in the south. In the north Syria had already accepted a UN ceasefire on 8 June, but when the Israelis persisted in their attacks to storm and capture the Golan Heights the Syrians withdrew the remains of their air force to defend Damascus. Only when Israel had achieved all her objectives did she agree to suspend hostilities.

Israel had won the war but failed to impose peace in the area. She had destroyed 286 Egyptian, 22 Jordanian, 54 Syrian, about 20 Iraqi and one Lebanese aircraft for the loss of between 45 and 60 of her own, as well as some 30 pilots killed or captured. There was to be no short-term reconciliation between Arab and Jew; both sides simply set about rebuilding their forces and embarked on the next, inevitable confrontation.

A flight of four Israeli air force Mirage IIICJ all-weather interceptors and day ground-attack aircraft, which was one of the many successful and effective types used by the Israelis during the Six-Day War.

THE SIX-DAY WAR

The close relationship between France and Israel meant that many French types were operated during the conflict. This Dassault Mystère IVA depicts the camouflage scheme carried by aircraft assigned to airfield attack. Three squadrons (60 Mystères) were involved, with only eight aircraft lost in total.

A Mikoyan-Gurevich MiG-17F 'Fresco-C' of the Egyptian air force. In numerical terms the most important aircraft in the Arab inventory, it could have proved highly effective if committed solely to the task of an interceptor, but losses were high when it was used for ground-attack and fighter-bomber roles.

One of the vital targets for the pre-emptive air strikes made by the Israeli air force on the morning of 5 June 1967 was Cairo West air base. This was home to the Egyptian Tupolev Tu-16 'Badgers' which, with the capability to launch large stand-off missiles, had to be knocked out at an early stage.

This Mil Mi-6 makes a morale-boosting flight over Cairo during the 1967 war. The Mi-6 was the largest helicopter available to either side, but could do little to stem the phenomenal advance of the Israelis.

Countries committed to the UARAF in the Six-Day War used stars on their original insignia. Three stars identified Syrian aircraft, in this case a MiG-19SF 'Farmer'. They were equipped with three NR-30 30-mm cannon and various stores, but despite their potential threat they were well contained by the Israelis.

One of the most numerically important and ultimately effective aircraft in service with the Israeli air force was the Dassault Mirage IIICJ. With various bomb and rocket stores combinations, the Mirage was involved extensively throughout the conflict in both ground-attack and interceptor roles.

While the jet-equipped squadrons stole the limelight with impressive sorties into enemy territory, some equally important aircraft were involved in troop movements. The Sikorsky S-58 helicopters provided the mobility essential for quick progress through the Egyptian defences in the Sinai.

WAR OF YOM KIPPUR 1973

The war of Yom Kippur (the Day of Atonement) was unleashed on 6 October 1973 against Israel by Egypt, not as an aggressor but as the liberator of Sinai, which had been occupied by the Israelis since the Six-Day War of 1967. By 1973 the air forces of both nations had undergone extensive modernization, that of Egypt thanks to support by the Soviet Union and that of Israel with massive assistance from the United States. The former included more than 400 MiG-21s and Su-7s, and many more MiG-17s the latter some 290 Skyhawks and Phantoms; this disparity was to a great extent offset by the Phantom's ability to carry up to 16,000 lb (7258 kg) of ordnance, seven times the load carried by a MiG-21 and 10 times that of the Egyptians' principal ground-support aircraft, the MiG-17.

Determined not to be surprised by pre-emptive action, as in the previous War, Egypt started massing her forces on the western bank of the Suez Canal on 5 October, a move immediately spotted by the Israelis who, unprepared and suddenly alarmed, began hurriedly to move their armour forward through Sinai. At 14.00 on 6 October 1,000 Egyptian guns opened up a massive barrage across the canal, its cover enabling assault infantry to cross at four points. Air battles began raging as Egyptian MiG-17s, covered by MiG-21s, ranged forward against the Israeli positions in Sinai; Israeli Skyhawks in turn attempted to attack Egyptian forces moving up to the west bank but were met by intense radar-predicted AA fire and a deep belt of surface-to-air missiles. In an attack on the first day against the Israeli command position at Bit Gifgafa, three Egyptian MiG-17s were destroyed by Hawk missiles; all told, the air fighting on 6 October cost the Israelis 11 aircraft, the Egyptians 100. The Egyptians had also attempted to bomb Tel Aviv, launching a 'Kelt' stand-off missile from a Tu-16, but the missile was shot down by a Phantom.

The next day the Israelis carried out heavy attacks on the Egyptian SAM sites, but did little damage to their concrete structures and lost about six Skyhawks. The Egyptians now launched airstrikes against the enemy's airfields in a vain attempt to destroy the Israeli air force on the ground, but suffered the loss of more than 30 aircraft. Elsewhere, under strong top cover, the Egyptians started airlifting further assault forces forward by helicopter. On 8 October the Egyptians in turn attacked missile sites at Baluza, Judi and Samarah, as the Israelis concentrated on defending their air bases and ground forces; both sides lost about a dozen aircraft.

By 10 October, following the destruction of the Israeli 190th Tank Brigade on the ground, the Egyptians deepened their defence line of SAMs by setting up mobile sites on the east bank of the canal. By 12 October, independent sources estimated that losses so far amounted to 99 Egyptian aircraft (including 17 helicopters) compared with 94 Israeli aircraft (including 16 helicopters). In the north Syria had joined battle against Israel and had suffered the loss of at least 80 aircraft.

The ground fighting on 14 October proved to be the turning point of the war. A massive tank battle in Sinai cost each side about 100 tanks destroyed, losses which forced the Egyptians to move forward their reserves of armour being held on the west bank of the Canal. Two days later the Israelis battered their way forward and succeeded in putting across armour into Egypt and establishing a bridgehead. Meanwhile, in reply to desperate Israeli calls for assistance, the United States had supplied 24 more Phantoms to replace those lost, as well as a large number of Shrike anti-radiation missiles, vital weapons in Israel's attacks on the SAM sites. Despite all attempts by the Egyptians to destroy the Israeli forces, now on the rampage west of the canal, the bridgehead held, and air battles overhead began to swing heavily against the Egyptians who lost 45 aircraft in four days. As the Egyptian 3rd Army faced encirclement and annihilation a ceasefire was agreed and eventually took effect on 24 October.

In the north the early Syrian attacks had also met with success, but the Arab forces had failed to cover their advance by moving forward adequate SAMs and thereafter suffered heavily from air attacks by Israeli Skyhawks. Some devastating raids were also carried out by bomb-carrying Phantoms deep inside Syria. After withdrawal by the Syrians from the commanding Golan Heights the outcome of the war was never in doubt, and the Israelis, having come close to disaster in its early stages, emerged victorious, albeit almost exhausted. There is little doubt that they had been saved by imaginative and courageous tactics and superior weaponry, not to mention the assistance rendered by the USA at the moment when disaster seemed imminent.

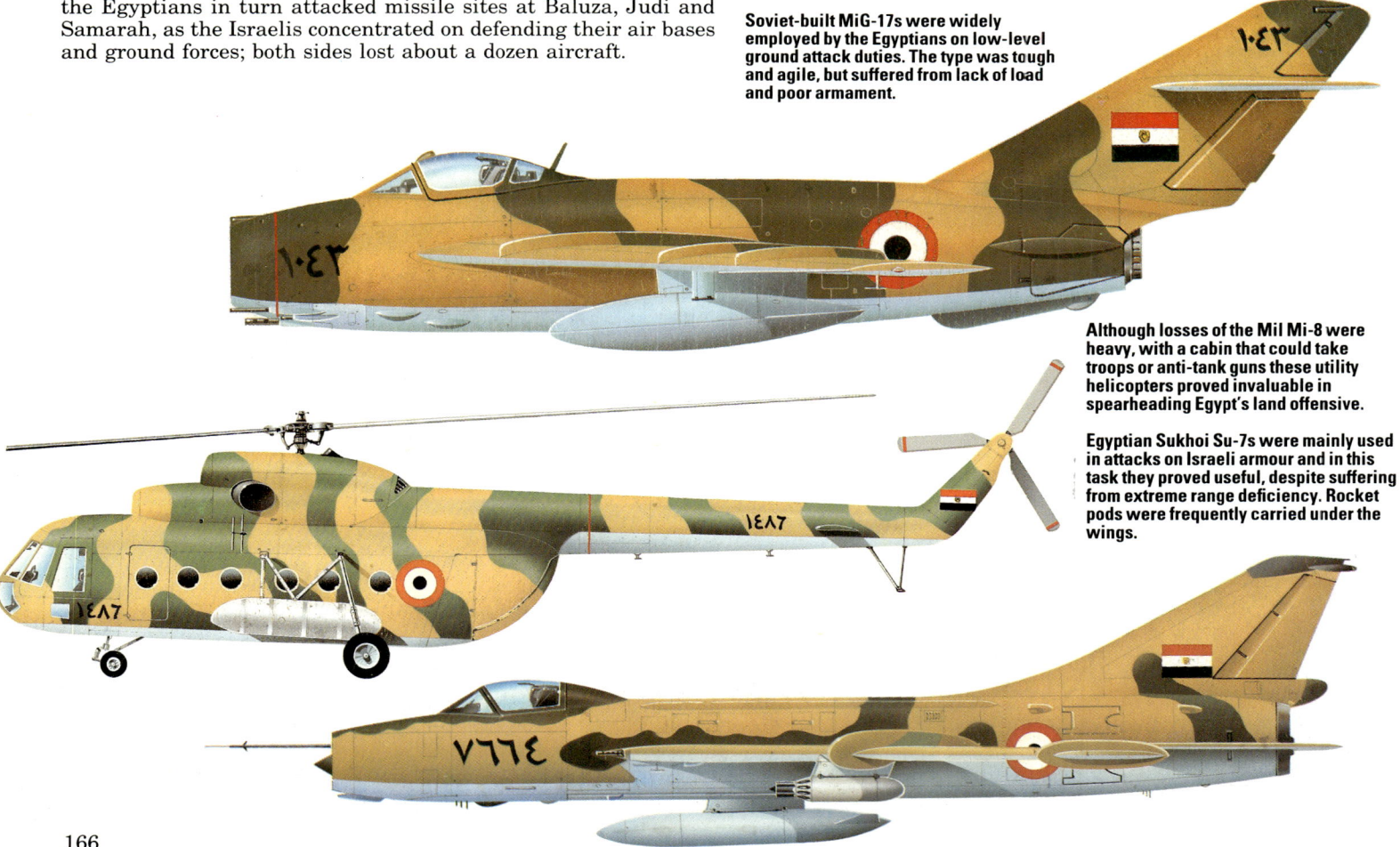

Soviet-built MiG-17s were widely employed by the Egyptians on low-level ground attack duties. The type was tough and agile, but suffered from lack of load and poor armament.

Although losses of the Mil Mi-8 were heavy, with a cabin that could take troops or anti-tank guns these utility helicopters proved invaluable in spearheading Egypt's land offensive.

Egyptian Sukhoi Su-7s were mainly used in attacks on Israeli armour and in this task they proved useful, despite suffering from extreme range deficiency. Rocket pods were frequently carried under the wings.

An Egyptian MiG-17 plunges towards the ground after being hit by a heat-seeking air-to-air missile. There was a curious dichotomy in the missile war, the SAM superiority of the Arab forces being balanced by the Israeli's total dominance in AAM firings.

One Tupolev Tu-16 'Badger-G' managed to launch a 'Kelt' missile at Tel Aviv, but this was shot down by an Israeli F-4 Phantom. The 'Badger'/'Kelt' combination represented Egypt's most potent striking force during the war, but was used only on this occasion.

The sheer logistics of the conflict put considerable strain on the transport fleets of both sides, with aircraft flying around the clock to support the forward forces. Illustrated is one of six Iraqi air force Antonov An-12 'Cub-As' that saw extensive use for troop and freight transport.

Despite the fact that they could be operated for close support, both the Syrian and Egyptian air forces restricted their MiG-21PF 'Fishbed-Js' to the air superiority role, providing top cover that allowed the MiG-17s and Su-7BMs to operate in relative safety on ground-attack missions.

The IDF/AF fleet of about 120 McDonnell Douglas F-4E Phantom IIs provided the ability to mount long-range strike missions against Arab strongholds, carrying a wide range of modern weapons.

An F-4E Phantom passes an Israeli gun emplacement at dawn. The Phantom was the decisive aircraft of the war, gaining air superiority over the MiG-21s fielded by Egypt, and making many punishing strikes deep in enemy territory.

AFRICAN AIR WARS 1952-83

At the end of World War II more than 85 per cent of Africa was distributed between the empires of the UK, France, Belgium and Portugal, or about to be administered by these nations under United Nations trusteeship. Within 30 years the entire continent, comprising almost 50 states, had divested itself of the trappings of colonial rule and was to a great extent independent of its traditional imperial parents. A more insidious style of imperial domination emerged, based on the strategic interests and embracing the world ambitions of the superpowers, the Soviet Union, the United States and communist China. But in varying degrees (depending on the relations that existed at the time of independence) many emergent states opted to retain defence agreements with their former colonial parents in exchange for economic and cultural aid.

First signs of the traumas of independence were signalled in 1952 in Kenya, whose long-standing nationalist faction fostered an uprising in the Kikuyu tribal area, a rebellion that was to last for three years and was to be suppressed by land and air forces which inflicted 11,000 casualties for the loss of 55 white lives. The use of air power escalated from the employment of 12 Harvard trainers in the ground attack role in 1953 to the deployment of Avro Lincoln heavy bombers, Vampire and Meteor jets and a host of support aircraft of the RAF, such as Valetta transports and Sycamore helicopters. After the end of the rebellion a well-administered transfer of government went ahead and by 1965 Kenya was able to assume self-sufficiency, albeit with a long-standing border dispute with neighbouring Somalia.

Meanwhile France had granted self-determination to Morocco and Tunisia, an act of preferential treatment that was coveted by Algeria, with the consequence of bloody civil war. In the instance of Morocco the path to independence was smoothed by the perpetuation of defence undertakings in return for use by the USA of a number of air bases. However, another long-standing dispute with Algerian-based Polisario rebels over border demarcation has resulted in persistent border clashes in which Moroccan aircraft have been shot down by Soviet-supplied SAMs.

In 1960 Nigeria gained independence from the UK and seemed set for a peaceful transition until in 1966 a bloody civil war between Biafra (which had seceded) and the federal government erupted. The latter turned to the communist bloc to equip its air force, receiving MiG-17s and Il-28 jets, which faced a motley collection of ancient aircraft flown almost exclusively by white mercenaries. The civil war ended in 1970, and the federal government has since decided to adopt a balance of political affiliation between West and East.

Also in 1960 the Congo acquired an over-hasty independence from a corrupt Belgian administration, and this was followed by the secession of the Katanga province; once more civil war ensued. After hesitant intercession by the UN, an international force including air force elements from India (Canberras), Sweden (Saab J29s) and Canada (Beavers and Otters) took part in operations against Katangese forces, and in a series of strikes by the J29s almost the entire rebel air force was eliminated by January 1963. A second attempt in 1977 to establish an independent state of Katanga was frustrated when, following the declaration of a state of emergency by President Mobutu, 1,500 Moroccan troops brought into the country by French Transall C.160 transports restored the situation. Here, as in so many other instances of conflict, the presence of Soviet-trained Cuban forces presented a sinister interpretation of communist ambitions in Africa.

Of all the other inter-state and civil wars, three occupied world headlines for many months. Indeed the strife in Rhodesia, following the 1964 unilateral declaration of independence by a white minority administration, was fuelled by foreign-based guerrillas against which the tiny air force was constantly in action, a handful of Hunters and Canberras which, in an extraordinary exercise of 'hand to mouth' logistics, remained in being for more than 15 years despite a UN-inspired blockade of the country. As part of this blockade, RAF Shackletons flew patrols over the straits between Madagascar and Mozambique on the lookout for oil supplies being shipped from the Middle East.

The worst of all horrors accompanied the civil wars in the Horn of Africa where natural disasters of repeated droughts, combined with indiscriminate air force action against innocent civilian populations, followed the decolonialisation by Italy, France and the UK of Ethiopia and Somalia. The political vacuum that followed the death of Emperor Hailie Selassie was filled by a Marxist administration, bolstered by Cuban forces, which quickly traded strategic bases with the Soviet Union in return for MiG-15s and MiG-17s (and later MiG-21s and Il-28s) which, when guerrilla war broke out against an Arab-backed Eritrean Liberation Front, were employed with the utmost ferocity and without regard for the safety of civilians.

Finally, and most recently, the previous French colony of Chad has been for 25 years wracked by internal strife, a situation ruthlessly exploited by the military regime of neighbouring Libya, whose forces invaded the northern area. This conflict was only partly controlled in 1982-3 by the intervention of elements of the French air force.

Allied with the Ilyushin Il-28 bomber, Nigeria's Mikoyan-Gurevich MiG-17 fighters were the most potent warplanes involved in the Nigerian civil war which lasted from 1966 until 1970.

English Electric Canberra B.Mk 52 of the Imperial Ethiopian air force, Asmara, 1970. Four, acquired in 1969, were used in attacks on the Eritrean Liberation Army and against the Somalis.

Among the air force of the so-called Organisation Nations-Unies du Congo (ONUC) was a small number of Indian Air Force English Electric Canberra bomber-intruders based at Luluabourg during 1961-2. The aircraft was found unsuitable for the low-level pinpoint strike operation needed in the Congo.

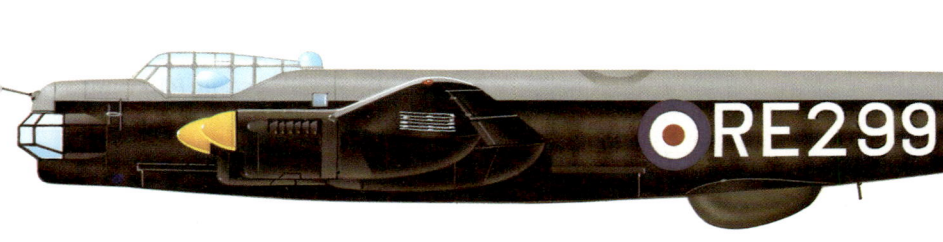

Avro Lincoln B.Mk 2 of No. 214 Squadron detached from the UK and based at Eastleigh, Kenya, during 1954. As in Malaya, the RAF soon discovered that widespread bombing of a Mau Mau terrorist area was far more effective than pinpoint attacks made by larger numbers of sophisticated jet fighters.

Canadian de Havilland Canada DHC-3 Otters were employed for liaison duties by United Nations forces during the civil war between the Belgian Congo and Katangese secessionists.

An Indian Canberra patrols over the Congo. This type flew alongside the Saab J29 on strikes against Katangese forces.

Mirage F.1CH of the Royal Moroccan air force (formally designated the Forces Armées Royales). Morocco acquired a batch of 25 F.1CHs, which were ordered in 1976 and delivered in 1978-9. Some of these aircraft have reportedly been used in fighting with the Polisario guerrillas for control of the western Sahara.

Invasion of the northern half of Chad by Libya in support of rebel forces fighting against the French-backed government in the south has seen Tupolev Tu-22 'Blinders' used on strike missions against government forces.

Six Ilyushin Il-28 bombers were supplied to the Federal Nigerian air force by Algeria and Egypt during the Biafran Civil War of 1967-9. They were flown originally by Egyptian and white mercenary pilots, and later by Nigerian nationals, but the standard of aircraft serviceability was very poor.

FERRETS AND RECONNAISSANCE 1947-84

At the end of World War II, the Americans realized that it was going to be difficult to keep up with Soviet military developments without using their superior aircraft technology to fly reconnaissance missions over and around the USSR and its satellites. The first result of this thinking was the re-activation of the 72nd Reconnaissance Squadron operating from Ladd Field, Alaska, with Boeing F-13A and B-29F aircraft. Both were reconnaissance variants of the Superfortress, and the B-29F version could remain aloft for over 30 hours. These probably flew over the Soviet Union with all manner of sensors on board, their extreme altitude capability and good cold-weather performance rendering them safe from interception.

Electronic sensors began to complement traditional reconnaissance methods on a large scale during this period, and this led to the 'ferret' missions. These entailed flying in a threatening manner towards Soviet airspace in order to provoke a reaction, which could then be monitored by the sensors on board the aircraft, gaining information about reaction times, radio and radar frequencies and the locations of the defences. Unfortunately, these reactions were on several occasions too quick for the 'ferret' and several aircraft were shot down. The first of these was a US Navy Lockheed P2V Neptune, shot down over the Baltic on 8 April 1950. The 'ferret' practice probably continues today, and has been marked by a series of attacks from Soviet interceptors and missiles. Aircraft types attacked have included the B-29 Superfortress, Boeing RB-47 Stratojet, Martin P4M Mercator, Douglas RB-66 Destroyer and a Lockheed C-130 Hercules. Several commercial airliners have also been attacked, culminating in the destruction of a Korean Air Lines Boeing 747 over Sakhalin Island in 1983. In some instances there has been evidence that the victim had been lured over the Soviet border by jamming of the aircraft's navigation equipment.

During the 1950s Soviet fighters had been developed to the point that modified bombers were not adequate for overflights of the USSR and the Central Intelligence Agency began using for this task a specially designed aircraft, the Lockheed U-2. This aircraft had incredible altitude performance which was hoped would keep it above missiles and interceptors. U-2s started operations with a civil registration under the pretence of flying NACA calibration and sampling flights. Their 'utility' designation hid further their true purpose. However, on 1 May 1960, a U-2 flown by Francis Gary Powers was shot down by a surface-to-air missile over Sverdlovsk, and the cat was out of the bag.

Cuba provided the real catalyst for the U-2 operations to come out into the open. The island had long been under surveillance by CIA U-2s and when the Soviet Union supplied SAMs to the Cubans, the CIA immediately feared another Powers incident, so all U-2 operations were handed over to the USAF. Their precautions were worthwhile as, on 27 October 1962, Major Rudolf Anderson Jr was shot

down in a 4080th SRW U-2. This still proved embarrassing for the Americans for, at the same time, a U-2 was intercepted over the Arctic. Fortunately, the pilot managed to turn back after entering Soviet airspace.

In the late 1950s it was becoming obvious to the CIA that the U-2 could no longer be expected to overfly heavily defended areas safely, and so a new aircraft was developed by Lockheed to carry on this role. This was the A-11, which was later developed into the SR-71. These aircraft were, and still are, the fastest, highest-flying aircraft in the world. Both A-11s and SR-17s operated a variety of CIA missions during the 1960s, and SR-71s fly on today with the USAF's 9th SRW as the spearhead of the West's reconnaissance force. Both U-2s and SR-71s undertook many missions during the war in South East Asia.

The Soviet Union did not undertake many overflying missions, although open surveillance of western navies is commonplace, with Tupolev Tu-142 and Tu-16 aircraft employed in large numbers. Electronic intelligence (Elint) and 'ferret' missions are also widely carried out in European skies, testing reaction times of NATO defenders. The United Kingdom's Phantom and Lightning force has been kept particularly busy for many years steering away and shadowing 'Bears' and 'Badgers' over the North Sea and the Atlantic. Other Soviet reconnaissance missions have been undertaken with the Yak-25RD 'Mandrake' (long-span, straight-wing derivative of the Yak-25 fighter) and the reconnaissance version of the MiG-25 'Foxbat' Mach 3 interceptor, which possesses some of the attributes of the SR-71 in having high speed and exceptional altitude performance. The Soviet Union is developing a U-2 type 'spyplane', known to NATO as 'RAM-M', and Aeroflot airliners are thought to be used on occasion.

Other nations to employ 'ferrets' and strategic reconnaissance types are the UK and Taiwan. The RAF's No. 51 Sqn has operated various versions of the Avro Lincoln, BAC Canberra, de Havilland Comet and British Aerospace Nimrod on a variety of secret electronic reconnaissance missions around the borders of the Warsaw Pact countries, while Taiwan has used U-2s supplied by the USA for overflights of the Communist Chinese mainland. A number of these Taiwanese aircraft have been downed by Chinese SAMs.

Although strategic reconnaissance, often using side-looking airborne radar, is still widely used by the USA and USSR, the two superpowers are now looking to space and satellites for their military intelligence.

Seen banking over its home base of Beale AFB in northern California, this Lockheed SR-71A of the 1st Strategic Reconnaissance Squadron, 9th SRW, was taking part in Global Shield 79, a worldwide exercise by Strategic Air Command that took place in July of that year. Note the Boeing KC-135Q tankers on the ground.

Featuring a redesigned nose and a bomb bay bulge housing three electronic specialists and their equipment, this Boeing ERB-47H is typical of many aircraft used by the US since the end of World War II on clandestine reconnaissance and ferret missions around the borders of the Soviet Union and its satellites.

The Lockheed U-2 was originally operated by the Central Intelligence Agency and flew in civil registrations. Operations were handed over to the USAF following the Gary Powers incident to avoid any future embarrassment caused by a repeat of that accident.

The United Kingdom has employed electronic intelligence-gathering aircraft for many years, but not in any large numbers. Present strength is three British Aerospace Nimrod R.Mk 1s based at Wyton. In common with all Elint aircraft, these sport a wide array of blisters and blade aerials for the sensors on board.

Lockheed U-2s have been flown by the Nationalist Chinese for many years over Communist territory. Many have been shot down by SAMs of the Chinese People's Republic, and this example is on display in Peking.

The Soviet Union assigns a large number of Tu-142 'Bear' aircraft to both maritime surveillance and ferret missions, especially around European coasts. This 'Bear-D' was intercepted by RAF fighters over the North Sea.

The world's most capable reconnaissance platform is the Lockheed SR-71. Operating at extreme altitude and at speeds over Mach 3, the SR-71 is still uncatchable, despite many rumoured attempts by several countries.

CENTRAL AMERICA

The supposed threat to the United States by air attack during the past 30 or so years has, perhaps to put it unkindly, become a subject pursued with hawkish paranoia. Nevertheless since the years of domestic McCarthyism the 'Red under the Bed' syndrome has materialized as a specific military threat based upon the island of Cuba, whose previous Batista administration was not only corrupt but was actively supported by the US government. Little wonder therefore that the Soviet Union should seize on the opportunity to actively sustain the Communist-inspired revolutionary government of Fidel Castro, and the sudden appearance of missile sites in Cuba following the 1961 Bay of Pigs fiasco, which itself was given limited American air support, was perhaps the logical Soviet ploy.

Although disclosure of the planned deployment of Soviet-made missiles and their eventual enforced return home may have reflected some credit on the Kennedy administration, the whole approach to a major power confrontation concentrated the Americans' minds wonderfully on the slow but steady spread of international communism into the American hemisphere.

Perhaps bearing in mind that modern Soviet aircraft, including long-range bombers, reconnaissance aircraft and fighters, have been known to be based on Cuba in recent years, the USA has suffered a constant and increasingly uncomfortable awareness of a potential military threat to what has become traditionally an American sphere of influence, particularly in the states bordering the strategically vital Panama Canal Zone. Indeed, the emergence of the Soviet navy as a 'blue water fleet' has spotlighted the significance of Cuba as a strategic base for all manner of threats to Allied naval forces in the North Atlantic, not least in anti-submarine forces.

Accordingly the US air arms (the USAF, US Navy, US Marine Corps and Air National Guard) are deployed and tasked to watch these threats. Apart from Cuba itself (where a Soviet-supplied air force of some 450 aircraft includes MiG-23s, MiG-19s and MiG-21s fixed-wing aircraft and heavily-armed Mi-24 'Hind-D' helicopter gunships), the nations of Central America are poor, and lacking external support of the Cuban type cannot support significant air forces, with the result that the United States has been engaged in propping up shaky administrations whose neighbours have displayed inability or unwillingness to withstand the infiltration of communist philosophies.

The geographically huge but relatively impoverished nation of Mexico has deliberately supported no more than a very small air force but, because of the threat posed by guerrilla activity in neighbouring Guatamala, has in recent years received a dozen F-5 Tiger II fighters and some Pilatus PC-7 armed trainer/COIN aircraft. Guatemala itself had for some years benefited from the supply of

American military aircraft until, following alleged violation of human rights, this was summarily suspended in 1977. Although a return to American favour in 1982 followed seizure of power by a more moderate regime, tension has continued as Guatemala has claimed sovereignty of the tiny state of Belize, itself guaranteed protection by the UK, whose RAF has maintained a detachment of Harriers and helicopters in situ for the purpose.

A far more serious situation has arisen in Honduras and El Salvador, their common border being the source of argument, fanned by active Communist sympathy for a left-wing guerrilla army in the latter country. As is so often the situation, the discredited right-wing regime has gained American military support (simply because it is fighting Communism), and matters were not improved when, in January 1982, the guerrilla forces attacked the main air base, destroying Ouragan fighters, C-47 transports and, more important, six Iroquois helicopters. The immediate response by the USA was to supply replacements to El Salvador and to undertake the modernization of three air bases in Honduras!

Compounding this dangerous situation, Nicaragua, on Honduras' southern side, seems to have submitted to political overtures from the Castro regime, and is believed to have received more than a dozen MiG-17s and MiG-21s, some 70 pilots having been trained in Bulgaria.

Thus far the Panama Canal Zone has been troubled little by outside politics, the United States being justified by treaty obligations in maintaining a low-key military presence there until 1999. However, as can be seen from the foregoing, the entire theatre is potentially ripe for political intrigue, and the suspicions aroused by the presence of Cuban workers on the site of a new air base on Grenada in the Windward Islands late in 1983 was quite adequate to spark instant and powerful intervention by all manner of American forces, from AC-130 gunships, C-141 transports, helicopters and fighter-bombers in an astonishing overkill operation, all on the pretext of supporting an established democratic administration whose authority was being endangered by Communist Cuba. Such is the delicately balanced political climate in Central America that, with poverty-stricken nations attracting the assumed benefits of Soviet-inspired revolutionary Communism, it seems that the United States is inevitably cast in the role of villain in its own backyard by lending support to bankrupt right-wing administrations whose corrupt economic policies have produced the endemic symptoms of discontent.

The Fairchild A-10 is deployed in substantial numbers in the south of the United States as a deterrent to any attack coming from Central America. Its obvious potential for counter-insurgency also renders this deployment favourable, given the delicate political situation in the region.

United States' worldwide commitments need the services of a large transport force for routine and emergency movement of men and equipment. Epitomizing this role is a Lockheed C-141B StarLifter, carrying supplies into Grenada in 1983.

The invasion of Grenada saw the first combat use of the Sikorsky UH-60 Black Hawk. Set to eventually replace the ubiquitous Huey family, the UH-60 was used in Grenada as an assault helicopter although casevac (casualty evacuation) was an important role.

Left: A highly mobile force, the US Army is well equipped with helicopters, one of which is the Sikorsky UH-60A Black Hawk. These UH-60s are carrying US troops to suppress resistance on Grenada by Cuban soldiers and others.

Though ostensibly deployed to meet a threat from the USA, Cuba could use its recently acquired MiG-23 'Flogger-Fs' to support guerrilla operations on the Central American mainland. Used in that theatre they would be in devastating contrast to the low-grade aircraft deployed by those mainland nations.

An unusual and exotic environment is provided by the jungles of Belize for a Puma HC.Mk 1 of the RAF's No. 33 Squadron. Under threat of invasion from Guatemala, Belize has been defended by British Harriers, Pumas and Gazelles, although a small local air arm has been formed with two Pilatus Britten-Norman Defenders.

SOVIET AIR POWER

Being espoused to a totalitarian philosophy, the Soviet Union is less constrained by economic considerations for the maintenance of gigantic armed forces, whose air defence elements alone are greater than the entire air forces of the UK, France, West Germany, Belgium and Denmark combined. Cast in the eyes of the West as an aggressor, the Soviet Union also possesses massive forces for offensive operations and, given the slightest provocation, has displayed no less a willingness to employ these in overkill situations than the USA. Such are the high stakes in the respective defence of Western democracy and international Communism.

Throughout the decades since World War II the Soviet Union has pursued a continuing policy of advancing technology and, on balance today, matches that of the West, particularly in the realms of space and aviation. Air Defence of the Nation is vested in the Voyska Protivovozdushnoy Obonony (PVO) which is tasked and organized with five responsibilities: fighter interception, surface-to-air missile defence, radio and radar warfare, interception of enemy rockets, and space warfare. This huge organization originated in 1949 with the introduction of the first MiG-15 fighters and SA-1 SAMs. In the past dozen years such aircraft as the Sukhoi Su-15 'Flagon' Mach 2.5 interceptor with 'Anab' air-to-air missiles and the MiG-23MF 'Flogger' with 85-mile (135-km) range 'High Lark' radar and long-range 'Apex' missiles have entered service. Currently appearing is the two-seat MiG-25 development (the so-called 'Super Foxbat'), a Mach 2.8 interceptor with an 80,050-ft (24400-m) ceiling. In all the PVO fields there are some 2,600 fighter aircraft. These aircraft and weapons have virtually closed the technology gap that for years existed between East and West.

Another element of the Soviet forces is Frontovaia Aviatsiya (Frontal Aviation, FA), established to provide a vast umbrella for the ground forces and comprising 5,000 combat aircraft and some 3,500 assault and gunship helicopters. Principal among the former are some 1,400 MiG-23/27s, about 1,200 MiG-21s and a fast-growing number of variable-geometry Su-24 'Fencer' low-level penetration strike aircraft; among the helicopters are the heavily-armed troop-carrying Mi-8 'Hip', the assault Mi-24 'Hind' and the enormous Mi-26, capable of carrying more than 100 troops.

Units of the FA were involved in the recent invasion of Afghanistan by the Soviet 40th Army, Mi-24 helicopters being much in evidence in attacks on the Afghan tribesmen. A new ground attack aircraft, the Su-25 'Frogfoot', also appeared in operational use for the first time, alongside the inevitable MiG-21s and Su-17s.

The majority of FA forces are not unnaturally deployed in the western areas of the USSR and in eastern Europe, although persistent suspicions that China harbours territorial ambitions in the East prompts the deployment of more than 1,700 fighters and fighter-bombers facing that country.

Bearing in mind the Soviet Union's preoccupation with sustaining the spread of communism worldwide through the dissemination of military equipment and 'advisers' to the new 'Russian Empire', another branch of the Soviet air force, the Voenno-Transportnaya Aviatsaya (V-TA) has in recent decades assumed new importance and is currently equipped with more than 1,000 transport aircraft distributed among six air divisions, as well as some 2,000 helicopters. This may also be supplemented, whenever necessary, by aircraft of the state-owned Civil Air Fleet, better known as Aeroflot. Roughly one-third of the V-TA's fleet comprises the Il-76 'Candid', a four-jet transport similar in performance and ability to the American C-141 StarLifter. Recently there appeared a new Soviet super-transport, the An-400 'Condor', an aircraft larger even than the American C-5 Galaxy.

Uniquely among world naval air forces the Soviet Aviatsaya Voenno-Morskogo Flota (AV-MF) supports a considerable long-range land-based strategic element which includes the Tu-95/142 'Bear', a very large aircraft which, using inflight refuelling, roams the ocean skies to plot the activities of the West's navies. Anti-shipping strike forces, which include aircraft such as the Tu-22M 'Backfire' and Tu-124 'Blinder' with ASMs, pose a major threat to Western warships.

In 1984 the US government published an appraisal of new Soviet aircraft currently entering service or shortly to do so. This disclosed that the new 'Blackjack' variable-geometry bomber would be armed with a cruise missile, that MiG-29 'Fulcrum' and MiG-31 'Foxhound' fighters are currently entering service, soon to be joined by the Su-27 'Flanker', and that a new attack helicopter, the Mi-28 'Havoc', is being developed. A recent estimate of Soviet fighter production in 1983 of about 950 aircraft (compared with a 1980 total of 1,300) does not reflect any diminution of Soviet military aspirations, merely a discontinuation of older aircraft such as 'Fitter', 'Fishbed' and 'Flogger' while the new generation gears up in the factories.

While such an imposing arsenal remains in being it is impossible to countenance any end to the terrifying wastage of man's resources.

Mil Mi-24s used in Afghanistan include the 'Hind-A' and 'Hind-D' models, the aircraft in the immediate foreground being a 'Hind-A'. Mi-24 tactics in Afghanistan show its potential for counter-insurgency operations, but they would not be workable if confronted with an effective air defence.

In its many variants the MiG-23/27 family has now taken over from the MiG-21 as the principal Soviet fighter, with around 2,000 in service. This example is a MiG-23MF 'Flogger-G' which is distinguished by a shorter dorsal fin than other models. This version is optimized for air defence.

Soviet intervention in Afghanistan has been supported by a massive airlift from the USSR to Afghanistan, and to outlying garrisons around the country. At the heart of this airlift is the Ilyushin Il-76, which has paradropping capability and excellent short/rough-field performance.

Newest type of aircraft to appear over Afghanistan is the Sukhoi Su-25 'Frogfoot' anti-armour and close support aircraft.

Spearhead of the Soviet Union's maritime strike force are the Tupolev Tu-22M 'Backfire-B' bombers, each carrying a 'Kitchen' air-to-surface nuclear missile under the fuselage. Prime targets for these aircraft would be the large carriers employed by the US Navy.

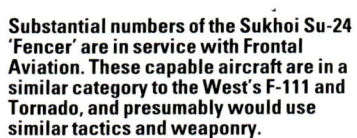

Substantial numbers of the Sukhoi Su-24 'Fencer' are in service with Frontal Aviation. These capable aircraft are in a similar category to the West's F-111 and Tornado, and presumably would use similar tactics and weaponry.

Now obsolete, the Tupolev Tu-22 'Blinder' is still in widespread use as a conventional and anti-shipping strike aircraft. It is believed 'Blinders' have been used for level-bombing over Aghanistan in concert with the older Tu-16 'Badger' and Tu-95 'Bear'.

ADVENTURES IN THE MIDDLE EAST 1976-80

The modern phenomenon of political blackmail by hostage ransom has in recent years come to be countered by the use of military force, the assault troops usually being delivered by air. Prototype of the armed rescue of hostages held by terrorists in an alien country was the audacious operation by Israeli commandos to secure the rescue of hostages held at Entebbe in Uganda following the hijacking of an airliner. Involving a round flight of more than 3,000 miles (4825 km), and by refuelling in Kenya, Hercules transports carried an assault force into a country whose hostile dictatorship threatened resistance but in the event proved unable to match the determination of the Israelis whose operation succeeded with relatively few casualties, having destroyed much of the Ugandan fighter force on the ground to prevent interference with the return flight. A similar adventure by Egyptian commandos, who attempted to secure the release of hostages held by hijackers at Larnaca in Cyprus on 19 February 1978, failed when the Egyptian Hercules was destroyed in the course of the assault.

A new scale of operations was undertaken to secure the release of American hostages held in Teheran following the overthrow of the Shah in 1979. Involving elements of the US Army, US Navy, US Marine Corps and US Air Force, the plan was to fly an assault force into Iran, release the hostages and then fly them out. To do this, the nuclear carrier *Nimitz* would sail into the Gulf of Oman with eight RH-53D Sea Stallion helicopters. These and eight C-130 Hercules, temporarily based at Masirah Island off the Oman coast, would then fly in darkness to a remote point, known as Desert One (previously reconnoitred and prepared by covert injection of American personnel beforehand) some 200 miles (320 km) south east of Teheran. The C-130s would disembark some 120 members of the counter-terrorist Delta Force and refuel the helicopters, which would then fly them to a hidden site about 30 miles (48 km) from the Iranian capital, lying up under camouflage during the first day. Delta Force would then be lifted into Teheran, secure the release of the hostages under cover of AC-130H gunships and then be airlifted out by helicopter to the Iranian airfield at Manzariyeh; this would have been secured by Rangers and held while C-141s landed and embarked hostages, rescue forces, helicopter pilots and US Rangers for withdrawal to Egypt. A C-9A Nightingale aeromedical aircraft was also deployed in case of casualties.

During the intensive planning and training phase, codenamed 'Rice Bowl' and involving numerous full-scale exercises in the USA, it was found that the US Navy helicopter pilots were not sufficiently experienced to undertake the difficult night flight from *Nimitz* to Desert One and, at a late stage, US Marine Corps pilots were substituted and then flown out to join the carrier in the Far East.

Staging through Europe and Egypt the Hercules of the 8th Special Operations Squadron and the 7th Airborne Command and Control Squadron, comprising four MC-130E command transports and four EC-130Hs equipped as tankers, arrived at Masirah Island on 21 April 1980. In the late afternoon of 24 April Operation 'Eagle Claw' began as the eight Sea Stallions launched from the *Nimitz* and the eight Hercules set out from Masirah. The C-130s arrived at Desert One some five hours later and landed to await the helicopters, which were due after 30 minutes. Encountering severe storms, however, only six helicopters completed the journey, one having been forced by technical trouble to return and another to land with rotor failure *en route*. The operation was still viable with a minimum of six Sea Stallions, and these eventually arrived at Desert One, 90 minutes late and therefore with insufficient time to reach the hide site before dawn. Nevertheless refuelling from the EC-130Hs got under way and Delta Force made ready to embark in the helicopters. Things then started to go badly wrong. One of the US Marine helicopter pilots reported hydraulic failure, and this straightaway posed a decision whether to go on with the operation with five Sea Stallions and leave some of Delta Force behind, a decision rendered academic when one of the remaining helicopters, while lifting away from its tanker, struck the side of the Hercules and erupted in a great fireball of exploding fuel.

It then remained only to re-embark everyone (including the US Marine pilots) in the C-130s and withdraw, leaving the surviving Sea Stallions to be destroyed by an air strike from the *Nimitz* (this in fact was never carried out for fear of reprisals against the hostages in Teheran). The remaining C-130s landed safely back at Masirah Island early on the morning of 25 April as signals to abort the entire operation were flashed to the US Rangers and to the C-141 and AC-130H crews.

Failure of 'Eagle Claw' was ascribed not to the helicopter pilots, who were among the best in the US Marine Corps, but to the fact that the entire operation involved too many different elements of the US armed forces in a complex plan without training together over a long period. Indeed the only adequate element of the rescue plan, Delta Force (painstakingly selected and trained in just the type of operation undertaken) never even reached the fighting stage for which it was intended.

Special paint schemes were adopted by the Sikorsky RH-53D Sea Stallion helicopters which took part in the abortive Iranian hostage raid. The aircraft were painted sand for desert operations, and all markings were removed in the interest of security.

Two HM-12 RH-53Ds fly past the aircraft-carrier USS *Nimitz* prior to the rescue attempt. These aircraft are seen before they acquired the sand scheme. The RH-53D is the Navy's standard minesweeping helicopter, and had been used in this task for clearing the Suez Canal after the Yom Kippur war in 1973.

Aircraft from the carriers *Coral Sea* and *Nimitz* were tasked with providing air cover for the rescue attempt. Most participant aircraft received coloured bands around one wingtip to help identification. These VA-97 Vought A-7 Corsair IIs would have been used for strikes on Tehran if this was needed.

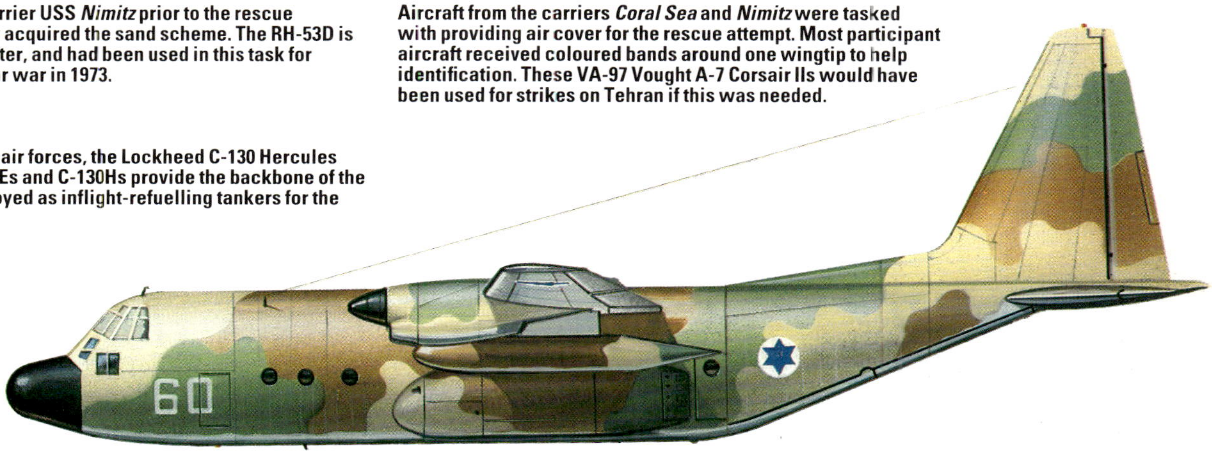

In Israeli air force service, as in many other air forces, the Lockheed C-130 Hercules fulfils two primary roles. Twenty-four C-130Es and C-130Hs provide the backbone of the transport fleet, and two KC-130Hs are employed as inflight-refuelling tankers for the front-line strike aircraft.

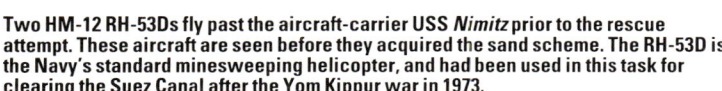

Disaster at Desert One: the charred remains of the RH-53D which hit the EC-130H Hercules, from which it had just refuelled. In the background is a deserted RH-53 left behind by the rescue force. A decision to destroy the helicopters with naval attack aircraft was dropped for fear of reprisals against the hostages.

TASK FORCE SOUTH 1982

Too small for independence and supposedly too remote to warrant protection by the UK, the Falkland Islands had for years been the subject of repeated wrangling with Argentina over sovereignty when, on 2 April 1982, several thousand troops from that country were put ashore at the capital, Port Stanley, from the carrier *Veinticinco de Mayo* and two modern destroyers, while Hercules transport aircraft disgorged other units to occupy the small airport nearby. After a three-hour battle with the tiny group of Royal Marines (who shot down an Argentine helicopter), the town was overrun and a build-up of Argentine forces in the islands began.

Caught largely unawares, the British government under Prime Minister Margaret Thatcher the following day ordered the assembly of a naval task force in British ports, as efforts were launched to settle the dispute through diplomatic channels and to persuade the Argentines to withdraw their forces. On 5 April the main fighting elements of the task force sailed from Portsmouth, comprising the flagship carrier *Hermes* (at that time due to be sold as scrap), the ramp deck-equipped carrier *Invincible* and a number of destroyers, frigates, support auxiliaries and other ships. Aboard the carriers were 20 of the Royal Navy's total inventory of 33 Sea Harriers of Nos 801 and 899 Squadrons, V/STOL aircraft whose normal function was air interception with guns and Sidewinder missiles, but whose pilots now engaged in ground-support training during the voyage south. Also embarked in the carriers were 18 Sea King helicopters of Nos 820 and 826 Squadrons.

Setting out later were large numbers of other ships, including the large liners *Queen Elizabeth II* and *Canberra*, hurriedly requisitioned and converted as troopships to carry British forces for the assault on and recapture of the far-off islands. Two large container ships, the *Atlantic Causeway* and *Atlantic Conveyor*, also sailed with Sea Harriers and RAF Harriers, plus Wessex, Lynx and Chinook helicopters. Other helicopters were carried in the destroyers and frigates.

Meanwhile, as No. 1 (Fighter) Squadron of the RAF based at Wittering was ordered to prepare for action in the South Atlantic, an intermediate base at Ascension Island, 600 miles (970 km) south of the equator in the central Atlantic, was being supplied by an air bridge of RAF Hercules transports; as the task force paused momentarily to allow other ships to catch up, further troops, weapons and stores were airlifted out of the force by helicopters from the island base. By the end of April a number of Victor tankers of Nos 50 and 55 Squadrons had arrived on Ascension in anticipation of a substantial inflight-refuelling commitment.

All the while, as the world watched the progress of the task force southwards and the diplomatic initiatives failed in their purpose, the Argentine forces in the Falklands were continuing to build up. The UK declared a 200-mile (320 km) radius war zone around the islands in which any Argentine vessel found was liable to be sunk.

As a preliminary to the assault on the Falklands themselves, British forces recaptured the dependency of South Georgia, a detachment from the task force, comprising the *Antrim, Plymouth, Endurance* and, later, *Brilliant*, arriving in the area in mid-April. Small assault parties of Royal Marines were put ashore by Wessex helicopters (two of which were lost in bad-weather accidents), and on 24 April the Argentine submarine *Santa Fe* was attacked in the approaches to Grytviken harbour by the *Antrim* and beached after further damage from attacks by the British helicopters. By 28 April South Georgia had been cleared of all Argentine forces.

As the task force arrived in the vicinity of the Falklands on the last day of April the RAF carried out the first of several strikes by single Vulcan bombers, an aircraft of No. 44 Squadron making the trip from Ascension with several inflight-refuellings during the night of 30 April/1 May; arriving over Port Stanley airfield in the small hours of 1 May the bomber dropped 14 1,000-lb (454-kg) bombs, scoring a single direct hit on the runway. The Vulcan returned safely to Ascension, with further *en route* refuelling, after one of the longest operational bombing sorties in history.

As dawn broke on 1 May the Sea Harriers of the task force carried out their first ground strikes at Port Stanley airfield and Goose Green (a small grass strip some 50 miles/80 km to the south west) in the face of brisk fire from small arms and a number of Tigercat surface-to-air missiles. Several aircraft were reported destroyed or damaged on the ground as all the raiding Sea Harriers returned safely to the carriers. The Argentine air force had reacted by sending a number of Mirage IIIs from the mainland and these were engaged by covering Sea Harriers; one was shot down by the British pilots and another by the Argentine ground defences. Later the same day four Argentine Canberras were intercepted by the Sea Harriers as they approached the islands, and one was shot down by a Sidewinder. It was estimated that about a dozen Argentine aircraft (FMA IA 58 Pucarás, Beech T-34C-1s and Aermacchi MB.339As) had been destroyed or damaged on the ground by the Sea Harriers' cluster bombs.

Much worse was to befall the Argentines on 2 May when the British nuclear submarine *Conqueror* torpedoed and sank the cruiser *General Belgrano* west of the Falklands with the loss of 300 lives. On 3 May Lynx helicopters from the task force attacked two Argentine patrol vessels, sinking one and damaging the other. Thus far the entire operation by the British forces had achieved success far beyond the most sanguine expectations.

Westland Wessex helicopters were instrumental in the recapture of South Georgia island, a prelude to the Falklands campaign. This Wessex HAS.Mk 3 flew from HMS *Antrim* and landed assault parties of Marines. Later it was involved with the attack and subsequent capture of the Argentine submarine *Santa Fe*.

Dassault Mirage IIIs and the unlicensed Israel Aircraft Industries Dagger copy were the principal attack aircraft employed by the Argentines. This Dagger carries bombs under the wings for attacking British shipping. These aircraft proved to be easy meat for the Sea Harriers.

The Westland Lynx helicopter was widely employed by the Royal Navy, and one is seen here flying close to East Falkland. It is equipped with Sea Skua missiles, the type with which one Lynx sank an Argentine patrol vessel in May.

One of the Victor tankers of Nos 55 and 57 Squadrons, RAF, at Wideawake, Ascension Island, which provided vital inflight-refuelling for all task force aircraft.

One of the five Dassault Super Etendards which, from an order for 14, had been delivered to Argentina before France imposed her arms ban. It is pictured in the markings of 2 Escuadrilla, 3 Escuadra Aéronaval.

The Vulcan B.Mk 2 XM607 of No. 44 (Bomber) Squadron which, under the codename of Operation 'Black Buck', bombed Port Stanley airport in May and June 1982.

At dawn on 1 May 1982, Sea Harriers from the Task Force attacked Argentine installations on East Falkland, including Port Stanley airfield.

FINAL VICTORY 1982

The first three weeks of May 1982 were spent by the British task force in preparations for the main assault landing, with assembly of the landing ships and with air strikes, sea bombardment, reconnaissance of and raids on the Argentine defences by British naval, air and ground forces. Royal Navy ships were posted to form a screen of anti-aircraft pickets against interference by the mainland-based Argentine air force, in the absence of any AEW aircraft in the Royal Navy. Moreover, so small was the force of Sea Harriers available that constant air cover for the entire task force (by now approaching about 100 ships) was impossible. It was one of these pickets, the Type 42 destroyer *Sheffield*, on 4 May was hit by an Exocet ASM launched from an Argentine Super Etendard; *Sheffield* later sank with the loss of 20 lives as she was being towed away. The same day a Sea Harrier was shot down during a low-level strike on Port Stanley, and a Vulcan carried out a second raid on the airfield, but with no more success than the first.

Four days later eight Harriers of No. 1 Squadron, RAF, landed on the carriers, having made the flight from the UK and landing only at Ascension on their way south. Although these aircraft had been adapted to carry Sidewinders they would, in the main, pursue their normal ground-support function while the Sea Harriers reverted to their accustomed air-defence duties.

On 12 May the Argentine air force started determined air attacks on the task force, scoring a direct hit on the frigate *Alacrity* with a 1,000-lb (454-kg) bomb which failed to explode, but losing at least three A-4 Skyhawks. On 15 May, under cover of a naval bombardment, a small force of SAS and SBS men went ashore at Pebble Island off the north coast of West Falkland, destroying with demolition chargers five Pucarás and three helicopters; all the British forces were recovered without loss. It was shortly after this that the SAS suffered tragic loss, about 30 men losing their lives when their Sea King helicopter crashed after an albatross struck its tail rotor.

By the date of the main landing assault, which took place at Port San Carlos on 21 May, the Argentine aircraft losses stood at about 28 (of an air force that had numbered more than 200), against British losses of three Sea Harriers and nine helicopters. As the Royal Navy assembled its screen of missile-armed ships in Falkland Sound, the assault vessels sailed into San Carlos Bay and began disembarking the first of 3,500 troops. Rapier missiles were quickly deployed on the shoreline as the first waves of Argentine fighters and fighter-bombers appeared on the scene. The frigate *Ardent* was sunk by a bomb, and the *Antrim* was struck by another which failed to explode. By the end of the day about 2,500 men had come ashore with scarcely a casualty.

In the air a Harrier had been shot down over Goose Green and three helicopters were also lost. On the following day, with an unexplained absence of Argentine air attacks, the liner *Canberra* sailed into San Carlos Bay to land a further 3,500 men. On 23 May the Argentine air force returned, sinking the frigate *Antelope* but losing at least seven aircraft; on the next day eight further raiders were destroyed, and on 25 May (Argentina's National Day) her air force scored twice, sinking the destroyer *Coventry* with bombs, and the freighter *Atlantic Conveyor* with an Exocet probably aimed at one of the task force carriers but deflected by chaff. Fortunately, the vital Sea Harriers aboard the latter ship had already been flown off, but almost her entire cargo of helicopters, including all but one of the heavy-lift Chinooks, went to the bottom.

On 27 May the British forces broke out of their beach-head and started a two-prong advance towards Port Stanley, 60 miles (97 km) to the east. Realizing that the Argentines could cover the entire area with a radar post set up in the central mountains, a number of strikes were launched by the Vulcan armed with Shrike anti-radiation missiles, and it was considered that at least one of these struck the radar.

A brilliant action by 650 British paratroops on 28 May resulted in the capture of Goose Green (together with about 1,500 Argentine troops), the landing strip subsequently being employed as a forward base by British aircraft. The same day two Sea Harriers were abandoned over the sea after sustaining combat damage, but their pilots were recovered safely. On 2 June the Argentine Skyhawks gained a notable, if lucky, success when their bombs struck the landing ships *Sir Galahad* and *Sir Tristram* in Bluff Cove as they were disembarking men of the Welsh Guards, 50 of whom died in the attack.

As a preliminary to the final assault on Port Stanley, one last Vulcan air strike was flown against the airport (which had remained in partial use by the Argentines throughout the campaign) on 11 June, the same day that a shore-launched Exocet struck and damaged the *Glamorgan* as she bombarded the harbour.

On 13 June the attack on Port Stanley by 6,000 men of the Parachute Regiment, Scots Guards, Welsh Guards and Gurkhas opened under cover of the Harriers and Sea Harriers and to the accompaniment of a heavy artillery barrage. The opposing air force was scarcely able to put in an appearance and, after 36 hours' fierce fighting, the Argentine commander, Brigadier General Menendez, surrendered to the British Major General Jeremy Moore. Some 9,000 Argentines laid down their arms.

The 74-day seizure of sovereign British territory had been ended. Beyond all reasonable odds the British forces, almost fatally weakened by years of political neglect, had sailed 8,000 miles (12800 km) across the world and, with support from a tiny force of aircraft, of which the Harriers gained their spurs, regained territory from a nation that possessed a large, land-based air force of modern aircraft.

Amid the desolation, an RAF Hercules approaches the runway at RAF Stanley after the end of hostilities. Aircraft abandoned by the Argentines include IA 58 Pucarás, Aermacchi M.B.339s and a Bell 212 helicopter.

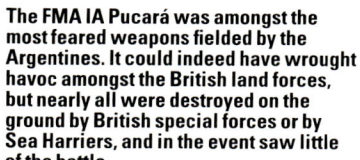

The FMA IA Pucará was amongst the most feared weapons fielded by the Argentines. It could indeed have wrought havoc amongst the British land forces, but nearly all were destroyed on the ground by British special forces or by Sea Harriers, and in the event saw little of the battle.

To bolster the Sea Harrier force, several RAF Harrier GR.Mk 3s were dispatched to the Falklands and these were soon in action carrying out strikes on Argentine positions with conventional stores, cluster bombs and laser-guided weapons. Several were converted to carry Sidewinder air-to-air missiles.

Scene of great courage as a naval Sea King plucks survivors of the stricken SS *Sir Galahad* from the waters of Bluff Cove. These pilots flew into the acrid smoke and, using rotor downwash, forced the life-rafts clear of the flames.

Only one Boeing Vertol Chinook survived the attack on the *Atlantic Conveyor*, which was transporting them to the battlezone. This aircraft performed sterling work around the islands both during and after the battle. It was the only heavylift capability available to the invasion forces.

Below: Argentine navy McDonnell Douglas A-4Q Skyhawks of 3ª Escuadrilla de Ataque, 3ª Escuadra, embarked in the carrier *Veinticinco de Mayo*, are believed to have flown alongside aircraft of the FAA during the Falklands operation.

An IAI Dagger of the Argentine air force attacks a Royal Fleet Auxiliary craft at anchor in San Carlos Water. These ships were vulnerable and volatile targets, loaded to the brim with fuel or ammunition and without defensive armament. Miraculously they all survived the San Carlos landings.

AIR POWER IN SOUTH AFRICA 1961-84

Following the withdrawal of South Africa from the British Commonwealth in 1961 that nation has, by exploitation of its own vast mineral and economic resources, proceeded along the road to self-sufficiency despite general condemnation of its apartheid racial policies. Indeed these external pressures, as well as scarcely-effective sanctions imposed internationally, have merely served to stiffen the white population's resolve to withstand what it interprets as the creeping Marxist infiltration of the continent's post-imperial vacuum. Spearheading this resolve has been the creation of an indigenous arms manufacturing industry capable of providing more than 80 per cent of the weapons and equipment required by the nation's armed forces. It remains extraordinary that the motives for the embargo of arms seem to have been deliberately blurred expressly to include arms patently relevant to national defence, whereas the condemnation of the republic from abroad centres almost exclusively on a repugnant internal social policy.

With no immediate maritime threat from neighbouring black African states, South Africa has been for two decades preoccupied with securing her northern borders, a seemingly nebulous task having regard to the ill-defined relations enjoyed with her immediate neighbours, Botswana, Zimbabwe (previously the war-racked Rhodesia) and Mozambique. Greatest current embarrassment is the huge ex-German colony of South West Africa which South Africa has administered since 1919 and which, as Namibia, seeks independence with active guerrilla support based in Angola.

Before the lapse of the Simonstown Agreement with the British government, and before the UK discontinued the supply of arms, South Africa purchased a small number of Canberra bombers and trainers, Buccaneer strike aircraft and Shackleton maritime reconnaissance aircraft. The nation then negotiated the continuing purchase and licence-production of large numbers of French Mirage IIICZ fighters, Mirage IIIBZ fighter-bombers and Mirage IIIRZ reconnaissance aircraft and these, together with subsequent Mirage F.1AZ and CZ aircraft, have dominated South African front-line defence equipment. In the counter-insurgency role (a vital element in the operations in Angola and Namibia) the Active Citizen Force flies licence-built Atlas M.B.326 Impala aircraft, five such squadrons being deployed throughout the republic. Thus far air combat

has not occurred, the opposing guerrilla forces conforming to the established pattern of jungle infiltration, the SWAPO forces using tactics introduced by the inevitable Cuban expeditionary force.

Considerable dependence rests on a sizable fleet of helicopters (again almost exclusively French) for the mobility of jungle assault forces, and the South African army is extremely adept in the classic anti-terrorist tactic and strike-and-pursue, with effecive support from the air.

In November 1975 Portuguese colonial rule in Angola ended, followed seemingly inevitably by civil war between the Marxist MPLA on the one hand and the FNLA and UNITA (with faint-hearted Western support) on the other. After the MPLA suffered early setbacks the Soviet Union intervened and Cuban advisers began arriving in Soviet aircraft which had staged through other African Marxist states. Almost the entire country was under Marxist control by March 1976, and with some 30 MiG-21 ground-attack fighters based within striking range of South African territory, an extremely delicate balance had to be struck by the SAAF between effective self-defence and the deployment of counter-terrorist air support aircraft. Such losses that South Africa has suffered among her helicopter fleet have been the result of ground fire.

It seems inconceivable that world pressures will fail to secure independence for Namibia, and it is clearly in South Africa's interests to retain good relations with its new administration if only to secure a buffer zone in front of the potentially hostile nation of Angola.

Elsewhere South Africa has managed to negotiate improving relations with her neighbours, although all are vulnerable to strongly nationalist factions which constantly express sympathy with the South African black population. And all the time the SAAF must retain and sustain a powerful air defence system against the possibility of the emergence of a Soviet-backed black Southern African air force. With such forces already in being in Libya, Ethiopia and Tanzania, it is little wonder that South Africa continues in its preoccupation with strength in the air.

Photographed against an impressive backdrop is an Aérospatiale Puma of the South African Air Force, a type used extensively in anti-guerrilla missions. Only 20 Pumas were delivered officially, but the SAAF's final total is nearer 67.

The Mirage IIICZ provides the South African Air Force with a potent force of fighter-bombers for ground attack duties along its borders. This aircraft flies with No. 2 Squadron, based at Waterkloof, which is the SAAF's main Mirage base. South Africa also operates the Mirage IIID2Z, the most powerful sub-series.

Left: South Africa operates the Aermacchi AM.3C on spotting and liaison duties. Known locally as the Bosbok, this light aircraft has proved particularly useful to the South African forces in fighting with guerrillas in Angola and Namibia.

Below: South Africa was the sole export customer for the Buccaneer, receiving 15 for No. 24 Squadron at Waterkloof in 1965-6. The SAAF S.Mk 50s were unique in having a retractable rocket-pack booster to improve take-off performance.

Lieutenant Adriano Bomba of the Mozambique air force defected to South Africa in a MiG-17 and is escorted to Hoedspruit AB by a Mirage F.1AZ.

EXCURSION INTO LEBANON 1982-84

With the implicitly-conditional realignment by Egypt with the West during the late 1970s, Israel's principal Arab antagonist automatically became Syria, which had for many years championed the cause of the Palestinians in their continuing efforts to secure a formally-recognized state of their own. Indeed, ever since the unequivocal defeat of Egypt by Israel in 1973 the Syrians had, if anything, become more firmly aligned with the communist bloc and particularly with the Soviet Union, which saw the likelihood of a future gateway through the Lebanon to strategic naval bases in the eastern Mediterranean. By 1982, with generous military assistance by the Soviet Union in the form of Su-7s and Su-20s, MiG-23BNs, MiG-25s, MiG-21PFs, MiG-21MFs and MiG-21bis all-weather fighters, the Syrian air force (SAF) was certainly regarded by Israel as the principal threat to her own military dominance in the Middle East. She had accordingly acquired from the USA McDonnell Douglas F-15As and F-15Bs plus General Dynamics F-16As and F-16Bs to add to her impressive arsenal of F-4Es, Mirage IIIBJs and Mirage CJs, and indigenous Kfir-C2s; the Israeli air force (IAF) was also equipped with a number of modern ECM aircraft, including Grumman E-2Cs and four Boeing 707ECMs; Lockheed C-130 Hercules doubled as transports and ECM aircraft.

Claiming exasperation at PLO terrorist activities against her nationals outside the Middle East, Israel on 2 June 1982 ordered a revenge raid by seven waves of aircraft, said to be F-16s (in defiance of previous American insistence that such aircraft were supplied for defence purposes only), against the PLO central office in Beirut, capital of the Lebanon, for it had long been established that this country was the unenthusiastic host of the stateless Palestinians. Shortly after this attack the IAF struck at PLO positions in southern Lebanon, provoking artillery fire on Israeli territory by the PLO.

For four days the IAF and PLO forces kept up intermittent attacks and retaliatory bombardments, culminating in a further attack on Beirut on 5 June. On the following day, risking possible armed intervention by a Syrian force of occupation that was present in the Lebanon, ostensibly to keep the peace and protect the PLO, Israel launched a full-scale invasion from the south, at first claiming its objective as being to establish a demilitarized buffer zone in front of her territory. In the face of further PLO actions, however, the Israelis were in no mood to restrain their forces, and massive land, sea and air bombardments against supposed pockets of PLO forces resulted in enormous civilian casualties. The world's attention was, however, diverted at this time by dramatic events in the tiny Falkland Islands in the South Atlantic.

On 7 June the Israelis launched an attack on the port of Sidon while overhead her covering F-16s were engaged by Syrian MiGs; Syrian jets also hit Israeli armour near Sidon itself. For her part Israel had hoped to avoid direct conflict with the Syrians, fearing an escalation that could not be contained, while the ground forces of both sides had hitherto avoided crossing the 'Red Line' which for some years had represented the southern limit of the Syrian 'peacekeeping' forces. But when Israeli armour was airlifted into the Shuf mountains the Syrians faced being outflanked, while an Israeli threat to cut the main Beirut-Damascus road would have isolated Syrian forces in the Lebanese capital. Accordingly SAF helicopters (probably SA 342 Gazelles with HOT anti-tank missiles) attacked Israeli armour as a number of air combats took place high over central Lebanon. Both sides made victory claims but the true losses by both sides were clearly 'doctored' for both tactical and political moves. In general, however, the Israelis by constant use of decoy flares and other countermeasures seemed capable of mastering the Syrian jets and certainly emerged with lower casualties. Be that as it may, the presence of large numbers of Syrian SAM batteries along the Bekaa valley posed a threat to the IAF, and on 9 June a major air battle developed as A-4s and F-4s attacked the missile sites and F-15s and F-16s engaged MiG-21s and MiG-23s overhead. The SAF later admitted losing 16 aircraft while claiming to have hit 26 Israli aircraft, a claim almost certainly confused by the IAF's use of Ryan Firebee RPVs; 19 Syrian SAM sites were claimed destroyed.

Continuous fighting went on for three days until a ceasefire eventually took tenuous effect on 12 June. Thereafter fighting flared up between further improvised ceasefires. Israeli reconnaissance revealed the arrival of mobile SA-8 SAM units in the Bekaa valley, and the IAF attacked these on 24 July killing, among others, 11 Soviet technicians. Subsequently the Syrians deployed SA-9s within 20 miles (32km) of Beirut. In attempts to dislodge PLO forces from the capital the IAF embarked on a ferocious air assault on the city, using napalm, cluster, fragmentation, phosphorus and high-velocity shrapnel bombs which caused the most hideous injuries to thousands of innocent civilians.

Following the eventual departure of the PLO from Lebanon, civil war broke out between Christian and Moslem factions, forcing the withdrawal of international peacekeeping forces from the capital, while world opinion focussed on the flagrant atrocities of the Israeli assault on Beirut, such that during the next two years Israel felt obliged to progressively withdraw her forces southwards, leaving Syrian political influence in the Lebanon as powerful as ever.

Loaded with bombs and Sidewinder missiles for self-defence, this IAI Kfir prepares for take-off on a mission against Lebanon. The Kfir was widely used as a fighter-bomber alongside the McDonnell F-4E Phantom.

Equipping two SAF regiments, the MiG-23BN 'Flogger-F' is the export counterpart of the USSR's MiG-27 'Flogger-D'. It retains the MiG-23MF interceptor's powerplant, variable-geometry intakes and GSh-23 twin-barrel gun in a belly pack. It can also carry stores on five weapons pylons.

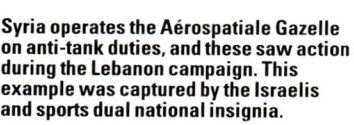

Syria operates the Aérospatiale Gazelle on anti-tank duties, and these saw action during the Lebanon campaign. This example was captured by the Israelis and sports dual national insignia.

Below: Airborne early warning and control, provided by Grumman E-2C Hawkeyes, was a decisive factor in the air fighting, enabling the highly trained Israeli pilots to engage the enemy on highly favourable terms.

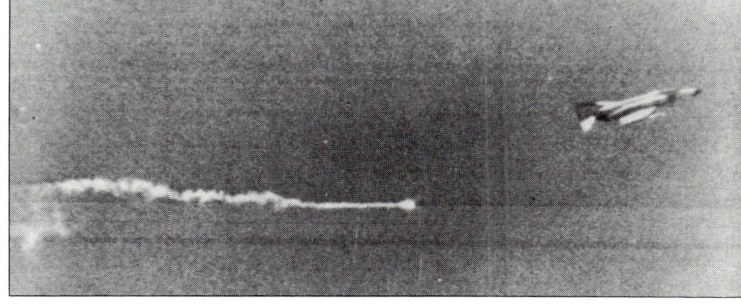

Israeli tactics were considerably better than those of Syria throughout the war, the most important of which were airborne control and ECM. This Phantom strike bomber releases a flare to divert heat-seeking missiles during an attack over South Beirut.

Air-to-air fighting over Lebanon was dominated by the General Dynamics F-16 (illustrated) and the McDonnell Douglas F-15 Eagle. These two types scored over 80 victories for no loss during the fighting.

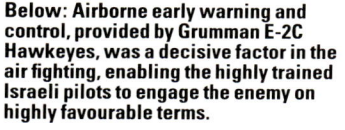

Below: An F-15 Eagle returns to base after a mission. The F-15 has been Israel's primary fighter since 1977 and has scored many victories over MiG-21s, 23s and 25s. Over Lebanon it accounted for over 40 victories.

HOLY WAR IN THE AIR 1980-84

Overthrow of the authoritarian Shah of Iran's rule by the Islamic revolution in February 1979 brought about the abrupt termination of American arms exports to that nation; these in recent years had assumed huge proportions, with the avowed purpose of bolstering Iran's capability to counter any Soviet threat to the West's oil supplies through the Persian Gulf. At the time of the revolution the Imperial Iranian air force possessed 80 F-14 Tomcats, more than 200 F-4 Phantoms and a like number of F-5s among a modern inventory of about 1,000 aircraft.

At a single stroke the arms embargo prevented delivery of 160 F-16s, 400 Bell helicopters and large numbers of Phoenix, HAWK, Standard and Harpoon missiles, as well as denying Iran maintenance back-up and spares for her existing aircraft. It was in the acrid diplomatic atmosphere that surrounded this isolation, nurtured by the Islamic leaders, that 53 US hostages were seized in Tehran, prompting the daring but ill-fated attempt at their rescue by American forces in April 1980 (Operation 'Eagle Claw').

Progressive westernization of the Iranian economy and society that had continued unchecked for half a century rendered the acceptance of Islamic law difficult to reconcile among all but the humble masses of Iranians, and it was among these people that the religious leaders sought and found support. It resulted in increasing isolation of the officer ranks of the armed forces, with dire results, particularly in the air force, which was already suffering technical privation through its isolation from the West. Moreover, while the Revolutionary Council declared its determination to avoid alignment with East and West alike, the Soviet Union was unwilling to intervene militarily, having condemned 'Eagle Claw' on the one hand but having itself gained worldwide condemnation for its invasion of neighbouring Afghanistan on the other.

The Iranian economy, dependent as always on its oil exports, now tottered towards collapse and it was at this point that Iraq, a powerful Soviet-aligned oil-producing state with a precariously short coastline on the Persian Gulf, found its seaward access to its oil port of Basra threatened by events in Iran; it seized the opportunity of disarray in that country and, on the pretext of opposing Islamic law, launched an attack towards the great Iranian oil complex at Abadan. Realizing this to be a serious threat to the new order, the Revolutionary Council in Tehran immediately declared a *Jihad*

(holy war), taking little account of the considerable weakness of its own armed forces.

Iraq on the other hand possessed a relatively powerful and well-trained army and air force. The latter fielded nine squadrons of Mirage F.1s and MiG-21PFM interceptors and MiG-23 fighter-bombers in addition to 11 squadrons of Hunters, Su-7s, Su-20/22s and MiG-17s, and two of Il-28 and Tu-22 bombers. However, although isolated air combats have occurred between the two air forces, and both have engaged in periodic raids on enemy towns, Iraq has refrained from concerted air operations for a number of feasible reasons: uncertainty of Iran's state of fighter opposition, fear of massive reprisal and of alienating potentially dissident elements of the Iranian population, and the possibility of attracting trade and arms sanctions in the West. And it was against a background of delicately balanced diplomacy that Iraq secured the purchase from France of a small number of Super Etendard strike aircraft with Exocet anti-shipping missiles in 1983. Even these highly potent weapons were to be expended very sparingly. Only in 1984 as both Iraq and Iran embarked on a series of attacks on shipping in the Persian Gulf in attempts to paralyse each other's oil export traffic (and to discourage other, smaller oil states from alleviating each other's oil blockades) was it evident that weapons such as the Exocet were being used.

In fact the Iranian air force has managed to sustain a credible level of air defence, largely through ruthless cannibalism of damaged aircraft, although it seems unlikely that more than a handful of Tomcats has survived. Aircraft such as the Iranian P-3F Orion sea surveillance aircraft have probably been flown sparingly to watch for oil traffic targets but, if still airworthy, have almost certainly been based well away from the war zone.

Unfortunately it has proved impossible to gain any accurate information of the true losses suffered by the two air forces as both sides constantly discredit their opponents' claims and, for obvious reasons, scarcely mention their own losses. One can only conjecture that Iran has almost certainly suffered far greater attrition.

Both Iran and Iraq have employed their helicopter gunships in support of army units fighting in the border areas. Iran's army was equipped with 202 Bell AH-1J SeaCobras, ordered by the Shah in 1972. Following the revolution and continuing Iran-Iraq war only about 10 per cent may remain serviceable.

Iraq has maintained good relations with Moscow, and consequently has received much Soviet equipment while still being able to buy Western hardware when it requires (mainly from France). This Ilyushin Il-76 is flown in quasi-civil markings (Iraqi Airways) but is used almost exclusively on military duties. The rear gun turret is a giveaway of its true role.

Training for the Iraqi air force is undertaken on the Pilatus PC-7 and the Czech-built Aero L.39 Albatros; both these types are believed to have been fitted with rocket pods and gun pods for use against Iranian forces. This Aero L.39 sports a typical desert scheme.

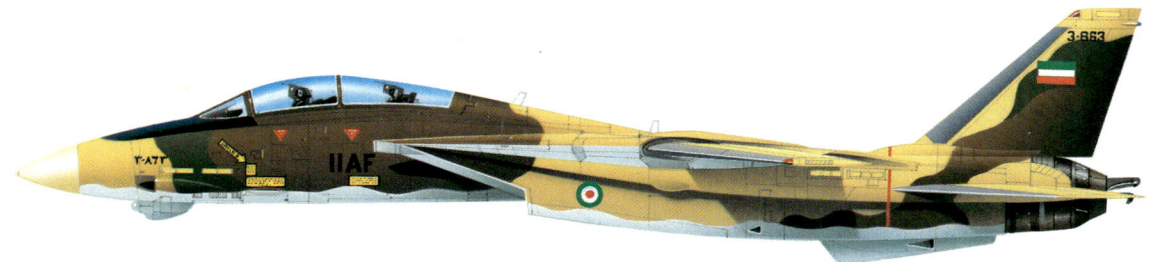

Eighty Grumman F-14A Tomcats were supplied to Iran during the days of the Shah, and these have seen action against Iraq. Only a handful are believed to be airworthy due to lack of spares, but it is thought that Iran is now manufacturing these herself.

Since the Iranian revolution the serviceability of the equipment of the country's once-strong armed forces has deteriorated very seriously for lack of maintenance and spares supply. Six Lockheed P-3F Orions were acquired for ASW patrol, but only two of these were reported operational in late 1984.

The Phantom is still one of the most potent aircraft involved in the Gulf War, and Iran has made many important strikes with this aircraft. Until recently, spares and technicians for the Phantom fleet have been provided by Israel, but this support has now been withdrawn. This F-4D sports a Vulcan gun pod under the fuselage.

INDEX